Reagan

versus

the Sandinistas

About the Book and Editor

The product of research and investigation by a team of sixteen authors, *Reagan versus the Sandinistas* is the most comprehensive and current study to date of the Reagan administration's mounting campaign to reverse the Sandinista revolution. The authors thoroughly examine all major aspects of Reagan's "low-intensity war," from the U.S. government's attempts at economic destabilization to direct CIA sabotage and the sponsorship of the contras or freedom fighters. They also explore less-public tactics such as electronic penetration, behind-the-scenes manipulation of religious and ethnic tensions, and harassment of U.S. Nicaraguan specialists and "fellow travelers." The book concludes with a consideration of the impact of these activities and their implications for international law, U.S. interests, U.S. polity, and Nicaragua itself.

Reagan versus the Sandinistas is designed not only for courses on Latin America, U.S. foreign policy, and international relations, but also for students, scholars, and others interested in understanding one of the most massive, complex efforts—short of direct intervention—organized by the United States to overthrow the government of another country.

Thomas W. Walker, professor of political science at Ohio University, is the author of *Nicaragua: The Land of Sandino* (second edition, 1986, Westview).

Nicaragua

Source: Thomas W. Walker, *Nicaragua: The Land of Sandino,* 2nd ed. (Boulder, Colo.: Westview Press), 1986.

Reagan

versus

the Sandinistas

THE UNDECLARED WAR ON NICARAGUA

edited by Thomas W. Walker

Westview Press
BOULDER & LONDON

The drawing on the paperback cover, entitled "Los Sandinistas, Blanco de Agresión," was done especially for this book by Leoncio Sáenz of Managua. Sáenz, whose works have been featured in exhibitions in New York and throughout the world, is a frequent artistic contributor to *Nicaráuac*, *Pensamiento Propio*, and other Nicaraguan publications.

Copyright © 1987 by Westview Press, Inc.

Published in 1987 in the United States of America by Westview Press, Inc.; Frederick A. Praeger, Publisher; 5500 Central Avenue, Boulder, Colorado 80301

Library of Congress Cataloging-in-Publication Data
Reagan versus the Sandinistas.
  Includes index.
  1. United States—Foreign relations—Nicaragua.
2. Nicaragua—Foreign relations—United States.
3. Nicaragua—Politics and government—1979–
4. United States—Foreign relations—1981–
5. Reagan, Ronald. I. Walker, Thomas W.
E183.8.N5R43 1987   327.7307285   87-2036
ISBN 0-8133-0371-0
ISBN 0-8133-0372-9 (pbk.)

Printed and bound in the United States of America

∞   The paper used in this publication meets the requirements of the American National Standard for Permanence of Paper for Printed Library Materials Z39.48-1984.

10   9   8   7   6   5   4   3   2   1

Lest history once again be written
by the rich and powerful
at the expense of the poor

Contents

ix

Tables and Figures

Tables

Figures

Preface

In mid-1986, both branches of the U.S. Congress voted approval of $100 million worth of overt, mainly military, aid to the counterrevolutionary (contra) forces fighting to overthrow the government of Nicaragua. The money itself was not important. Since November 1981 when the Reagan administration first decided to create a surrogate army to harass the Sandinistas, it had been quite successful in channeling hundreds of millions of dollars to the "freedom fighters," as Reagan would come to call them. Some of this money had been initially allocated by the U.S. Congress to help interdict an alleged flow of arms from Nicaragua to the Salvadoran rebels. (The contras, in fact, never interdicted anything.) Some may have come through unmonitored CIA slush funds. Other assistance appears to have been laundered through Israel and pro-U.S. military establishments in the region. Large quantities of U.S. military supplies were simply left behind to be picked up by the contras following each of a series of joint U.S.-Honduran military maneuvers close to the Nicaraguan border. Finally, a very successful "private" contra fund-raising campaign had been organized under the close supervision of an office in the White House. What was important about the $100 million, if not the money itself, was the fact that passage of that appropriation gave formal bipartisan approval to Ronald Reagan's longstanding crusade to overthrow the Sandinistas. It was essentially a declaration of war. From this point onward, a long, bloody conflict—with unspeakably tragic consequences for both the United States and Central America—seemed very likely. For those of us who had studied the Sandinista revolution from within, the possibility that Nicaragua could be subdued without tremendous bloodletting was essentially zero. Yet congressional approval was sure to give legitimacy and virtually irreversible momentum to the anti-Sandinista program already in advanced stages of implementation by the CIA, the Pentagon, the Department of State, and others. Though the situation in Nicaragua would not be identical to that in Vietnam—history rarely repeats itself exactly—it seemed destined to rank as one of the great human tragedies of the second half of the twentieth century.

If not yet fully guaranteed, this scenario had loomed as a clear probability from early in the Reagan presidency. Even then, it appeared extremely unlikely that Washington would agree to a negotiated peace—though that option was always tantalizingly present. Therefore, against this backdrop in mid-1985 I began mulling over ways of systematically documenting and disclosing what had already become the most massive effort—short of direct intervention by U.S. troops—ever mounted by the United States to overthrow the government of another country. The urgency of the matter and the need to research simultaneously a bewilderingly wide range of topics led finally to a decision to organize a group effort. Accordingly, within the next few months I designed a chapter outline, enlisted authors—most of them researchers already at work on their topics—and signed a contract with the publisher. By late that fall the book was under way. This volume, the manuscripts for which were completed in mid-1986, is the product of that team effort.

This book is designed to examine systematically the undeclared war on the Nicaraguan revolution. Part 1 examines the direct assault on Nicaragua: the covert war, military encirclement, economic strangulation, electronic penetration, the manipulation of religious and ethnic tension, and the diplomatic assault. Part 2 looks at the waging of the war in the United States: the use of deceptive analysis, the management of the U.S. media and Congress, and the harassment of Nicaraguanist scholars and fellow travelers. Part 3 focuses on impact and implications—for Nicaragua, international law, U.S. foreign policy, and the U.S. polity and society.

Thomas W. Walker

ONE

Introduction

THOMAS W. WALKER

Background

Located at the geographic center of Central America, Nicaragua is the largest country in the region. Even so, its 91,943 square kilometers of surface make it only slightly larger than the state of Iowa. And its population of a little over 3 million is also only slightly greater than Iowa's 2.8 million. Given Nicaragua's low population density, abundant natural resources (good land, timber, gold, petroleum), access to two oceans, and long-recognized potential as a site for a transoceanic waterway, one would expect Nicaraguans in general to be prosperous. In fact, however, when the Sandinistas overthrew Anastasio Somoza Debayle in 1979, the social conditions of the majority of Nicaraguans ranked that country with the two or three most backward of Latin America. The explanation for this apparent paradox lies in Nicaraguan history—one of the most unfortunate of the hemisphere.[1]

Two major factors had combined to produce this situation: (1) elite irresponsibility flowing out of a highly unequal social system and (2) endemic foreign intervention or manipulation. The inegalitarian nature of Nicaraguan society had its roots in the Spanish conquest in the early sixteenth century. In contrast to neighboring Costa Rica where the Spaniards either killed or expelled the Indians, the conquerors of Nicaragua drastically decimated, but did not completely destroy, the native population. As a result, in Nicaragua there was an underclass of nonwhites who could be used as virtual slaves in the income-concentrating economic activities of the European minorities. In Costa Rica, the Europeans had no ethnically distinct underclass to exploit. Thus, over the centuries, Costa Rica developed the relatively more egalitarian society that gave birth in the twentieth century to liberal democracy whereas Nicaragua and the other Central American countries to the north—with which it shared sociohistorical characteristics—produced an endless chain of elite-run dictatorships. Although the natural resources of the country were exploited by the elite to produce export products to generate wealth for its members, the human condition of the bulk of the population actually declined as the country's rulers used law and brute military force to promote their already lopsided class advantage. In Nicaragua, the last of these income-concentrating regimes were those of the Somoza dynasty—Anastasio Somoza García (1937–1956), Luis Somoza Debayle and puppets (1956–1967), and Anastasio Somoza Debayle (1967–1979). By the time Anastasio Somoza Debayle (with a net worth estimated well in excess of US$0.5 billion) was finally overthrown, the poorer 50 percent of his country's people were struggling to make do on a per capita income of around US$250 per year.

Parallel to, and often intimately connected with, this history of elite exploitation was a long experience of foreign intervention and meddling. During the colonial period, the Spaniards on the Pacific Coast and later the British in the Atlantic region exercised control over what is now Nicaragua. Although Spanish rule in the west came to an end in 1822, the British were only finally expelled from the east in the 1890s.

Decades before, the Americans had also begun meddling in Nicaraguan affairs.[2] In the 1850s a U.S. filibuster, William Walker, briefly imposed himself as president of Nicaragua and actually won diplomatic recognition from Washington. Later, in 1909, the United States encouraged and assisted the minority Conservative party in overthrowing Liberal nationalist president José Santos Zelaya. Subsequently, to keep elite pro-American governments in power, U.S. troops occupied Nicaragua from 1912 to 1925 and from 1926 to 1933. In return, these client regimes signed treaties giving away Nicaragua's right to have its own transoceanic waterway (which would have meant competition for the U.S. canal in Panama) and relinquishing its claims to San Andrés and other offshore islands (which Colombia demanded in apparent compensation from the United States for its involvement in engineering the independence of the Colombian province of Panama in 1903). During the second occupation, the United States created the Nicaraguan National Guard to preserve pro-American stability. After the U.S. troops departed, the National Guard's first Nicaraguan commander, Anastasio Somoza García, wasted little time in creating a pro-American dictatorship, which with abundant U.S. assistance was to last until 1979. By the time the dynasty was finally overthrown, its National Guard—one of the most corrupt and exploitative military establishments in the hemisphere—was also the most heavily U.S.-trained in all of Latin America.[3]

Not surprisingly, the centuries-old themes of elite exploitation and foreign meddling produced numerous incidents of grass roots or nationalist resistance. Several heroic Indian leaders resisted the Spanish conquistadores. Centuries later, in 1881, thousands of Indians lost their lives in the War of the Comuneros in futile resistance to the seizure of their ancestral lands by Nicaraguan coffee planters. In 1912, Liberal nationalist Benjamín Zeledón lost his life after leading an unsuccessful revolt against the U.S.-imposed Conservative regime. From 1927 to 1932, Augusto César Sandino lead a long guerrilla campaign to liberate his country from both the U.S. occupiers and the client regime they had imposed. Though his effort was partially successful in that it forced the United States to withdraw its troops, Sandino—who had signed a peace agreement with titular president Juan B. Sacasa—was subsequently murdered by Anastasio Somoza's National Guard.

The final—this time successful—resistance began in 1961. That year, frustrated with the lack of nationalism of the Nicaraguan Socialist party (PSN)—the local pro-Soviet Communists—several young Marxists split from the PSN to form the Sandinist Front for National Liberation (FSLN). Relatively unsuccessful in their initial guerrilla activities of the 1960s, the Sandinistas gained popularity and strength in the 1970s as Somoza rule became harsher and even Catholic clergy—following the suggestion of the Latin American bishops at their second international conference at Medellín, Colombia, in 1968—began organizing and raising the social and political awareness of the masses. Finally, after an unprecedented eighteen-month War of Liberation in 1978 and 1979, Somoza's army was defeated and the Nicaraguan revolution came to power.

The War of Liberation had cost Nicaragua around 50,000 lives, or approximately 2 percent of its people. In the United States, that would be the equivalent of a loss of around 4.5 million people, or over seventy-five times the U.S. death toll in the entire Vietnam conflict. But as Nicaraguans reminded me on my trip there a few days later, freedom, justice, and national dignity are sometimes worth such a price.

The First Seven Years of the Revolution

The new system was inevitably controversial both at home and abroad. Though ardently nationalist and in many cases deeply religious, most Sandinistas were also openly Marxist or Marxist-Leninist in that they found the writings of Marx and Lenin useful in understanding the history of Latin America. Consequently, they were automatically viewed with suspicion both by Nicaragua's middle- and upper-class minority—who feared the immediate imposition of a Soviet-style state and economy—and by foreign-policy makers in Washington—who were worried about the specter of a "second Cuba." Internally, these fears led to a rapid class polarization, rumor mongering, and a notable lack of cooperation in the reconstruction effort on the part of the private sector. Internationally, especially after the election of Ronald Reagan in the United States, these perceptions produced a multifaceted program to destroy the Sandinista revolution, including a campaign of propaganda and disinformation[4] depicting the government of Nicaragua as a grim, totalitarian Communist regime and an instrument of Soviet expansionism in the Americas. Although most of these allegations were either completely groundless or very nearly so, the U.S. mass media and opposition politicians (perhaps fearing to appear "naive," "liberal," or "biased") rarely challenged the carefully cultivated "conventional wisdom." Reagan's tactics for dealing with the Sandinistas could be criticized but not the administration's picture of the Nicaraguan regime itself.

For U.S. scholars who did research in Nicaragua during this period, the discrepancy between what was heard in the United States and what was seen in Nicaragua proved stark and frustrating. Far from being a coterie of wild-eyed ideologues, the Sandinistas behaved in a pragmatic and indeed moderate fashion throughout the first seven years. Although they were forced increasingly to rely on the Socialist Bloc for trade and aid, they did not impose a Soviet-style state or a Communist, or even socialist, economic system. They succeeded in carrying out innovative and highly successful social programs without inordinately straining the national budget. And contrary to the "conventional wisdom," their performance in the area of human rights—though not flawless—would probably rank Nicaragua at least in the top third of Latin America states.[5]

The Sandinistas enjoyed a number of political assets at the time of their victory, but their power was not limitless. Their greatest asset was the fact that their victory had been unconditional. The old National Guard had been defeated and disbanded. The new armed forces were explicitly Sandinist— that is, revolutionary and popularly oriented. Moreover, the mass organizations created in the struggle to overthrow the dictator gave the Sandinist Front of National Liberation (FSLN) a grass roots base that dwarfed the organized support of all potential rivals. Finally, the new government enjoyed broad international support. Nevertheless, the country's new leaders were well aware that their revolutionary administration faced certain geopolitical and economic constraints. The Soviet Union had made it clear that it was not willing to underwrite a second Cuba. Hard currency would not be forthcoming from that source, nor would military support in the event of a U.S. invasion. Furthermore, unlike Cuba, Nicaragua was not an island. Its long borders were highly vulnerable to paramilitary penetration, and any attempt to impose a dogmatic Marxist-Leninist system would certainly have generated a mass exodus of people. Finally, the Catholic Church in Nicaragua was so important and Catholics had played such a crucial role in the War of Liberation that the Sandinistas were neither inclined nor well situated to attack the Catholic traditions of their country. For these reasons, it is not surprising that for the next seven years the Sandinistas, in fact, attempted to govern in a pragmatic, nonideological fashion.

Sandinista rule was marked by a high degree of consistency and continuity—owing at least in part to the fact that the overall political trajectory of the revolution was set during these years by the same nine-person Sandinista Directorate (DN). Decisions made by the DN were based on consensus or near consensus. Reportedly, important decisions were never made on a five to four vote. This inherently conservative style of revolutionary stewardship meant that domestic and international policy, though adaptive in detail, remained consistent in overall characteristics and goals. During the entire seven years, the Sandinistas promoted (1) a mixed economy with heavy participation by the private sector, (2) political pluralism featuring interclass dialogue and efforts to institutionalize input and feedback from all sectors, (3) ambitious social programs, based in large part on grass roots voluntarism, and (4) the maintenance of diplomatic and economic relations with as many nations as possible regardless of ideology.

However, in spite of such overarching continuity, it is possible to divide this period into three subperiods that were clearly conditioned by the country's international environment. The first, which lasted until the election of Ronald Reagan in November 1980, was a time of euphoria and optimism. The second, spanning the nearly two years from that election to spring 1982, was a period of growing awareness of, and concern with, the hostile intentions of the new administration in Washington. In the third, during the little over four years that had elapsed from spring 1982 through summer 1986, Nicaragua would meet the full brunt of an unprecedentedly massive surrogate invasion, direct Central Intelligence Agency (CIA) sabotage, and economic strangulation.

THE QUIET BEFORE THE STORM

The first year (1979–1980) was the quiet before the storm. Jimmy Carter was still president of the United States. Though not pleased with the Sandinista victory, his administration had decided to make the best of it, offering economic aid with strings attached in the hopes of manipulating the Sandinistas in a direction acceptable to Washington. During this period, the FSLN consolidated the revolution politically by promoting the growth of grass roots organizations, reorganizing the Sandinista armed forces, and reequipping them with standardized military materiel. Much of the latter was obtained from the Socialist Bloc: The United States had earlier refused an arms purchase request by the Sandinistas. Nevertheless, the Sandinista Army was quite small (15,000 to 18,000 soldiers) and the civilian militia— little more than an association of patriotic marching units—hardly constituted a credible addition to the country's defensive force.

In economic affairs, the Sandinistas decided to honor Somoza's foreign debt in order to maintain Nicaraguan creditworthiness in Western financial circles. Lengthy negotiations with the international banking community led to concessionary terms for repayment. Public loans and aid poured in from a wide variety of countries. And, although the government immediately confiscated properties owned by the Somozas and their accomplices, it respected the rest of the private sector and even offered it substantial financial assistance (in the form of reactivation loans, preferential access to foreign exchange, and so on).

In line with the decision to preserve a large private sector, the revolutionaries created an interim government in which all groups and classes in society, including the privileged minority, could have a voice. The plural executive (Junta of National Reconstruction), created shortly before the victory, included wealthy conservatives as well as Sandinistas. The interim legislative body (Council of State) gave corporate representation to most parties and organizations of significance in Nicaraguan society. This was also a time of ambitious social programs—most notably the 1980 Literacy Crusade, which was carried out at relatively low cost to the government owing to its ability to mobilize massive voluntary participation.

The period was not without tension, however. Class polarization had set in almost immediately. Many in the minority privileged classes were certain that totalitarian communism was just around the corner. Accordingly, some fled immediately to Miami whereas others first illegally decapitalized their industries, transferred money abroad, and then fled. Moreover, a crisis of sorts occurred early in 1980, when conservatives on the Junta resigned in a pique over the fact that the organizations representing their class had been given representation on the new Council of State that was only slightly larger than the equivalent of the minority percentage that they represented in the population as a whole. At the same time, the independent daily, *La Prensa*, was taken over by a conservative wing of the Chamorro family and from then on took a critical position, playing on the fears of the privileged classes.

On balance, however, these were not bad times. Other conservatives were found to replace those who had resigned from the Junta. Human rights in general were respected. And *La Prensa* was allowed to make scurrilous and frequently false attacks on the system with virtual impunity. Former Somoza military personnel and accomplices were subjected to legal investigation and trial rather than execution. Indeed, the death penalty itself was immediately abolished.

THE GATHERING STORM

The second period, one of growing concern and apprehension, began in fall 1980 with the election of Ronald Reagan. That summer the Republican party platform had "deplor[ed] the Marxist-Sandinista takeover of Nicaragua" and had promised to end all aid to that country. Campaign aides to Reagan had advised using on Nicaragua the full gamut of techniques (e.g., economic destabilization, surrogate invasion) employed by the United States in the past to destroy Latin American regimes of which Washington did not approve. In fact, the new administration wasted little time in implementing these suggestions. Early in 1981, U.S. economic assistance to Nicaragua was terminated and the administration began to allow anti-Sandinista paramilitary training camps to operate openly in Florida, California, and the Southwest.[6] That December, President Reagan signed a directive authorizing the CIA to spend $19.8 million to create an exile paramilitary force in Honduras to harass Nicaragua.[7] Although some counterrevolutionary (contra) attacks occurred as early as 1981, such activity increased markedly in 1982, as bridges, oil-refining facilities, and other crucial infrastructure, in addition to civilian and military personnel, were targeted. That same year, the United States used its central position in the World Bank and the Inter-American Development Bank (IDB) to cut off the flow of badly needed multilateral loans to Nicaragua (see Chapter 4).

This growing external threat was clearly reflected in Nicaragua in increased class polarization, greater emphasis on austerity and defense, and some—albeit still relatively mild—government infringements on human rights. The acceleration of class polarization began almost immediately after the Reagan victory. Many in the privileged classes then apparently saw even less need than before to accommodate themselves to the new revolutionary system. Within days of Reagan's victory, representatives of the Superior Council of

Private Enterprise (COSEP) walked out of the Council of State. On November 17, Jorge Salazar, vice-president of COSEP and head of the Union of Nicaraguan Farmers (UPANIC), was killed in a shootout with state security forces while allegedly meeting with gun runners in preparation for armed counterrevolutionary activities. Even though the government televised highly damaging evidence against him, Salazar immediately became a martyr for the privileged classes.

From then on, tension mounted steadily as the conservative church hierarchy, the opposition microparties, COSEP, and La Prensa—all working in obvious coordination with the U.S. Embassy—showed less and less inclination to engage in constructive dialogue and an ever greater tendency to obstruct and confront. This behavior, in turn, generated resentment in the masses. In March 1981, for instance, Sandinista Defense Committees (CDSs) "in effect challenged the authority of the Ministry of the Interior by [staging demonstrations] blocking plans by the opposition MDN [Nicaraguan Democratic movement] to hold a political rally [at Nandaime] that had been presented by the government as proof that pluralism was still viable in Nicaragua."[8]

In addition, an increased emphasis was placed on military preparedness. The Sandinista Army was almost immediately expanded to around 24,000 persons, the level at which it would stay until 1983. Recruitment and training for members of the militia were stepped up markedly and obsolete Czech BZ-52 ten-shot rifles were imported to arm them. Socialist Bloc tanks, anti-aircraft equipment, helicopters, and troop transport vehicles were also imported. Moreover, there was talk of obtaining Soviet MiG fighter jets. This buildup, however, was clearly defensive, as noted in a staff report of the House Committee on Intelligence, when, in September 1982, it chastized the U.S. intelligence community for making dramatic public statements about Nicaragua's offensive intentions and capabilities while at the same time secretly briefing high-level administration officials to the contrary.[9] Meanwhile, there was a general belt tightening as the importation of nonessential goods was restricted and salaries were held down.

All government social programs were continued. Indeed, in 1981 over 70,000 young people participated in a voluntary primary health crusade. But, overall, the people of Nicaragua were beginning to feel the negative effects of the Reagan assault on their country.

As is true in all states in time of war or threat of war, certain human rights were gradually infringed upon in the name of national security. Late in 1981, in response to contra activity in the region, the government ordered the involuntary evacuation of some 8,500 to 10,000 Miskito Indians from isolated communities along the Rio Coco. Although careful investigations into this matter indicate that the evacuation itself was carried out in a humane fashion, in isolated incidents during subsequent security activities on the Miskito Coast individual commanders or soldiers disobeyed orders to respect the lives of prisoners and were apparently responsible for the execution or permanent "disappearance" of as many as 150 individuals.[10]

Also apparent was a deterioration in the right to due process for political prisoners in general and on the Miskito Coast in particular. Finally, on a half-dozen occasions, *La Prensa* was closed for two-day periods. This action was taken under the terms of a press law decreed by the original Junta (of which, ironically, *La Prensa* owner Violeta Chamorro had been part)—a law calling for such action in the event that an organ of the media was found to have disseminated material that was not only false but also destabilizing. However, even with these shutdowns, *La Prensa* continued to operate freely and in bitter opposition to the government more than 95 percent of the time. Moreover, at no point during this period did human rights infringements in Nicaragua even remotely approach the wholesale abuses prevalent in a number of other Latin American countries. In fact, late in 1982, the U.S. ambassador to Nicaragua, Anthony Quainton (a Reagan appointee), admitted candidly to a group of which I was a part that the human rights situation there was better than that in El Salvador or Guatemala—ironically two countries that Washington was then trying to portray as having made great strides in this respect.

WEATHERING THE STORM

The third period, from early 1982 through mid-1986, might aptly be labeled "weathering the storm." The storm, in this case, was the Reagan administration's massive and multifaceted campaign to destabilize and over-throw the Sandinista government, which, by the onset of this period, was covert in name only. The CIA-coordinated recruitment, training, arming, and disgorging of contras into Nicaragua had escalated rapidly from the force of 500 originally envisioned in the CIA finding of late 1981 to over 15,000 by 1984 (a proportionately equivalent invasion of the United States would number over 1,280,000) (see Chapter 2). Direct involvement by CIA personnel was also evident in the destruction of Nicaraguan oil-storage facilities late in 1983 and the mining of Nicaraguan harbors early in 1984 (see Chapter 2). Furthermore, an ever-larger number of U.S. military personnel participated in nearly continuous, highly menacing joint military maneuvers in Honduras and in naval "exercises" off both Nicaraguan coasts.

Accompanying these military and paramilitary efforts was an escalating program of economic strangulation. Washington continued to block approval of Nicaraguan loan requests before the World Bank and the IDB. U.S. trade was at first drastically curtailed (the Nicaraguan quota for exporting sugar to the United States was cut by 90 percent in May 1983) and then, in May 1985, embargoed completely. Washington also made an effort—though only partially successful—to pressure its allies to follow suit.

These activities had a clear impact on Nicaragua, though not always one that U.S. policy makers would have desired. In economic matters the country was hurt but by no means brought to its knees. Although the economy grew steadily during the first four years of Sandinista rule (except in 1982, when a severe flood occurred, followed by drought), problems inherited from Somoza, combined with a sharp decline in the world prices of

Nicaragua's export commodities and the enormous direct and indirect cost of the contra war, meant that by this third period Nicaragua was having increasing problems in servicing its debt. Accordingly, Venezuela ceased (1983) and Mexico drastically curtailed (1984) supplies of oil to the country. As a result, by 1984 and 1985 the Sandinistas were forced to turn to the USSR for most of their petroleum needs. The scarcity of foreign exchange also meant severe shortages of imported goods or of products manufactured in Nicaragua from imported materials or with imported machinery. Of course, such shortages also triggered rampant inflation and spiraling wage demands, which could not be satisfied given the tremendous diversion of government revenues into defense.

Social services were also negatively affected. As increased emphasis was placed on defense, government spending on health, education, housing, food subsidies, and so on had to be cut back. Further, the contras were deliberately targeting the social service infrastructure. Many government employees in health, education, and cooperatives were kidnapped, tortured and killed; schools, clinics, day-care centers and grain-storage facilities were destroyed. However, if all of this activity was designed to so damage the living standards of most Nicaraguans that they would become angry with their government and ultimately overturn it, someone had badly miscalculated. Although the human condition did decline during this later period, support for the government actually appears to have grown—as measured by levels of membership in pro-Sandinista grass roots organizations.[11] In the aftermath of the Triumph (1979–1980), such membership reached a peak of about 250,000 to 300,000 persons. Thereafter, it declined for a few years—as a result, perhaps, of apathy or a sense of lack of fulfillment of unrealistically high expectations for the revolution. However, by late 1982, grass roots membership had begun to climb again, and by 1984 it had doubled or tripled over the previous highwater mark. By then, around half of all Nicaraguans aged sixteen or older were in such voluntary support organizations.[12] In my opinion, the intervening variable was the contra war, the effects of which really began to hit home late in 1982. Simply put, Nicaraguans had come together to support their government in this time of national emergency and foreign threat.

During the same period, the military underwent a significant buildup. Nicaragua stepped up its purchase of military hardware such as helicopters, propeller-driven aircraft, artillery, anti-aircraft equipment, troop transports, and light weaponry—mainly from the Socialist Bloc (the United States had applied pressure to dissuade other potential suppliers such as France). By 1983 or 1984, the Sandinista Army, which had held constant at around 24,000 strong since 1981, was increased to over 40,000; in addition, a military draft was instituted. At the same time, the Sandinista Militia—a lightly trained body of over 60,000 civilian volunteers who had previously been armed with liberated Somoza-era weaponry and obsolete Czech BZ-52 rifles—was largely reequipped with Socialist Bloc AK-47 automatic rifles.

At first, the political response of the Sandinistas to the external threat was predictably defensive. In spring 1982 following contra attacks on important Nicaraguan infrastructure and the disclosure in the U.S. media of President Reagan's earlier authorization of funding for CIA-sponsored paramilitary operations against its country, the government declared a state of prewar emergency under which certain civil and political rights were temporarily suspended. Some measures (such as the short-term preventive detention of suspected subversives) had actually begun during the previous period; others (such as precensorship of the printed media) were new. The implementation of these measures was relatively mild. The short-term preventive detention measure affected only a few hundred persons at any one time. And *La Prensa*, though now heavily censored, continued to function until June 1986, when it was finally closed in the wake of the House approval of the $100 million. (In El Salvador the only real opposition papers had long since been driven completely out of business through the murder or exile of their owners.)

Another new political measure, decreed in July 1982, was the massive decentralization of government. Under it, the country was divided into six regions and three special zones for all governmental functions. The main purpose of this reform was to avoid the stifling effects of centralized bureaucratic control by creating institutions for local decision making and public policy implementation; another important objective was to institute a system of government that could continue functioning even if communications were badly disrupted or if Managua were occupied by enemy troops.

Eventually, however, as more and more Nicaraguans rallied around their government, the Sandinistas came to show renewed confidence in the people and to take a more relaxed approach to domestic politics. Late in 1983, the government actually passed out many tens of thousands of automatic weapons to civilians so that they could help defend their families, farms, villages, and neighborhoods.[13] Meanwhile, the government, in consultation with all political parties and groups that chose to enter into dialogue, had been working to create a mechanism to implement the Sandinistas' oft-repeated promise to hold general elections. Eventually, in September 1983, with considerable opposition input, a political parties law was hammered out and enacted. Three months later the government announced that the elections would be held in 1984. Early in 1984, November 4 of that year was set as the election date, and in March an electoral law modeled after "key components of the French, Italian, Austrian, and Swedish electoral systems"[14] was enacted. The Reagan administration denounced the Nicaraguan election in advance as a "Soviet-style farce," hyped businessman Arturo Cruz (whom they apparently knew had no intention of running) as the only viable opposition candidate, and reportedly pressured certain other candidates to withdraw from the contest at the last moment.[15] Nevertheless, the election was held as scheduled, and, though either ignored or panned by the U.S. media, it was certified as being a meaningful, clean, and relatively competitive election (given the difficult circumstances under which it was held) by a number of observer delegations representing Western European parliaments and governments, the U.S.-based Latin American Studies Association, and so on.[16] Although voting was not obligatory, 75 percent of those registered (93.7 percent of the voting-age population had registered) cast ballots. Although six opposition parties—three each to the Right and the Left of the FSLN—appeared on the ballot, the Sandinistas captured 63 percent of the vote. That gave the presidency and vice-presidency to Daniel Ortega and Sergio Ramírez, and sixty-one of the ninety-six seats in the new (constituent) National Assembly to the FSLN.

The National Assembly had a variety of functions but clearly the most important was that of producing a constitution. U.S. citizens familiar with President Reagan's description of Nicaragua as a "totalitarian dungeon" might imagine that the FSLN would simply have written a constitution and presented it to the National Assembly to be rubber-stamped. But this did not happen. The people who had designed the electoral law had deliberately selected a Western European system of proportional representation that tended to overrepresent minority parties. In addition, they had included a provision whereby all losing presidential candidates would get seats in the National Assembly. The end result was that although the Sandinistas got sixty-one seats, the six opposition parties got a substantial thirty-five. This division meant that the FSLN had just barely the 60 percent necessary to pass the constitution. Furthermore, the same practical considerations that had caused the Sandinistas to pursue dialogue, feedback, and pluralism during the Government of National Reconstruction were very much present as the constitution was being written.

In 1985 and 1986 the National Assembly proceeded with the task of producing a constitution. Subcommittees—in which minority opposition parties were deliberately overrepresented—were set up to deal with the different subject areas. Heated debate developed on a variety of issues. Finally, early in 1986 a preliminary draft constitution was produced, and a process of national and international consultation began. Seventy-eight open meetings—organized according to geographical region or interest identification (women, labor, small farmers, Christians, the military)—were held throughout Nicaragua to elicit feedback. And, as this process of "national consultation" was taking place, the draft constitution was submitted to international scrutiny. Large multiparty delegations from the National Assembly went to various countries to seek expert advice on that document. For instance, at a National Conference on the Nicaraguan Constitution (co-sponsored by Rutgers University, the City University of New York, the *New York University Journal of International Law and Politics*, and others), hundreds of prominent experts on U.S. constitutional law, human rights, and Nicaraguan affairs, organized into workshops concerned with eleven principal themes, met for three days to examine and criticize that document. When all of the data from both the national and international consultations were gathered, the original document underwent extensive rewriting and, in January 1987, a final constitution was formally promulgated. Though it drew heavily on the legal traditions of Western Europe and the United

States, the new basic law was also very "Nica" in that it was very much in tune with the social, cultural, and economic characteristics of Nicaragua. Ironically, though Nicaraguans had ample reason to be proud of both the elections of 1984 and the very open constitution-drafting process that followed, very few people in that war-torn country found these years to be a time of joy. The war itself was destabilizing the Nicaraguan economy and inflicting death, destruction, and suffering on the Nicaraguan people. And the Reagan administration pushed for—and eventually got—congressional approval for a vastly accelerated war. Virtually the entire U.S. media by the mid-1980s had adopted a "patriotic agenda"[17] in covering events related to the president's chosen enemy. In the wake of the 1984 election almost no U.S. media coverage was given to the generally positive reports produced by the various prestigious international election observer teams previously mentioned. Instead, for the next several weeks, the United States was gripped by war hysteria sparked by a series of skillfully timed (though utterly groundless) Reagan administration "leaks" to the effect that Soviet-built MiGs were en route by sea to "Communist" Nicaragua.[18] Thereafter, since the Reagan portrayal of the Nicaraguan elections as a Soviet-style farce was never seriously contradicted, the constitution drafting process could be ignored (though invited, the U.S. media were conspicuous in their absence from the New York Conference on the Nicaraguan Constitution) or, more ironic still, portrayed as an obstacle to peace (the United States, which arbitrarily broke off bilateral talks with Nicaragua in 1985, arrogantly insisted that these negotiations could not be resumed until Nicaragua stopped the constitution-drafting process and began negotiations with the contras).

Low-Intensity War and Historical Precedents

U.S. behavior toward Nicaragua in the 1980s was by no means an aberration either from traditional patterns in the U.S. treatment of Latin American countries or from the behavior of great powers in general. It appears to be a sad truism of international relations that hegemonic powers have always displayed the least creativity, sensitivity, and humanity in dealing with signs of change emanating from smaller countries within their spheres of influence. Certainly in twentieth-century Latin America, the United States—despite high-sounding rhetoric to the contrary—has consistently been an obstacle to change. Fearing the uncertain outcome of autonomous change Washington has instead advocated guided "moderate" reformism under the auspices of traditional client elites, which in fact have clung stubbornly to the status quo. The failure of the Alliance for Progress in the 1960s is only one dramatic example of the futility of such reformism.

Further, in those few cases where autonomous change began to develop in spite of U.S. policy, Washington has consistently worked to reverse such processes. U.S. troops made incursions into Mexico during the early years of its populist revolution. And, though President Franklin Roosevelt had the good sense to resist the idea, the U.S. Congress actually approved an invasion of that country when the "Mexican Bolsheviks" had the audacity to nationalize their country's own subsoil resources in 1938. The United States recruited and prepared the surrogate exile invasion forces that helped overthrow the democratically elected, mildly revolutionary government of Guatemala in 1954 and that attempted to reverse the Cuban revolution in 1961. It trained the local military establishment that gave the coup de grace to the middle-class revolutionary experiment in Bolivia in 1964. It sent U.S. Marines to the Dominican Republic in 1965 to block the return to power of centrist social democratic forces that it mistook for "Communists." And it used economic destabilization and CIA covert action to prepare the "ambient" for the military coup that overthrew the democratically elected government of Chilean socialist Salvador Allende in 1973.

Because of its actions, the U.S. government bears a heavy burden of responsibility for the negative impact of many of them. Where U.S. efforts were successful—in Guatemala, Bolivia, Dominican Republic, and Chile—the defeat of progressive forces was followed by oppressive dictatorship and campaigns of demobilization featuring the murder or disappearance of thousands, sometimes tens of thousands, of civilians at the hands of government security forces, associated "death squads," or both.[19] Also, in each of these cases the movement toward greater social justice was immediately and indefinitely halted. Where the United States failed—in Mexico and Cuba—Washington's counterrevolutionary behavior contributed to popular resentment against the United States, and in my opinion such behavior in the case of Cuba may have been a significant contributing factor in the restriction of traditional civil liberties in the name of national security.

U.S. techniques for the containment and destruction of chosen enemies underwent considerable change in the twentieth century. The direct use of U.S. troops—common until the early 1930s—was seldom seen thereafter. In the first three decades of this century, Cuba, the Dominican Republic, Haiti, and Nicaragua all suffered U.S. occupation as part of an expanded interpretation of the Monroe Doctrine first popularized by Teddy Roosevelt in his "big stick" policy. However, by the early 1930s, Sandino's patriotic resistance in Nicaragua had so delegitimized the idea of direct intervention that President Franklin Roosevelt finally declared a "good-neighbor" policy. Subsequently—with the notable exceptions of the Dominican Republic (1965) and Grenada (1983)—U.S. combat troops seldom set foot in Latin America.

Nevertheless, though it did come to practice relative restraint in the use of U.S. troops, Washington would continue to work in other ways to destroy its perceived enemies in the hemisphere.[20] Some of the many devices it employed were legal and above board; others were not. Usually both types were used in combination. Covert devices—usually employed by the CIA—included planning assassinations; conducting dirty tricks; inventing and disseminating "black propaganda"; funding or bribing opposition groups (church, labor, press, party); training and arming of surrogate native "rebel" forces; and carrying out of selective acts of sabotage often in the name of those "freedom fighters." More overt activities took the form of official warnings or expressions of displeasure, diplomatic maneuvers aimed at isolating the target regime, and a variety of devices designed to cause economic collapse (the cutting of normal U.S. trade and aid relationships, pressure to restrict the flow of funding from multilateral lending agencies, the use of travel bans to curtail tourism, etc.).

Often, the particular combination of techniques employed appeared to be chaotic, ad hoc, and poorly thought out. The amateurish and comical surrogate invasion of Guatemala in 1954 succeeded only through bluff and because the regular Guatemalan army was not loyal to the elected president. Having "succeeded" on that occasion the United States then mounted the ill-fated surrogate invasion of Cuba in 1961. The latter failed not, as some have argued, because President Kennedy refused to provide sufficient air cover but rather because a couple of thousand surrogate troops—no matter how well armed or protected—simply cannot overthrow a mass-based revolutionary government.

By the mid-1980s, however, indirect strategies for the destruction of "enemy" regimes had undergone considerable refinement. Indeed, a whole school of thought concerned with "low-intensity warfare" had come into being and was very much in vogue among the ultraconservative policy planners and advisers of the Reagan administration.[21] Advocates of low-intensity (as opposed to atomic or conventional) warfare argued that the war in Vietnam had been lost not because the United States failed to send sufficient human resources and materials but rather because it chose to fight a conventional war in a situation calling for low-intensity techniques. The heavy use of U.S. troops and equipment not only alienated the Vietnamese people but, equally important, exhausted the patience of the U.S. electorate. The employment of low-intensity techniques using native (surrogate) troops and a careful program of covert and overt activities aimed at building grass roots support and discrediting the enemy could, they argued, have been sustained indefinitely at relatively low cost and would ultimately have led to victory.

When the Reagan administration came to office in 1981 there was a clear cold war consensus that "communist" incursions into the Third World—especially into "our back yard"—should be rigorously combated. However, there was no immediate agreement on techniques. Secretary of State Alexander Haig seemed to advocate a crudely conventional military approach. Advising the president that Central America was "one [he could] win,"[22] Haig talked of "go[ing] to the source,"[23] and in El Salvador, U.S.-trained and -advised security forces used brutal search and destroy techniques, thus greatly alienating the rural population.

By 1983, however, Haig and many other early Reagan administration advisers were out, and advocates of a more subtle low-intensity approach were in. In El Salvador, security forces were being trained in civic action, the CIA was reportedly disseminating disinformation about the insurgents,[24] and a patina of democracy was being applied to a system that, in fact, remained extremely repressive and nondemocratic.[25] In Nicaragua, too, the dream of a quick military victory—possibly directly using U.S. troops—was apparently abandoned by the mid-1980s. In its place was a strategy of prolonged low-intensity conflict involving propaganda and disinformation, surrogate "insurgency," economic strangulation, and so forth. Since the human and material expense to the United States—and, therefore, the political costs—were expected to remain low, it was felt that a war of this sort could be carried out indefinitely.

Notes

1. For more detailed information about Nicaragua's early history than can be presented in this book, see John A. Booth, *The End and the Beginning: The Nicaraguan Revolution*, ed. 2 (Boulder, Colo.: Westview Press, 1985), and Thomas W. Walker, *Nicaragua: The Land of Sandino*, ed. 2 (Boulder, Colo.: Westview Press, 1986).

2. The best study of the 150-year history of U.S. interference in Nicaraguan affairs is Karl Bermann, *Under the Big Stick: Nicaragua and the United States Since 1948* (Boston: South End Press, 1986).

3. Richard Millett, *Guardians of the Dynasty: A History of the U.S.-Created Guardia Nacional de Nicaragua and the Somoza Family* (Maryknoll, N.Y.: Orbis Books, 1977), p. 252.

4. For some specific examples of the use of disinformation against Nicaragua see Thomas W. Walker, "The Nicaraguan-U.S. Friction: The First Four Years, 1979–1983," in Kenneth M. Coleman and George C. Herring, eds., *The Central American Crisis* (Wilmington, Del.: Scholarly Resources, 1985), pp. 181–186.

5. Throughout the first seven years, the Nicaraguan government invited various human rights monitoring organizations to conduct investigations in Nicaragua. Consequently, there are a number of extensive reports on human rights under the Sandinistas. Most are critical of certain violations, but the abuses they identify are relatively mild compared to those of many other Latin American states. See Amnesty International (AI), "Nicaragua Background Briefing: Persistence of Public Order Law Detentions and Trials" (London: AI, 1982); Amnesty International, "Prepared Statement of Amnesty International USA on the Human Rights Situation in Nicaragua Before the Subcommittee on Human Rights and International Organizations," U.S. House of Representatives, September 15, 1983 (mimeograph); Inter-American Commission on Human Rights, Organization of American States (OAS), *Report on the Situation of Human Rights of a Segment of the Nicaraguan Population of Miskito Origin* (Washington, D.C.: OAS, 1984); and Americas Watch, *Human Rights in Nicaragua* (New York: Americas Watch, 1984). Americas Watch eventually confronted the stark discrepancy between what the Reagan administration was charging and what these reports state, in Americas Watch, *Nicaragua: Reagan, Rhetoric and Reality* (New York: Americas Watch, 1985).

6. The story of the contra training camps first became public in Eddie Adams, "Exiles Rehearse for the Day They Hope Will Come," *Parade Magazine* (March 15, 1981), pp. 4–6.

7. "U.S. Plans Covert Operations to Disrupt Nicaraguan Economy," *Washington Post*, March 10, 1982, and "U.S. Said to Plan 2 C.I.A. Actions in Latin Region," *New York Times*, March 14, 1982.

8. Jack Child, "National Security," in James D. Rudolph, ed., *Nicaragua: A Country Study* (Washington, D.C.: Government Printing Office, 1982), p. 202.

9. Staff Report, Subcommittee on Oversight and Evaluation, Permanent Select Committee on Intelligence, *U.S. Intelligence Performance on Central America: Achievements and Selected Instances of Concern*, September 12, 1982, (mimeo.), p. 43.

10. Inter-American Commission on Human Rights, *Report on the Situation of Human Rights*.

11. My estimates of grass roots organization memberships are rough. They are based on conversations held during eleven visits to Nicaragua with individuals working in mass mobilization and on Luis H. Serra, "The Sandinista Mass Organizations," in Thomas W. Walker, ed., *Nicaragua in Revolution* (New York: Praeger Publishers, 1982), pp. 95–114, and Luis H. Serra, "The Grass Roots Organizations," in Thomas W. Walker, ed., *Nicaragua: The First Five Years* (New York: Praeger Publishers, 1985), pp. 65–89.

12. Interestingly, this estimate is essentially corroborated by an in-house U.S. Embassy estimate for late 1984, which places grass roots membership at 7 to 8 hundred thousand. This information was revealed by an official in the U.S. Embassy to a group of which I was a part on June 25, 1985.

13. Mary Vanderlaan states that the campaign to hand out rifles to civilians began in 1984 and that by 1986 "nearly 300,000 rifles" had been distributed (Mary B. Vanderlaan, *Revolution and Foreign Policy in Nicaragua*, Boulder, Colo.: Westview, 1986), p. 272. My conversation with Sandinista officials and other informed Nicaraguans would generally confirm these observations. The only minor correction I would make concerns Vanderlaan's starting date: During a visit to the northern war zone in December 1983, I was informed—and could readily observe—that this program had already begun.

14. Latin American Studies Association (LASA), *The Electoral Process in Nicaragua: Domestic and International Influences*, Report of the Latin American Studies Association Delegation to Observe the Nicaraguan General Election of November 4, 1984 (Austin, Tex.: LASA, 1984), p. 29.

15. LASA, *The Electoral Process*, p. 29–32.

16. LASA, *The Electoral Process*; Thom Kerstiens and Piet Nelissen (official Dutch government observers), "Report on the Elections in Nicaragua, 4 November, 1984" (photocopy); Irish Inter-Party Parliamentary Delegation, *The Elections in Nicaragua, November, 1984* (Dublin: Irish Parliament, 1984); Parliamentary Human Rights Group, "Report of a British Parliamentary Delegation to Nicaragua to Observe the Presidential and National Assembly Elections, 4 November, 1984" (photocopy); and Willy Brandt and Thorvald Stoltenberg, "Statement [on the Nicaraguan elections in behalf of the Socialist International]," Bonn, November 7, 1984.

17. This term was apparently coined by Edward S. Herman in his excellent article, "'Objective' News as Systematic Propaganda: The New York Times on the 1984 Salvadoran and Nicaraguan Elections," *Covert Action Information Bulletin*, Spring 1984, no. 21, pp. 7–13

18. See *Washington Post* and *New York Times* from November 6 through late November 1984.

19. These and other demobilization operations elsewhere in Latin America (Brazil, Uruguay, Argentina, etc.) bore some resemblance to the CIA-coordinated Phoenix program in Vietnam, which in 1969 alone took the lives of over 20,000 alleged Viet Cong suspects. The fact that the United States had extensive police and security force training programs in each of the countries involved suggests that those similarities may not have been accidental.

20. For an introduction to the techniques (short of direct U.S. invasion) that the United States has employed in the past to destroy chosen enemies throughout the

world and in Latin America in particular see Philip Agee, *Inside the Company: CIA Diary* (London: Bantam Books, 1976); Richard H. Immerman, *The CIA in Guatemala: The Foreign Policy of Intervention* (Austin: University of Texas Press, 1982); Seymour M. Hersh, "The Price of Power: Kissinger, Nixon and Chile," in *The Atlantic Monthly*, December 1982), pp. 31–58; Victor Marchetti and John D. Marks, *The CIA and the Cult of Intelligence* (New York: Dell Publishing Company, 1975); Stephen Schlesinger and Stephen Kinzer, *Bitter Fruit: The Untold Story of the American Coup in Guatemala* (Garden City, N.Y.: Anchor Books, 1982); John Stockwell, *In Search of Enemies: A CIA Story* (New York: W. W. Norton, 1978); U.S. Congress, Senate, Staff Report of the Select Committee to Study Governmental Operations with Respect to United States Intelligence, *Covert Action in Chile* (Washington, D.C.: Government Printing Office, December 18, 1975); and Armando Uribe, *The Black Book of American Intervention in Chile* (Boston: Beacon Press, 1974).

21. For the best discussion of low-intensity warfare as applied to Central America see the entire April/May 1986 issue of *The NACLA Report on the Americas*. For other source material on the subject see Deborah Barry, "Los conflictos de baja intensidad: Reto para los Estados Unidos en el Tercer Mundo (El Caso de Centroamérica)," in *Centroamérica: La Guerra de Baja Intensidad* (Managua: Coordinadora Regional de Investigaciones Económicas y Sociales (CRIES), 1986); Tom Barry and Deb Preusch, *The Central America Fact Book* (New York: Grove Press, 1986); Arthur H. Blair, Jr., et al., "Unconventional Warfare: A Legitimate Tool of Foreign Policy," *Conflict* 4, no. 1 (1983):59–81; Richard A. Hunt and Richard H. Schultz, Jr., *Lessons From Unconventional War: Reassessing U.S. Strategies for Future Conflicts* (New York: Pergamon Press, 1982); Bill Keller, "'Essential,' they say, but 'repugnant'" (Department of Defense conference on little wars—'low intensity conflict'), *New York Times*, January 20, 1986, p. 12ff.; F. Kitson, *Low Intensity Operations: Subversion, Insurgency, Peace-Keeping* (Harrisburg, Pa.: Stackpole Books, 1971); Brad Knickerbocker, "U.S. Military Surveys Central America Turf; Some Officers Say U.S. Unready for Demands of 'Low-Intensity Conflict,'" *Christian Science Monitor*, May 15, 1985, p. 1; James Berry Motley, "'Grenada: Low Intensity Conflict and the Use of United States Military Power," *World Affairs*, 146, no. 3 (Winter 1983–1984):221–238; G. Reed, "Low Intensity Conflict: A War for All Season," *Black Scholar* 17, no. 1 (1986):14–22; Sam C. Sarkesian, *The New Battlefield: America and Low Intensity Conflicts* (Westport, Conn.: Greenwood Press, 1986); Sam C. Sarkesian and William L. Scully, *U.S. Policy and Low Intensity Conflict* (New Brunswick, N.J.: Transaction Books, 1981); Raúl Vergara, José Rodolfo Castro, and Deborah Barry, "Nicaragua: Escalada agresiva y movilización defensiva: Informe final del proyecto 'Violencia, Derechos Humanos y Sobrevivencia Cultural en América Latina.'" Unpublished manuscript (Managua: Coordinadora Regional de Investigaciones Económicas y Sociales [CRIES], 1986); Caspar W. Weinberger, "Low Intensity Warfare," *Vital Speeches*, February 15, 1986, p. 258.

22. Lawrence Barrett, *Gambling With History* (Garden City: Doubleday, 1983), p. 207.

23. William M. LeoGrande, "The United States and Nicaragua," in Thomas W. Walker, ed., *Nicaragua: The First Five Years* (New York: Praeger, 1985), p. 428.

24. "America's Secret Warriors," *Newsweek* 102 (October 10, 1983):39.

25. For a brief discussion of the flaws of the Salvadorean elections as opposed to those carried out in Nicaragua see Walker, *Nicaragua: The Land of Sandino*, pp. 116–119.

PART 1

The Assault on Nicaragua

Introduction

The Reagan administration's attack on Nicaragua was thorough and multifaceted. First and most obvious was the paramilitary war. In Chapter 2, Peter Kornbluh describes the history of the U.S.-sponsored contra war as well as the various sabotage actions carried out directly by the CIA—often in the name of the contras. Eva Gold in Chapter 3 details the military encirclement of Nicaragua: the tremendous U.S.-sponsored armed buildup in Costa Rica and particularly in Honduras from 1981 onward, a buildup that, though obviously designed in part to alarm the Nicaraguans and make them act "paranoid," could not be completely discounted as a possible prelude to direct U.S. invasion. Michael Conroy turns in Chapter 4 to the economic war, demonstrating how the destruction and dislocation caused by the contra war were used to intensify the negative effects of other more traditional forms of economic aggression including the severance of U.S. trade and aid and the blocking of badly needed loans from international lending agencies such as the World Bank and the Inter-American Development Bank. Next, in Chapters 5 and 6 Martin Diskin and Betsy Cohn/Patricia Hynds provide descriptions of the U.S. manipulation of ethnic and religious tensions in Nicaragua. The authors demonstrate that, as the Reagan administration and various like-minded "private" groups were distorting and propagandizing about real and imaginary Sandinista abuses against the Church and ethnic minorities, they were also extremely active behind the scenes in promoting and exacerbating the conflicts they were publicly denouncing. In Chapter 7 on electronic penetration Howard Frederick describes the ever expanding radio and television infrastructure—clandestine, commercial, and governmental—used by the Reagan administration and its private and public allies to inject anti-Sandinista propaganda across Nicaragua's borders. He shows that the revolutionary government with its primitive and weak telecommunications infrastructure was at a clear disadvantage in the electronic war of words. Finally, in Chapter 8 William Goodfellow details the history of the U.S. effort to "coopt [the] negotiations issue" in order to avoid any peaceful settlement of its dispute with Nicaragua.

TWO

The Covert War

PETER KORNBLUH _____

It is much easier and much less expensive to support an insurgency than it is for us and our friends to resist one. It takes relatively few people and little support to disrupt the internal peace and economic stability of a small country.

—CIA Director William Casey
March 13, 1982[1]

As the Sandinista revolution triumphed in Nicaragua on July 19, 1979, the U.S.-sponsored counterrevolution began. A DC-8 jet, disguised with Red Cross insignia, landed in Managua to evacuate commanders of the Nicaraguan National Guard, a force the United States had created more than fifty years before. Over the next few days, U.S. operatives airlifted remnants of Anastasio Somoza's praetorian army to Miami from where they could reorganize to renew their fight against the Sandinistas in the future.[2] Unnoticed at the time, this operation marked the opening salvo in what would eventually become the paramount symbol of U.S. policy toward Nicaragua—the CIA's "covert war."

Genesis of the Covert War

By the time Ronald Reagan assumed office in 1981, the Carter administration had already expended $1 million in covert funds to organize and bolster internal opposition groups in Nicaragua. Nevertheless, Carter's limited efforts to manipulate the course of the Nicaraguan Revolution were considered insufficient by the new administration hardliners who viewed the Sandinistas' very existence as a challenge to U.S. hegemony in the Western Hemisphere. Achieving a modus vivendi with the Sandinist Front of National Liberation (FSLN) was all but ruled out from the beginning. Instead, the new team in Washington decided to make Nicaragua a test case of the Reagan Doctrine of taking the offensive against revolution in the Third World.

Within the incoming administration a general consensus existed on the objectives of U.S. policy in Central America—to "excise the cancer of communism" in the words of the president—but not on the means to accomplish that goal.[3] In early meetings of the National Security Council, Alexander Haig, Reagan's first secretary of state, counseled "a determined show of American will and power" and a "high level of intensity at the beginning."[4] To bolster his case that the United States needed to go "to the source" of revolution in Central America, Haig ordered then–State Department adviser Robert McFarlane to draw up an options paper, "Taking the War to Nicaragua," that weighed the possibility of the open use of force against Cuban ships and planes and a naval blockade against Nicaragua.[5]

Yet the president's advisers, including Vice-President George Bush, Secretary of Defense Caspar Weinberger, and the Joint Chiefs of Staff, vetoed Haig's call to war. Any overt display of force, they reasoned, would conjure up the image of "another Vietnam" in the mind of the public, divert resources from more important battlefields in Europe and the Middle East, and jeopardize the administration's efforts to garner congressional support for its domestic and foreign policy agenda.[6]

The decision to opt for a covert tack against the Sandinistas reflected the tension between Reagan's commitment to "project American power abroad" and the political constraints on sending U.S. troops into a Central American quagmire. Against the backdrop of the "Vietnam Syndrome"— widespread public opposition to U.S. military involvement in Third World conflicts—CIA operations emerged as the centerpiece of a low-intensity warfare strategy that incorporated economic destabilization, psychological operations, and diplomatic pressures.[7] But between 1981 and 1986 the administration's so-called covert war—a misnomer since it became public virtually at its inception—passed through three distinct phases: (1) the creation of a surrogate army; (2) direct CIA attacks on Nicaragua; and (3) a National Security Council–sponsored campaign to maintain the contras despite the ban on official aid.

Initiation of the Proxy War

The Reagan administration's strategy depended on the creation of a proxy force of exiles such as the one the CIA had used to overthrow the Arbenz government in Guatemala in 1954 and in its failed effort to oust Fidel Castro at the Bay of Pigs in 1961. Accordingly, in 1981 a new generation of CIA-backed counterrevolutionaries emerged. The contras, as this force came to be known, could bring direct pressure on Nicaragua's fragile economic institutions, complementing U.S. efforts to undermine the economy from abroad. Moreover, implementing U.S. policy through a surrogate paramilitary army enabled Washington to invoke a "plausible denial" of responsibility for the contra's actions, shielding the administration from accountability to Congress and the U.S. public.

Publicly, the Reagan administration depicted the contras as an "interdiction force" meant to halt arms allegedly flowing from Nicaragua to Salvadoran rebels. Privately, however, policy makers held both optimal and minimal expectations for the contra war. Some officials believed that the contras might evolve into a credible invasion force, inciting a popular uprising that would topple the Sandinistas. In one scenario presented to the Congressional Intelligence Committees by Assistant Secretary Thomas Enders and CIA director William Casey, contra forces would launch a pincer-style assault "picking up more and more popular support, which will produce desertions in the Nicaraguan military, all setting the stage for a drive on Managua that forces the government out of power."[8]

Even if such optimistic projections did not come true, the contras served Washington's policy objectives. At a minimum, they provided a weapon to destabilize and discredit the Sandinista's revolutionary experiment, weakening the regime's ability to govern internally and undermining its image internationally. At CIA Langley, Virginia, headquarters, according to David MacMichael, an agency national intelligence analyst from 1981 to 1983, officials expected that the contra incursions

would provoke border attacks by Nicaraguan forces and thus serve to demonstrate Nicaragua's aggressive nature and possibly call into play the Organization of American States's provisions [for collective defense]. It was hoped that the Nicaraguan government would clamp down on civil liberties within Nicaragua itself, arresting its opposition, demonstrating its allegedly inherent totalitarian nature and thus increase domestic dissent within the country.[9]

The strategy was to force the Sandinistas to become in reality what administration officials called them rhetorically: aggressive abroad, repressive at home, and hostile to the United States. "The theory was that we couldn't lose," as one U.S. diplomat summarized the purpose of the contra war:

If they took Managua, wonderful. If not, the idea was that the Sandinistas would react one of two ways. Either they'd liberalize and stop exporting revolution, which is fine and dandy, or they'd tighten up, alienate their own people, their international support and their backers in the United States, in the long run making themselves more vulnerable. In a way, that one was even better—or so the idea went.[10]

The Evolution of the Covert War

"The Project," as the covert war was known within the intelligence community, officially began on March 9, 1981, when Reagan submitted his first "Presidential Finding on Central America" to Congress authorizing CIA covert operations in the region. The authorization provided $19.5 million for the CIA to significantly expand the Carter administration's clandestine assistance to "moderate" opponents of the Sandinistas, including private business groups, organized labor, political parties, and the press. In addition, the "Presidential Finding" called for a covert "arms interdiction program" to halt weapons Reagan claimed were flowing from Nicaragua to leftist guerrillas in El Salvador, Honduras, and Guatemala.[11]

Reagan's authorization gave the CIA a green light to lay the foundation for a covert paramilitary operation in Nicaragua. In spring 1981, agency operatives established contact with a number of small anti-Sandinista exile groups in Miami and Central America. U.S. special envoy Vernon Walters was dispatched to enlist the support of Argentina, Honduras, and other Central American governments in fostering secret war against the Sandinistas. In May, the CIA provided $50,000 to Argentine military intelligence officials to be funneled to the incipient contras as incentive to unite under one anti-Sandinista banner.[12] By then, Washington was openly sanctioning the existence of paramilitary training camps for Nicaraguan exiles in Florida, California, and Texas—even though their activities appeared to flaunt the 1794 Neutrality Act.[13]

In August, the CIA began to draw up contingency plans for clandestine operations in Nicaragua. William Casey appointed Duane Clarridge—"a real doer, a real take charge guy"—to oversee CIA operations against the Sandinistas.[14] Clarridge joined a Restricted Interagency Group, also known as the Core Group, made up of Enders, General Paul Gorman, and Lt. Colonel Oliver North, constituted to recommend and coordinate a covert warfare policy in Nicaragua.

The Core Group presented a series of option papers to the National Security Council in November. Among them was a CIA proposal to organize, arm, and train an action team of 500 Latin American commandos who would "engage in paramilitary and political operations in Nicaragua" and supplement a force of 1,000 Nicaraguan exiles already being trained in Honduras by the Argentine military government. The CIA requested $19.95 million as seed money for its paramilitary program. As the operation evolved, the agency predicted, "more funds and more manpower will be needed."[15]

On November 23, President Reagan signed National Security Decision Directive 17 granting the CIA authority to build a 500-person paramilitary force, collaborate with foreign governments in the region, and foster a broad opposition front to the Sandinista government. For congressional consumption, however, Reagan's second "Presidential Finding" depicted these operations as limited in scope and purpose. On December 1, CIA Director William Casey informed the Congressional Oversight Committees that the agency's paramilitary force would be restricted in numbers, that no Americans would be involved, and that no economic targets would be attacked. Instead, Casey indicated, the primary targets would be Cuban support structure in Nicaragua and arms supply lines to Salvadoran guerrillas.[16]

Whereas actions by small isolated bands of Somocista guardsmen had been previously limited to sporadic, ineffectual incidents along the border region, with the influx of U.S. personnel, equipment, and money the frequency and destructiveness of the contra attacks escalated rapidly. On March 14,

1982, CIA-trained and -equipped saboteurs blew up two vital bridges in the Chinandega and Nueva Segovia provinces near Honduras—marking an unofficial declaration of war. "In a 100 day period from 14 March to 21 June, at least 106 insurgent incidents occurred within Nicaragua," the Defense Intelligence Agency (DIA) reported. Contra operations during this period "involved the following types of operations":

- Sabotage of highway bridges and attempted destruction of fuel tanks.
- Sniper fire and attacks against small military patrols.
- Attacks by small guerrilla bands on individual Sandinista soldiers and the assassination of minor government officials and a Cuban adviser.
- Burning of a customs warehouse, buildings belonging to the Ministry of Construction, and crops.[17]

By spring 1982, the administration judged the covert war to be successfully under way. The young revolutionary regime in Managua had reacted as predicted, declaring a state of emergency after the first major contra attack in March, censoring the opposition press, and mobilizing troops along the Nicaraguan-Honduran border—all of which lent credence to Reagan's ever louder declarations that the Sandinistas were "totalitarian" aggressors. "In Nicaragua, the Sandinistas are under increasing pressure," proclaimed a classified National Security Planning Group summary paper in April, "as a result of our covert efforts."[18]

The CIA and the Contras

The original control structure of the proxy war was known as La Tripartita— a joint U.S., Argentine and Honduran effort. At first, the CIA dispersed hundreds of thousands of dollars in cash and military hardware through two Argentine military intelligence officials, Colonel Osvaldo Ribeiro, and Julio Villegas, who, along with high Honduran military officials, acted as go-betweens with the contra hierarchy. But when U.S.-Argentine relations soured after the Malvinas-Falklands war in April 1982 and divisions within the rebel leadership became a serious problem, U.S. operatives assumed direct command and control of the paramilitary campaign.[19] Under Ambassador John Negroponte, a former assistant to Henry Kissinger on the National Security Council and political officer in Saigon during the Vietnam War, dozens of U.S. agents worked out of Tegucigalpa; a handful, known to the contras as "Colonel Raymond," "Major West," "Alex," "George," "John," "Thomas," and "Donald," supervised the rebel force, overseeing the administration, logistics, and tactical operations of the war effort.[20]

Under their direction, motley bands of former national guardsmen and peasants were transformed into a paramilitary army equipped with trucks, planes, automatic weapons, and artillery. U.S. officials forged the main contra coalitions, determined their leadership, supplied the contra forces, paid the salaries of both commanders and foot soldiers and planned their missions. Through the power of the purse and the provision of equipment, the CIA controlled the size and activities of the contra forces. Within a year of NSDD 17, Casey's original 500-person "action team" had increased eightfold to 4,000 persons. By July 1983, CIA officials informed Congress that the contra army was 10,000 strong and growing.[21]

Initially, the contra forces broke down into two main coalitions: the Nicaraguan Democratic Force (FDN), based in Honduras, and the Democratic Revolutionary Alliance (ARDE), which operated out of Costa Rica. Miskito Indian contra forces split into two organizations: MISURA, which joined the FDN, and MISURASATA, which was part of ARDE.

The FDN was founded in Guatemala City on August 10, 1981, when, at the behest of the CIA, the original Honduran-based contra group known as the September 15 Legion and the Miami-based Union Democratica Nicaragüense (UDN) agreed to merge their efforts. From its inception, former officials of Somoza's widely despised Nicaraguan National Guard dominated the FDN's leadership. A "secret" Defense Intelligence Agency report, dated July 16, 1982, noted that the FDN "is reportedly led by Col. Enrique Bermúdez—former GN [National Guard] member and last Nicaraguan military attache to the US under the government of President Anastasio Somoza—and other ex-GN officers. It is based in Honduras and operates primarily in northern Nicaragua. It is the largest, best organized and most effective of the anti-government insurgent groups."[22]

ARDE, by contrast, was founded in Costa Rica in September 1982 by two former members of the Sandinista government: Edén Pastora, the legendary guerrilla fighter known as Commandante Zero, and Alfonso Robelo, a millionaire businessman who had been a member of Nicaragua's ruling junta until April 1980. Its anti-Somocista credentials made ARDE a potentially more credible force against the FSLN than the National Guard–ridden FDN. Hence, in April 1982, Duane Clarridge approached Edén Pastora and offered to make him "the star of the second revolution as he had been the star of the first."[23] Pastora accepted, according to the *Wall Street Journal* "on the condition that he have absolute deniability because his credentials as a nationalist would be weakened if his CIA ties were revealed."[24]

By April 1984, the CIA was funneling $400,000 a month to Pastora's forces fighting from bases in northern Costa Rica.[25] But when Pastora refused the agency's demand that ARDE join in a two-front war alliance with the FDN, the CIA abandoned him. In the aftermath of a May 30 attempt to assassinate Pastora, apparently carried out by anti-Castro Cubans acting in concert with members of the FDN, Robelo and half of ARDE's troops joined the FDN.[26] Two years later, CIA operatives lured Pastora's remaining troops away with a promise of military assistance if they would join an FDN-ARDE coalition. Isolated and demoralized, Pastora announced he would retire from the contra movement and return to his prerevolutionary occupation as a shark fisherman.[27]

Despite its Somocista orientation, the FDN received the bulk of U.S. resources and therefore emerged as the vanguard of the counterrevolution.

Both the organization and its leaders, according to Edgar Chamorro, the former FDN director of public affairs, became "nothing more than executioners of the CIA's orders."[28] In December 1982, the CIA organized a civilian directorate for the FDN and in October 1983 selected a long-time agency "asset," Adolfo Calero, to be the FDN's chair and spokesperson.[29] U.S. special forces personnel trained FDN task force commanders at the Lepaterique base outside of Tegucigalpa. Under the cover of the Pentagon's military "exercises" in southern Honduras, U.S. Army engineers constructed logistical command posts at El Aguacate and Jamastran from which the CIA managed the war effort. From sanctuary bases stocked with U.S. military materials along the Honduran-Nicaraguan frontier, FDN forces conducted raids into northern Nicaragua almost at will.

What Reagan administration officials depicted as a campaign to "harass" and "pressure" the Sandinistas into halting their alleged export of revolution in practice translated into vicious attacks on small villages, state-owned agricultural cooperatives, rural health clinics, bridges, electrical generators, and, finally, people. Far from living up to their billing in Washington as "freedom fighters," FDN troops established a reputation for abject brutality and gross violations of human rights. By the end of 1985, the Nicaraguan Ministry of Health estimated that 3,652 civilians had been killed, 4,039 wounded, and 5,232 kidnapped during contra raids.[30] FDN forces, the human rights monitoring organization *Americas Watch* reported, "systematically engaged in the killing of prisoners and the unarmed, including medical and relief personnel; selective attacks on civilians, and indiscriminate attacks; torture and other outrages against personal dignity."[31] Their actions, as former CIA Director Stansfield Turner testified before Congress in April 1985, "have to be characterized as terrorism, as State-supported terrorism."[32]

The Reagan administration dismissed reports of FDN atrocities as "Sandinista disinformation" and maintained the mythology of the contras as "good" guerrillas. Yet, the CIA's own training manuals for the FDN advocated various tactics of terrorism. One handbook, *The Freedom Fighters Manual*, left behind after an attack on the city of Ocotal in June 1984, provided instructions for thirty-eight forms of "sabotage tasks" against government-owned property including how to commit arson by using match books and cigarettes as slow fuses and how to construct Molotov cocktails for setting police stations and fuel depots on fire.

A second CIA manual, *Psychological Operations in Guerrilla Warfare*, prescribed more extreme forms of terrorism—including assassinating civilians. The ninety-page booklet was written in October 1983 by a U.S. Army counterinsurgency specialist on contract to the CIA who called himself "John Kirkpatrick" and then cleared by officials at the CIA's Langley, Virginia, headquarters.[33] The agency printed 2,000 copies; 200 were distributed to the FDN for use in training courses on psychological warfare.

Rather than counsel indiscriminate violence, the *Psychological Operations* manual encouraged the contras to regulate their savagery—to use terrorism for political advantage. It stressed the counterinsurgency concept of "armed propaganda"—employing implicit terror to win the hearts and minds of the Nicaraguan peasantry. As for explicit terror, the CIA booklet issued concrete instructions for the "selective use of violence" against civilian leaders associated with the Sandinista government. "It is possible to neutralize carefully selected and planned targets, such as court judges, magistrates, police and state security officials, etc. For psychological purposes, it is necessary . . . to gather together the population affected, so that they will be present, take part in the act, and formulate accusations against the oppressor."[34]

Advocating murder violated the president's Executive Order 12333, which states that "no person employed by or acting in behalf of the United States Government shall engage in or conspire to engage in assassination" and "no agency may request any person to undertake activities forbidden by this order."[35] Publicly, therefore, the White House denied that it endorsed such a practice or that it even occurred.[36] Behind closed doors, however, the CIA admitted that the contras were committing such atrocities. In late 1983, Duane Clarridge conceded in a closed briefing for the House Intelligence Committee staff that the contras had killed "civilians and Sandinista officials in the provinces, as well as heads of cooperatives, nurses, doctors and judges." "After all," Clarridge reportedly reasoned, "this is a war."[37]

The CIA's War

The contras proved adept at vanquishing undefended villages and killing unarmed civilians, but they were incapable of establishing themselves as a viable guerrilla force. In December 1982 and again in March, August, and October 1983, FDN troops mounted coordinated attacks on northern Nicaraguan villages in an effort to secure a "liberated zone" and set up a provisional government. Although the raids wrought severe economic damage and left many casualties, the contras failed to generate any popular support and were eventually driven back into Honduras by the Sandinista Popular Army (EPS).[38]

These losses sparked a major review of the covert war within the CIA. In July and again in October 1983, Clarridge traveled to Tegucigalpa to pressure FDN leaders to make a better showing on the battlefield.[39] One CIA national intelligence estimate submitted to the congressional oversight committees in fall 1983 concluded, however, that "there are no circumstances under which a force of U.S.-backed rebels can achieve a military or political victory over the leftist Sandinista government."[40] Within the agency, one senior intelligence official recalled, "there was a push to have some kind of success in Nicaragua." The prevailing attitude, he explained, was that "if the FDN and Pastora's people can't really do things that hurt, it's got to be worked out another way."[41]

In its original November 1981 proposal to initiate the covert war, the agency had forecast its own direct role in attacking Nicaragua: "In some circumstances CIA might (possibly using U.S. personnel) take unilateral action against special . . . targets."[42] To "do things that hurt," therefore, the CIA initiated its own war of sabotage and destruction against Nicaragua. Between September 1983 and April 1984, the agency carried out at least twenty-two attacks on vital installations.[43] CIA pilots bombed Nicaraguan targets, frogmen sabotaged port facilities and commandos planted mines— all missions deemed too sophisticated for the contras to accomplish. U.S. officials ordered the FDN and ARDE to take credit for these operations. In reality, the contras played no role other than as a cover for direct U.S. aggression.

The CIA supplemented its own agents with a specially trained force of "unilaterally controlled Latino assets" (UCLAs)—contract operatives recruited from Salvador, Honduras, Chile, Argentina, Ecuador, and Bolivia. Supervised by agency personnel, the UCLAs received training in unconventional warfare from U.S. special forces in Panama, the United States, and Honduras. "Our mission was to sabotage ports, refineries, boats, bridges," one Honduran UCLA explained, "and try to make it appear that the contras had done it."[44]

Sophisticated military technology added a James Bond–like element to the CIA's operations. Two "mother ships"—large oil service-type vessels with long flat sterns for helicopter pads—served as floating bases for air and sea attacks on Nicaraguan harbor facilities. Piranhas (high-speed motor boats provided by the U.S. Drug Enforcement Agency) were converted into lethal attack craft equipped with mortars and machine guns. Twin-engine Fairchild Merlin IV airplanes with sophisticated infrared radar provided reconnaissance intelligence during CIA raids. As part of ongoing "psy-ops" against Nicaragua, the agency also deployed floating gunfire simulators offshore, in a design to exacerbate tensions among Sandinista troops guarding coastal installations.[45]

On September 8, 1983, the CIA launched a series of direct attacks on Nicaraguan port facilities. Speedboats manned by UCLAs and launched from a base ship anchored 12 miles off shore struck at Puerto Sandino. Five weeks later Latino frogmen returned to sabotage an underwater oil pipeline.

The second major attack took place on October 10 at Corinto, Nicaragua's largest commercial port. Agency commandos fired mortars and grenades at five huge oil and gasoline storage tanks, igniting 3.4 million gallons of fuel. Over one hundred people were injured in the raid, according to Nicaraguan authorities, and 25,000 inhabitants of the city had to be evacuated while a fire raged out of control for two days.[46]

In the wake of these dramatic attacks, President Reagan approved a December 1983 NSC proposal to escalate "harassment" operations against ports, power plants, bridges, and other installations.[47] A month later, in January 1984, U.S. personnel conducted a helicopter raid on the Nicaraguan port of Potosí, killing one Nicaraguan and wounding eight.[48] On February 2, 1984, UCLA pilots flying U.S. military planes bombed a communications center and a military training camp in Northern Nicaragua leaving four dead.[49]

On March 7, and again on March 30, CIA pilots flying Hughes 500 helicopters provided what one CIA combat summary called "suppressing rocket fire" to back up an attack by UCLA-driven piranha boats at the petroleum storage facility at San Juan Del Sur and Puerto Sandino. When on April 9 ARDE forces seized the oceanside village of San Juan del Norte for forty-eight hours, agency helicopters flying off the CIA base ship along the coast furnished rocket and gunfire support against Sandinista positions. "ARDE was satisfied with the fire display," the CIA report stated. "No known casualties."[50]

Mining the Harbors

The Reagan plan also authorized the mining of Nicaragua's harbors.[51] Manufactured by the CIA Weapons Group—a munitions division within the agency—with assistance from the Naval Surface Weapons Center in Silver Spring, Maryland, the underwater charges deployed in Nicaragua consisted of large metal cylinders packed with 300 pounds of C-4 plastic explosives—enough to sink small fishing boats and damage larger vessels.[52] UCLA commando teams, operating once again from a CIA intelligence ship anchored offshore, deposited the mines in the shipping channels of Nicaragua's major Atlantic and Pacific Coast ports in January, February, and March 1984.

As in previous cases of CIA/UCLA actions, the contras were told to take public credit for sowing the mines. "At 2 A.M. on January 5, 1984," Edgar Chamorro recalls, "George [the deputy chief of the CIA mission] woke me up at my safehouse in Tegucigalpa and handed me a press release in excellent Spanish." "I was surprised to read that we—the contras—were taking credit for having mined several Nicaraguan harbors. George told me to rush to our clandestine radio station and read this announcement before the Sandinistas broke the news. Of course, we played no role in the mining of the harbors."[53]

U.S. policy makers assumed that once the contras announced that the harbors had been mined no civilian cargo ship would dare run such a gauntlet, impeding trade and dealing a serious blow to Nicaragua's already fragile economy. FDN radio broadcasts warned Lloyds of London, the shipping insurance company, that merchant vessels should stay away from dangerous Nicaraguan waters. "We find it strange that Lloyds of London and the owners and ships' captains have unnecessarily exposed themselves to financial and physical loss by not taking our warning seriously," stated one communiqué after commercial shipping to Nicaragua had failed to halt. "Only the FDN has the capacity and the necessary knowledge to deactivate the mines and only the FDN knows how many and where they are. The mines will be removed only when Nicaragua is freed of communist totalitarianism."[54]

By the first week of April, ten commercial vessels had struck the CIA-sown mines. Six of those were non-Nicaraguan. Ships registered to Japan, the Netherlands, Liberia, and Panama—as well as the Soviet oil tanker *Lugansk*—sustained damage; five Russian seamen were among the fifteen sailors injured by the exploding underwater charges. Two Nicaraguans were killed.

As ships began to sink in Nicaraguan waterways, the administration invoked its cover story, pointing the finger of blame at the contras. In response to a diplomatic protest from the Kremlin condemning the United States for an "act of banditry and piracy," the State Department issued a carefully worded denial: "We note that the anti-Sandinista forces have widely advertised that certain Nicaraguan ports have been mined. We have no further information on this incident."[55]

The Surrogate Supply Network

Revelations of CIA responsibility for the mining of Nicaragua's harbors provoked an avalanche of criticism at home and abroad. Around the world, Washington's allies openly castigated the CIA's action as a flagrant violation of international law. In Congress, even staunch Republican supporters of the contras such as Chairman of the Senate Intelligence Committee Barry Goldwater joined liberal Democrats in expressing outrage.[56] Both the House and the Senate passed bipartisan resolutions condemning the mining operation.

The political uproar marked a turning point in Congress's willingness to look the other way while the Reagan administration violated international codes of conduct in pursuit of overthrowing the Sandinistas. As it became apparent that the Democrat-controlled House of Representatives would not, in 1984, pass further aid for the contras, administration officials turned to other options for sustaining the war effort.

Between 1984 and 1986, two interrelated tactics were pursued. Abroad, U.S. officials initiated contact with third countries such as Israel, Saudi Arabia, Brunei, and Guatemala to enlist their support for the contras.[57] At home, President Reagan approved a National Security Council plan to create a surrogate network that would provide funds, training, and armaments to the contras when and if Congress refused to back the war. The plan called for Lt. Col. Oliver North, an aide to National Security Advisor Robert McFarlane, to work through designated intermediaries to keep the FDN financially, materially, and militarily afloat.[58] When Congress declared a moritorium on further aid to the contras on October 10, 1984, the administration's shadow contra aid network was already in place.

Circumventing the new legislation—again named for Representative Boland—which explicitly barred U.S. intelligence officials from "directly or indirectly" assisting the contras, Colonel North, Assistant Secretary of State Elliott Abrams, and Alan Fiers, director of the CIA's Central American Task Force, oversaw an operation codenamed "Project Democracy."[59] A key NSC contact, retired General John K. Singlaub, met with North once a month to discuss the FDN's needs and domestic fund-raising efforts.[60] Retired

Major General Richard V. Secord supervised the acquisition of arms and the contra resupply missions. Secord associates purchased hundreds of tons of grenades, explosives, rifles, and bullets in Portugal and employed a former CIA-owned air charter company, Southern Air Transport, to ship the equipment to Central America.[61] Through a complex maze of international bank accounts, corporate fronts, arms brokers and shipping companies, a cabal of former Pentagon special operations personnel and ex-CIA agents covertly maintained the flow of arms to the contras.[62]

Although the bulk of what the administration falsely portrayed as private aid to the contras arrived covertly through these channels, open support came from sympathizers of the United States. In the aftermath of the congressional ban, supporting the contras became a cause célèbre for the new Right. Encouraged by President Reagan's rhetoric, dozens of contra charities sprang up around the United States. Established right-wing organizations, such as the Christian Broadcasting Corporation, the Unification Church, and Veterans of Foreign Wars, joined newly formed ultra-Right groups such as Citizens for a Better America, Refugee Relief International, and the Nicaraguan Freedom Fund in raising money, medical supplies, clothing, foodstuffs, and other materials. To avoid openly violating the Neutrality Act, these groups classified their assistance as "humanitarian aid" for Nicaraguan refugees.

Working in concert with Colonel North, General Singlaub emerged as the driving force behind an ostensibly private nationwide fund-raising campaign for the contras. As chairman of the U.S. Council for World Freedom, an organization chartered in 1981 to aid "freedom fighters around the world," General Singlaub became the principal generator of nonlethal aid to the contras in the United States, claiming by late 1984 to be raising $500,000 a month.[63] Through his position as head of the World Anti-Communist League (WACL), moreover, he collaborated with North to raise funds from Asian countries for the contra campaign. Singlaub also contributed—along with paramilitary groups such as Soldier of Fortune and Civilian Military Assistance—men to the contra cause. During a trip to Central America in March 1985, the general met with FDN leaders and promised to recruit "a few American trainers" with "specific skills" to fill in for CIA agents legally prohibited from working with the contras. Singlaub informed North that "these will be civilian (former military or CIA personnel) who will do training only and not participate in combat operations."[64]

Through Singlaub's fundraising and the administration's solicitation of third country support, more than $50 million flowed into contra coffers during the official moratorium on aid. And, by the fall of 1986, $10 to $30 million more had been added through the diversion of profits from clandestine arms sales to Iran. This money paid for approximately 2000 tons of weapons for the contras procured through the Administration's surrogate network. It also financed the purchase of cargo planes, ships, safehouses, maintenance facilities, and communications gear necessary for the resupply missions. In the spring and summer of 1986, White House-directed crews conducted dozens of clandestine airdrops of ammunition, rifles, grenade launchers, and other equipment to contra bands operating along Nicaragua's northern and southern borders. U.S. ambassadors and CIA and Pentagon officials in Central America assisted these supply operations. According to telephone records from El Salvador, Colonel North maintained contact with key operatives directing the missions. On October 5, 1986, when one of the network's planes was shot down by Sandinista troops, the NSC-run contra program was halted.[65]

The Humanitarian Aid Era

The Reagan administration's surrogate support system enabled the contras to expand their ranks, acquire new weapons, and launch scattered but not insignificant attacks inside Nicaragua. Most important, the aid network salvaged the contras from political extinction in Washington, buying time for the administration to mount an effective propaganda campaign aimed at forcing Congress to renew U.S. assistance. In April 1985, Reagan's initial proposal for $14 million in military aid was narrowly rejected. But, prompted by Daniel Ortega's ill-timed trip to Moscow in May and by the administration's creation of yet another civilian front for the contras, the United Nicaraguan Opposition (UNO), the House of Representatives reversed itself in June and voted $27 million in nonlethal aid.

The new legislation maintained the ban on CIA participation in the war other than to provide intelligence data to the contras. The assistance was to be administered overtly, and the legislation called for a "detailed" accounting of the program's expenditures. To distribute the clothing, food, medicine, and transportation vehicles that Congress had authorized, in September 1985 President Reagan created a new agency, the Nicaraguan Humanitarian Assistance Office (NHAO).

The NHAO became another vehicle for the administration to skirt the law. The principal air freight company contracted by the NHAO to ferry "humanitarian" supplies to the contras was controlled by members of the NSC network. The firm, Airmach, received over $180,000 to fly between the United States and Central America. Once there, however, its planes were used by U.S. operatives to drop guns and ammunition into Nicaragua.[66]

Suspected abuse of NHAO funds quickly became an issue of contention between Congress and the Reagan administration. In December when the House Subcommittee on Western Hemispheric Affairs asked the General Accounting Office (GAO) to verify how the humanitarian aid moneys were being spent, the NHAO initially refused to cooperate. NHAO records of hundreds of thousands of dollars in U.S. payments to various grocery shops, pharmacies, and clothing shops in Central America for contra supplies turned out to be inaccurate; journalists discovered that many of the stores had conducted only a fraction of the business cited by the NHAO or none at all.[67] In March and again in May and June 1986, GAO investigators testified before the committee that millions of dollars that the NHAO claimed to have paid to suppliers and brokers in Miami, Honduras, and Costa Rica could not be traced. Finally, after the subcommittee had subpoenaed bank records of NHAO expenditures, it found that $1.5 million had been paid to the Honduran Armed Forces, including a January 10, 1986, $450,000 payment to then–commander in chief, General Walter López, and that over $6 million had disappeared into obscure bank accounts in Miami, Panama, and the Cayman Islands.[68]

Besides the implications of widespread corruption uncovered by the GAO, in spring 1986 other scandals threatened to undermine the administration's new campaign to obtain $100 million in military and nonmilitary assistance for the contras. Reports that some contra members were involved in cocaine trafficking began to appear in the press.[69] In May, a mercenary named Jack Terrell, who had worked at a contra base in Honduras in 1985, publicly accused FDN leaders of corruption and brutal atrocities and implicated them in the assassination attempt on Edén Pastora's life.[70]

A group of twenty former FDN officials added their voices to the charges against the contra leadership. "A cool, dispassionate analysis of the six years of struggle," the so-called CONDOR group wrote in a March 1986 letter to General Singlaub, "brings us to the following conclusions": the FDN hierarchy was "politically inept," abused power, indulged in "croneyism and nepotism," and had resorted to "improvised quackery in conducting the war."[71]

Indeed, after six years and more than $130 million in U.S. aid, by spring 1986 the contra movement was in its worst military condition since its formation. Aside from a flurry of ambushes in August and September 1985, the contras had virtually ceased to fight. Although President Reagan claimed a force of 20,000, contra sources admitted their ranks had dwindled to 12,000, almost all of whom were forced back into Honduras by a superior Sandinista military.

On the political front, squabbling between the three UNO civilian leaders, Arturo Cruz, Adolfo Calero, and Alfonso Robelo, over power had produced cracks in the contras' civilian facade that would eventually lead to the breakup of the organization. "The Nicaraguan resistance remains without a political infrastructure inside Nicaragua or a clear political message to give to the Nicaraguan people," a House Select Committee on Intelligence evaluation stated in March 1986. "It has never developed urban support. In fact, years of United States assistance have not produced an insurgency capable of sustaining itself among the population in Nicaragua." According to the classified assessments of the CIA and DIA, the Intelligence Committee noted, "only United States forces could truly resolve the conflict in Nicaragua on a military basis."[72]

Yet the teflon nature of the Reagan presidency seemed to rub off on the contras; despite the corruption, human rights atrocities, the lack of political appeal or military prowess of the contras, on June 26 the U.S. Congress acceded to the administration's intense pressure and authorized $100 million to renew the war on Nicaragua. Far more important than the amount of money, the vote lifted all previous restrictions on CIA involvement in the paramilitary campaign. Nor did Congress reimpose any limitations on the purpose for supporting the Contras. For the first time, U.S. legislators unequivocably endorsed the administration's strategy of low-intensity warfare against the Sandinista government.

Indeed, the House of Representative's reversal of its previous opposition to the Reagan administration's course marked a watershed in the not-so-secret covert war. Almost immediately, the White House began to implement a comprehensive war plan designed to rejuvenate the contras and spread their violent attacks throughout the countryside and into urban centers including Managua. The plan called for establishing new contra bases on small islands located off Nicaragua's Atlantic Coast. The Pentagon would assume a prominent role in the war effort by training contra forces in the tactics of special warfare and civic action at bases in Honduras, Panama, and the United States. By November 1986, the first team of seventy contras had arrived at Eglin Air Force base in Florida. Moreover, the CIA planned to revive its Unilaterally Controlled Latino Assets program and begin anew its own direct involvement in the war effort.[73]

As the CIA's proxy campaign entered its seventh year it was clear that the Reagan administration intended to escalate its policy of punishment against Nicaragua. Although the contras brashly predicted crippling the Sandinistas by mid-1987, they remained politically and militarily distant from taking power. Revelations in November 1986 that administration officials had illegally skimmed off millions of dollars from arms sales to Iran for the contras threatened future congressional appropriations. Nevertheless, increased U.S. intervention on the contras' behalf reflected Washington's determination to wage a war without end in Nicaragua, spreading ever more death and destruction over a country that the administration claimed to want to save.

Notes

1. Casey is quoted in the *Washington Post*, May 8, 1983. For a fuller treatment of the covert war and the other facets of U.S. policy toward the Sandinistas, see Peter Kornbluh, *The Price of Intervention: Reagan's "Total War" on Nicaragua* (Washington, D.C.: Institute for Policy Studies, 1987).

2. For a description of this mission, see Christopher Dickey, *With the Contras* (New York: Simon and Shuster, 1986) pp. 51–55.

3. For a description of early debates within the administration, see the *Wall Street Journal*, March 5, 1985. See also, William M. LeoGrande, "The United States and Nicaragua," in Thomas W. Walker, ed., *Nicaragua: The First Five Years* (New York: Praeger, 1985), pp. 425–446.

4. See Haig's memoirs, *Caveat* (New York: Macmillan, 1984) p. 129.

5. *Los Angeles Times*, March 3, 1985.

6. Haig describes the objections of Reagan's advisers in *Caveat*, pp. 129, 130.

7. For an analysis of low-intensity warfare as a new military strategy of intervention, see Sarah Miles, "The Real War: Low Intensity Conflict in Central America," North American Congress on Latin America (NACLA), May/June 1986.

8. *New York Times,* May 23, 1983.

9. See MacMichael's testimony before the World Court, September 13, 1985, p. 8 of transcript.

10. Quoted in Allan Nairn, "Endgame," *NACLA,* May/June 1984, p. 29.

11. The "Presidential Finding" is described in the *New York Times,* April 8, 1983, and the *Washington Post,* May 8, 1983.

12. The Argentines began supporting small bands of contras in Guatemala in early 1981 after a handful of ex-Guardia officials undertook a sabotage mission against Radio Noticias del Continente, a leftist radio station outside of San José, Costa Rica. See Dickey, *With the Contras,* p. 91. See also Shirley Christian, *Revolution in the Family* (New York: Random House, 1985), p. 198.

13. *New York Times,* Jan. 18, 1982.

14. *Wall Street Journal,* March 4, 1985.

15. The CIA proposals are cited in the *Washington Post,* May 8, 1983.

16. Ibid.

17. See Defense Intelligence Agency, "Weekly Intelligence Survey," July 16, 1982, pp. 20, 21.

18. The NSC document, "United States Policy in Central America and Cuba Through F.Y. 84, Summary Paper," is reprinted in the *New York Times,* April 7, 1983.

19. For a description of Argentina's early role in supporting the contras, see the *Miami Herald,* December 19, 1982.

20. These names were cited by former members of the FDN during interviews in Miami, June 4, 1986.

21. The size of the contra forces was overinflated by the CIA for propaganda purposes, according to Edgar Chamorro, the FDN's former director of public relations. In April 1984, for example, CIA officials reported to Congress that the size of the contra forces stood at 15,000; yet internal contra memoranda written two months earlier put the figure at closer to 6,000.

22. See the Defense Intelligence Agency, "Weekly Intelligence Survey," p. 22.

23. Dickey, *With the Contras,* p. 149.

24. See the *Wall Street Journal,* March 4, 1985.

25. "ABC Weekend Report," April 22, 1984.

26. One of the journalists who was injured in the bomb blast that was meant to kill Pastora conducted a major investigation into the assassination plot and arrived at these conclusions. See Tony Avirgan and Martha Honey, *La Penca: Reporte de una Investigación* (Lima, Perú: Ediciones El Gallo Rojo, 1985).

27. *Washington Post,* May 30, 1986.

28. Chamorro's comments are printed in the Center for National Security Studies, *First Principles,* "Running the Nicaraguan War," September/October 1985, p. 7.

29. Administration and contra sources identified Calero as CIA in the *New York Times,* March 6, 1986.

30. These statistics are cited in David Siegel, "Nicaraguan Health: An Update," *LASA Forum,* winter 1986, p. 30.

31. See Americas Watch, *Human Rights in Nicaragua: Reagan, Rhetoric and Reality* (New York: Americas Watch, July 1985), p. 16.

32. Stansfield Turner is quoted from his testimony before the House Subcommittee on Western Hemispheric Affairs. See House, Subcommittee on Western Hemispheric Affairs, "U.S. Support for the Contras," 99th Cong., 1st Sess., April 16, 1985, p. 4.

33. Kirkpatrick essentially translated the manual from a 1968 lessons book, "Armed Psyop," used at the Army Special Warfare School at Fort Bragg, North Carolina.

Parts of the manual were word for word from lesson plan 168, which among other things called for the use of selected violence against civilians. See the *Washington Post*, October 24, 1984.

34. The contras followed these instructions. FDN units, according to Edgar Chamorro, "would assemble all the residents in the town square and then proceed to kill—in full view of the others—all persons suspected of working for the Nicaraguan government." See Chamorro's affidavit before the World Court, signed on September 5, 1985, p. 10. For the quotations from the manual see *The CIA's Nicaragua Manual: Psychological Operations in Guerrilla Warfare* (New York: Vintage Books, 1985).

35. The statute is cited in *The CIA's Nicaragua Manual*, p. 104. It is an extension of a 1975 executive order, signed by President Ford in the aftermath of the Church Committee findings that the CIA had participated in assassination plots around the world.

36. President Reagan, for example, dismissed the controversy over the manual as "much ado about nothing." In his interpretation, the passage advocating the "selective use of violence" meant simply firing someone from his or her position. To "neutralize" someone, according to the president, "You say to the fellow who's sitting there in the office, 'You're not in the office anymore.'"

37. Clarridge's testimony is reported in the *Miami Herald*, October 20, 1984.

38. For periodic updates on fighting inside Nicaragua, see the Central American Historical Institute *Updates*.

39. Interview with Edgar Chamorro, June 10, 1985.

40. Cited in the *Washington Post*, November 25, 1983.

41. Dickey, *With the Contras*, p. 258.

42. *Washington Post*, May 8, 1983.

43. Nineteen of these attacks are listed in a CIA after-action report obtained by the *Wall Street Journal*, March 6, 1985.

44. This man, who remains unidentified, was interviewed by Gillian Brown for her documentary, "The Pentagon Republic," an Insite Production, 1985.

45. A CIA report citing the use of this equipment is quoted in the *Wall Street Journal*, March 6, 1985.

46. *Washington Post*, April 18, 1984.

47. See the *Washington Post*, April 11, 1984.

48. *Wall Street Journal*, March 6, 1985.

49. *New York Times*, May 3, 1985.

50. See the *Washington Post*, December 20, 1984, and the *Wall Street Journal*, March 6, 1985.

51. Duane Clarridge takes credit for the idea for sowing the mines. His historical knowledge of the 1904–1905 Russo-Japanese war where mining tactics had been used, Clarridge told the Joint Chiefs of Staff, prompted him to consider mines as a weapon against the Sandinistas. See the *Wall Street Journal*, March 6, 1985.

52. *New York Times*, June 1, 1984.

53. See Edgar Chamorro's article, "Confessions of a Contra," in *The New Republic*, August 5, 1985, p. 22.

54. Communicado, Oficina de Prensa, Centro de Comunicaciones, Fuerza Democrática Nicaragüense, undated.

55. *New York Times*, March 22, 1984.

56. In a scathing letter to Casey, Goldwater wrote that he was "pissed off" at not being fully informed about an operation that he called "an act of war" and a "violation of international law." See *Time*, April 23, 1984.

57. In July 1984, Saudi Arabia began to funnel $1 million per month into contra bank accounts and by the spring of 1986, according to the Senate Select Committee's report, "Preliminary Inquiry," had contributed over $31 million. In August 1986, Elliott Abrams solicited a $10 million dollar donation from the Sultan of Brunei—money that was deposited in a Swiss bank account set up by Lt. Col. Oliver North. Israel provided weapons seized from the PLO in Lebanon. At the request of NSC advisor Robert McFarlane and Lt. Col. North, Guatemala agreed to supply false documentation for the network to purchase arms in Portugal. See The Senate Select Committee on Intelligence, "Report on Preliminary Inquiry," January 29, 1987, p. 49. See also the President's Special Review Board, Report of the Special Review Board, February 26, 1987 (hereafter referred to as the *Tower Commission Report*.).

58. For a description of the plan see the Associated Press, June 10, 1986. For an overview of the NSC network see Robert Perry and Brian Barger, "Reagan's Shadow CIA," *The New Republic*, November 24, 1986.

59. See the Associated Press, January 14, 1987.

60. See the Associated Press, June 10, 1986.

61. For Cline's role see the *Wall Street Journal*, January 2, 1987. See also the *Washington Post*, January 17, 1987, for a description of the number of weapons sent from Portugal to the contras.

62. The network also included Robert Dutton and Richard Gadd, both retired military officials with Air Force Intelligence backgrounds. In El Salvador, missions were overseen by two former CIA Cuban Americans, Felix Rodriquez, a Bay of Pigs veteran, and Luis Posada Carilles, who is believed to have masterminded the October 1986 bombing of an Air Cubana jetliner over Barbados, which killed seventy-three people. On Secord's role see the *New York Times*, December 6, 1986. See also the *Washington Post*, December 7, 1986.

63. The council's 1985 tax forms, however, show grants totaling only $270,745. See Internal Revenue Service Form 990, statement of Program Services Rendered, 1985.

64. *The Tower Commission Report*, p. C-4.

65. *Washington Post*, December 7, 1986.

66. Internal NHAO memoranda show payments of $182,000 to Airmach, a company owned by Secord associate Richard Gadd, and another $80,000 to Vortex Air, a Miami-based company with no planes. For a description of their activities see the Associated Press, November 13, 1986. See also, the *New York Times*, December 4, 1986.

67. See the *Miami Herald*, May 9, 1986, and June 1, 1986.

68. See statement of Frank C. Conahan, U.S. General Accounting Office, before the House Subcommittee on Western Hemispheric Affairs, June 11, 1986. See also the *New York Times*, December 6, 1986.

69. For two such stories, see the *San Francisco Examiner*, March 16, 1986, and the *New York Times*, April 11, 1986.

70. Terrell has been interviewed by the American Broadcasting Company and the National Broadcasting Company news, National Public Radio, and several newspapers. For a summary of his story, see James Ridgeway, "Contragate?" *Village Voice*, May 20, 1986.

71. See Nicaraguan Coalition of Opposition to the Regime, (CONDOR), "The Nicaraguan Situation," undated.

72. See the House of Representatives, Permanent Select Committee on Intelligence, *Adverse Report*, March 12, 1986, pp. 5, 6.

73. For details of the war plan see the *Miami Herald*, June 27, and October 23, 1986.

THREE

Military Encirclement

EVA GOLD

U.S. militarization of Central America in the 1980s continued a history of U.S. military intervention in Latin America: Nicaragua, Guatemala, Honduras, El Salvador, Panama, and Mexico, as well as Haiti, the Dominican Republic, Cuba, Grenada, and Chile, were among the Latin nations that had been invaded by U.S. Marines, occupied by U.S. troops, or subject to U.S.-sponsored covert actions in the nineteenth and twentieth centuries.[1] Following the success of revolutions in 1979 in Nicaragua and Grenada the United States accelerated its program of military exercises and inflated its security assistance programs. By the mid-1980s U.S. military policy in the region, supplemented by secret wars and covert actions, formed the backbone of the Reagan Doctrine—an all-out counterrevolutionary campaign.

In 1979 there were three major U.S. bases in the Caribbean Basin—in Panama, Guantanamo Bay, Cuba, and Roosevelt Roads, Puerto Rico—with nearly 15,000 U.S. troops stationed in the area.[2] Additional U.S. troops were deployed in the region for several weeks annually, for military exercises in the Caribbean Sea, for practice in defense of the Panama Canal, and, less frequently, for joint exercises in Honduras. Military training was offered, primarily through the U.S. Army School of the Americas in Panama, where approximately 1,000 Latin officers attended classes each year.[3] No more than a dozen U.S. military personnel were assigned to each U.S. Embassy in Central America, the Caribbean, and South America. Security assistance programs in the region were small. Several, such as those for El Salvador and Guatemala, had been terminated because of failure to comply with U.S. human rights criteria.

Toward the end of his presidency, Jimmy Carter turned to a more militaristic foreign policy. In 1979 he responded to the purported discovery of a Soviet combat brigade in Cuba with a call for a greater U.S. military presence in the Caribbean; in 1980 he authorized the resumption of assistance to the Salvadoran military despite its responsibility for continuing human rights violations.[4] With the Reagan presidency Central America became a testing ground for the new administration's commitment to contain and turn back revolutionary Third World movements. The Central American landscape and the capabilities of local military forces were reshaped in the first half of the 1980s; U.S. troops with giant earthmovers built or improved airstrips and roads, dug wells and tank traps, and erected radar stations, piers, and barracks. In Honduras, the logistical center of U.S. military operations, there were rarely fewer than 1,000 U.S. troops from 1983 on, while tens of thousands more cycled through in an unbroken sequence of military exercises.[5] Additional U.S. troops were involved in exercises in Panama and Costa Rica and in the Caribbean Sea, at times bringing thousands more to the region. Military assistance programs—grants and loans for military training, equipment, and weapons—escalated from $10 million for El Salvador, Honduras, Costa Rica, and Guatemala in fiscal year (FY) 1980 to nearly $200 million in FY 1985.[6] Although assistance to El Salvador, the largest recipient of U.S. military aid in the region, was directed primarily toward defeat of internal insurgency, the purpose of military assistance programs for Honduras and Costa Rica was twofold: to prepare local troops to deal with any internal insurgency and to play a role should there be military intervention in Nicaragua. It also helped create a climate of hostility toward Nicaragua, both in the region and in the United States, and the appearance of regional support for U.S. policy.

The buildup in Central America was part of the Reagan administration's pledge to enlarge the U.S. military presence worldwide. According to Secretary of Defense Caspar Weinberger's 1985 Annual Report to Congress, military construction through 1989 would "move us considerably closer to our goal of being able to deploy major forces and sustain combat operation in two or more theaters simultaneously."[7] U.S. bases were expanded in the Persian/Arabian Gulf, Indian Ocean, and Mediterranean Sea as well as in the Caribbean Basin. U.S. Readiness and Special Operations Forces were strengthened, and the U.S. Army upgraded its light infantry divisions to prepare for quick deployment.[8] Military exercises toned up U.S. troops; U.S. military muscle was flexed with deployments in the Middle East, confrontations with Libya, and the invasion of Grenada.

At first portrayed by U.S. policy makers as a quick and easy solution to a crisis in Central America, intervention proved to be a long-term commitment with far-reaching implications. From the first the Reagan administration had carefully built in both Washington and Central America diplomatic and military leadership committed to military solutions of the regional crisis, assigning go-getter, anti-Communist ideologues with wide-ranging experience in Vietnam and in CIA-managed covert activities world-wide. The U.S. military command post for Latin America was elevated to a four-star post, and the size of the U.S. Embassy staff in Honduras mushroomed, turning it into one of the largest U.S. diplomatic missions in Latin America.[9] The National Security Council, which became the administration's point group for the region, doubled in size, rivaling even Henry Kissinger's operation under Nixon.[10] Any foreign service officers, such as former Assistant Secretary of State Thomas Enders and ex-ambassador to Honduras John Ferch, who were seen as pragmatists or open to the possibility of negotiated solutions, were dismissed. By the mid-1980s the United States had invaded Central America with its military presence, techniques, and weapons. Two main instruments of U.S. military policy—military exercises and security assistance programs—had been reduced to minor points of debate in Congress, of only occasional interest to the media.

Beginning in the early 1960s, the United States had staged worldwide U.S. military exercises, known as war games. Planned and announced well in advance, war games were designed to give U.S. troops practice in simulated war situations, to train them in skills they might be called upon to use in a war, and in some cases to develop coordination with friendly militaries.[11] As the United States geared up for intervention in the Third World, it expanded its military exercises, as seen in the Caribbean, where in 1981 the United States had practiced its eventual invasion of Grenada, and in Central America, a laboratory for the new interventionist strategy.[12] Land exercises, primarily staged in Honduras, were continuous beginning in August 1983. In 1985, however, land exercises lasting longer than the traditional several weeks were carried out in Panama as well. Periodically, smaller exercises also took place in Costa Rica.[13] On occasion land and naval maneuvers overlapped, as in spring 1984 with the coincidence of Ocean Venture '84 and Grenadero I, which brought 33,000 U.S troops to the region and in spring 1985 when Big Pine III and Universal Trek together brought 7,000 to 11,000 U.S. troops to Honduras and its coastal waters.[14]

Honduras

The *Congressional Presentation for Security Assistance Programs* for FY 1979 noted that the Honduras military "as a group has historically been friendly to the United States."[15] The FY 1986 congressional presentation justified the U.S. program for Honduras: "It would be extremely difficult to defend U.S. interests in Central America without the cooperation of Honduras. . . . With this [U.S.] aid, higher operational readiness rates can be attained and the positive military-to-military relationship between our two countries will be furthered."[16] The new scale and scope of U.S. military exercises in Honduras led to continuous deployment of large numbers of U.S. troops and construction of military, logistical, and intelligence-gathering infrastructure. In addition, military equipment left behind following exercises and facilities, such as the airstrip upgraded at Aguacate, were used by the CIA for covert support for the contra (counterrevolutionary) war against Nicaragua.[17] The exercises were ostensibly to signal Nicaragua that the United States would stand by its allies. Tensions in the border area between contras and Sandinista troops provided a pretext for U.S. accusations that Nicaragua planned an invasion, despite testimony by U.S. military personnel stationed in the region and U.S.-based military analysis as to the unlikelihood and military infeasibility of such an invasion.[18]

Initially the military exercises in Central America practiced large-scale war scenarios in a broad geographic zone: invasions of the Puerto Rican island of Vieques; evacuations from Guantanamo Bay, Cuba; mock bombing runs and aerial dogfights in the Gulf of Mexico. With the concentration of the exercises in Honduras they increased in frequency and focused not only on practice of war scenarios but also on quick deployment and construction, counterinsurgency training, and civic action.

The military exercises in Honduras familiarized large numbers of U.S. troops with local conditions and military personnel. Troops came from bases all over the United States, from units stationed at the U.S. Southern Command (SOUTHCOM) in Panama, and from Puerto Rico. Reservists and state National Guard units also participated. The mobilization of the state National Guard became a subject of debate in the United States. National Guard spokesperson Major John Smith defended their deployment: "It's a part of the total readiness picture. We're doing . . . a disservice to our soldiers if we leave them unprepared to fight."[19] Massachusetts Governor Michael S. Dukakis, along with other governors, as commander-in-chief of his state's National Guard, had refused to allow his units to participate in military exercises. A spokesperson for Dukakis stated: "If the United States wants to send troops into Central America, that ought to be something that the President asks the Congress and the Congress debates and votes. . . . Barring that, I don't think there ought to be this subterfuge of sending Guard units down from the various states."[20]

Some members of Congress also suspected that the military exercises in Honduras extended well beyond routine military maneuvers and congressional intentions. Representative William V. Alexander, Jr. (D.-Ark.), asked the General Accounting Office (GAO)—the congressional watchdog agency—to investigate whether the exercises were a vehicle by which the Pentagon was usurping functions that properly came under congressional authority. The GAO issued reports in 1984 and 1985 questioning the scope of the military exercises in three areas: construction, counterinsurgency training for Honduran troops, and civic action.[21] Funding for the military exercises came directly from the Pentagon and was supposed to be limited to operational needs. For example, any single construction project that was part of a military exercise was to cost no more than $200,000. Decisions on larger construction projects were assigned to the congressional military construction subcommittees because of their implications for U.S. policy. The GAO found that during Big Pine II in 1983-1984 and afterward the Pentagon had evaded this limit in two ways. First, construction projects were broken up into discrete pieces, each costing less than $200,000. An example was the San Lorenzo base in southeast Honduras, where the barracks were considered a separate project from the post exchange and dining facilities—all built to service U.S. military personnel stationed there. Second, the GAO determined that the Pentagon was manipulating its accounting. Some expenses traditionally considered part of the cost of a project were transferred to other categories; in exercises after Big Pine II only the cost of materials was counted. The GAO estimated that a $133,626 project executed during Cabanas exercises would have cost $265,000 under the accounting used during Big Pine II. The GAO also pointed out that had the cost of the project been accounted for without any allowances, including those accepted during Big Pine II, the total cost would have been closer to $635,000.[22]

Honduras became the base for an elaborate U.S. military complex. Throughout the country U.S. troops upgraded and constructed airfields, two of which could accommodate the most sophisticated planes in the U.S. arsenal; built base facilities, including barracks, mess halls, showers, latrines, and recreational facilities; erected radar stations that could monitor air, land, and sea traffic over much of Nicaragua, Honduras, and El Salvador; and set up headquarters for Joint Task Force Bravo, an intraservice operational center for support and control of deployed U.S. forces. Honduras became a base of operations for intelligence-gathering overflights into El Salvador and Nicaragua and could easily be converted into an operational center for broad U.S. military action in the region.[23]

After the buildup had become an accomplished fact the Pentagon was ready to broach to Congress its long-term plan for a U.S. military presence in Honduras. In March 1986 Nestor D. Sanchez, deputy assistant secretary of defense for inter-American affairs, presented to the House Appropriations Subcommittee on Military Construction a request that included $5 million for a facility in Honduras to support a U.S. Army Aviation unit involved in intelligence collection. At the same hearing General John R. Galvin, then commander-in-chief of SOUTHCOM, stated that he was aware of congressional concern about the "indefinite temporary" U.S. presence: "It may take two years or five years or more," he told the subcommittee.[24] The administration had revealed a month earlier a $50 million plan through 1991 for upkeep and extensive construction projects in Honduras, including expansion of facilities for U.S. troops and construction of ammunition supply points in remote areas, warehouses for secure storage, and improved runways.[25]

The GAO also found problems with the large amount of counterinsurgency training provided as part of the military maneuvers and with the implementation of a vast civic action program. Counterinsurgency training was built into numerous exercises. Congressionally authorized military assistance to Honduras grew from $4 million in FY 1980 to over $60 million in FY 1985—weapons, military-related equipment, aircraft, and training.[26] The training was done at U.S. military bases or in country by Mobile Training Teams (MTTs)—usually Special Forces deployed to provide instruction in specific skills or techniques. Training by Special Forces during exercises, particularly of Honduran troops, went far beyond the congressionally approved program.

Humanitarian aid—medical care and supplies, food, clothing, and educational materials—was yet another carrot offered to Honduras. Representatives of both the Honduran government and the private sector laid before U.S. policy makers the desperate economic situation and their need for U.S. assistance. The forthcoming assistance provided by Congress fell far short of what Hondurans felt was their due, given the strategic role of their country in U.S. regional policy.

One way to compensate for the shortfall was through exercise-related civic action programs, largely the delivery of medical, dental, and veterinary services to rural Honduras. During Big Pine II, 53,000 rural Hondurans received medical or dental care, 200,000 immunizations were given, and 37,000 animals were treated.[27] The official purpose of the program was to provide U.S. military medical personnel with training in the treatment of tropical diseases. The GAO observed, however, that "after-action reports indicated that the program itself was primarily a civic action, rather than a training program" and considered the funds used to pay the costs of these civic actions as "improperly" disbursed.[28] Following Big Pine II medical and veterinary services continued at the rate of one or two forays weekly.[29]

Civic actions served several other purposes. First, U.S. troops gained familiarity with the climate, terrain, and people of rural Honduras. They practiced the complex tasks of transporting equipment and personnel, located helicopter landing pads, identified village leaders, and took a census of patients and family members.[30] Second, they helped hold in check the discontent of the Honduran people with their desperate economic and social conditions. As a U.S. Embassy economic adviser put it, "Neither the Honduran government nor the United States has a program to reverse economic stagnation. The best that can be accomplished is direct aid to help close the budget gap and food to feed the increasing number of hungry people."[31] One enthusiast for civic action, Captain Robert S. Perry of SOUTHCOM, wrote: "Civic actions build an important people-to-people reservoir of trust and confidence in their government and the U.S. . . . and cast the military in the role of a positive social agent."[32] The program was intended to build popular support in Honduras for the military exercises and ensure a sympathetic rearguard for the U.S.-supported contras. In an invasion of Nicaragua, it would ensure that the Honduran people identified their interests with those of the United States.

However, the civic action program did not always spread good will. Many Hondurans felt the program was for show and did not address the country's deep-rooted problems. Dispensing vitamins, aspirin, and antiworm medication to last no more than three months could do little to alleviate malnutrition, poor hygiene, lack of potable water, and the other plagues of poverty.[33]

The exercises frequently bred resentment as Hondurans found themselves abruptly evicted from their land when the United States decided to build a road, airfield, or other military-related facility. The U.S. press gave some attention to a U.S. citizen from Puerto Rico who lost his Honduran cattle ranch in 1983 when the United States set up the Regional Military Training Center (RMTC) on the Honduran Atlantic Coast; the case was tossed back and forth between the Honduran government and the U.S. Embassy. By summer 1986 the man had not been paid for his property.[34] Little publicity, however, was given to the plight of Honduran peasants thrown off their land in clean-up operations prior to the setting up of the RMTC. (According to the Honduran daily La Tribuna 101 peasants received a total of $221,000 two years later.[35]) In April 1986 the National Association of Honduran Campesinos (ANACH) charged that peasants in Yoro had been removed from their land while troops practiced parachute jumping. Although the director of the National Agrarian Institute claimed the situation was temporary and that the army would pay for all damages, ANACH protested that on previous occasions farmers who had been given similar assurances had received nothing.[36]

Social problems were another legacy of the U.S. troops stationed in Honduras, including sexually transmitted diseases well known in South Vietnam during the Indochina War and in the Philippines where thousands of U.S. troops were based. In the town of Comayagua, near Palmerola Air Base—the nucleus of the U.S. military presence—discos, bars, brothels, and begging flourished. In March 1986 articles began to appear in the Honduran press with titles like "Comayagua: Sodoma y Gomorra?" blaming U.S. troops for sexual abuse of children, promotion of drug and alcohol abuse, and the introduction of AIDS to the Honduran population.[37] Victor Meza, then director of the Honduran Documentation Center, an independent research and publications group based in the Honduran capital of Tegucigalpa, explained to one journalist, "We have no real benefit from the American military. All we get is beer and whores."[38]

The U.S. military exercises brought about in a short time the dramatic growth of the U.S. presence in Honduras, U.S. support for the Salvadoran armed forces and the contras through the back door, and the acclimatization of the U.S. public to the presence of U.S. troops in the region. Simultaneously, through the traditional channels of military assistance, the United States had bolstered the Honduran armed forces: Honduran military and security forces more than doubled from 11,000 in 1979 to 23,000 in 1985. The Honduran air fleet, which had been the best equipped air force in the region even before 1980, was built up with Huey helicopters and A-37 attack and O-2 reconnaissance planes.[39]

In addition to aircraft, howitzers, M-16 rifles, and other weaponry, the United States supplied Honduras with radios and communication gear, trucks and other ground vehicles, and personnel equipment ranging from boots and canteens to parachutes and sunglasses.[40] These items both modernized the Honduran armed forces and increased their interoperability with U.S. armed forces and other U.S.-supplied military forces in the region.

The expansion of the Honduran armed forces was complemented by training. Between 1980 and 1984 the numbers of Honduran officers and cadets trained at the U.S. Army School, then in Panama, increased from a few hundred to well over 500 a year; the number of Hondurans attending the school was second only to the number of Salvadorans. Special courses were designed to redress deficiencies in the Honduran as well as in the Salvadoran military.[41] Several thousand additional Honduran troops were also trained at the RMTC from June 1983 until it was closed in September 1984, as well as by dozens of mobile training teams (MTTs) who went to Honduras every year.[42] One Honduran unit trained by the United States was used as a sabotage and assassination squad inside Nicaragua.[43]

The CIA was deeply involved in training and in the inner workings of the Honduran military. Along with a Special Forces unit from Fort Bragg, it had trained in strict secrecy a Honduran "anti-terrorist" unit in an operation code-named "Operation Quail Shooter."[44] A *New York Times* article by James Lemoyne implicated the CIA in human rights abuses in Honduras: "The Central Intelligence Agency aided Honduran security forces that it knew were responsible for having killed a number of people they detained for political reasons between 1981 and 1984."[45] A similar accusation was made in testimony before the Senate Intelligence Committees and individual members of Congress by Honduran Major Ricardo Zúñiga Morazán, who was killed not long after his visit to the United States.[46] Zúñiga alleged that Honduran intelligence agents and members of the U.S.-backed Nicaraguan Democratic Forces (the largest contra group) had committed human rights abuses with the knowledge of U.S. intelligence officers. Further, Ramón Custodio López, a leading human rights activist, charged that former U.S. Ambassador to Honduras John Dmitri Negroponte had directed "a terrorist ring" in Central America whose mission was elimination of leftist opposition in Honduras and support for the contras.[47] Between 1981 and 1985 there were some 200 disappearances in Honduras, primarily of Salvadorans and Hondurans identified as leftists or as student, peasant, or union leaders.[48]

Many human rights abuses took place while General Gustavo Alvarez Martínez, known for his strong-arm tactics and support for U.S. policy, was commander-in-chief of the Honduran Armed Forces. While he was commander-in-chief Honduras got its nickname, "the U.S.S. Honduras."[49] In March 1984 a coup within the military sent him into exile and installed Walter Reyes López, who maintained a cooperative relationship with the United States despite efforts by the Honduran military to obtain better terms for Honduras in exchange for permitting the U.S. military presence. These efforts led to shutting down the RMTC, established in Honduras primarily to provide training for Salvadoran troops. The RMTC had been a thorn in the side of many members of the Honduran military who had regarded the Salvadoran military as an enemy following defeat in a border war with El Salvador in 1969. The Honduran government also sought renegotiation of its treaties with the United States to ensure protection against invasion and publicly objected to the flow of assistance to the contras through Honduras. A few days after the 1986 Honduran presidential elections Reyes López resigned his position as commander-in-chief and Humberto Regalado Hernández stepped in. In the first several months following the elections and installation of Regalado as commander-in-chief, Honduran officials began to talk openly, for the first time, of the existence of contra bases along the border with Nicaragua.

Despite this apparent official acquiescence to U.S. policy, in spring 1986 the largest demonstration ever in protest of the U.S. presence in Honduras took place in the capital city of Tegucigalpa. Five thousand Hondurans demanded the cancellation of Honduran military treaties with the United

States, adoption of a neutral policy toward Nicaragua, expulsion of the contras, and a full accounting for the disappeared.[50]

Costa Rica

As in Honduras, exercises, security assistance programs, and the CIA had all been instruments for increasing the U.S. military presence in Costa Rica. In FY 1980 Costa Rica received no U.S. military assistance; between FY 1981 and 1983 U.S. military aid to Costa Rica totaled $21 million.[51] Although Costa Rica initially had resisted any significant U.S. military presence as compromising its commitment to neutrality in the region's conflicts, by the mid-1980s Costa Rica had conceded to greater U.S. military influence.

Sometimes referred to as the "Switzerland of Central America," Costa Rica disbanded its armed forces in 1949 after adopting a new constitution. In the following decades Costa Ricans carved out a prosperous existence, in the midst of a poverty-ridden region, by supporting a generous welfare system and providing free health care and hospitalization, education, housing, child care, and retirement benefits to a majority of the people. Government subsidies placed many foods and services within reach of most Costa Ricans. The public sector employed 20 percent of the people and was the controlling interest in a number of financial and industrial enterprises.[52]

However, Costa Rica could not escape the world economic recession of the 1970s, which grew to crisis proportions throughout Latin America by 1980. In August 1981 Costa Rica became the first Latin American country to cease payments on its international debt. Only through U.S. economic assistance—infusions of relatively large amounts of money in proportion to its small economy—did Costa Rica stay afloat, becoming the second largest recipient of U.S. aid in Latin America after El Salvador, and the second highest per capita recipient of U.S. assistance worldwide after Israel.[53]

Costa Rica's dependency on U.S. aid left it particularly vulnerable to U.S. demands, which fell primarily into two areas: (1) that Costa Rica wean itself from its democratic social welfare system to a free market economy and become the Reagan administration's model for Latin America; and (2) that Costa Rica cooperate with U.S. regional military plans.[54]

On both counts Costa Rica wavered in its willingness to follow the U.S. lead and abandon its historical commitments. Oscar Arias, elected president in spring 1986, embodied the national ambivalence. Even though he stated he would permit the continued upgrading of Costa Rica's security forces with U.S. aid and training, he reaffirmed his country's pledge of neutrality. He also firmly stated that Costa Rica's welfare system was not to be dismantled: "we preferred a welfare state to a garrison state."[55]

Although still a far cry from a garrison state in 1986, Costa Rica had begun a process of militarization. Costa Rica was exempted from the U.S. congressional prohibition against assistance to foreign police forces, and in 1981 U.S. training programs to Costa Rica's national and rural guard were resumed. Thirty-seven members of the security forces attended schools in

Panama. By FY 1985 U.S. training programs had increased threefold; 104 Costa Ricans went to U.S. military schools under the International Military and Educational Training program. In February 1985 an additional thirty-four members of the security forces attended an eight-week leadership course in Honduras at the RMTC.[56]

In spring 1985, a border incident with Nicaragua in which two Costa Rican guardsmen were killed and nine others wounded served as a pretext for increased U.S. military aid and a break in relations with Nicaragua. In May 1985 twenty U.S. Special Forces were dispatched to the Murciélago base in Costa Rica, 20 kilometers from the border with Nicaragua, to train 750 guardsmen, apparently not only in basic military skills but also in ideology.[57] It was reported that the new recruits were instructed in war chants such as "Comunista Bueno, Comunista Muerto" (A good Communist is a dead Communist).[58] That same spring saw an infusion of U.S. aircraft, weapons, and military-related equipment: helicopters, light observation planes, M-16 rifles, rocket launchers, machine guns, antitank weapons, mortars, ammunition, and spare parts.[59] Earlier that year a Voice of America relay station was inaugurated; security for the station—high-tension wire, double storm fencing, microwave sensors, TV cameras, and sandbags—led some to observe that the station looked more like a military communications installation than a radio station.[60] In early 1986 Costa Rica permitted the first military exercises involving construction; over 150 U.S. Army Engineers arrived to upgrade bridges and highways.[61]

By the mid-1980s significant steps had been taken to accommodate U.S. military pressures. Training, upgrading of weaponry and aircraft, military exercises, military civic action, and port calls by U.S. war ships were all established facts. Costa Rica's 8,000-member guard, which had been made up of political appointees who changed after the elections every four years, was turning into a professional military force.

As in Honduras, the CIA was entrenched in Costa Rica through programs of support for the contras. Though primarily based in Honduras, the contras also had a southern front in Costa Rica. To help establish a receptive environment in Costa Rica for the contras, the CIA made contacts with government officials and local guardsmen and arranged drop-off points for supplies and bases from which the contras could launch attacks and to which they could retreat. CIA influence was said to extend as high as the offices of the Costa Rican Ministry of Security and the Department of Intelligence and Security. The CIA was accused of setting up incidents to promote tension between Costa Rica and Nicaragua.[62]

The Costa Rican media carried on continuous agitation against the Sandinistas. The rationale of conservative Costa Rican press and politicians was parallel to that of Honduras—that Costa Rica needed to take precautions to protect itself from Nicaraguan-sponsored subversion or invasion. Juan José Echeverría, a former public security minister, challenged this assumption, charging that conservative Costa Rican businesspeople wanted a strengthened police force to quell any rebellion caused by continuing economic hardship.[63]

Middle- and upper-class supporters of Arias as against Rafael Angel Calderon, his virulently anti-Communist opponent in the presidential race, felt that Costa Rica was compromising its traditional neutrality and its future by becoming a base for the contra war or for an invasion of Nicaragua by U.S. troops.

> If the Sandinista government were ever driven out of Managua and into the mountains the war would spread to Costa Rica, with safehouse and smuggling by pro-Sandinista forces and probably bombing of Costa Rica by U.S. forces trying to break up Sandinista supply routes. A U.S. invasion wouldn't be the end of our problems with the Sandinistas, only the beginning.[64]

Among Arias's first initiatives after winning the presidency was an agreement with Nicaragua on a proposal to establish a peacekeeping force on their common border, to provide "permanent inspection and surveillance" in order to prevent border incidents.[65] However, over a year later this agreement still had not been implemented.

The Region

Beginning in 1981 the United States tried to facilitate formation of agreements among Central American military forces excluding Nicaragua.[66] Reconstitution of past military accords or fabrication of new ones was part of the strategy of isolating Nicaragua by casting it as a military threat. In addition, in case of dramatic U.S. military escalation or invasion, such agreements might provide troops from the area, allowing early withdrawal of the bulk of U.S. forces. The United States failed in its initial attempts to forge such an alliance. Nationalist sentiments created obstacles, primarily the hostility between the Salvadoran and Honduran militaries and the anger of the Guatemalans at U.S. condemnation of their human rights record, which made them unwilling to be associated with any plan that appeared to be U.S. inspired. The United States did succeed, however, in opening up some areas of cooperation: Military leadership from Honduras, El Salvador, and Guatemala did meet periodically; Guatemala and Honduras agreed that their countries would not provide sanctuary to Salvadoran guerrillas; Hondurans did support the Salvadoran military during offensives in zones along their common border. Such integration of local militaries with U.S. policy objectives inevitably contributed to a willingness to support the contra war: The Guatemalan military provided assistance to the contras despite an official position of neutrality; Honduras and El Salvador were named as third countries providing aid to the contras when the U.S. Congress cut off assistance from October 1984 to July 1985; El Salvador allowed the CIA to launch air and sea attacks against Nicaragua in 1984 and by 1986 had become a regular conduit for supplies to the contras; the expansion of the Salvadoran navy and its inclusion in military exercises in the Gulf of Fonseca led to speculation that it might play a role in any invasion of Nicaragua;

and in December 1986, after Nicaraguan troops pursued contras to their camps in Honduras, Honduran jets bombed inside Nicaragua.[67]

Conclusion

The overall purpose of U.S. policy in Central America during the early 1980s was to disarticulate the political and social forces that had developed to counter decades of poverty and injustice. The U.S. strategy evolved into what military analysts identified as "low-intensity conflict"—warfare employing a range of diplomatic, economic, social, psychological, and political pressures along with military force.[68] The concept "low-intensity" was the designation of the level of military engagement at which Pentagon strategists saw the conflict in Central America—a stage where it might be possible to achieve the desired ends without having to introduce large numbers of U.S. combat troops. By the mid-1980s the intention of the U.S. government to defeat the guerrilla movement in El Salvador and to remove the Sandinista government in Nicaragua was clear; though officially at peace the United States was engaged in a strategy of war.

The 1980s saw expansion of U.S. military capabilities to wage low-intensity war: growth of unconventional forces and the CIA, coordination of CIA activities with the Pentagon, utilization of mercenary forces and private organizations, development of Army light infantry forces and other quick strike units.[69] Low-intensity conflict required the U.S. public to tolerate evasion of U.S. and international law, violence against civilians, support of dictatorships, military forces and regimes guilty of human rights violations, and "limited" military strikes and to ignore the ever present danger that U.S. troops would be drawn into direct combat.[70]

By the mid-1980s it appeared that key government agencies—the Department of Defense, the CIA, and the National Security Council—had reached consensus around this strategy. Congress passed legislation that set up structures to support the implementation of low-intensity conflict doctrine, and a Small War Operations and Research Division (SWORD) was established at SOUTHCOM. Many factors still existed, however, that could hamper its effectiveness: the response of the Nicaraguan government to U.S. aggression, the resistance of the U.S. public and some members of Congress to deepening U.S. military involvement, and ambivalence in Honduras, Costa Rica, and other Latin countries toward U.S. policy.

Continuous military maneuvers in Central America and the militarization of Honduras and Costa Rica were designed to convince Nicaragua that there would be a U.S. invasion backed by other countries in the region. At the same time the U.S. public was assured that the maneuvers were only for training purposes and that military assistance for Honduras and Costa Rica was a response to a call for help from allies.

The Sandinistas organized their armed forces to fight the war at hand and to protect the population, as much as possible, from contra attacks in addition to a military buildup to defend against invasion. Their strategy relied upon autonomous military units with decentralized decisionmaking capabilities, greatly augmenting the number of people directly involved in the war against the contras. This complemented a nationalist upsurge among Nicaraguans who remembered earlier U.S. invasion and occupation.[71] The majority of Nicaraguans rejected the contras because of the predominance of former members of the dictator Anastasio Somoza's National Guard among contra military leadership and their record of pillage and brutality against the Nicaraguan people, especially teachers, health workers, and cooperative leaders, who represented progress and change from the years under the Somozas.[72]

Fifty percent of Nicaragua's budget was directed toward the war effort, diverting resources from programs to transform the society and reform the economy.[73] The Reagan administration put pressure on its European allies and on international financial institutions to dry up sources of funds for Nicaragua, further strangling the economy, waged a vitriolic propaganda campaign against the Sandinistas, and exerted diplomatic pressures to isolate Nicaragua from its neighbors, other Latin countries, and Western Europe. Yet the Sandinistas did not appear to be unraveling.

The U.S. strategy of low-intensity conflict was undercut by the lack of a viable political alternative to the Sandinistas, which left only the prospect of unending war. Some members of the U.S. Congress and a substantial portion of the press and public feared that the deepening U.S. military involvement would result in invasion and another Vietnam-like quagmire. The administration was seeking a formula to rally public opinion. As far back as 1981 then–Secretary of State Alexander Haig had warned before a meeting of the Organization of American States that the United States would do whatever was "prudent and necessary" to prevent any nation in Central America from becoming a "platform for terror and war."[74]

In spring 1986 the United States attacked Libya in retaliation for its alleged support of terrorists. In the United States support for the air strike was overwhelming. Although European allies were at first reserved they soon rallied behind the United States. Months earlier Nicaragua, along with Cuba, North Korea, Libya, and Iran, had been listed as terrorist nations by President Reagan in a speech before the American Bar Association.[75] In the following months the portrayal of Nicaragua as a sponsor of terrorism and akin to Libya was fully integrated into the Reagan administration's vilification campaign. That same spring the United States charged Nicaragua with invading Honduras when Nicaraguan troops pursued contras across the border. Although Honduras initially ignored the incident, within a few days they nominally accepted the charge, and U.S. troops and helicopters ferried a Honduran battalion to the border area, bringing U.S. forces closer yet to direct involvement in combat.[76]

The United States had put in place in Central America the military infrastructure to support either limited military strikes or invasion. Though support of regional allies for U.S. policy was not totally predictable, Honduras and Costa Rica had taken significant steps toward compliance with U.S.

wishes and President José Napoleón Duarte of El Salvador was virtually a captive of U.S. policy demands. The ability of Nicaragua to thwart U.S. plans on the battlefield and diplomatically remained a serious problem for U.S. policy, as did public ambivalence toward support for the contras and deepening U.S. military involvement. Whether or not the Reagan administration had broadened its military options with its orchestration of a global antiterrorist campaign was not certain. But continued failure to reverse the Nicaraguan revolution through low-intensity warfare would confront the United States with the old choice: negotiate or invade.

Notes

1. Jenny Pearce, *Under the Eagle: U.S. Intervention in Central America and the Caribbean* (London: Latin America Bureau, 1982); Noam Chomsky, "The Fifth Freedom," *Turning the Tide, U.S. Intervention in Central America and the Struggle for Peace* (Boston: South End Press, 1985).

2. *Defense '81—Special Almanac Issue* (Arlington, Va.: American Forces Information Services, September 1981), pp. 22–23.

3. Gerald F. Seib, "U.S. Military Training of Hemispheric Allies Is Spurred in Panama," *Wall Street Journal*, August 3, 1981; Christopher Dickey, "U.S. Prizes Its School for Latin Military," *Washington Post*, May 23, 1983.

4. Cynthia Arnson, "Cold War in the Caribbean," *Inquiry*, December 10, 1979; Thomas Conrad and Cynthia Arnson, "The Aid for El Salvador is Called Nonlethal," *New York Times*, June 15, 1980.

5. Fred Hiatt, "Entrenching in Honduras," *Washington Post*, February 18, 1986.

6. *Invasion: A Guide to the U.S. Military Presence in Central America* (Philadelphia: NARMIC/American Friends Service Committee, 1985), pp. 4–5.

7. *Annual Report to Congress of Secretary of Defense Caspar W. Weinberger*, Fiscal Year 1985, p. 178.

8. Sam C. Sarkesian, "Low-Intensity Conflict: Concepts, Principles and Policy Guidelines," *Air University Review* 36, no. 2 (January-February 1985):8; Michael T. Klare, "The 'In-Between' Deployment Force," *The Nation*, September 22, 1984; "America's Secret Soldiers: The Buildup of U.S. Special Operations Forces," *The Defense Monitor* 14, no. 2 (Washington, D.C.: Center for Defense Information, 1985).

9. Loren Jenkins, "U.S. Officer Influential in Latin Region," *Washington Post*, January 3, 1984; Bill Keller, "Army General Chosen as New Latin Commander, *New York Times*, January 12, 1985; Loren Jenkins, "Honduras on the Edge," *The Atlantic*, August 1982.

10. Leslie H. Gelb, "Where Anonymous Power Accrues," *New York Times*, June 4, 1985.

11. "War Games," *The Defense Monitor* 13, no. 7 (Washington, D.C.: Center for Defense Information, 1984).

12. Catherine A. Sunshine, *The Caribbean: Survival, Struggle and Sovereignty* (Washington, D.C.: Ecumenical Program for Interamerican Communication and Action (EPICA), 1985), p. 122.

13. *Congressional Presentation: Security Assistance Programs*, FY 1979, p. 335.

14. *Congressional Presentation: Security Assistance Programs*, FY 1986, p. 401.

15. *Invasion*, pp. 12–15.

16. Memorandum for Correspondents, Pentagon Public Affairs, March 22, 1984; "Land of Eternal Maneuvers," *Central America Report* (Guatemala: INFORPRESS),

vol. 12, no. 15, April 26, 1985; "Granadero I Begins," *Central America Report* (Guatemala: INFORPRESS), vol. 11, no. 14, April 6, 1984; Edward Cody, "Exercises in Honduras Go Forward Despite Ouster of Generals," *Washington Post*, April 8, 1984; James LeMoyne, "Army Games Due with Hondurans," *New York Times*, March 25, 1985; Michael Wiesskopf, *Washington Post*, "U.S., Honduras Planning Their Largest Exercises," March 22, 1985.

17. Jeff Gerth and Philip Taubman, "U.S. is Reported to Skirt Curbs in Latin Moves," *New York Times*, May 18, 1984; Gillian Brown, *Pentagon Republic* (VHS video) (New York: Icarus Films, 1986).

18. John B. Oakes, "Treating Honduras as a Vassal State," *New York Times*, January 11, 1985; interview by Eva Gold, San Lorenzo Base, Honduras, November 1983.

19. "National Guard Troops Draw Fire," *USA Today*, February 11, 1986.

20. Fred Hiatt, "Governors Wary of Sending Guard Troops to Honduras," *Washington Post*, April 5, 1986.

21. Comptroller General's decision, B-213137, June 22, 1984, and "DoD Use of Operations and Maintenance Appropriations in Honduras" (Washington, D.C.: General Accounting Office, January 30, 1986).

22. Ibid., January 30, 1986, pp. 11–19.

23. Eva Gold, "High Stakes: The Cost of the U.S. Military Buildup in Honduras," *Sojourners Magazine*, August 1984; Bill Keller and Joel Brinkely, "U.S. Military Is Termed Prepared for any Move Against Nicaragua," *New York Times*, June 4, 1985.

24. Statement of General John R. Galvin, U.S. Army commander-in-chief, U.S. Southern Command, before the House Appropriations Committee, Subcommittee on Military Construction, Caribbean Basin Construction Program, March 12, 1986, p. 7.

25. Fred Hiatt, "U.S. Outlines Plans for Base in Honduras," *Philadelphia Inquirer*, February 8, 1986.

26. *Invasion*, pp. 4–5, 18.

27. "DoD Use of Operations and Maintenance Appropriations in Honduras," p. 29.

28. Ibid., pp. 29 and 31.

29. Robert J. McCartney, "GIs Aid Villagers in Honduras," *Washington Post*, February 12, 1986.

30. Eva Gold and Mary Day Kent, "The Ahuas Tara II Exercises," a supplement to *A View of the U.S. Role In the Militarization of Central America* (Philadelphia: NARMIC/American Friends Service Committee, February 1984).

31. Interview by Eva Gold, November 1983.

32. Robert S. Perry, "Civic Action and Regional Security," *The Disam Journal of International Security Assistance Management* 5, no. 3 (spring 1983):34–35.

33. Gold and Kent, "The Ahuas Tara II Exercises"; and McCartney, "GIs Aid Villagers in Honduras."

34. "American in Honduras Sues over Land," *Baltimore Sun*, July 25, 1983; Edith Evans Asbury, "American in Honduras in Fight of Life," *New York Times*, December 20, 1983; "Court Gets Latin Ranch Suit," *New York Times*, April 26, 1984; Joanne Omang, "U.S. To Shut Honduras Training Site," *Washington Post*, March 16, 1985.

35. Douglas Kincaid, "The Honduran Agrarian Reform: Still Under Arrest," *Honduran Update*, (Somerville, Mass.) 3, nos. 10–11 (July/August 1985); Committee for the Defense of Human Rights in Honduras (CODEH), "The Human Rights Situation in Honduras: 1985 Report" (excerpts), *Honduras Update* 4, no. 5 (February 1986); *La Tribuna*, May 29, 1985, as reported in *Honduras Update* 3, nos. 10–11 (July/August 1985).

36. "Land of Eternal Maneuvers."

37. "Comayagua: Sodoma y Gomorra?" *El Tiempo*, March 10, 1986; "No Ocultamos Informacion Sobre 'SIDA': Villeda B." and "10 Son Las Prostitutas Portadoras del 'SIDA'," and "Hematologo Asegura Existencia de 11 Casos positivos de SIDA," *La Tribuna*, March 12, 1986.

38. Edward R. F. Sheehan, "The Country of Nada," *New York Review of Books* 33, no. 5, March 27, 1986.

39. Jozef Goldblat and Victor Millan, "The Honduras-Nicaragua conflict and prospects for arms control in Central America," *SIPRI Yearbook 1984: World Armaments and Disarmament* (London and Philadelphia: Taylor and Francis, 1984), p. 525; *Invasion*, p. 18.

40. *Invasion*, p. 18.

41. *Congressional Presentation, Security Assistance Programs*, FY 1982, p. 434; *Congressional Presentation, Security Assistance Programs*, FY 1983, p. 409; Mary Day Kent and Eva Gold, "The U.S. Army School of the Americas," a supplement to *A View of the U.S. Role in the Militarization of Central America* (Philadelphia: NARMIC/American Friends Service Committee, May 1984), p. 2.

42. Patricia Flynn, *Honduras: Base for Intervention—Report on a Fact-Finding Trip* (Berkeley, Calif.: Center for the Study of the Americas, February 3–19, 1984), p. 11; Edward Cody, "Honduras Seeks Change in Base Pact," *Washington Post*, May 26, 1984; Leslie Parks, Jonathon Marshall, and Michael T. Klare, "Background Information on U.S. Security Assistance and Military Operations in Honduras," *Update*, no. 9 (Washington, D.C.: Institute for Policy Studies, May 30, 1984), p. 8.

43. Gillian Brown, *Pentagon Republic* (New York: Icarus Films, 1986).

44. Joe Pichirallo and Edward Cody, "U.S. Reported Training Anti-terrorists," *Philadelphia Inquirer*, March 26, 1985.

45. James LeMoyne, "CIA Accused of Tolerating Killing in Honduras," *New York Times*, February 14, 1986.

46. Dennis Volman, "Killing of Honduran Army Officer Linked to Testimony on U.S," *Christian Science Monitor*, November 19, 1985; "CIA Accused of Tolerating Killings in Honduras," *New York Times*, February 14, 1986.

47. G. Ivan Santiago, "Honduras: Despite Military Investigation, Repression, Disappearances Continue," *Latinamerica Press* (Lima, Peru) 17, no. 33, September 12, 1985.

48. "CIA Accused of Tolerating Killings in Honduras"; Santiago, "Honduras: Despite Military Investigation, Repression, Disappearances Continue."

49. Allan Nairn, "The United States Militarizes Honduras," in Nancy Peckenham and Annie Street, ed., *Honduras: Portrait of a Captive Nation* (New York: Praeger Publishers, 1985).

50. "U.S. Troops and Honduran Army Under Fire," *Central America Report* (Guatemala: INFORPRESS), vol. 13, no. 12, April 4, 1986.

51. Tim Goldin, "Costa Ricans Complacent and They Like it That Way," *Miami Herald*, January 31, 1986; *Invasion*, p. 4–5.

52. Roger Lowenstein, "Costa Ricans Cheerfully Absorb U.S. Aid Sent as Immunization Against Nicaragua," *Wall Street Journal*, September 19, 1985; Marc Edelman, "Back from the Brink," *NACLA: Report on the Americas* (New York) 19, no. 6 (November/December 1985).

53. Edelman, "Back from the Brink."

54. "Back from the Brink"; *Report on Costa Rica, 1985* (Philadelphia: American Friends Service Committee, September 1985).

55. "Costa Rica," in *Mesoamerica* (San Jose, Costa Rica: Institute for Central American Studies, February 1986).

56. *Invasion*, p. 11.

57. "Behind the War Games," *New York Times*, June 4, 1985; Goldin, "Costa Ricans Complacent and They Like It That Way."

58. Jean Hopfensperger, "U.S. Policy, Regional Developments Nudge Costa Rica to the Right," *Christian Science Monitor*, January 14, 1986; *Report on Costa Rica, 1985*.

59. *Invasion*, p. 16; "Costa Rica Presses U.S. on Weapons," *Newark Star-Ledger*, June 6, 1985.

60. *Report on Costa Rica 1985*; letter from Committee of U.S. Citizens Resident in Costa Rica, April 11, 1985.

61. "Costa Rica," in *Mesoamerica* (San José, Costa Rica: Institute for Central American Studies, March 1986); "News Briefs," *Latinamerica Press* (Lima, Peru) 18, no. 7, February 27, 1986.

62. Martha Honey and Tony Avirgan, "The Carlos Files," *The Nation*, October 5, 1985; Caitlin Randall, "Charges of Contra Aid are Denied," *The Tico Times* (San Jose, Costa Rica), July 5, 1985; "Jailed Foreign Rebels Tell Their Story," *The Tico Times*, July 5, 1985. Jean Hopfensperger, "U.S. Policy, Regional Developments Nudge Costa Rica to the Right"; *Report on Costa Rica, 1985*.

63. Andrew Maykuth, "Costa Rica Takes a Disputed Step with New Brigade," *Philadelphia Inquirer*, August 12, 1985.

64. *Update* 5, no. 8 (Washington, D.C.: Central America Historical Institute, March 7, 1986).

65. Ibid.

66. Marlise Simons, "3 Armies Collaborate in Central America," *Washington Post*, September 27, 1981; "Setback for CONDECA Revival Plan," *Latin America Regional Report: Regional Reports—Mexico and Central America*, RM-81-09, September 23, 1981. Loren Jenkins, "U.S. Officer Influential in Latin Region," *Washington Post*, January 3, 1984.

67. Raymond Bonner, "Friction Reported in Honduran-Salvadoran Drive," *New York Times*, July 4, 1982; Philip E. Wheaton, "Collaboration Between Salvadoran and Honduran Military Forces Is Now an Offensive Strategy" (Washington, D.C.: EPICA, December 1, 1981); "Hondurans Reported in El Salvador," *Philadelphia Inquirer*, July 4, 1982; "Rebels Say Honduran Jets Are Supporting Salvador," *Philadelphia Inquirer*, March 21, 1983; Philip Taubman, "Nicaragua Rebels Reported to Have New Flow of Arms," *New York Times*, January 13, 1985; James LeMoyne, "U.S. Is Said to Aid Contras Via El Salvador," *New York Times*, February 13, 1986; interview by the author in El Salvador with an analyst based in the region, November-December 1985. Richard J. Meislin, "Guatemala Aided Contras Despite Denials, Panel Says," *New York Times*, February 28, 1987; Steven Danziger, "Nicaraguan Leader Claims Honduras Attacked Under U.S. Pressure," *Christian Science Monitor*, December 10, 1986.

68. For background on low-intensity conflict theory and strategy, see Frank B. Barnett, Hugh Tovar, and Richard H. Shulz, eds., *Special Operations in U.S. Strategy* (New York: National Defense University Press, 1984); Tom Barry, *Low Intensity Conflict: The New Battlefield in Central America* (Albuquerque, N.M.: Inter-Hemispheric Education Resource Center, 1986); Sara Miles, "The Real War, Low Intensity Conflict in Central America," *NACLA: Report on the Americas* 20, no. 2 (April/May 1986); and Michael T. Klare, "The New U.S. Strategic Doctrine," *The Nation*, December 28, 1985.

69. Barry, *Low Intensity Conflict;* "America's Secret Soldiers: The Buildup of U.S. Special Operations Forces"; Peter H. Stone, "The Special Forces in 'Covert Action,'" *The Nation,* July 7–14, 1984; Charles Mohr, "To Modernize the Army Is Bringing Back Light Infantry," *New York Times,* November 25, 1984; Sarkesian, "Low-Intensity Conflict," p. 8; Klare, "The 'In-Between' Deployment Force."

70. Sarkesian, "Low-Intensity Conflict," pp. 9–13; Ramsey Clark, "Libya, Grenada and Reagan," *The Nation,* May 3, 1986.

71. "US 'War Games' in Central America: What's Behind the Strategy?" an interview with Deborah Barry, a U.S. analyst who works with the Regional Center for Socio-Economic Research in Managua, *Envío* 4, no. 54 (December 1985); William I. Robinson and Kent Norsworthy, "Nicaragua: The Strategy of Counterrevolution," *Monthly Review,* December 1985.

72. *Who Are the Contras? An Analysis of the Makeup of the Leadership of the Rebel Forces and the Nature of the Private American Groups Providing Them Financial and Material Support,* April 1985, and *The Contra High Command, An Independent Analysis of the Military Leadership of the FDN,* March 1986, research reports prepared for the members of the Arms Control and Foreign Policy Caucus; *Update* 4, no. 1 (Washington, D.C.: Central American Historical Institute, January 29, 1985).

73. Steve Stecklow, "After a Year Nicaragua Is Suffering from the U.S. Trade Embargo," *Philadelphia Inquirer,* May 11, 1986.

74. Excerpts from Haig's address at OAS meeting from *New York Times,* December 5, 1981, as quoted in William M. LeoGrande, "The United States and Nicaragua," in Thomas W. Walker, ed., *Nicaragua: The First Five Years* (New York: Praeger, 1985), p. 435.

75. Bernard Weintraub, "President Accuses 5 Outlaw States of World Terror," *New York Times,* July 9, 1985.

76. James LeMoyne, "Honduran Tells of U.S. Pressure," *New York Times,* April 3, 1986.

FOUR

Economic Aggression as an Instrument of Low-Intensity Warfare

MICHAEL E. CONROY

The economy of Nicaragua represented the point of greatest external vulnerability for the Sandinista revolutionary government throughout its first seven years in power. And the policies implemented by the Reagan administration in the United States consciously focused upon that vulnerability. The very concept of low-intensity warfare evolved and became a leading military doctrine of the U.S. government precisely during the period when the administration's attention was agonizingly focused on overthrowing the Sandinista government.

In this chapter I will argue that traditional policies of economic aggression against Latin American regimes out of favor with Washington constituted an important part of the initial policy response of the Reagan administration to the consolidation of the Sandinista government. By the second half of the 1979–1986 period, however, the use of the surrogate counterrevolutionary forces based in Honduras became the most important part of this economic war. In fact, the Nicaraguan experience of counterrevolutionary low-intensity warfare can be understood best from the perspective of its actual and potential impact upon the increasingly vulnerable economic sphere, rather than as either an attempt to organize and seat a politically viable alternative

This chapter was prepared as a paper for presentation at the September 1986 annual meeting of the Midwest Association for Latin American Studies Association Annual Meetings in St. Louis. It includes a substantial updating and reworking of material previously published in an article entitled "Economic Dependence, External Assistance, and 'Economic Aggression' Against Nicaragua" that appeared in *Latin American Perspectives*, issue 45, vol. 12, no. 2 (spring 1985):39–67.

government or as a predominantly military effort designed to defeat the Sandinistas.

Although the full economic impact of the contras remains a closely guarded secret in Nicaragua, ample evidence on theoretical, inferential, and anecdotal bases links the initial vulnerability of the postinsurrection economy to the deliberate policies of the Reagan administration to destabilize it and to evaluate the contra war as a continuation, extension, and deepening of that predominantly economic attack.

Prerevolutionary External Economic Vulnerability in Nicaragua

The full extent of Nicaraguan external dependence prior to the revolution has seldom been demonstrated or documented thoroughly. In fact, standard overviews of the Nicaraguan economy prior to 1979 rarely raised the issue.[1] Analyses at that time by the UN Economic Commission for Latin America (ECLA) provided a clearer portrait of the growing disequilibrium.[2] ECLA's more recent overview of the nature of the Central American crisis provides insight into this problem, without focusing explicitly on the dimensions of real (production-based) and financial dependence.[3]

Nicaraguan dependence can be seen first in the relative importance to the economy as a whole of its export products and in their vulnerability to fluctuations in production and market prices. The Nicaraguan economy in the 1960s and 1970s, ECLA noted, suffered from the same structural problems that afflict the other Central American economies to this date. Having linked their post–World War II growth to the expansion of markets for their traditional exports in the industrialized countries, such economies encountered rapidly growing import and export coefficients (proportions of national product) after 1960. The evolution of the external sector "determined the global economic behavior of the economy," and the restrictions found in that sector "marked the limit on the rate of domestic economic activity." There resulted a "direct relationship between the level of exports on the one hand and the rates of economic expansion, capital accumulation, investment, procurement of fiscal revenue, level of employment, and import capacity, on the other."[4]

On the financial side the growing external orientation was less obvious but equally profound. The 1960s and 1970s were a period characterized by increasing availability of foreign financial assistance and direct investment flows to offset the ever-widening gap between foreign exchange earnings and the demand for foreign exchange. "When weakening of external demand coincided with restrictions on the flow of external financing," ECLA noted, "the external sector had the effect of inhibiting economic growth and even bringing about a contraction in economic activity in real terms."[5] Furthermore, increasing flows of repatriated profits and interest payments and the amortization of growing international private and public debt absorbed rapidly increasing shares of export earnings.

Nicaragua had a distinctly open economy prior to 1979; exports and imports constituted very large shares of total production and total consumption. And it remained relatively open after seven years of revolutionary policy. Total exports of goods and services constituted an average of nearly 24 percent of total demand in the economy just prior to the insurrection. Exports represented Nicaragua's principal source of foreign exchange. And they were, oddly enough, the foreign exchange source over which Nicaragua had the greatest control, albeit still very limited control. Foreign exchange needs vary from year to year depending not only on the levels of imports but also on the levels of outflow of profits and interest on private direct and portfolio investment, amortization of public and private debt, and the volatile demand for short-term capital movements. One can measure external imbalance in the economy by comparing the supply of foreign exchange from export earnings with the demand for foreign exchange generated by those four items.

When the external balance, as measured in this manner, proves to be negative, a country must find ways other than through exports to cover the exchange deficit. None of those ways, however, is free from international political pressure. The least political method of covering the deficit is to draw down foreign reserves (deposits of foreign currency, gold, etc.) from the country's holdings at home or abroad, to whatever extent they exist when needed. Private and public foreign borrowing offers another alternative, but the nation must then meet the explicit economic and implicit political criteria of potential lenders. Foreign private long-term investment affords a further method for covering the foreign exchange gap. But the strictures that this last solution places upon domestic economic policy may be the most sensitive of all. Unless a nation offers a set of political and economic conditions that are competitive with all other potential destinations for that private investment, the investment is unlikely to be forthcoming. Long-term dependence on such foreign investment to resolve short-term shortages of foreign exchange leads to the creation of very severe limitations on the ability of governments to implement social and economic policies that are not in the explicit interest of the investors. A government's interest in improving social legislation, in mandating occupational, health, and environmental conditions, and in raising the incomes earned by wage and salary workers is often diametrically opposed to the interests of investors who simply wish to obtain labor or access to markets at the lowest possible costs. In this sense, the problem of covering foreign exchange shortages represents the cutting edge of external dependence.

During the four years prior to the Nicaraguan revolution, imports exceeded exports by large margins (see Table 4.1). Foreign exchange required simply for repatriation of profits and interest exceeded an average of $70 million each year (more than 10 percent of total exports). Total public debt service added an additional $75 million per year (12.5 percent of average export

60   Michael E. Conroy

TABLE 4.1
Basic Indicators of External Dependence in Prerevolutionary Nicaragua, 1975–1978

	1975	1976	1977	1978
1. Total exports of goods and services				
(US$ million)	448	630	733	732
(Total demand)	26.4%	23.6%	18.0%	26.7%
2. Total imports of goods and services				
(US$ million)	720	678	926	766
(Total supply)	24.6%	22.6%	26.7%	28.6%
3. Net outflow of profits and interest				
(US$ million)	54	67	76	76
(Export earnings)	12.1%	10.6%	10.4%	10.4%
4. Total debt service (US$ million)	50.4	76.2	101.9	99.2
(Export earnings)	11.3%	12.1%	13.9%	13.6%
5. Capital flight: Private short-term capital movements (US$ million)	29.9	5.0	-79.5	-226.7
6. External balance: Total exports less total foreign exchange requirements (US$ million)	-346.5	-186.2	-450.4	-435.9

Sources: Items 1, 2, and 4: World Bank, World Debt Tables, 1982-1983 edition, p. 195. Item 3: UN Economic Commission for Latin America, Economic Survey of Latin America, 1978, p. 391. Item 5: IDB, Social and Economic Progress in Latin America, 1982 edition, p. 383.

earnings). And short-term capital movements changed from small flows into the country to massive hemorrhaging from the country between 1975 and 1978. The result in theory, as well as that shown on Table 4.1, is that Nicaragua was not only dependent upon export markets for 25 percent of its national income prior to the revolution; it also suffered from a chronic need for additional external financial assistance of more than $350 million, on average, each year for its imports and debt servicing. During 1977 and 1978 this external financial imbalance averaged more than $440 million each year.[6]

Nicaraguan external dependence, however, was not limited to this imbalance reflected in balance of payments data; for the balance of payments data do not reveal whether the imbalance was the product of temporary and readily remediable events or policies (such as import increases related to sudden expansion of export industry investment) or whether they reflect deeper, chronic problems. In Nicaragua both the banking system and the central government itself had become heavily dependent upon continued high levels of short-term foreign borrowing. Although the Nicaraguan banking systems as a whole had levels of resources and levels of debt no larger than those of a single bank of medium size in the industrialized world, that banking system was heavily dependent upon foreign debt and, especially, upon short-term foreign debt.

TABLE 4.2
External Dependence of the Nicaraguan Banking System: 1976-1978

	1976	1977	1978
Total bank system debt (US$ million)	175.1	229.7	328.8
Total foreign bank debt (US$ million)	94.1	141.1	188.4
Foreign bank debt as % of total:	53.98	61.40	57.32
Short-term foreign (US$ million)	41.1	94.6	151.2
Short-term foreign as a % of total bank debt	23.41	41.64	45.97
short-term foreign as % of total foreign	43.37	67.81	80.21

Source: Basic data from the Banco Central de Nicaragua, "Informe Anual, 1978," p. 18; conversions to US dollars at 7.026 Córdobas per dollar, as taken from the IMF "International Financial Statistics," April 1984, p. 278.

The foreign debt of the Nicaraguan banking system averaged more than $140 million from 1976 to 1978 (see Table 4.2). And the level of the debt doubled between 1976 and 1978. This debt constituted an average of 57 percent of all banking system debt in the country. Although in 1976 less than a quarter of the total debt was short-term foreign debt (loans with a maturity of one year or less), by 1978 short-term foreign debt constituted 46 percent of total bank debt. Even more significantly, the short-term portion of bank debt to foreigners increased from 43 percent to 80 percent between 1976 and 1978.[7]

What this meant for Nicaragua was quite simple. Nicaraguan bankers were required to renegotiate continually nearly 40 percent of the total outstanding bank debt of the country, either rolling over that much debt in foreign banks on a continuous basis or facing the possibility of a tumultuous multiplied contraction of the nation's financial system. Foreign bankers could refuse to roll the debt over if any untoward events occurred in the country that might raise their concerns or if any changes in government policies displeased them. Nicaraguan borrowing, although large in the context of the small Nicaraguan economy, represented miniscule proportions of the global credit market; thus there was little or no incentive for foreign banks to be reticent about lessening their lending exposure in Nicaragua at any given moment. Nicaraguan debt to all major U.S. banks in 1978, for example, constituted only one quarter of one percent (0.262 percent) of total U.S. bank lending abroad at the close of that year.[8]

Prior to 1979 the Somoza government also tended to rely upon foreign borrowing to finance its government programs (see Table 4.3). From 1975 to 1977 the government deficit averaged 38 percent of total expenditures, and an average of 94 percent of that deficit was financed with foreign borrowing. The fragility of this form of solution was seen in 1978 when

62   Michael E. Conroy

TABLE 4.3
External Financing of Government Deficits: Nicaragua, 1975-1978

		1975	1976	1977	1978
Total govt. expenditures	(US$ million)	300	313	438	439
Government deficit	(US$ million)	-111	-95	-189	-225
Def. as % of expenditures		37.2%	30.5%	43.2%	51.3%
Externally financed		104	88	180	86
Foreign financed as % of deficit		93.7%	92.4%	95.2%	38.3%

Source: UN Economic Commission for Latin America, "Estudio Económico de América Latina, 1982: Nicaragua," E/CEPAL/1.286/add.4, p. 395; conversions to U.S. dollars at 7.026 Córdobas per dollar, as taken from the IMF, "International Financial Statistics," April 1984, p. 278.

the government was only able to finance 38 percent of the deficit through foreign borrowers. The scarcity of credit that year is reflected in the capital flight noted in Table 4.1: more than $225 million.

The combined effects of these overlapping dimensions of external structural and financial dependence were rooted deeply in the Nicaraguan economy inherited by the Sandinista government in 1979. Patterns of production in the nation's best agricultural land, the training that was embodied in large portions of the labor force, and the nature of the capital equipment available at that time were all products of the evolution of the external sector in the preceding years. The financial imbalance produced by that system of production represented a form of long-term economic mismanagement, but it was not an imbalance that could be removed by fiat. Under the very best circumstances, the new government would have required many years to restructure and reorganize the economy to eliminate imbalances of that magnitude. Under the best of circumstances, the new government was going to need to depend heavily upon the export sector and on significant quantities of external assistance to avoid precipitous decline in the standard of living.

The chronic imbalance in the Nicaraguan economy was exacerbated by the actions of the Somoza regime as it abandoned the country in 1979. Capital flight during the final months of the insurrection exceeded $500 million according to the first World Bank mission that visited Nicaragua after the Sandinista government took power.[9] The banking system had been "completely decapitalized"; it was left virtually insolvent because many transactions during the last months of the conflict were, according to ECLA analysts, "of doubtful legality or completely illegal."[10] But the foreign private debt of the banking system was still due. Both the World Bank and ECLA noted that the foreign public debt inherited from the Somoza regime, approximately $1.6 billion, was a particularly acute problem, for there had been extensive short-term borrowing during the last two years of the Somoza era to finance arms purchases, to counteract capital flight, and to finance the government deficit.

The crucial and immediate need for external financial assistance in 1979 was emphasized by both organizations. The very viability of the financial and monetary system and, as a result, the possibilities for economic stabilization in general depended upon obtaining ample new foreign resources to rehabilitate the nation's productive capacity.

Reactivation of the economy became the highest priority of the Sandinista economic policy during the last half of 1979 and throughout 1980. Production had virtually ceased throughout the country during the months of June and July, key planting months. Real gross domestic product fell by 25 percent in 1979; exports decreased by 12 percent in 1979, and, reflecting the consequences of disruption during the fall planting period, they fell by a further 20 percent in 1980. This export-dependent, nearly bankrupt economy began the transition to a "new economic and social system" from a profoundly disadvantageous starting point.

The Vulnerability of Exports in Sandinista Nicaragua

Nicaragua did not have a large number of clear models to emulate in the reorganization of its economic system. Nicaraguan planners were most interested in adapting policies from a variety of socialist and social democratic experiences. Although all prior attempts since 1950 to construct a socialist system had occurred in small, open economies that were, like Nicaragua, significant exporters of primary products, the experiences of other nations had historical specificity that limited the transferability of their experiences. The body of theoretical literature potentially relevant to the design of a new social and economic order in Nicaragua was extremely limited, whether one searched among the histories of nations that had made a recognized transition to more-socialist forms of organization or in the Marxist theories of transition to socialism. Those analyses that were subsequently directed to the problems of transition in Nicaragua, however, were virtually unanimous in their interpretation of the crucial role of the export sector.[11]

Primary product exports in Nicaragua are the heavy industry of the country, according to FitzGerald. They are the relatively capital-intensive earners of foreign exchange and the vehicle for the insertion of the economy into the world market system. And they are, ultimately, "a (or perhaps the) crucial determinant of the model of growth and distribution."[12]

The export sector was also the most likely source of surplus within the society. Part of that surplus was generated from the profits on the large amount of capital dedicated to that sector; part of it accrued because the costs of agricultural production in Nicaragua, even after the improvements in the total wage package for farmworkers, were significantly lower than those of other producers in the world market. Given the revolutionary government's goals of increasing substantially the availability of locally produced wage goods (basic food stuffs, transportation, housing) and the concrete programs to sustain and improve the standard of living of the peasantry and urban and rural wage workers by subsidizing the prices paid for basic commodities, there was little opportunity to accumulate surplus in that sector. The heavy damage done to industrial production during the last phase of the insurrection and the heavy import requirements of rebuilding and then serving those industries made them equally unlikely candidates for generating a surplus with which to cover the costs of subsidies in other areas and for new investment projects.

The production of exports, however, was one portion of the Nicaraguan economy that was furthest from direct government control. Most estimates suggest that the proportion of production controlled directly by the public sector amounted to little more than 40 percent of Nicaraguan gross domestic product by the 7th Anniversary. But the Nicaraguan public sector controlled only 25 percent of the production of the agricultural export sector. Although the distribution of exports across specific products fluctuated from year to year, 1981 data are representative. In 1981 five primary agricultural products accounted for 72 percent of all Nicaraguan exports: coffee (27 percent), cotton (25 percent), sugar (10 percent), beef (6 percent), and bananas (4 percent).[13] Large-scale private producers accounted for 30 percent of all agricultural export production; small-scale private production accounted for 42 percent; and only approximately 28 percent was derived from state-sector production.[14]

The private control of export production forced the Sandinista government to face the stiffest test of its resolve to maintain private production in the bulk of the economy. The conflict was theoretical as well as practical. The urgent need to expand export production, "an absolute priority" according to Irvin, led the government to introduce preferential treatment for those producers, including special access to foreign exchange, reductions in the original highly-progressive export taxes, and reduced interest rates.[15] These export-oriented policies were considered by some as creating a class of "privileged" producers.[16]

The special treatment, however, reflected the need to create incentives for that particular group of producers that compensated for the effects upon them of other government policies. Given that one fundamental goal of the Nicaraguan model was to use a broad range of economic policies to redistribute income toward the working class and the peasantry, these redistributive policies may have conflicted with the need for export expansion unless they were somewhat offset by special treatment. Irvin noted in a contemporaneous analysis, for example, that "the danger is that with the bulk of export production still in private hands, further redistribution (via higher taxation, a fixed exchange rate, and the disappearance of imported consumer goods) may lead to export stagnation."[17]

The terms of trade for Nicaraguan exports deteriorated after 1979 as a result of world market conditions. The value of Nicaraguan exports fell by nearly 23 percent from 1979 to 1986 but not because of shortfalls in the production of agricultural exports. The physical volume of production increased, in fact, by 11.2 percent during the first five years. The growth in export production in Nicaragua contrasts with the decline elsewhere in Central America that averaged 19 percent over the same period.[18] The decline in export earnings in Nicaragua was a clear and direct function of the decline in world prices for its export commodities.[19]

Economic measures undertaken by the U.S. government to undermine the Nicaraguan economy, discussed in greater detail in later sections, further worsened Nicaraguan export earnings by forcing the government to develop new markets through price concessions. Expectations for the 1984-1985 harvest year were pessimistic because of the severity of the attacks on coffee growing areas by the CIA-organized contras. Periodic increases in overflights by contra and U.S. aircraft forced limitations on aerial spraying in cotton-growing areas, reducing yields and exportable harvests. Despite Sandinista successes in the 1985-1986 harvest year in clearing the contras out of coffee-producing areas—so that deaths of harvesters in those areas attributable to the contras fell from thirty-five in 1984-1985 to zero in 1985-1986—these actions were only a small part of the overall attempt by the U.S. government to exploit Nicaragua's inherited dependency by "making its economy scream."[20]

U.S. Economic Policies as Economic Aggression

Economic aggression is not a term found in the glossaries of most U.S. economics texts. It is not a theoretical concept that has been well defined, analyzed, characterized, or typified. There is a strong tendency among U.S. academic economists to dismiss the term as the reflection of concepts or approaches in the realm of political science but certainly not in the domain to which traditional analytical tools of economists may be applied legitimately. This rather ingenuous approach reflects, I believe, both an act of faith in the nature of market economies and a deeply held moral belief that the U.S. government does not engage in such practices. In the case of Nicaragua, however, that naivete may have met its overdue end.

Prior to the onset of the new doctrines of low-intensity warfare, policies of economic aggression were designed and implemented in a manner fundamentally independent of overt military strategy. One of the best analytical treatments of the notion of economic aggression was provided by Pedro Vuskovic in a little known essay first published by *Le Monde Diplomatique* and reproduced in *El Nuevo Diario* (June 4, 1981). Vuskovic was himself a victim of the U.S. destabilization policies against Chile while he served as minister of the economy under Salvador Allende. He wrote the essay in early 1981 at a time when the Reagan administration had begun to announce its opposition to aid to Nicaragua but when the magnitude and full characteristics of its anti-Sandinista economic policies had not been made apparent. His analyses were prescient.

Vuskovic discussed the nature and the objectives of U.S. programs of economic destabilization with reference to a relatively wide variety of nations and national experiences. Economic aggression, he noted, has ranged from simple warnings and notices that policies might be enacted to the open implementation of deliberate policies designed to have a direct effect on particularly vulnerable areas of an economy. The objectives ranged from "dissuading" a government from a planned or proposed policy to "delegitimizing" whole governments by using less visible, more "normal" tools. Under conditions where elections are about to occur, for example, Vuskovic showed that the U.S. attempted to create a tangible worsening in the social and economic conditions of that country to lessen the likelihood that the ruling government would be retained in power. He cites not only the overt attempts to depose Fidel Castro through the U.S. economic embargo, but also U.S. economic policy toward the Goulart government of Brazil just prior to its overthrow in 1964, the measures taken by the Nixon administration to limit and restrain economic policies of the Velasco Alvarado government in Peru, the pressures that led to the overthrow of the Torres government in Bolivia in 1971, the deliberate destabilization attempts made against Allende in Chile, the policy changes that hurt the Peronist government of Argentina from 1973 to 1976, and comparable but lesser destabilization efforts directed at General Torrijos of Panama, Prime Minister Manley of Jamaica, and the Echeverría regime in Mexico.

All of these experiences share a set of common characteristics, Vuskovic noted, that is useful for understanding the coherence behind the policies that were then beginning to be enacted against Nicaragua:

1. The economic aggression is articulated through policies that link the interests of international institutions, such as the IMF, with the economic interests of local elites, who attempt to claim representation of broader social groups, such as small businesspersons or the salaried professional class.
2. The destabilization programs are developed gradually and at first discretely, beginning with actions that may create an adequate response and then escalating the nature and the public defense of the policies with deliberately misleading demagoguery to justify increasingly open economic aggression.
3. The initial phases are accompanied by a campaign of delegitimization, claims of "inefficiency," charges that the government is violating nationalist commitments, and demands for change as great as possible (effectively eliminating any possibility that they will be met), while linking the opposition to "private enterprise."
4. At intermediate stages, repeated in most of the cases cited, conditions are created that encourage destructive behavior on the part of businesspeople in the country, based on campaigns of fear about the future: liquidation of assets, capital flight, reduction of inventories, postponement of maintenance, and the gradual increase in shortages created simply by a hoarding mentality. As the inflationary pressures are brought to bear and domestic production

suffers from the climate of fear and uncertainty, international finance is increasingly blocked or delayed, and demands for protection of private enterprise are escalated.

5. In its most ferocious stages, the coordinated policies become open, public, international economic aggression: sources of international finance are deliberately blocked; concerted efforts are made to deny access to international markets for essential products; and conditions are created so that entrepreneurial class in the country refrains from rational economic activity, producing as little as possible, hoarding, and, in general, disrupting normal production and commerce.

If we define *economic aggression* as the introduction of political and economic policies designed to disrupt or injure the economy of another country, including the deliberate withdrawal of economic assistance with an intent to injure, there is little doubt that U.S. policies toward Nicaragua constituted blatant aggression. The list of the specific elements of those policies is too long to reproduce completely at this point, but they have been outlined extensively elsewhere.[21]

The United States began its economic pressure immediately after Ronald Reagan was inaugurated. Disbursement of the last $15 million in committed economic assistance was halted, and a much needed shipment of wheat was stopped. By late 1981 the United States was publicly organizing in the Inter-American Development Bank to block one loan after another, especially in the Fund for Special Operations, the concessional loan facility over which the United States has unusually great influence.[22] An October 1980 World Bank mission, named by out-going World Bank president Robert McNamara, provided a fundamentally supportive analysis of the Nicaraguan situation and the need for substantial and immediate assistance. This report, completed in February 1981 and circulated for eight months before being published in October of that year, unintentionally provided, it now seems, the blueprint for the Reagan administration's aggression against Nicaragua.[23]

The Bank's October 1980 mission reported that the damaging economic consequences of the insurrection were real and persistent. "Per capita income levels of 1977 will not be attained, in the best of circumstances," it noted, "until the late 1980's." It envisaged high probabilities of debt-servicing and financing problems, but it noted that "if Nicaragua can obtain substantial financing in the near term, a considerable improvement in its creditworthiness three to four years hence [could] be foreseen."[24] And the report urged that "it would be highly desirable for the country to receive external assistance at concessional terms and in excess of the foreign exchange component." The consequences of withholding financial support were also clear: "any untoward event could lead to a financial trauma, since the country would not be able to obtain commercial financing as a buffer. Moreover, it would be very difficult indeed to restrain consumption for such a long period."[25]

Shortly after that World Bank team returned from Nicaragua, Robert McNamara retired and was replaced by William Claussen, previously president of the Bank of America. Ronald Reagan was inaugurated, the presidential transition team expressed much concern about World Bank lending to socialist countries, a new team was sent to Nicaragua, and a radically different report was written. The report was labeled "confidential" and was intended for use within the World Bank alone.[26]

This new report admitted that the World Bank had taken on the role of negotiating for the private sector in Nicaragua, insisting on new "clear and consistent rules of the game for the private sector," acceptable to the Bank, as a precondition for any further bank lending. The new report termed Nicaragua only "marginally creditworthy," a rating blamed primarily on problems in the growth rate of export earnings, and said that Nicaragua's foreign exchange shortages are the "overwhelming medium-term problem." It then argued against funding most of the projects that the Nicaraguan government had requested.[27] Noting that Nicaragua "is likely to be a very controversial client," the new report recommended ending all lending for water supply projects, road building, or education programs and offering only limited financial assistance for agricultural credit programs "directed to the private sector." It then called for slowing the processing of the request for even those funds, awaiting the Sandinista government's responses to its demands with respect to the private sector.[28]

The International Development Association (IDA) is the "soft-loan" or concessional branch of the World Bank; its functions are similar to those of the Fund for Special Operations of the International Development Bank (IDB). The United States has made considerable donations to this fund, and it exercises effective veto control. The application of that veto was never publicly announced, although Nicaragua did not receive any funds from the IDA after 1980. The February 1982 World Bank report also included a tacit admission that the United States had, by that date, blocked all loans and grants to Nicaragua from IDA.[29]

The United States attempted to undercut Nicaragua's export earnings in more direct ways as well. In 1983 the United States unilaterally reduced Nicaragua's quota of sugar for U.S. markets by 90 percent, an act designed to cost Nicaragua more than $23 million in differential sugar prices. The United States was a founding member of GATT (General Agreement on Tariffs and Trade), the international organization charged with policing fairness in trading relations. The United States had depended heavily on GATT, over the years, to condemn "unfair" dumping and subsidizing of Japanese and Third World products being sent to U.S. markets. The Nicaraguans complained to GATT that the arbitrary reduction of the sugar quota constituted an "unfair practice." GATT ruled that it was, indeed, a violation of binding agreements, but the U.S. decided to ignore this decision.[30]

The U.S. government used a plethora of harassment techniques to slow, delay, or deter Nicaraguan trade with the United States. According to officials interviewed at the Ministry of Foreign Commerce, they ranged from restrictions on exports of chemical feedstocks to Nicaragua because of their alleged use in products traded with Cuba, inconsistently scrupulous and exaggerated agricultural inspections, the closing of the Nicaraguan consulates to lessen the ability of U.S. producers to meet Nicaraguan import technicalities, and pressure on U.S. firms to avoid dealings with Nicaragua. The mining of all Nicaraguan harbors and undeveloped "anchorages" in January and February 1984 represented an even more direct form used by the United States to inhibit all trade with Nicaragua, one that was criticized by even the Reagan administration's closest European ally, Margaret Thatcher. The consequences were far greater than the much-heralded damage to some vessels. Representatives of the Ministry of Planning indicated that during the first two months after the mining, shippers with contracts to deliver goods to Nicaragua off-loaded many of them in Costa Rica and shipped them overland to Nicaragua, often with delays of many weeks. Several shipping lines declined future shipments until it could be demonstrated that the mines had been cleared; shipping insurance costs were increased; and the already precarious foreign supply of goods was further disrupted. Although the U.S. government agreed to cease the placement of new mines in March 1984, the mines were not removed. They continued exploding through summer 1984.

The formal imposition of an embargo on all trade with Nicaragua on May 7, 1985, was, therefore, little more than a formalization of policies implemented much earlier. Its principal immediate impact was psychological and political, and it was criticized by virtually every ally of the Reagan administration. One year after its implementation, it was respected by no country except the United States. Nicaragua had been quite successful in the diversification of its trade, especially with respect to the number and relative importance of trading partners. The total elimination of U.S. trade had the ironic impact of shifting ever-larger proportions of Nicaragua's trade to a small number of new trading partners, especially Japan, Canada, and the Netherlands.[31]

The most important deterrent to Nicaraguan trade, however, was the collapse of private credit links for both imports and exports. These were simple transactions credits[32] rather than the borrowing more commonly recorded under public borrowing, and there was no international system for recording them or evaluating their magnitude. The pervasiveness of international credit in the financing of even the simplest transactions between the United States and many Third World nations represented a form of hidden dependency that cost Nicaragua dearly. Much of this dependence is never manifested in international statistics, for it is based on links to the actual importing or exporting firms.

It is often the U.S. firm, for example, that arranges for the credit needed to consummate an international transaction with Third World importers and exporters. The U.S. firm uses its domestic lines of credit with U.S. banks to finance shipments or receipts of goods, rather than requiring that the Third World party to the transaction obtain a loan that produces a recorded international transaction. Prior to the revolution, for example, a Nicaraguan importer of fertilizer could often obtain six-month credit terms directly from the manufacturer; the manufacturer would obtain the financing in its name from a local bank. The distributor then extended comparable credit to the farmer until the crop was harvested. Once the crop was in, the distributor was paid by the farmer, the manufacturer by the distributor, and the bank in the United States was repaid. A similar process was often used for Nicaraguan exports: U.S. importers would obtain loans from U.S. banks to provide advances to Nicaraguan producers; the advance would be deducted from payment due for the crop itself; and the bank would be repaid without a recorded international credit transaction. There was not necessarily any fear of the recorded credit transaction; however, international statistics understate the extent of this hidden dependence.

When the Ministry of Foreign Trade was organized in 1979 to control all imports and exports (specifically to avoid the capital flight that occurs surreptitiously through "over-invoicing" procedures), the first great problem that it encountered was the complete breakdown of that suppliers' credit system. There is no way to know precisely how much of Nicaragua's imports and exports prior to the revolution were financed with this kind of short-term credit. The ministry later conservatively estimated that if 50 percent received such financing, the loss in credit amounted to more than $500 million. For a nation to lose all such credit almost instantaneously is devastating; it forces the nation onto a totally cash basis, causing dramatic contractions in spending until the needed cash can be accumulated.

In theory Nicaragua should have then been able to turn directly to the banking community for loans to replace the suppliers' and importers' credits that were lost. Whereas credit had previously been extended to myriad small businesses in Nicaragua on a strictly private basis, the state was now willing to offer formal state guarantees for short-term import and export credits. Nicaragua should have been viewed as an especially good credit risk for most banks, for the new government had taken the unusual step of officially accepting responsibility for the $1.6 billion Somoza-era debts and had succeeded in restructuring and refinancing the vast majority of its debts.[33]

The restructuring was precedent setting: Nicaragua was given until 1986 to resume principal payments, and the interest payments on most loans were lowered to 7 percent for that period with the difference between that rate and the actual rate on the loan capitalized into the principal.[34] In fact, the World Bank reported that Nicaragua had brought itself up to date on all international debt payments by early 1980;[35] and Nicaragua was reported in the North American press as "one of the few countries in Latin America that continues to pay its debts on time."[36]

The pattern of economic aggression, however, included State Department efforts to discourage bank lending to Nicaragua. These activities appear to have been very widespread, and they are epitomized by the history of a loan that was organized by the Bank of America and announced in December 1982. The loan amounted to approximately $30 million for ninety days, and it was guaranteed by an effective mortgage on a share of the nation's cotton crop. It would have been "the first significant bank loan to Nicaragua since 1979."[37] The loan was sought to meet interest payments due on foreign debt, but the Nicaraguans committed themselves to making those payments whether or not the loan was finalized. The loan was stopped. Later reports indicated that the State Department took an active role in discouraging the loan, calling Bank of America loan officers and threatening to call members of the bank's board of directors. The official State Department response was that it had not formally blocked the loan but that it had made certain that the bank's officers knew what the administration's feelings were about such loans.[38]

Under normal circumstances the process of restructuring existing debt is undertaken so that a nation is once again considered creditworthy for additional short-term and medium-term borrowing. Revolutionary Nicaragua, however, has encountered an almost total withdrawal of short-term financing, precisely the form of financing on which the Somoza regime had become so totally dependent. In December 1978, 73.3 percent of all the bank debt owed by Nicaraguans to U.S. banks was short-term debt, debt that had to be renegotiated or repaid in one year or less. That short-term share was 15 percent of the region-wide average of 62.8 percent, and it was one of the highest encountered in Central America for the entire period for which data are available.[39]

As the medium-term loans of the Somoza era came due, the proportion increased to 75.5 percent in mid-1980. Thereafter the total absence of short-term lending by U.S. banks was reflected in the plummeting of the share of Nicaragua's debt that was short term. From June 1980 to June 1983 the share fell to 10.5 percent, a condition that was totally inconsistent with relative economic indicators, totally inconsistent with the banks' lending policies in the rest of Central America, and totally inconsistent with the expressed preferences of the Nicaraguan government. Despite the near total collapse of the economy of El Salvador, the refusal of the Costa Rican government to agree to an IMF adjustment program and the burgeoning there of the highest debt in Central America, and massive capital flight from Honduras, the banks continued to make short-term loans to each of these countries in relatively constant shares of total borrowing.

In July 1983 a Reagan administration spokesperson, James Conrow, the Treasury official responsible for U.S. votes in the Multilateral Banks, announced that the United States would vote against all loans for Nicaragua "unless the revolutionary Sandinista government takes steps to 'revitalize the private sector' and 'improve the efficiency of the public sector.'"[40] These are, of course, precisely the policies that the Nicaraguan government was pursuing most vigorously, even amid criticism from the Left.[41] The same news report that announced the policy also noted its inconsistency. The United States regularly votes in the World Bank for loans to countries with predominantly socialist economies, such as Yugoslavia, and it supported policies in El Salvador that it criticized in Nicaragua, such as the nationalization of the banking system. There is virtually no explanation for depriving

Nicaragua of its access to credit from the United States, whether supplier's credits or bank credit, other than a conscious policy of economic aggression.

Economic Aggression and Low-Intensity Warfare

The organization of dissident exile Nicaraguans in Honduras and Costa Rica to conduct guerrilla raids across the borders into Nicaragua began in 1981, but most generally perceived it to be a separate, distinctly military attempt to harass the Sandinista government, comparable to the harassment of Cuba by exiles based in Florida during the 1960s. Although they received hundreds of millions of dollars in direct and indirect assistance from the CIA, the contras were distinctly unsuccessful in any traditional military sense. During their first five years of operations, they did not succeed in capturing and holding a single town or other significant military objective. Their principal objectives were interpreted as political harassment, demonstrating that the Sandinista government could not defend all the population all the time. Although the destruction of some economically important targets such as granaries, road construction equipment, coffee *beneficios,* and newly formed cooperatives was a clear component of the tactics, the strategy of the contra was generally not perceived as principally economic.

By early 1986, however, the use of such irregular forces against politically progressive governments of which the Reagan administration disapproved was recognized as a "new U.S. strategic doctrine."[42] This doctrine had evolved out of the "post–Viet Nam syndrome" to replace and to complement preexisting doctrines of the use of conventional forces against "brushfire wars" and insurgencies. Contributors to its formulation included military officers specialized in Special Operations[43] as well as conservative think-tank analysts.[44] The doctrine featured three principal dimensions: (1) classic counterinsurgency activities of the sort developed and practiced by the Kennedy-inspired Special Forces in Vietnam to provide political, economic, and psychological operations to neutralize peasant support for insurgents in countries whose governments were supported by the United States; (2) an active defense against terrorism including U.S. military raids on suspected terrorist strongholds; and (3) support for "anti-Communist" insurgencies against leftist governments.[45]

The economic significance of this last form of low-intensity warfare was understated in the analyses of its application to Nicaragua prior to 1986. It is useful to focus, first, on the theoretical potential for damage that such an insurgency might have against an economy such as that of Nicaragua. But first one must reflect on the nature of the Nicaraguan productive system.

Nicaraguan production, as I have noted, remained fundamentally in private-sector hands in 1986. Much of it, especially the production of basic grains, cattle, and coffee, took place over vast expanses of mountainous terrain scarcely penetrated by roads or other infrastructure, especially in the departments of Jinotega, Matagalpa, Boaco, and Chontales. The Sandinista government developed extensive systems to purchase, store, and distribute basic grains through state distribution enterprises that replaced price-gouging middlemen and distributed through the existing private retail food system. And this system involved the deployment of numerous trucks, jeeps, purchasing agents, and other state employees to the most remote harvesting and transshipment points accessible. At the same time, unregulated parallel markets for all products continued to function throughout the country.

Agricultural production, especially on the most remote agricultural frontiers but also throughout the more developed interior, depended increasingly upon family labor. The agrarian reform had soaked up much of the previous labor surplus, so that even without conscription there were labor shortages at crucial planting and harvesting times.

The maintenance and expansion of private sector agricultural production levels depended crucially upon convincing individual farmers to invest in seed, plowing, planting, cultivation throughout the growing season, harvesting, and the equipment needed for these phases as well as for processing and transportation. Any activity that disrupted the likelihood of final marketing of products lessened the incentive to invest in each phase of production.

In agriculture, as well as in nonagricultural production in Nicaragua, pricing of inputs and of final products sold for export involved extensive negotiations between government representatives and representatives of principal producer and labor organizations. And producers always had the option of producing as little as possible to forestall expropriation if the negotiated prices did not seem adequate to generate a profit.

Within this context an armed guerrilla force attacking from across nearby borders threatens the economy, in theory, in numerous direct and indirect ways:

- Direct damage to roads, bridges, vehicles, and farm storage structures requires replacement that diminishes the availability of investment, whether public or private, for the maintenance and expansion of production.
- Such direct damage further increases costs of production in unpredictable ways, lowers profits, undermines the price negotiations that determine profits in government-subsidized agricultural channels, and raises the prices of products in parallel markets, thereby increasing the real wages needed for subsistence by agricultural labor.
- Defense requirements tap significant proportions of an already shrunken labor force, lessening its availability for all production and forcing the costly mobilization of poorly trained and less productive volunteer labor.
- To the extent that the guerrillas can force relocation of the rural population in defensive settlements away from production areas, or even somewhat more distant from fields, the amount of time that farmers can spend on their lands is diminished and the availability of other family farm labor is reduced.

- To the extent that the fundamental viability of the government is questioned, producers are provided with an incentive for postponing or withholding investment while they await the outcome.
- Under conditions where foreign exchange is scarce, the foreign exchange needed to replace damaged or destroyed imported equipment reduces the availability of foreign exchange for directly productive needs, such as fertilizers, seed, other farm chemicals, and the imported components of all other production.
- To the extent that the guerrilla activities are successful, directly and indirectly, in reducing the production of exportable products or in increasing the need for imports, the worsening of the balance of payments will discourage new lending by lenders in other countries, whether public or private, whether banks, agencies, or direct suppliers, and will make more difficult the renegotiation or restructuring of existing debt.
- To the extent that the government responds to the various dimensions of economic crisis attributable to the war by expanding the role of the state in production, the already delicate balance between state and private sector, the confidence of private producers, and their willingness to invest may be diminished.

The full extent of economic damage to Nicaragua from the low-intensity war may never be known. For obvious reasons the best estimates of the direct links between contra activity and economic problems have been kept highly confidential by the Nicaraguan government; it has had little interest in giving that ammunition to the contra leaders in their campaign to convince the U.S. government to provide further assistance. But the evidence available on the mode of operation of the contras lends considerable credibility to the hypothesis that their long-term objectives were most closely associated with inflicting economic damage. And the anecdotal evidence of their success was abundant by the end of 1986. In fact, the specific pattern of contra attacks seemed clearly designed to affect Nicaragua most severely in those economic areas of greatest vulnerability: agricultural exports, basic grains production, and international lending.

The contra concentrated their attacks on outlying communities in the strictly agricultural frontier areas. They attacked numerous cooperatives, effectively terrorizing the residents, by raining mortar shells indiscriminately among the clusters of homes that normally characterize a cooperative settlement. These attacks created more than 100,000 internal refugees, most of whom were engaged in agricultural production.[46] Many of these farmers continued to attempt to till their fields, but the frequency with which they could reach them and the availability of family labor were sharply reduced. Residents of one settlement camp near Ocotal indicated that they were forced to reduce the number of visits per month to their farms to only eight or ten, rather than the twenty-five to thirty that they would normally make, because government vehicles and military escorts were available only that often. And because of both the distance and the danger, they seldom took other members of their families with them.[47]

The contra adopted a deliberate policy of seeking out and attacking those farmers who cooperated with the government in terms of loans for investment and production. To own and use a new vehicle, such as a late-model diesel-powered jeep or truck, available at subsidized prices to large-scale producers who participated in government production and marketing programs, was to make oneself a target. And there were numerous cases of farmers who were singled out by contra ambush squads and murdered apparently because they were found in such symbols of production.[48]

The contra also made it a policy to "interview" farmers, indicating their preferences. Farmers in Jinotega and Nueva Segovia were told that any sign of participation in agrarian reform programs or in government-sponsored cooperatives would submit them to the risk of attack. One result was that farmers in Nueva Segovia consistently resisted the efforts of agriculture ministry and agrarian reform teams to get them to form cooperatives as a precondition to the distribution of lands under the agrarian reform. The ministry responded by distributing parcels to individual farmers with a minimum of fanfare.[49] Farmers in Boaco and Chontales were told that production at the absolute-minimum levels needed to avoid expropriation would be condoned but that any production beyond that or any sign of collaboration with the government would lead to destruction of farm structures and the risk of death for the farmer and his family.[50]

Government vehicles were prime targets for contra attack, whether military vehicles or not. This meant that the ability of government programs to provide secure markets for basic grain producers in remote areas was substantially reduced, and the ability of the government to distribute other commodities that kept the cost of living low (thereby keeping the rural subsistence wage low) was also affected. The severe shortage of basic grains, especially of beans and corn, during the months of April, May, June, and July 1986 was largely attributable to these production and distribution problems that were caused, at least in part, by the relative success of the contra in the previous year at planting and harvesting times.[51]

Perhaps the most tragic of the distortions created in the economy by war, and in this case by the low-intensity war, is the misallocation of human resources. After five years of increasing conflict, large proportions of the labor force of Nicaragua had been diverted away from directly productive activities in ways that were tangible. Nicaragua's total available labor force was less than 1.5 million persons in the mid-1980s, including all men and women between the ages of fifteen and fifty-five. There were no official figures on the total size of the armed forces, but it was commonly believed that between 100,000 and 150,000 persons had been mobilized in the regular army, the standing reserves, and the active militias; that is from 7 percent to 10 percent of the labor force, and the youngest and healthiest of those, especially young men.

Nicaragua entered the 1980s with a severe scarcity of skilled labor, especially in the technical and professional areas. In Managua, after five years of war, the greatest opportunities for advancement, the greatest employment challenge, and the greatest social needs were found in jobs in the government in general and especially in the security forces and other armed forces. The caliber of the personnel working in those positions was noteworthy, and conversely, the relatively lower caliber of those who were left in positions in the nongovernmental productive economy was equally visible. One whole generation of younger Nicaraguans and the best of the older generations were seeing their lives allocated to defense against the contra.

Conclusion

Nicaragua may have been the leading testing ground for the emerging concepts of low-intensity warfare in the mid-1980s and for its application against "unfriendly" governments in power. In the economic sphere, the sphere in which the contra war was probably most successful, the design of the policies dovetailed almost perfectly with the more traditional forms of economic aggression practiced prior to the melding of the low-intensity war concept. That they represented a new and frightening extension of older policies practiced by the U.S. government against Latin American governments is clear. But there was little evidence that low-intensity warfare could be successful against the Sandinista regime on any level other than the economic.

The five-year history of measures taken to "strangle" the Nicaraguan economy had a telling effect. We will never know what the Nicaraguan economic experiment might have evolved into without this external pressure. We will never know whether the new forms of mixed economy and basic-needs orientation implemented in the first years of the revolution could have led to long-term growth and stability; for the distortions created by the war economy after 1983, the critical labor shortages, the lack of investible resources, the growth of state production in response to war-related shortages— all would take many years to correct. The destruction of productive property, the erosion of institutions, the allocation of the "best and the brightest" of the labor force to state-based tasks of production and defense all militated against the growth and successful evolution of the private sector in Nicaragua. Once again, the very institutions that the U.S. administration claimed to be advocating were those most damaged by the policies with which that advocacy was implemented.

Notes

1. See, for example, the Inter-American Development Bank reports on Nicaragua in its *Economic and Social Progress in Latin America* series for 1975–1977.

2. UN Economic Commission for Latin America (ECLA), *Economic Survey of Latin America, 1977,* Santiago, Chile, 1979, pp. 345–365.

3. UN ECLA, *The Crisis in Central America: Its Origins, Scope, and Consequences*, E/CEPAL/G.1261, September 15, 1983.

4. Ibid., pp. 5–6.

5. Ibid.

6. The negative signs on the capital flight levels indicate that there was net movement out of the country; inflows of funds are subtracted from line six of Table 4.1 and outflows are added to it.

7. Banco Central de Nicaragua, *Informe Anual, 1978*, Managua, pp. 18–25.

8. See Federal Financial Institutions Examination Council, *Statistical Release F-26: Country Exposure Lending Survey* (Washington, D.C.: FFIEC, 1979).

9. World Bank, *Nicaragua: The Challenge of Reconstruction*, Report 3524-NI, October 9, 1981 (Washington, D.C.: World Bank, 1981), p. 2.

10. UN ECLA, *Nicaragua: Repercusiones Económicas de los Acontecimientos Politicos Recientes*, E/CEPAL/G.1091, August 1979, p. 24.

11. See, for example, E.V.K. FitzGerald, "The Economics of the Revolution," in Thomas W. Walker, ed., *Nicaragua in Revolution* (New York: Praeger Publishers, 1982), pp. 203–221; George Irvin, "Nicaragua: Establishing the State as the Centre of Accumulation," *Cambridge Journal of Economics* 7 (1983):125–139; and E.V.K. FitzGerald, "Planned Accumulation and Income Distribution in the Small Peripheral Economy," in K. Martin, ed., *Readings in Capitalist and Non-Capitalist Development* (London: Allen and Unwin, 1983).

12. FitzGerald, "Planned Accumulation," p. 1.

13. UN ECLA, *Estudio Económico de América Latina, 1982: Nicaragua*, E/CEPAL/L.286/Add.4, 1982, p. 15.

14. Ibid.

15. Rose J. Spalding, "State Economic Expansion in Revolutionary Nicaragua," paper presented at the 25th Anniversary Meeting of the International Studies Association, Atlanta, Georgia, March 29, 1984, typescript.

16. Forrest D. Colburn and Silvio DeFranco, "Privilege, Production, and Revolution: The Case of Nicaragua," paper presented at the 25th Anniversary Meeting of the International Studies Association, Atlanta, Georgia, March 29, 1984, typescript.

17. Irvin, "Nicaragua," p. 138.

18. Michael E. Conroy, "False Polarisation? Differing Perspectives on the Economic Strategies of Post-Revolutionary Nicaragua," *Third World Quarterly* 6, no. 4 (October 1984):993–1032.

19. UN ECLA, *Centroamérica: Evolución de sus Economias en 1983*, Mexico City, 1984, typescript.

20. The reference, of course, is to the terms used by President Richard Nixon in 1970 when he directed CIA Director Richard Helms to orchestrate U.S. economic policies against the elected government of Salvador Allende in Chile.

21. See, for example, John Cavanaugh and Joy Hackel, "U.S. Economic War Against Nicaragua," *Counterspy*, March-May 1984, pp. 12–17; Jim Morrell and William Jesse Biddle, "Central America: The Financial War," *International Policy Report*, March 1983, pp. 7–11; and Richard Sholk, "U.S. Economic Aggression Against Nicaragua," paper presented jointly with Sylvia Maxfield at the Eleventh International Congress of the Latin American Studies Association, Mexico City, October 1, 1984 typescript.

22. Sholk, "U.S. Economic Aggression," p. 9.

23. World Bank, *Nicaragua: The Challenge of Reconstruction*.

24. Ibid., p. 47.

25. Ibid.

26. World Bank, "Country Program Paper: Nicaragua," Washington, D.C., February 16, 1982.

27. Ibid., p. 12.

28. Ibid., pp. 16–17.

29. While discussing loans for educational projects, frequently covered by IDA, the report notes on page 14 that "no IDA resources can be allocated to Nicaragua." There is no basis other than a U.S. veto for denying access of any country to IDA funds.

30. *New York Times*, April 16, 1984.

31. See Michael E. Conroy, "Patterns of Changing External Trade in Revolutionary Nicaragua: Voluntary and Involuntary Trade Diversification," in Rose J. Spalding, ed., *The Political Economy of Revolutionary Nicaragua* (New York: Allen and Unwin, 1986).

32. I am indebted to Linda Hudgins for suggesting this apt distinction.

33. The decision to accept responsibility for Somoza's debt remains controversial in Nicaragua. It was made deliberately to maintain contacts with the international financial community upon which Sandinista leaders knew Nicaragua would have to depend for many years into the future. As the costs of that commitment have come due under conditions of considerable financial isolation, the wisdom of the initial decision continues to be questioned.

34. IMF, *Recent Multilateral Debt Restructurings with Official and Bank Creditors*, Occasional Paper 25, Washington, D.C., December 1983.

35. World Bank, "Country Program Paper."

36. *Washington Post*, December 18, 1982.

37. *New York Times*, December 14, 1982.

38. *New York Times*, February 21, 1984.

39. FFIEC, Statistical Release E.16(126): "Country Exposure Lending Survey," various dates.

40. *Washington Post*, July 1, 1983.

41. See Conroy, "False Polarization?"

42. Although researchers at Coordinadora Regional de Investigaciones Económicas y Sociales (CRIES) in Managua had been pursuing the theme for more than a year, some of the earliest national attention to it in the United States was provided by Michael T. Klare, "The New U.S. Strategic Doctrine: Low Intensity Conflict," *The Nation*, December 28, 1985/January 4, 1986, pp. 699, 710–716. For the CRIES perspective, see Deborah Barry, Raul Vergara, and José Rodolfo Castro, "Aproximación al Conflicto Centroamericano desde la Perspectiva de la Guerra de Baja Intensidad (1980–1985)," paper presented at the February 1985 conference at the University of Southern California entitled "The United States and Central America: An Overview of the Last Five Years, 1980–85." A particularly complete analysis of its application to Central America may be found in Sara Miles, *NACLA Report on the Americas* 20, no. 2 (April/May 1986).

43. See Colonel John Wagelstein, "Post-Vietnam Counterinsurgency Doctrine," *Military Review*, January 1985, pp. 42–48.

44. See Ernest Evans, "Revolutionary Movements in Central America: The Development of a New Strategy," in *Rift and Revolution: The Central American Imbroglio* (Washington, D.C.: American Enterprise Institute, 1984).

45. See Klare in *The Nation*.

46. Interview with Reynaldo Téfel, minister of social welfare.

47. Interview at the Santa Rosa resettlement camp, June 1986.

48. Interview with Juan Tijerino, National Union of Farmers and Cattlemen (UNAG) representative and cattle rancher from Boaco, May 1986.
49. Interview with Paul Rice, Ministry of Agriculture and Agrarian Reform (MIDINRA) staff, Estelí, June 1986.
50. Interview with UNAG officials in Boaco, May 1986.
51. See Michael E. Conroy et al., "Internal Migration, the War, and the Regional Outreach of the Nicaraguan State," paper presented at the 1986 Latin American Studies Association Congress, Boston, October 24, 1986.

The Manipulation of Indigenous Struggles

MARTIN DISKIN _____

I am a Jew in a world still threatened by anti-semitism, I am an Afghan, and I am a prisoner of the Gulag. . . . I am a Laotian, a Cambodian, a Cuban, and a Miskito Indian in Nicaragua. I, too, am a potential victim of totalitarianism.

—Ronald Reagan
May 6, 1985[1]

President Reagan's examples show a remarkable selectivity.[2] He might have identified himself with the Big Mountain Navajo who were being forcibly relocated by the federal government or with the Mapuche people of Chile whose land rights were being violated by their government. Reagan's examples were not chosen at random. They were consistent with the Reagan Doctrine of pushing back what he called "communism" by actively supporting its enemies. Any situation that fit the bill was fair game; those that did not were of no interest. A good example of this selective concern is the Reagan administration's use of the issue of the "persecution" of the Miskitos in its attack on its chosen enemy, the Sandinista government of Nicaragua.

The Reagan administration devoted significant resources to make the best case for its foreign policy toward Nicaragua. Among these were the State Department's Office of Public Diplomacy, whose mission was to discredit Nicaragua through public pronouncements, leaked and sometimes classified information, and even disinformation.[3] A reader of these statements, particularly in the cases of indigenous struggles on Nicaragua's Atlantic Coast, must conclude that the U.S. government went beyond trying to make its case using facts. Rather, it indulged in massive misinformation to a public whose tax money it spent on this effort. Further, while distorting or inventing facts, it tried to support these statements by supplying arms and training to foment and intensify discontent there, regardless of the suffering it caused.

The tensions between Atlantic Coast people and their government were used to make Reagan's point about totalitarianism. The use of indigenous and ethnic struggles to support Washington's anti-Nicaragua policy distorts the intrinsic meaning of these struggles. For the Reagan administration, the Miskito and other groups from the Atlantic Coast of Nicaragua counted only as another means of discrediting the Sandinistas. The administration showed the shallowness of its commitment to indigenous struggles, particularly in Central America, through its refusal to condemn the significantly worse systematic government assault on the indigenous populations of Guatemala.[4]

By considering human rights abuses only when convenient, the Reagan administration also diluted the impact of serious monitoring of the world human rights situation. For example, by its consistent characterization of the human rights situation in El Salvador as "improving,"[5] it disqualified itself as an objective watchdog of human rights. Although the Reagan administration did not, properly speaking, monitor human rights, it accused and attacked any group that did if its conclusions differed from Washington policy. And nowhere was more mischief caused than by the use of the peoples of the Atlantic Coast, especially the Miskitos, to bash the "evil empire."

Historically, relations between indigenous people and nation states have been asymmetrical. The state, through its monopoly of force, defined the rights of those who inhabited the land since time immemorial. This relation is well exemplified in the case of the United States. The westward movement of European-derived settlers meant the systematic displacement of the original populations and often their physical destruction. In committing ethnocide and genocide, the new country freely violated its own treaty obligations, made to pacify those who were injured.[6] What most states, including the United States, offered their indigenous populations was a dubious "citizenship" in exchange for any remaining historic rights.

The bearers of Hispanic culture spread their hegemony throughout what came to be called Latin America along with the systematic extinction of hundreds of cultures, peoples, polities, and societies. Now, in the late twentieth century, to be an Indian in America is to be part of a minority. The popular conception holds that this minority must yield to the wishes of the majority. Not even in countries with huge Indian populations, such as Guatemala, Bolivia, Colombia, Ecuador, Peru, Chile, and Mexico, were the indigenous peoples accorded a dignified position. In countries in which Indians were a small fraction of the population (i.e., survivors of prior violence), such as Canada, United States, Brazil, and El Salvador, the situation was even worse.[7]

At the outset of the Sandinista revolution in Nicaragua, the new government applied its revolutionary ideas on the Atlantic Coast in a mechanical, sometimes brutal way. This gave an opening for U.S. policy makers to seize on this issue and make indigenous-state relations another front in the war against Nicaragua. Although the Sandinistas made serious mistakes, they subsequently made strong efforts to respond to the needs of the people of the Atlantic Coast. But U.S. policy was aimed at keeping the tension high by mentioning the mistakes and problems, not the improvements. As a result the legitimate aspirations of Atlantic Coast people in their efforts to achieve autonomy were damaged. To accomplish the overthrow of the Sandinista government, the Reagan administration appeared willing to sacrifice whole peoples.

Background

Separated by formidable geographic barriers, even in the 1980s the people of the Atlantic Coast still refer to those from the Pacific side as "Spaniards." Since Europeans first attempted to appropriate the territory, resources, and labor of the New World, first the Spanish, then the English, and then Pacific Coast Nicaraguans vied for hegemony over the Atlantic Coast. The Spanish saw the coast as peripheral to their ambitions to dominate the dense, productive, highland indigenous populations. For them, it was an unhealthy environment with a sparse population, difficult communication, and little wealth. During the seventeenth century, the British, in their effort to compete with the Spanish beachhead in the Caribbean and Central America, raided the "Spanish Main" and established a small presence in what is now Belize, Honduras, Nicaragua, Costa Rica, and Panama.[8]

The British presence had a profound impact. Shortly after contact, they developed close cooperation with the Miskitos. The Sumus were the largest indigenous group. But, since the Miskitos lived along the coastal littoral and on the banks of the Río Coco, they were more accessible to the British. Through their relations with the British, in return for crewing and provisioning British ships they were rewarded with muskets and other weapons. With this new technology and their strategic position as intermediaries with the British, they were able to subjugate and decimate the Sumus. One historic consequence of this process was the eventual domination in numbers and political influence of the Miskitos over the Sumus. Contact with the British reinforced the cultural distance of coastal people from the Hispanic seat of power, even after independence from Spain in 1823. British influence lasted until the end of the nineteenth century, although Nicaraguan sovereignty was recognized in 1860. The British established a Miskito king (rey Mosco),[9] and, although kingship never seemed to be significant, there was a feeling among twentieth-century Miskitos that their golden age was unjustly terminated.

As an enclave within a colony and then within a modern state (Nicaragua), the Miskitos generally lived in a condition of neglect. In the twentieth century, when foreign commercial interests sought to exploit the natural resources of the coast, the door was open. Tropical hardwoods, minerals, bananas, fish, turtles, and shrimp were freely exported. The turtles, bananas, and pine forests were virtually destroyed to satisfy foreign demand.[10] Although it generated some employment, this activity damaged the environment and, by increasing the importance of cash in the region, ultimately reduced the level of the people's welfare.[11] This period of open exploitation of the Atlantic Coast was not perceived by coastal people as a new Conquest, although it probably should have been. Rather, it was remembered as a time of some excitement, when cash flowed and commerce was vigorous. Older people discussed this period in terms of consumer goods. The commissaries of U.S. companies were full of items not available in Nicaragua. Those coastal people with adequate funds were more attuned to Galveston, New Orleans, and Miami than to Managua.

The coast has always been a multi-ethnic environment. In addition to the Miskito and Sumu populations, there are Ramas, another Amerindian group, now almost extinct, Garífonas (so-called Black Caribs), English-speaking Creoles, mainly in the South, and, in the second half of the twentieth century, mestizo (Hispanic) peasant migrants from the Pacific side of the country.

The "opening up" of the Atlantic Coast by foreign corporations served to create an ethnic stratification that placed foreigners (white) on top, Creoles (black) in managerial and supervisory positions, and indigenous peoples (Miskito, Sumu) on the bottom. These values were part and parcel of this period. So, although some Miskitos, Sumus, Ramas, and Creoles benefited from the presence of foreign commercial interests, most coastal people learned they were inferior to foreigners.[12]

The Somoza period was not a time for liberation movements. Somocista peace and order were obtained through the president's National Guard in most of the country. On the Atlantic Coast, such measures were not as necessary since order prevailed through a mixture of neglect and increasing integration into a cash economy. Through a system of traders, storekeepers, and buyers, local produce was marketed.[13]

During the 1960s and 1970s, there were stirrings of group organization along cultural lines. Two groups arose to express these concerns. One, CORPI (Consejo Regional de Pueblos Indígenas de Centroamérica, México y Panamá) tried to organize on behalf of all Central American indigenous groups. In Nicaragua, ALPROMISU (Alianza de Progreso de los Miskitus y Sumus) and SUKAWALA (Asociación Nacional de Comunidades Sumu) were founded in the early 1970s.[14] During this time more coastal youths were educated through the Moravian Church and the National University. As a result, many of them became even more conscious of themselves as coastal, indigenous people and assumed positions of prominence and leadership when they returned to the coast.

The Sandinista Revolution

Very little of the fighting in the revolution took place on the Atlantic Coast. With the euphoria that prevailed after the ouster of the Somoza dynasty on July 19, 1979, the new government seemed ready to recreate the entire society. The consequences of *somocismo* (the Somoza style of rule) on the

Pacific side were quite different from the situation on the Atlantic Coast. The Atlantic Coast did not have an exploited peasantry dominated by large landowners, nor did it suffer from land shortage, nor was it "unorganized." There was sufficient land available for use. In many communities there was a pattern of communal land tenure whereby any community member could clear land not in use. Public affairs in many Miskito, Sumu, Garífona, and Creole communities were regulated by local institutions. For the Miskitos these institutions were the Moravian Church, especially village pastors (almost all of whom were Miskitos) and village elders. Most of the environments of the coast, humid tropics, are propitious for the cultivation of fruits and vegetables and for fishing. Because marketing arrangements were dominated by intermediaries, there was a chronic imbalance in the terms of trade for most people. To obtain basic goods (rice, kerosene, clothing, tools) people sold their crops or fish for low prices to traders and storekeepers and bought their necessities at high prices.[15] National services never reached most coastal people. These were left in the hands of church social action agencies, private voluntary groups, and random charitable gestures by individuals.

In hindsight, the Sandinista government clearly should have adapted its program to achieve coastal goals with maximal participation of coastal people. The organizational forms could well have taken on a coastal identity and Sandinismo could have had a *costeño* variant.

Instead, in an enthusiastic and dedicated way, Sandinista cadres—almost all Pacific people—"sacrificed" themselves to bring the revolution there. Tirelessly they preached the agrarian reform and tried to implement "modern" ideas about agriculture, health, and education. Their goal was to assimilate the Atlantic Coast into national life—to "Pacificize" the coast.

They also brought their prejudices about coastal life. For the first Sandinista "missionaries," the Atlantic Coast people were primitives, backward in all respects. Their cultural and religious practices were often ridiculed and depreciated. Like most missionaries, the Sandinistas assumed a blank page of primitivism that needed to be written on by modern civilization.

Although these efforts produced more tension, they also stimulated local groups to focus their goals on the emerging situation. The most significant indigenous organization emerged at that time. It was created in direct response to a visit by Daniel Ortega (then a Junta member) to Puerto Cabezas in November 1979, barely four months after the revolution. Instead of implanting the organizational apparatus of Sandinismo as it was then emerging, Ortega met strong sentiment to recognize the representatives of the indigenous groups of the Atlantic Coast, and MISURASATA (Miskito Sumu Rama Sandinista Asla Ta Kanka or Miskito, Sumu, Rama, and Sandinistas Working Together) was formed on the spot. Granted recognition as a "mass organization" of equivalent status as the women's organization (AMNLAE), the farm workers (ATC), or industrial workers (CST), MIS-URASATA began operating vigorously at once.

One of its first goals was to change the Literacy Crusade to include Miskito and English (*alfabetización en lenguas*). MISURASATA's participation in the literacy campaign also enabled it to grow as an organization. Many Miskito literacy workers became MISURASATA cadres. During this time, Miskito consciousness and militancy grew as well. In 1980 and 1981, some of the MISURASATA leadership spoke freely of sovereignty, self-determination, and autonomy for Atlantic Coast indigenous people.

The Sandinista leadership was not prepared for the intensity of the new organization, nor was it aware of how to cooperate with people as different as the coastal people were. It sensed that things were moving too fast, and, as warnings, it jailed some Miskito leaders, usually for a few weeks. At the close of the literacy crusade in February 1981, violence broke out in Prinzapolka: Four soldiers and four Miskitos were killed in a shootout caused by the insensitivity (or racism) of the soldiers and strong local feeling against the government. Other incidents followed, such as the killing of government soldiers at San Carlos.

In 1981 tensions and violence increased. MISURASATA leaders were developing the arguments for territorial claims and were increasing their rhetoric of dissatisfaction with the government. Steadman Fagoth Mueller, a powerful orator and influential MISURASATA leader, was jailed in 1981, accused of having been a member of Somoza's secret police during his student days. Released from jail on his agreement to study abroad in a socialist country, he promptly left Nicaragua for Honduras. There, he joined one of the earliest contra groups, the "15th of September." He broadcast regularly on their radio, attacking the Sandinistas as Communists, and preached resistance to the Sandinistas. After Fagoth's move to Honduras, there were more military actions across the Coco River.

The government accused MISURASATA of supporting a plan for separatism. This plan, called Red Christmas, was to be implemented on Christmas 1981. Leading up to this date were increasing numbers of attacks from Honduras. The villages along the Coco River, the boundary between the two countries, were particularly hard hit, and the government military, sent to repel these attacks, was always at a disadvantage. At this time it was widely believed that a "covert" military operation was part of the CIA operation in the region.[16]

In late 1981 and early 1982, the Sandinista government responded to the situation in the Miskito part of the Atlantic Coast, especially the Río Coco, by forcibly relocating the villagers who lived along the river. They were sent to a newly created settlement called Tasba Pri (Free Land).

Within two years, then, after centuries of second-class status and inequality, coastal people created a vigorous organization, military conflict began, and many local communities experienced direct conflict with the state. Whether this happened because of the seizure of MISURASATA by separatists, along with collaboration by some in the U.S.-sponsored contra war, or because of an excessively harsh response by the Sandinistas to a new and novel situation, will take a long time to sort out. It did, however, initiate the darkest period of Sandinista-coastal relations.

During this period, a series of human rights violations were reported by several responsible monitoring organizations.[17] Human rights are stipulated in various international conventions, usually ratified by member countries of international organizations such as the United Nations or the Organization of American States.[18] The serious monitoring groups keep tabs on trouble spots by sending teams that take testimony from the victimized people and government officials. Thus, through this process, the killings of Miskitos in Leimus by government troops in December 1981 and the San Carlos killings of Sandinista troops by local insurgents in 1981 are both acknowledged violations of human rights.[19] All human rights abuses are inexcusable although the ones cited in these reports were consistently of lesser degree than those regularly committed by the governments of Guatemala against its indigenous population and El Salvador against its entire population.

The Distortions

From the outset, there was a strident campaign to characterize Sandinista policy on the Atlantic Coast as the destruction of coastal peoples and their cultures. Jeane J. Kirkpatrick, exambassador to the United Nations, said that the "'assault' on thousands of Miskito Indians in Nicaragua by that country's Sandinista government is 'more massive than any other human-rights violation that I'm aware of in Central America today.'"[20] In a now famous gesture that backfired, Alexander Haig, then secretary of state, claimed that a photograph he displayed during congressional testimony showed a scene of Miskito bodies being burned by Sandinista troops. The nearly four-year-old photograph actually showed the burning of corpses of people killed during the Somoza period.[21]

The State Department Office of Public Diplomacy's 1984 attack on the Nicaraguan government[22] is a good example of administration falsehood and innuendo. It said that the majority ("perhaps 150,000 to 165,000") of inhabitants of the Atlantic Coast are Miskitos, Sumus, and Ramas, with "a number of blacks." The total number of indigenous people was difficult to determine since there was no census for the Atlantic Coast, but the most recent government estimates claimed about 67,000 Miskitos, 5,000 Sumus, and about 800 Ramas. The black (Creole) population numbered about 25,000 to 30,000 and lived mostly in and around Bluefields. There were about 1,500 Garífonas. The mestizo population, post–World War II peasant migrants from the Pacific side, numbered 172,000 people, or an absolute majority of the Atlantic Coast population.[23]

By characterizing the problem as the assault of the state against Indians, the United States represented the situation as easy to solve by giving the Indians land and independence. The only problem, according to this version, was an intransigent state that wanted to eliminate Indians. But, in fact, any solution to coastal demands would face multiple and competing claims and would have to avoid any solution that would create even greater injustice than at present. For example, the creation of a Miskito territory would be seen as unjust by the Sumu. And if the entire coast became Indian country, the mestizo and Creole populations would be reduced to second-class status. The report continued, "The people of Zelaya [the Atlantic Coast province] traditionally speak English, since the area was long a British protectorate." In fact, English is spoken, especially among the Creole population, but the most widely spoken language since long before the Sandinista revolution is Spanish. Miskito is universally spoken in the Miskito communities as is Spanish among the mestizos. Although Spanish may not be the native language for many groups, it tends to be the lingua franca for all.

By citing statements out of context and freely editorializing, the State Department report represented everything the Sandinista government was doing as evil. For example, a 1980 FSLN document to its cadres, discussing the consolidation of the revolution on the coast, was taken to be a sinister plot. The goals of creating state-run fishing, industrial and mining enterprises and pursuing "programs that bring the revolution to the masses, giving priority to the peasant population"[24] were described as a kind of invasion rather than the political platform of victorious revolutionaries.

The report also purported to show that "Indian rights have been badly violated,"[25] but it did not state what those rights are. It presented rights that are not supported by any laws or conventions (e.g., "Indian rights to self-government").[26] Later, in presenting part of the summary of the OAS Commission on Human Rights report on the Atlantic Coast, the State Department account neglected to include the OAS discussion of those rights, particularly the finding that "the Commission believes that in the current status of international law the claim [by Misurasata] is supported only with respect to the preservation of their culture, practise of their religion and the use of their own language, but it does not include the right to self-determination or political autonomy."[27] The massive relocation and movement of the Indian population of Guatemala received no such condemnation from the State Department.[28]

The State Department report implied that systematic killing had taken place. By speaking of "surviving" Indians or referring to the inhabitants of half the Miskito and Sumu villages being "killed, 'relocated,' or driven away,"[29] it suggested mass murder. In general, the tendentious and instrumental use of existing information makes this a piece of propaganda rather than a document that can teach the U. S. people. Naturally, findings from groups like the Organization of American States (OAS), Inter-American Commission on Human Rights, or Americas Watch were not mentioned. If they had been, it would have become clear that the relocations, although hard on the people, were an exercise of a right of national sovereignty. Americas Watch and the OAS reports accepted the possibility that national sovereignty was really being violated by combatants (armed and trained by the United States) who crossed the Río Coco from Honduras. Both acknowledged that states have that right and stated what they believe is the correct way to exercise it. Americas Watch cited precedents from recent U.S. history of massive relocation of people, such as the internment of over

100,000 Japanese Americans during the World War II.[30] The OAS report found a threat to national security from "former members of the National Guard."[31] To go back further in U.S. history, the Cherokee removal, a death march forced on Indians by the U.S. government, was far more cruel and without justification other than greed for land.[32]

Backing Away from the Abyss

The period from 1979 to 1984 saw a worsening of relations and an increase in violence and military encounters. However, in the second half of 1984, several developments signaled a major shift in relations between the government and the people of the Atlantic Coast.

During the opening of the UN session in September 1984, through the good offices of Senator Edward Kennedy (D.-Mass.) exiled MISURASATA leader Brooklyn Rivera was invited to go back to Nicaragua, travel throughout the coast region, and hold conversations with the government. He did so in October, and, by December, a formal negotiation apparatus was set up. The first negotiation session convened in Bogotá, Colombia, in December. After his stay in Nicaragua, Rivera went to Honduras to contact the many Indians who had left Nicaragua and discuss the possibilities for a negotiated end to the hostilities. On arrival in Tegucigalpa, in the presence of numerous witnesses, he was detained, interrogated, and finally expelled from the country without being permitted to visit the Honduran Mosquitia. It was widely believed that he was expelled with U.S. approval since Rivera's efforts could have threatened the U.S. policy of maintaining armed hostility on the Nicaraguan border.

During the course of the negotiation sessions held in December 1984 and January, April, and May 1985, several steps were agreed to that relieved the tension on the coast. Most important was an agreement in April 1985 in Mexico City to "not initiate offensive actions." Negotiations broke down in May 1985 amid mutual recriminations.

The Sandinista government announced in May 1985 that it would permit those who were moved in 1982 to return to their villages on the Río Coco. At the same time, it also announced that a cease-fire agreement had been signed with a group of Indian guerrillas connected to MISURA, Steadman Fagoth's CIA-supported organization. These fighters, led by comandante Eduardo Pantin, were actively seeking a nonmilitary solution to coastal problems. Finally, a government autonomy commission, created in December 1984, issued the first draft of a proposed autonomy statute in June 1985.[33]

The government was doing its best to channel resources to the area to help people return to their communities. It supplied transportation for people from Tasba Pri to carry their houses, piece by piece, for reassembly on the Río Coco.[34] It promised food for the new returnees for one year. And it continued to hold dialogue with Indian guerrillas. The agreements did not require them to disarm, simply to not fight so that the discussion of autonomy could proceed peacefully.[35]

During this time, the U.S. contribution consisted of financing the contra effort through a $27 million "humanitarian aid" plan. A new Indian guerrilla group, Nicaraguan Coast Indian Unity (KISAN), formed in September 1985, joined UNO (United Nicaraguan Opposition), the umbrella contra group supported by the United States, and asked for and received some of the aid money. In spite of the "humanitarian" designation, some of the funds they received went for the purchase of weapons.[36] KISAN also excluded Brooklyn Rivera and MISURASATA from its founding meeting, suggesting further how inconvenient it was for the United States to include any group or individual who had shown interest in negotiation with the Nicaraguan government.

The United States claimed that its support for anti-Sandinista forces in the Atlantic Coast region was meant to help achieve Indian self-determination by the overthrow of the Sandinistas. But, aside from the few direct military engagements with the Sandinista Army, most of the U.S.-financed action was aimed at destroying the economic infrastructure and impeding people from resuming their normal lives. In October 1985, a unit of KISAN guerrillas destroyed a suspension bridge over a deep gorge at Sisin. This action severed the only route taken by people returning to their villages on the Río Coco.

In March and April 1986, people from a series of villages on the Río Coco fled to Honduras. The KISAN spokesperson in Honduras, Roger Herman, said that this crossing was the result of Sandinista attacks on Miskito villages. According to this reasoning, the return to the river, the discussion of autonomy, and the support of returning communities with building materials, tools, and seed were all a ruse to renew a military assault on them. Yet, if that had been its goal, the government could have achieved it more easily in Tasba Pri itself. A 1986 State Department pamphlet about the Atlantic Coast repeated the KISAN version.[37] Not mentioned in the State Department pamphlet was the fact that KISAN fighters began infiltrating the communities from Honduras as soon as people arrived from Tasba Pri. This tactic was well known to the government but not acted upon since other armed KISAN fighters (a group known as KISAN por la paz) were engaged in active dialogue with the government. The government hoped to engage the infiltrated KISAN fighters in talks and swell the ranks of the KISAN pro-dialogue group. The tension among the KISAN por la paz, the FDN, and the Reagan administration was well expressed in a recent interview with Juan Salgado, a leader of KISAN por la paz. "We are not the soles of the FDN's feet," he said. "CIA pressure converted our fight into a struggle over dollars. We were not fighting for the Miskitos, but for Ronald Reagan. Our people demand peace through talks and not killing."[38]

Those KISAN fighters not engaged in dialogue were not harassed since government policy was to provide conditions to facilitate dialogue. The unspoken condition was that the KISAN fighters not initiate combat and that they maintain a low profile and not engage in provocative actions. The villagers who returned to the stretch of the Río Coco between Bilwaskarma and Kum entered the process of resettlement with enthusiasm. They planted bananas, beans, and rice and began reconstructing their houses. Many Miskito communities expressed unwillingness to see fighting break out again. They told KISAN combatants that their presence would be permitted only if they did not fight.[39] Eventually, the continued presence of KISAN fighters in the river communities led to problems. The fighters could not simply resume the life of village agriculturalists indefinitely since to do so would be to disobey their orders from the contra-controlled Honduras-based KISAN leadership. In this zone there were about three Sandinista army posts, all outside of communities. KISAN told the local people that they would ultimately have to cross the river into Honduras because fighting would break out. At the same time it engaged in a series of provocations with the Sandinista Army that elevated the level of tension. When combat actually started, it was between KISAN combatants and the army. But KISAN had prepared to capitalize on this and facilitate and aid a mass exodus across the river. That is exactly what happened. In late March (Easter week) a large number of villagers crossed the Río Coco into Honduras.

Although most villagers were frightened, few civilian casualties were reported. Some observers saw the exodus as a move designed to disorient local people and maintain a high level of distrust and suspicion toward the government. Those who saw the arriving villagers on the Honduran side noted the presence of KISAN and its effort to coach the new arrivals to say that they were victimized by bombs and attacked by the army. The Americas Watch report stated that "evidence was lacking of new Sandinista abuses that caused their flight. Rather, we and the journalists [from the *Philadelphia Enquirer* and the *Boston Globe*] found that an Indian *contra* organization KISAN . . . had spread fear as part of a deliberate plan to evacuate the Miskitos from Nicaragua to Honduras."[40] The Reagan administration was about to dispatch Vice-President Bush to the scene and tried to orchestrate a massive press presence by preparing two helicopters to fly journalists there. However, in spite of these efforts, this movement of people did not receive the notoriety hoped for by the United States. In fact, a relief worker in the area called it "the worst public relations job I've ever seen."[41] Furthermore, roughly half of those who left in March-April 1986 returned by August of the same year.[42]

When I interviewed a group of repatriating Miskitos in the holding camp in León, Nicaragua, in July 1986, they all said that they left their villages because of fear of the sounds of combat. Very few, though, actually saw any fighting. All said that they were taken across by KISAN ("led," "kidnapped," "crossed," were their words). They were unhappy with the depressed conditions in Honduras and, when faced with the possibility of becoming permanent refugees, opted to return home as soon as possible. Their fear of continued turmoil was considerably less than the prospect of living in the Honduran limbo, subject to an uncertain food supply as well as to personal insecurity. For many Miskitos, life in Honduras meant exposure to the competition for leadership of Indian fighters vying for U.S. support. KISAN in particular had forcibly recruited Miskitos and taken reprisals against those who wished to remain neutral or those who supported the position of Brooklyn Rivera.[43]

In the remote department of Gracias a Dios, where the Honduran Mosquitia is located, the Honduran Army, U.S. "advisers," USAID, and various North American private voluntary organizations were operating. The only official agency charged with caring for refugees was the UN High Commission on Refugees (UNHCR). Its policy was to resettle refugees who crossed the border, providing they moved at least 50 kilometers (about 30 miles) from the border. This stipulation was designed to preserve the neutrality of this UN agency and to ensure the security of the refugees against cross border conflicts.

But the no-man's-land between the border and the UNHCR jurisdiction was of great strategic interest to the United States. It was the redoubt where Indian guerrillas, first of MISURA, Steadman Fagoth's group, and later of KISAN, withdrew after raiding northern Zelaya in Nicaragua. There, supplies, training, and command were given to local leaders from the CIA liaison who moved between Tegucigalpa and the zone, presumably in coordination with the American Embassy.

USAID, which operated freely in this zone, built roads, a large landing strip, and a radio station. Also, a civilian aid organization called Friends of the Americas was located there. Set up in 1984 by Louisiana State Representative Louis "Woody" Jenkins and his wife, Diane Jenkins, it worked principally in the Mosquitia and further west, near the FDN main base camp, also inside Honduran territory. Friends of the Americas focused its Miskito operations in Rus Rus, the community that, for some time, served as the headquarters for Fagoth's MISURA. FOA supplied aid to KISAN fighters and their families, the people who crossed the border and did not go to the UN camps. Friends of the Americas raised its funds through public solicitations.[44] The rhetoric used in FOA's Shoe Boxes for Liberty Campaign (small boxes of personal supplies) expressed the hope that "the small things in this box are useful in your struggle for liberty."[45] Its supplies were transported on military planes under the provisions of the Denton amendment. Before that, the organization's shoe boxes and other supplies were carried to Honduras by Mississippi and Louisiana Air National Guard units.[46] Obviously, the choice of whom to help and especially where to concentrate their help qualified the Friends of the Americas more as friends of the contras. "AID plays a key role in keeping Nicaraguan Miskitos in Honduras and in supporting the work of Friends of the Americas."[47] Indicative of the coordination between FOA and the U.S.-supported Indian contras *The Friends Report* of March 12, 1986, states, "Miskito Indian leaders report that *an additional 3,500 Miskito refugees may attempt to cross the Coco River into Honduras in coming weeks*" [emphasis in original].[48]

Another group operating in that region was CAUSA USA (Confederation of the Associations for Unity of the Society of the Americas), which worked primarily in what it called a "war of ideology." Founded in 1980 as the political arm of Rev. Sun Myung Moon's Unification Church in the West, it shared interest in Central America with several other Unification Church fronts (International Relief and Friendship Foundation, Nicaraguan Freedom Fund, Freedom Leadership Foundation, and the Washington Institute for Values in Public Policy). These groups received public exposure through the *Washington Times*, also owned by the Unification Church.[49] CAUSA USA produced a highly tendentious film entitled, "Nicaragua Was Our Home," which purported to show Sandinista atrocities against the Miskitos. It was aired as a documentary on the Public Broadcasting Stations (PBS) as part of a major CAUSA media campaign (in spite of the fact that its use in the United States was, for technical reasons, of questionable legality).[50] Therefore, though nonmilitary support for U.S. policy against the Sandinistas appeared for a while to be in the hands of nongovernmental groups, it obviously received approval from the government in much the same way as did military assistance to the contras.

The Atlantic Coast of Nicaragua acquired enormous significance in Reagan's war against Nicaragua. By 1986 the major contra front, further to the west, had failed militarily and had become known for numerous violations of human rights and the laws of war.[51] Therefore, by 1986 it appeared unlikely that, even with the additional $100 million voted by Congress that summer, the contras in the west would be the route to the overthrow of the Sandinista government. A much more likely scenario seemed to be an attempt to bring about a military penetration of the Atlantic Coast region, in order to capture a community such as Puerto Cabezas and declare a provisional government through which to pump additional resources and (perhaps) U.S. troops.[52] With the failure of the FDN contra, KISAN might be the favored force to accomplish this end. The administration's ideological supporters, such as the American Security Council, called publicly for a withdrawal of recognition of the Nicaraguan government and for the recognition of the contra.[53]

The enormous military buildup, accomplished through the constant maneuvers, left installations such as airfields and roads close to the border. The cooperation among the U.S. military, USAID, and private groups such as Friends of the Americas to keep Miskitos near the border in opposition to the UNHCR guidelines was maintaining the conflict there. Ideologically, the activities of CAUSA USA reinforced anti-Nicaragua feeling in the United States. The justification for all this was the alleged concern for Miskito self-determination and protection of the indigenous population against the depredations of the Sandinistas.

Conclusion

Against the backdrop of U.S. government treatment of its own Indian population, many would argue that Reagan administration support for Atlantic Coast people was for strategic rather than humanitarian ends. Since the use of the Miskito example was not in the service of genuine liberation or real indigenous autonomy, the "victory" of Reagan's policy (the overthrow of the Sandinista government) was not likely to benefit the Miskitos or the other peoples of the Atlantic Coast. On the contrary, by maintaining the tensions in the region, the United States was actually frustrating efforts to solve the real problems. It was unlikely indeed that any contra government that might replace the Sandinistas would grant autonomy in any greater measure than that agreed to by the Sandinistas in the 1987 constitution.[54] The best that could be hoped for would be the old benign indifference until the region once again assumed economic importance.

The one-sided and distorted account of human rights in Nicaragua was more propaganda than fact. "In effect, the Reagan Administration [was using] human rights criticism of Nicaragua as an instrument of warfare," said Americas Watch, which regarded the Reagan human rights policy toward Nicaragua "as worse than a failure: it is a degradation of the human rights cause to make human rights criticism an instrument of military policy."[55] "With respect to the problem of the Miskitos, this is compounded by the Administration's unabashed use of half-truths and of outright lies."[56]

Two serious negative outcomes might result from this pattern of blatant government distortions. First, it might reinforce the already prevalent view that human rights concern is merely one tool in an ideological war.[57] That would further desensitize the U.S. public to the great significance of human rights as a legitimate foreign policy consideration. More important, however, was the erosion of U.S. public confidence in its national leadership. With the 1986 revelations about deliberate government disinformation toward Libya[58] and unfolding evidence of presidential disregard for the will of congress and the American people in the wake of the Iran-contra scandal, the many deliberate untruths repeatedly told in order to demonize Nicaragua would haunt our body politic for a long time to come. Honesty, or its absence, in foreign affairs has an immediate reflection at home.

Notes

1. Remarks outside Bergen-Belsen Concentration Camp, quoted in Americas Watch, *Human Rights in Nicaragua: Reagan, Rhetoric, and Reality* (New York: Americas Watch, 1985), p. 49.

2. The mention of these oppressed people became necessary only after Reagan was publicly embarrassed by his plan to praise fallen Germans, including members of the Waffen SS who were centrally involved in genocide.

3. *Miami Herald*, October 13, 1986.

4. Americas Watch, *Civil Patrols in Guatemala* (New York: Americas Watch Committee, August 1986); Americas Watch, *Guatemala: A Nation of Prisoners* (New York: Americas Watch, January 1984).

5. Department of State, "Report on the Situation in El Salvador" (Washington: Department of State, January 16, 1984), pp. i–iv. Also Department of State, "Report on the Situation in El Salvador with Respect to the Subjects Covered in Section 728 (d) of the International Security and Development Act of 1981, P.L. 97-113" (Washington, D.C.: Department of State, July 27, 1982).

6. Vine Deloria, Jr., and Clifford M. Lytle, *American Indians, American Justice* (Austin: University of Texas Press, 1983).

94   Martin Diskin

7. Roxanne Dunbar Ortiz, *Indians of the Americas: Human Rights and Self-determination* (New York: Praeger Publishers, 1984), pp. 1–26.

8. Ralph Lee Woodward, Jr., *Central America: A Nation Divided* (New York: Oxford University Press, 1976). Also, Troy S. Floyd, *The Anglo-Spanish Struggle for Mosquitia* (Albuquerque: University of New Mexico Press, 1967).

9. Martin Diskin, Thomas Bossert, Salomon Nahmad Sitton, and Stefano Varese, "Peace and Autonomy on the Atlantic Coast of Nicaragua," *LASA Forum* 16, no. 4 (spring 1986):6–7; Mary W. Helms, "Of Kings and Contexts: Ethnohistorical Interpretations of Miskito Political Structures and Functions," *American Ethnologist* 13, no. 3 (1986):506–523; Philip S. Dennis and Michael D. Olien, "Kingship Among the Miskito," *American Ethnologist* 11, no. 4 (1984):718–737.

10. Jorge Jenkins Molieri, *El Desafío Indígena: El Caso de los Miskitos* (Mexico City: Editorial Katun, 1986); Phillipe Bourgois and Jorge Grunberg, "La mosquitia y la revolución: informe de una investigación rural en la costa atlántica norte" (Managua: MIDINRA, 1980).

11. Bernard Nietschmann, *Between Land and Water: The Subsistence Ecology of the Miskito Indians, Eastern Nicaragua* (New York and London: Seminar Press, 1973).

12. Charles Hale, "Institutional Struggle, Conflict and Reconciliation: Miskitu Indians and the Nicaraguan State (1979–1985)," paper presented at conference on "Ethnic Groups and the Nation-State: The Atlantic Coast of Nicaragua," Stockholm, Sweden, February 1986.

13. Mary W. Helms, *Asang: Adaptation to Culture Contact in a Miskito Community* (Gainesville: University of Florida Press, 1971).

14. Consejo Regional de Pueblos Indígenas de Centroamérica, México y Panamá, "Manifiesto del Consejo Regional de Pueblos Indígenas de Centroamérica, México y Panamá (CORPI)," in Guillermo Bonfil Batalla, ed., *Utopía y Revolución: El Pensamiento Político Contemporáneo de los Indios en América Latina* (Mexico City: Editorial Nueva Imagen, 1981), pp. 365–366; Jenkins Molieri, *El Desafío Indígena*, pp. 183–188.

15. For example, see Helms, *Asang*; Nietschmann, *Between Land and Water*; and Bourgois and Grunberg, "La Mosquitia y la revolucion."

16. *Washington Post*, February 14, 1982; see also Judy Butler, *Trabil Nani* (Managua: Centro de Investigacíon y documentacíon de la Costa Atlántica (CIDCA), May 1984), pp. 19–33.

17. Organization of American States, Inter-American Commission on Human Rights (OAS-IACHR), *Report on the Situation of Human Rights of a Segment of the Nicaraguan Population of Miskito Origin* (Washington: General Secretariat, OAS, May 16, 1984) [original in Spanish, November 29, 1983]; Americas Watch, *The Miskitos in Nicaragua, 1981–1984* (New York: Americas Watch Committee, 1984).

18. Americas Watch Committee and the American Civil Liberties Union, *Report on Human Rights in El Salvador* (New York: Vintage Books, 1982), pp. xxviii–xliv. This contains an excellent definition of internationally recognized human rights. In the specific case of the Miskitos in Nicaragua, see OAS-IACHR, *Report on the Situation*, pp. 75–128, 28.

19. OAS-IACHR, *Report on the Situation*, p. 129; Americas Watch, *Violations of the Laws of War by Both Sides in Nicaragua, 1981–1985* (New York: Americas Watch Committee, 1985), pp. 4–5.

20. *Washington Post*, March 2, 1982.

21. *Le Canard Enchaine* (Paris), February 24, 1982, exposed the misuse of this photograph.

22. U.S. Department of State, Office of Public Diplomacy, *Broken Promises: Sandinista Repression of Human Rights in Nicaragua* (Washington: Department of State, October 1984), pp. 19–21.

23. CIDCA, *Demografía Costeña: Notas Sobre la Historia Demográfica y Población Actual de los Grupos Etnicos de la Costa Atlántica Nicaragüense* (Managua: CIDCA, 1982). These figures, based on household surveys, must be given a wide margin of error.

24. U.S. Department of State, *Broken Promises*, p. 20.

25. Ibid., p. 21.

26. Ibid., p. 20.

27. OAS-IACHR, *Report on the Situation*, p. 129.

28. Americas Watch, *Civil Patrols*.

29. U.S. Department of State, *Broken Promises*, p. 22.

30. *The Miskitos in Nicaragua 1981–1984*, pp. 24–34.

31. OAS-IACHR, *Report on the Situation*, pp. 112–127, especially p. 116: "The Commission finds that the security of the Nicaraguan state was truly threatened by the incursions of the groups of former members of the National Guard, which justified the declaration of a state of emergency and its maintenance."

32. Deloria and Lytle, *American Indians*, chap. 1.

33. Comision Nacional de Autonomía de la Costa Atlántica, *Principios y Políticas Para el Ejercicio de los Derechos de Autonomía de los Pueblos Indígenas y Comunidades de la Costa Atlántica* (Managua: Comisión Nacional de Autonomía de la Costa Atlántica (Managua: Comisión Nacional de Autonomía de la Costa Atlántica, 1985).

34. Martin Diskin, Thomas Bossert, Salomón Nahmad Sitton, and Stéfano Varese, "Peace and Autonomy on the Atlantic Coast of Nicaragua," *LASA Forum* 18, no. 2 (summer 1986), pp. 8–13.

35. Clifford Krauss, "Sandinistas Promote Peace With the Indians on Rebel-Held Coast," *Wall Street Journal*, March 6, 1986.

36. *Miami Herald*, October 24, 1986.

37. U.S. Department of State, Office of Public Diplomacy, *Dispossessed* (Washington: State Department, 1986), p. 1.

38. KISAN comandante Juan Salgado quoted in William Gasperini, "Miskitos Divided in Allegiances to Sandinistas and to Homeland," *In These Times*, September 3–9, 1986, p. 9.

39. Author's interview with KISAN comandante "Ráfaga," Reynaldo Reyes, January 1986, Puerto Cabezas. He said that this message was given to him in numerous Miskito communities when he was sent there by the KISAN high command from Honduras in fall 1985, in his capacity as second in command of the intelligence division. The communities' unwillingness to permit Miskito fighters to start combat again convinced him to initiate dialogue with the Sandinista government.

40. Americas Watch, *With the Miskitos in Honduras* (New York: Americas Watch), pp. 1–2.

41. *Boston Globe*, April 7, 1986.

42. Personal communication with a journalist who visited there in August 1986.

43. *Washington Post*, August 24, 1986.

44. Its *Friends Report* stressed that its aid went to victims of communism; numerous quotes from President Reagan support this notion; for example, *Friends Report*, (Baton Rouge: Friends of the Americas), summer 1985, p. 9. In a series of investigative articles in the *State Times* of Baton Rouge, documentation is introduced showing that the political nature of this group was more significant than its humanitarian

impulses. Further, it had been plagued by problems of unaccounted expenditures. See, for example, *State Times* (Baton Rouge, La.), May 26–30, 1986.

45. Tom Barry, Deb Preusch, and Beth Sims, *The New Right Humanitarians* (Albuquerque: Inter-Hemispheric Education Resource Center, 1986), p. 54.

46. Ibid., p. 54. The Denton amendment, passed in 1984, authorized AID to spend $7.5 million on Miskito refugees in Honduras. Further, it permitted the use of U.S. government planes to carry supplies on a space-available basis.

47. "The Contras, Miskito Indians, and the U.S.A.," *Resource Center Bulletin* (Albuquerque: Inter-Hemispheric Education Resource Center, winter 1986).

48. Friends of the Americas, *Friends Report* (Baton Rouge: Friends of the Americas), March 12, 1986, p. 1.

49. Barry, Preusch, and Sims, *The New Right Humanitarians*, pp. 48–49.

50. A report in *Indigenous World* presents evidence that this film also received support from the U.S. Information Agency (USIA). If so, the acceptance of this support would raise legal issues since "USIA-produced materials may not, by their own charter, be distributed domestically, directly or through another organism," *Indigenous World* (San Francisco), June 2, 1986, pp. 1–4.

51. Americas Watch, "Violations of the Rules of War by Both Sides in Nicaragua, 1981–1985" (New York: Americas Watch, 1985), pp. 4–9. Reed Brody, "Attacks by the Nicaraguan *Contras* in the Civilian Population of Nicaragua," report of a fact-finding commission, September 1984–January 1985 (mimeo).

52. William Gasperini, "Miskitos Divided in Allegiances to Sandinistas and to Homeland," *In These Times*, September 3–9, 1986, pp. 8–9.

53. *New York Times*, October 6, 1986.

54. See chapter VI, articles 89, 90, and 91, República de Nicaragua, "Constitucíon Política," *La Gaceta Diario Oficial* (Managua), January 9, 1987, pp. 46 and 47.

55. Americas Watch, "Failure: The Reagan Administration's Human Rights Policy in 1983" (New York: Americas Watch, 1984), pp. 46–47.

56. Americas Watch, "The Miskitos in Nicaragua, 1981–1984" (New York: Americas Watch Committee, November 1984), p. 57.

57. Lawyers Committee for Human Rights, the Watch Committees, *The Reagan Administration's Record on Human Rights in 1985* (New York and Washington: Lawyers Committee for Human Rights, the Watch Committees, January 1986); Americas Watch, Helsinki Watch, Lawyers Committee for International Human Rights, *Critique: Review of the Department of State's Country Reports on Human Rights Practices for 1984* (New York: Americas Watch, Helsinki Watch, Lawyers Committee for International Human Rights, May 1985); Americas Watch, Helsinki Watch, Lawyers Committee for International Human Rights, " . . . in the face of cruelty," *The Reagan Administration's Human Rights Record in 1984* (New York: Americas Watch, Helsinki Watch, Lawyers Committee for International Human Rights, January 1985); Americas Watch, *Managing the Facts: How the Administration Deals With Reports of Human Rights Abuses in El Salvador* (New York: Americas Watch, December 1985); Americas Watch, *Guatemala Revised: How the Reagan Administration Finds "Improvements" in Human Rights in Guatemala* (New York: Americas Watch, September 1985); Americas Watch, *U.S. Reporting on Human Rights in El Salvador: Methodology at Odds With Knowledge* (New York: Americas Watch, June 1982).

58. *New York Times*, October 5, 1986.

SIX

The Manipulation of the Religion Issue

BETSY COHN and PATRICIA HYNDS _____

From the moment the Reagan administration came to office in 1981 it devoted considerable attention and energy to the accentuation of religious tension and the denunciation of alleged religious persecution in Nicaragua. In this effort it found strong allies in Nicaragua's predominantly conservative Catholic hierarchy and growing fundamentalist Protestant movement as well as among various conservative religious groups in the United States. The Vatican, too, cooperated with Washington in this anti-Sandinista crusade. To understand how an ultraconservative administration in Washington was able to use religion and the religious issue as a weapon against Nicaragua we must first examine the history of religion in that country before and after the Sandinista Front of National Liberation (FSLN) victory in 1979.[1]

The History of Religion in Nicaragua

THE CATHOLIC CHURCH

With the exception of the Indian (Miskito, Sumu, Rama) and English-speaking Creole minorities on the Atlantic Coast, most Nicaraguans traditionally identified themselves as Roman Catholic. The Catholic Church permeated their culture and committed them to observing certain traditional rites. Its role nevertheless was limited. François Houtart, a Belgian priest who directed the first sociological study of the church in Latin America in the 1950s, noted "In Nicaraguan Catholicism, . . . few of its expressions are institutional. This is easily explained by the scant presence of the ecclesiastical institutions among the majority of the population. There have been few priests, so the social pressure of the church has been presented far more in the political apparatus of society than in the popular pastoral field, at least for the last century." Discussing the attitudes of Nicaraguans toward the clergy, Houtart noted: "Overall, they may be very critical of the

97

church authorities and of their political activities without rejecting thereby the necessity for certain institutional religious roles—but at the same time without granting them too much importance. . . . Nicaraguan Catholicism is characterized by a profound religiosity and by its largely noninstitutional nature."[2]

A group of Nicaraguan priests and religious, meeting in 1969, described a conservative, divided hierarchy distant from the people and lacking initiative. Diocesan priests were few and poorly trained. They held antiquated ideas, did not engage in dialogue with the people, and were primarily concerned with their own economic well-being. Because of their small numbers and orientation, most parish priests limited their ministry to celebrating the Eucharist and administering the sacraments. Their work rarely touched most Nicaraguans who, though notably committed to popular religiosity, were little concerned with formal religious practice, including church marriage and attendance at mass.[3]

In many senses the nature of Catholic religious institutions and religiosity in Nicaragua in the 1960s was not unlike the situation elsewhere in Latin America. Throughout their four and a half centuries of activity in Latin America, the Catholic clergy had tended generally to identify with the privileged classes. Accordingly, they had normally advised the region's suffering majority to accept their lot in life in return for the promise of reward in heaven.

By the mid–twentieth century, however, voices for change were being heard within Latin American Catholicism. In the early 1960s the Vatican itself—under the progressive leadership of Pope John XXIII—called for basic structural changes that would uplift the temporal lot of the world's poor. These ideas, in turn, were reflected and amplified in the published conclusions of the Second General Conference of Latin American Bishops (CELAM) of Medellín, Colombia, in 1968.[4] That document gave support to a current of thought emerging in the Latin American church, which became known as liberation theology. This perspective emphasizes the social reality of a people in their relationship to God and clearly recognizes institutional and structural, as well as personal, sin. It calls for the church to make a preferential option for the poor in their struggle for liberation from both structural and personal evil. Medellín also endorsed Christian Base Communities (CEBs), which were formed throughout Latin America by small groups of Christians whose subsequent reflections on their lives and the Gospel often led to community action.

By the 1970s, Medellín had started to have an impact even on Nicaragua. Priests and religious at the lower levels began training "Delegates of the Word," members of the Christian communities, to lead them in worship when a priest was not available. These delegates and clergy organized CEBs, and the latter in turn promoted the formation of various grass roots organizations that made demands on behalf of Nicaragua's common citizenry. Predictably, the Somoza dictatorship and its U.S.-trained National Guard employed violence against this process of popular mobilization. CEBs were attacked, and in some cases, delegates were killed. Radicalized by this experience, many Catholics joined or began cooperating with the FSLN. By the time of the revolutionary victory, the Catholic grass roots and revolutionary movement had merged into one powerful expression of popular will.

Given this history it is not surprising that many in Nicaragua felt that the new revolutionary system should reflect a Nicaraguan—and strongly nationalistic—blend of Christian and Marxist principles. "Between Christianity and Revolution there is no contradiction" was the popular refrain. Accordingly, the new government guaranteed freedom of religion, promoted religious festivals, put "In God We Trust" on newly minted coins on the flip side of the image of Sandino, subsidized parochial education, appointed several priests to cabinet posts, invited the Pope to make an official visit to their country, explicit and repeatedly rejected adherence to the old Marxist dictum that religion is "the opiate of the people," and, in the preamble to the 1987 Constitution, included laudatory mention of "Christians who, from their faith in GOD, have committed themselves to the struggle for the liberation of the oppressed."

Nevertheless, though the vast majority of Nicaraguan Catholics and a large number of lower level clergy welcomed the revolution, not all the clergy—especially in the hierarchy—were pleased. By 1983, a survey showed that of 220 priests who responded (nearly all the priests in the country), 46 percent supported the revolutionary process begun in 1978, whereas the others opposed it in varying degrees. Opposition was highest among the Nicaraguan (mostly diocesan) priests, whose training and institutional ties were with the Nicaraguan bishops.[5] The strongest support, conversely, came from foreign clergy and religious, many of whom originally came to Central America to fight communism but subsequently had been made socially and politically aware (conscientizados) by their work with the poor.

Nicaragua's bishops had been ambivalent about Somoza, even after the abuses connected with the handling of aid to the 1972 earthquake victims. They spoke out occasionally against Somoza abuses and in January 1977 even questioned the legitimacy of the regime. Yet, in July of that same year, they offered a solemn Te Deum and Mass for Somoza after his heart attack. During Somoza's final days in power, Archbishop (later to become Cardinal) Miguel Obando y Bravo worked to retain the National Guard and avoid a revolutionary outcome. Obando was one of the Nicaraguan "moderates" who went to Caracas in July 1979 to try to negotiate the status quo "solution" then being advocated for Nicaragua by the United States.

It is true that in June 1979, when the collapse of the regime was clearly inevitable, the bishops withdrew all remaining support in a statement affirming the right of the people, as a last resort, to take up arms against tyranny. And four months after the victory, in November 1979, they issued a joint letter tentatively recognizing the legitimacy of the new government and saying that its social programs were in keeping with the Christian faith. But it was not long before the bishops as a body led by Archbishop

Obando began to distance themselves from the revolution. They were worried that both the revolution and the grass roots movement within the church might threaten their hierarchical influence and control—their *magisterium*.[6] For several years the bishops repeatedly ordered the priests to resign. The latter, however, insisted on dialogue with the hierarchy and the Vatican. In 1981 an agreement was reached whereby the priests would remain in government on the understanding that they would not publicly or privately exercise their priestly functions. As this chapter was being written, the dialogue was still going on. Meanwhile, the hierarchy worked to undermine what it derisively labeled "the popular church" by pressuring religious orders to withdraw many foreign priests friendly to the revolution and by reassigning native progovernment clergy to positions in which they could have little impact. In addition, after the contra war heated up from late 1981 on, Obando—often speaking in the name of the bishops—repeatedly criticized alleged Sandinista human rights abuses while studiously ignoring the well-documented and much more deplorable behavior of the contras. Later, as the escalated fighting forced the government to impose a wartime military draft, the bishops—or at least Obando speaking in their name— issued a pastoral letter decrying the new measures and counseled conscientious objection. By the mid-1980s, Obando had even succeeded in pressuring many Nicaraguan priests into refusing to say funeral masses for dead soldiers.

Although Obando frequently spoke in the name of Nicaragua's bishops, some of the latter made it clear on occasion that they did not completely share his ideas. Bishop Rubén López Ardón of Estelí, for example, stated in November 1985 that "all peoples have the right to free self-determination. As a sovereign and independent country, Nicaragua has this right, and everyone must respect the Nicaraguan people's right to self-determination."[7] Even earlier, in 1984 an American Capuchin in Bluefields, Bishop Paul Schmitdz, said that "in my view any direct aggression would be a disaster for the Nicaraguan people. As a priest, as a Capuchin, as a Christian, I cannot be in favor of U.S. intervention."[8] About the same time, in a discussion of President Reagan's policies, Bishop Carlos Santi of Matagalpa said: "I am really not in agreement with any government which intervenes in the affairs of another government."[9]

Nevertheless, these voices of episcopal dissent were the exception. The protestations of Obando and other vehemently anti-Sandinista bishops were much louder and much more frequent. Therefore, though at first reluctant to confront the powerful church hierarchy, the Sandinistas eventually took measures to control what they saw as increasingly confrontational behavior on the part of certain clergy. One of the first such acts was the termination in mid-1981 of the airing of Obando's increasingly political Sunday masses on Sandinista TV (SSTV). This move was made after the archbishop refused to budge on an SSTV request that the masses be rotated among priests and bishops with various viewpoints.[10] Later, in 1984, the government arrested and tried a priest whom government security forces had videotaped in the act of planning violent subversive activities. Then, when antigovernment priests participated in an illegal protest march in support of the arrested cleric, offending foreign clergy were expelled from the country. In 1985, anti-Sandinista Radio Católica was closed after repeatedly disobeying government directives. And in 1986, Monsignor Bismarck Carballo and Bishop Pablo Antonio Vega were expelled from Nicaragua after engaging in openly seditious behavior at home and cooperating in the United States in the Reagan administration's effort to secure congressional approval of funds for the contras.

THE PROTESTANTS

Diversity and disagreement were also evident among Nicaragua's Protestant minority. Before the overthrow of Somoza, Protestants/evangelicals— terms used interchangeably in Nicaragua—constituted only a small segment of the population. The major concentrations of Protestants were the Moravians among the Miskito and other Indians and the Anglicans among the English-speaking Creoles. Pentecostal and fundamentalist churches from the United States had been present in Nicaragua since 1910 when the Protestant churches divided Latin America for purposes of evangelization. Because of their tradition and their U.S. leadership, these churches identified with U.S. values and often were sympathetic to U.S. foreign policy interests from the time they entered Nicaragua.

The identification with U.S. interests—which in practice involved support of the Somoza regime—became less solid, however, as these churches developed their own national leadership. This process accelerated after the 1972 earthquake with the creation of an umbrella aid agency that nearly all the Protestant churches joined: The Evangelical Committee for Aid and Development (CEPAD), as did other Nicaraguans, saw the rapaciousness with which Somoza and his colleagues diverted funds intended for earthquake relief, and many young evangelicals were awakened politically and socially and came to play an active role in the overthrow of the dictator.

New factors came into play once Somoza was thrown out. Alarmed by Washington's failure to prevent the Sandinistas from reaping the fruits of their victory and disturbed by the growing popular movements in El Salvador and Guatemala, conservative forces in the United States quickly flooded all Central America, including Nicaragua, with fundamentalist preachers. Heavily subsidized and using effective "revivalist" techniques, they quickly won many adherents among peasants who were nominally Catholic but who actually had little relationship to the church. In consequence, although many evangelicals left the country shortly after July 1979, the total number of Protestants in Nicaragua increased dramatically from 78,400 in 1979 to 376,851 in 1982. The growth continued, and the number of Protestants rose from 3 percent of the population in 1979 to at least 15 percent by 1985.[11]

Although CEPAD and many mainline Protestants in Nicaragua remained critically supportive of the revolutionary process, the new conservative fundamentalists were not. Many of their preachers had little formal training. They tended to promote an otherworldly approach to religion and to discourage their members from participating in the social campaigns promoted by the revolutionary government, including the literacy and health campaigns and the volunteer harvest brigades. Many of them also resisted the compulsory military service declared in 1983.

The attitudes of these newly arrived Pentecostal groups were shared by some of the older Protestant communities for reasons explained by Assembly of God pastor Miguel Angel Casco: "The theological formation of the sects and some Protestant denominations form part of a pro-American ideological plan. . . . In the majority of the biblical education centers, control of education was in the hands of North American missionaries, which meant that the nationals were recipients of a theology with a heavy North American ideological emphasis, and this was fortified with anti-communist, anti-Marxist material."[12] As a result, the Protestant churches were divided in their attitude toward the revolution, much like the Catholic Church.

Nicaragua's largest Protestant denomination is the Moravian Church, to which most Miskito Indians belong. Because of admitted abuses by the government in its treatment of the Miskito Indians in 1981–1982, the Moravian Church was in an excellent position to assess the accuracy of charges of religious persecution. Moravian church leaders were outspoken in their criticism of government mistakes and abuses toward the Miskitos but were equally vocal in denouncing U.S. intervention and support for the contras. They also insisted that the Miskito problems with the government were not problems of religion. Reverend Fernando Colomer, superintendent of the Nicaraguan Moravian Church, while visiting the United States in October 1983, expressed dismay over "the wave of propaganda, documents of disinformation, speeches, and a real campaign leading up to an invasion in my country some time soon." On the issue of religious freedom, he said: "We Christians are not forbidden to congregate for the worship of God; the Catholic, Evangelical, and Protestant Churches in Nicaragua have full freedom to meet in their churches for worship and to carry out church activities."[13]

The treatment of other Protestant groups also belied the alarmist picture of religious persecution so prevalent in the United States. The Nicaraguan Episcopal Church, for instance, ordained its first native bishop, Sturdie Downs, in 1985. In May of the following year, as Washington invective over alleged religious persecution in Nicaragua became ever more strident and imaginative, Downs stated unequivocally: "There is no religious persecution." Describing tension between the conservative Catholic hierarchy and the Sandinista state as a struggle over "power," he said: "If I am a religious leader and I say 'so-so-so' about the government, and the governments gets up and says 'so-so-so' about me, I think what we are doing is playing politics. I can't say 'they are persecuting me.'"[14]

Religion as a Weapon: Historical Precedents

Before discussing Reagan administration involvement in and manipulation of the religious issue in Nicaragua, it is essential to examine earlier patterns of the U.S. use of religion as a political tool in foreign policy. And since the Vatican came to play an important role in the post-1979 religious debate in Nicaragua—one that frequently bolstered the anti-Sandinista cause—it is also important to consider the history of U.S.-Vatican cooperation in international affairs. At the end of World War II, Soviet armies had come to occupy Poland, Czechoslovakia, Hungary, and Romania. Yugoslavia had opted for socialism and had not yet broken with Stalin. Italy's Communists— the backbone of resistance to Mussolini and Hitler—threatened to sweep Italy into the socialist camp. But Vatican backing of the Christian Democrats, with massive U.S. overt and covert aid, helped ensure Christian Democratic victory and dominance in Italian politics since that time.

Meanwhile, as Washington supported Vatican objectives in Italy, the Vatican accepted the growing role of the United States in Latin America, especially since the rising authoritarian and dictatorial regimes were consistently portrayed as bulwarks against "godless communism." Cardinal Francis Spellman, archbishop of New York at that time and simultaneously head of Catholic chaplains in the U.S. armed forces, maintained an informal but effective liaison between Washington and Rome on Latin American issues. He had close personal ties with such dictators as Fulgencio Batista in Cuba, Rafael Trujillo in the Dominican Republic, Alfredo Stroessner in Paraguay, and the Somozas in Nicaragua. He is credited with having influenced Archbishop Mariano Rossell Arellano of Guatemala to issue a pastoral letter in 1954 calling on Guatemalans to rise up against "the enemy of God and country." The letter was a major CIA weapon in its successful plot to overthrow the democratically elected government of Jacobo Arbenz.[15]

Elected pope in 1958, John XXIII startled the world by making overtures to the Soviet Union and encouraging Latin American bishops to promote social change. Washington was not pleased. A 1962 CIA report warned that the United States could no longer automatically assume that the Vatican was an ally, and CIA director John McCone went to Rome to register President Kennedy's displeasure with this "leftward drift."[16] Simultaneously, the CIA stepped up its programs designed to infiltrate church personnel throughout Latin America.[17] Many Catholic and Protestant missionaries from the United States became regular sources of information in the areas in which they worked, often unaware that they were being used by the U.S. officials with whom they associated. In addition, according to Penny Lernoux, a journalist who has written extensively on the church in Latin America, the CIA "used religious groups in Latin America for its own secret ends. At the same time it contributed to the persecution and division of Latin America's Catholic Church by supporting right-wing Catholic groups, and financed and trained police agencies responsible for the imprisonment, torture, and murder of priests, nuns, and bishops, some of them U.S. citizens."[18]

However, in spite of the efforts of the U.S. government and of Latin American dictators, progressive trends continued to develop in the church and were given official approval. Most notable was the landmark document of the Conference of Latin American Bishops at Medellín in 1968 that called for real structural change and endorsed an emerging theology of liberation. Nelson A. Rockefeller noted these changes and the threat they implied for U.S. interests in his 1969 report to President Nixon. The Catholic church, he wrote, had entered "a new role" in Latin America, becoming one of "today's forces for social and political change," after recognizing "a need to be more responsive to popular will." It was, he warned, "vulnerable to subversive penetration, ready to undertake a revolution if necessary to end injustice."[19]

In 1975 the CIA helped formulate what became known as the Banzer Plan. This campaign was designed to sharpen internal divisions within the church, smear and harass progressive church leaders, and cause the arrest or expulsion of foreign priests or nuns who supported social change. Intensively promoted throughout Latin America, the plan got its name from Bolivian dictator Hugo Banzer whose government described it in a memo submitted to an international meeting of anti-Communist organizations in Paraguay. Care must be taken, the memo insisted, to attack "only the church's progressive sector, . . . not the church as an institution or the bishops as a group." In the campaign to undermine the progressive sectors, it was essential to "insistently repeat that they preach armed struggle, that they are linked with international communism, and that they were sent to Bolivia with the sole purpose of moving the church toward communism."[20]

The Banzer Plan simply formalized a long-standing CIA practice of subsidizing such right-wing organizations as Tradition, Family, and Property, a group that helped destabilize the democratic government in Brazil in 1964, paving the way for a military dictatorship. It sought to promote Christian Democracy throughout Latin America as a means of domesticating and deradicalizing movements of social reform. Here the most thoroughly documented program was that carried out in Chile in the 1960s with the cooperation of West Germany's Christian Democratic government and the German bishops whose Miseror and Adveniat mission and relief agencies were heavily subsidized by their government.[21] Belgian Jesuit Roger Vekemans, later to emerge as a bitter enemy of liberation theology, served as a channel for at least $25 million a year from the Germans and a further $5 to $10 million in CIA and U.S. Agency for International Development funds.[22]

After the 1970 electoral victory of Socialist Salvador Allende in Chile, Vekemans moved to Bogotá. In the more sympathetic climate of Colombia's ultraconservative church, he teamed up with a young bishop, Alfonso López Trujillo, who shared his aversion to liberation theology. In 1972 the previously progressive staff of the Latin American Bishops' Conference was replaced by a much more conservative group under the direction of López Trujillo as secretary general. These changes were welcomed by the Vatican where by this time conservative forces were once again in the ascendency. Though these changes implied new possibilities for cooperation between Washington, Rome, and conservative forces in the Latin American church hierarchy, they also ensured a profound and painful polarization within Latin America Catholicism itself.

The U.S. Manipulation of
Religious Issues in Nicaragua

When a group of Reagan advisers met in Santa Fe, New Mexico, in early 1980 to formulate their presidential candidate's Latin America policy, they expressed concern over the continued growth of social activism in the church. The Santa Fe Document, edited by Lewis Tambs, former U.S. ambassador to Colombia and eventually U.S. ambassador to Costa Rica (1985–1986) called for a high level of intervention. "U.S. foreign policy," it said, "must begin to counter (not react against) liberation theology as it is utilized in Latin America."[23] Ignoring the fact that the religious media were overwhelmingly controlled by López Trujillo and his allies whereas the secular media were similarly dominated by conservative elements, it explained social activism as a result of the "manipulation of the information media through church-affiliated groups and other so-called human rights lobbies." Such manipulation, it asserted, "has played an increasingly important role in overthrowing authoritarian, but pro-U.S., governments and replacing them with anti-U.S., Communist or pro-Communist dictatorships of a totalitarian character."[24]

Upon gaining office, the Reagan team acted quickly to make religious issues an element of its war on Nicaragua. Part of this attack was covert. During the first term of the Reagan administration, the press revealed that the CIA produced two documents designed to guide the contras. The first was a comic-book-style "Freedom Fighter's Manual," aimed at teaching contra fighters how to commit sabotage against the "treasonous Marxist state." The second, entitled "Psychological Operations in Guerrilla Warfare," was a more sophisticated and lengthy piece intended to instruct contra leaders in the latest techniques of psychological warfare. Both manuals urged the "freedom fighters" to accentuate religious tension. The comic book, for instance, in exhorting its readers to "paint anti-Sandinista slogans," illustrated this idea with a picture of a young person writing "Long Live the Pope" on a wall.[25] In "Psychological Operations," the CIA's surrogate "commandos" were instructed that if they killed a civilian they should explain that, although like all "Christian guerrillas" they espoused nonviolence, the action was necessary to prevent "the repression of the Sandinista government against innocent people."[26]

The authors of "Psychological Operations" also instructed their surrogates to express "indignation over the lack of freedom of worship, and persecution, of which priests are victims" and over the participation of priests such as Miguel D'Escoto and Ernesto Cardenal in the Sandinista government "against the explicit orders of his Holiness, the Pope." The recommended slogans played on the popular religiosity: "God, Homeland and Democracy," "With

God and patriotism, we will overcome communism," "Because we love Christ, we love his bishops and pastors."[27]

Contra radio stations, financed in part with U.S. dollars, operated from both Costa Rica and Honduras and used religious themes, heaping praise on Obando—the "Cardinal of Peace"—and broadcasting his Sunday homilies. The Nicaraguan Democratic Forces (FDN) posters proclaimed, "God is on our side" and "The Pope is with us." The FDN promoted the figure of Obando and devoted its September/October 1985 bulletin, distributed in the United States, to the cardinal. The December 1985 cover had Obando's picture and the exclamations, "Long live our Cardinal!" and "With God and Patriotism, we shall defeat Communism."

In addition to these efforts to convince the Nicaraguan people that the Sandinistas were enemies of their church, the CIA also apparently put at least some of its abundant resources into efforts to propagandize within the United States. According to Edgar Chamorro, an FDN contra leader in the early 1980s, the CIA in 1982 set up the so-called Puebla Institute in Garden City, Michigan, under the formal direction of former *La Prensa* editor Humberto Belli.[28] Belli then produced a number of alarmist publications depicting the alleged Sandinista persecution of religion. At least one of these, *Nicaragua: Christians Under Fire,* was distributed free of charge to members of Congress. The *New York Times* even published a Puebla Institute op.-ed. piece and, in the box describing the author, referred to that organization as "a Roman Catholic human rights group."[29]

Covert means were not the only techniques employed in the Reagan administration's war against Nicaragua. There was also a very public war of words featuring numerous speeches by the president and other administration spokespersons as well as printed material in the *White House Digest* and other U.S. government publications. In addition, in an effort to influence U.S. religious leaders, the White House, beginning in May 1983, held weekly briefings on Central America.

To convince the U.S. public of the validity of its policy in Central America the administration had to conduct a well-planned, deliberate distortion of the facts.[30] An August 22, 1982, op.-ed. in the *Washington Post* written by State Department official Elliott Abrams (eventually to be promoted to the post of assistant secretary of state for inter-American Affairs) is illustrative. In it, Abrams charged that Nicaraguan Bishop Salvador Schlaefer had been detained by the Sandinistas (Schlaefer publicly stated that he had never been detained); that *La Prensa* had been prohibited from publishing a papal letter for two weeks (it was two days); that Managua's auxiliary bishop Bosco Vivas had been beaten by a Sandinista mob (in fact, he was pushed and fell in a scuffle when he came to remove the tabernacle from a church where angry parishoners were holding a vigil to protest the hierarchy's decision to transfer their very popular pastor); that Monsignor Bismarck Carballo had been marched naked through the streets of Managua to jail and that his interview with *La Prensa* was censored (in fact, in no account of the Carballo incident was he marched naked through the streets to jail.

And, Carballo's version of the incident was published in full in *La Prensa* before any government account of it was released).

The White House and the religious Right in the United States worked systematically to discredit the Sandinistas and to play up the divisions within the churches and between the churches and the government. Their approach made use of propaganda channels with direct support of U.S. church figures and institutions opposed to the Sandinistas; press conferences set up by the White House itself or by the Heritage Foundation, the Institute on Religion and Democracy (IRD), the Puebla Institute or other like-minded groups; speaking tours arranged for Nicaraguan defectors and opposition and contra figures such as Edgard and Geraldine Macias, Humberto Belli, and Alvaro José Baldizón. A concerted effort was also made to discredit any entity that had an opinion on the Nicaraguan situation that was not adamantly anti-Sandinista; thus the World Council of Churches, the National Council of Churches, the Methodist Church, Catholic and ecumenical centers in Nicaragua, Witness for Peace, Washington Office on Latin America, and others were publicly attacked. The Reagan administration also tried to obtain support for its policy by "wooing the Catholic leadership, especially the country's three hundred bishops who [were] the recipients of several 'Your Excellency' mailings."[31]

Although thoroughly discredited by investigative journalists and human rights organizations, the administration's charge that the Nicaraguan government was anti-Semitic was one of the most continually used allegations of "religious persecution." In July 1983, four days before Reagan's White House briefing on Central America to Jewish leaders, the U.S. embassy in Managua cabled Secretary of State Shultz, disclosing that the "evidence fails to demonstrate that the Sandinistas have followed a policy of anti-Semitism or have persecuted Jews solely because of their religion."[32] Ignoring this confidential cable, Reagan charged that "after the Sandinista takeover, the remaining Jews were terrorized into leaving. . . . The Sandinistas seem always to have been anti-Semitic." On December 14, 1985, Reagan repeated, "A tiny population of Jews was bullied and driven out."[33] And, in the 1986 campaign to secure funding for the contras, the same discredited charge was used over and over again.

The *White House Digest* of February 29, 1984, used allegations by contra partisans and Sandinista defectors to repeat totally unsubstantiated charges that portray a brutal, antichurch regime in Nicaragua. The *Digest* quoted ARDE leader Edgard Macías as saying that priests who have "expressed a desire to leave the regime have been told by the Junta that they cannot resign from their posts." Macías also charged that "the Sandinistas are even trying to create a new religious rite, the Sandino-Christian rite, complete with icons to Augusto Sandino, prayers to a new pantheon of martyred Sandinistas who are to be revered as saints, and even the beginnings of a cult of resurrection." North American church personnel living in Nicaragua testified to the absurdity of such charges.[34]

A November 6, 1985, White House report on Nicaragua decried the church situation there. It charged that "thousands of worshippers have been

prevented by force from attending masses given by Cardinal Obando."
Theologian Juan Hernandez Pico challenged the accusation: "While Cardinal
Obando, with the State of Emergency in October 1985, has been denied
permission to hold outdoor processions, he has travelled extensively throughout the country, saying mass wherever he goes. Nobody has been prevented
from attending his masses."[35]

The administration's wholesale deviation from fact in justifying its foreign
policy eventually came under strong criticism from Americas Watch. In its
July 1985 report on Nicaragua, it stated categorically, "The issue of religious
persecution in Nicaragua is without substance, although it is evident that
the political conflict between the Catholic Church and the government has
included cases of clear abuses, such as the expulsion of ten foreign priests.
There is not a policy of anti-Semitism, nor are Christians—Catholic or
Protestant—persecuted for their faith."[36]

Reagan's disregard for the truth increased with each congressional fight
for renewed military aid to the contras. In a radio address on December
14, 1985, he included this assessment of the church in Nicaragua:

> No institution more deeply embodies or glorifies or seeks to perfect the
> moral and spiritual goodness of man than the Church in all of its
> denominations. Yet, in Nicaragua, the Church is the enemy. . . . Cardinal
> Obando y Bravo, a great hero of truth and courage, is prevented from
> speaking freely to his flock. The State Police have expelled foreign priests
> and drafted seminarians who are virtual prisoners in the Sandinistas' armed
> forces. . . . The truth is, these men are nothing but thugs, a gang of hard-
> core communists to whom the word of God is a declaration of liberation
> that must be stamped out.[37]

Reagan's Domestic Allies

THE INSTITUTE ON RELIGION AND DEMOCRACY

Working with the Reagan administration in the ideological war were
organizations and individuals of the religious Right in the United States.
One of the pillars was the Institute on Religion and Democracy (IRD). In
an IRD founding statement, Richard Neuhaus declared that "because America
is a large and influential part of His creation, because America is the home
of most of the heirs of Israel of old, and because this is a land in which
His church is vibrantly free to live and proclaim the gospel to the world,
we believe that America has a peculiar place in God's promises and
purposes."[38] However, according to Martin Lee in a 1983 exposé published
in *Mother Jones*, the IRD "was established in 1981 with funding from right-
wing institutions, including the Smith Richardson and Sarah Scaife Foun-
dations," both of which he asserts "have served as CIA financial conduits."[39]
At least initially, the IRD was designed to mobilize Protestant opinion
against what its founders regarded as a dangerous swing to the Left in the
major mainline U.S. Protestant churches.

An IRD report published in 1981 asserted that the Catholic Church was "the only institution in Nicaragua which seems to have much prospect of holding the country back from the drift toward totalitarianism. Whether or not it succeeds may depend on the kind of moral support—and, possibly material assistance—it gets from the Christian churches throughout the world."[40] Other IRD documents attacked the Sandinista government, the Jesuits, the Evangelical Committee for Aid and Development (CEPAD), the Antonio Valdivieso Ecumenical Center, the Central American Historical Institute in Managua, Father Uriel Molina, the "popular church," liberation theology, and so on. The documents frequently used the analysis and sources employed by the Reagan administration: ARDE members Geraldine and Edgard Macias, former *la Prensa* editor Humberto Belli, defectors Miguel Bolaños Hunter and Alvaro José Baldizón, journalist Shirley Christian, and *Reader's Digest*.

Throughout the Reagan administration, IRD-U.S. government cooperation was extensive. In May 1985, the IRD and the U.S. State Department cosponsored a conference on the state of religious liberty around the world, held at the State Department. The U.S. Information Agency (USIA) provided some $45,000 to fly in foreign religious leaders, and President Reagan addressed the conference. IRD founders Michael Novak and Penn Kemble (also an adviser to USIA and a founder of the procontra Citizen's Committee for the Pro-Democratic Forces in Central America—PRODEMCA) were major proponents of the contras in the mid-1980s and organized forums and arranged meetings on Capital Hill for contra leaders.

According to James M. Wall, writing in the *Christian Century*, although evangelists such as Jerry Falwell were getting considerable media attention, the White House–IRD alliance was the connection to watch. "The Reagan Administration may give lip service to a prayer amendment, but its real commitment is to waging war against communism (or what it perceives to be communism). The IRD is Reagan's religious arm in the campaign to cut off funds from American churches to countries like Nicaragua."[41]

CONSERVATIVE CATHOLICS

Some of Reagan's allies in the fight against Nicaragua came from a network of wealthy conservative Catholics who played a role in Washington-Vatican relations that dated at least from World War II. Many of them belonged to the prestigious Knights of Malta, who trace their origins to medieval times. Because wealth and power are prerequisites for being invited into the Knights of Malta and because of its ties to the Vatican, its influence is considerable in both political and religious circles. Among U.S. knights, the best known and most prominent for many years has been J. Peter Grace, head of W. R. Grace, a company long active in shipping, agricultural, and industrial activities in Latin America. He was long-time president of the American Institute for Free Labor Development (AIFLD), an organization jointly sponsored and underwritten by the U.S. government and U.S. big business. Its stated purpose was to depoliticize trade union activity throughout

Latin America. In practice, it created divisions within organized labor and facilitated right-wing counterrevolutionary projects, of which the best known was the overthrow of President Salvador Allende in Chile in 1973.[42] Inducted into the Knights of Malta in January 1986, Lewis Lehrman, a recent convert to Catholicism, was one of the most vocal supporters of Reagan's Central American policy. Lehrman (of Rite-Aid Drug) served on the board of the Heritage Foundation and as chairman of Citizens for America brought together "freedom fighters" from around the world in June 1985.

Other U.S. Knights and Dames of Malta include William Casey, James Buckley, Lee Iacocca, William Buckley, Alexander Haig, William A. Wilson, Clare Booth Luce, William E. Simon, Senator Jeremiah Denton, John McCone (player in the overthrow in Allende and in the Diem assassination), Frank Ortiz (ambassador to Guatemala from 1979 to 1981, later to Argentina), and Patrick Frawley (who was born in Nicaragua and used part of his fortune from Schick razors to back the conservative *National Catholic Register*).

Michael Novak of the IRD was one of the most prolific writers and speakers of the religious Right. His favorite targets included the U.S. bishops' pastorals on peace and on the economy, the Sandinistas, and liberation theology. As Cornell historian Walter LaFeber put it:

> Novak saved his sharpest knives for the radical priests and bishops who used dependency theory to explain the [Central American] crisis, and who urged greater state involvement to break Latin American dependence on capitalist powers. He warned that their approach could lead to a "new union of Church and state (this time on the left)" that might well end in "economic decline" and the suppression of individual freedom.[43]

THE REST OF THE RELIGIOUS RIGHT

A November 22, 1985, IRD bulletin denounced alleged persecution of evangelical clergy in Nicaragua including the Nicaraguan Campus Crusade for Christ representative. The Campus Crusade had a spiritualist doctrine and was expressly against liberation theology and progressive pastors. Partially funded by conservative beer magnate Adolf Coors, much of its focus was political with a religious veneer; it viewed liberation movements or governments as atheistic, materialistic, and communistic. Headed by Bill Bright, the crusade was one of the prime movers to link Christianity to support for Reagan's U.S. foreign policy, to the extent that a good Christian had to support the MX missile program and aid to the contras. As early as 1976, *Sojourner* magazine had discredited Bright's brand of Christian politics and pointed out that Bright had long been criticized for crusades in countries with right-wing military dictatorships that he praised for their "Christian governments."[44]

The themes used by television evangelists are often highly political, and, according to sociologist Jeffrey Hadden of the University of Virginia, they "have greater unrestricted access to media than any other interest group in America."[45] Evangelist Jerry Falwell used his popularity on television to found Moral Majority, which was subsumed in February 1986 under the new Liberty Federation, a more overtly political body. This group enabled Falwell to throw his full weight behind Reagan's agenda, including the contra aid vote. Television evangelist Pat Robertson and his 700 Club were also influential in Reagan's war, generating much of the income of the Christian Broadcasting Network (CBN), a major private funder of the contras. Said Pat Robertson, "The U.S. has a moral obligation to support 'freedom fighters' who battle 'satanic' Communism. . . . I think that if we have the opportunity to assist these wars of liberation, as in Afghanistan or Nicaragua or Angola, we should do that. We have no obligation to assist the enemies of the United States or the enemies of the Lord or the enemies of freedom."[46] Lesser known anti-Communist fundamentalist or Pentecostal groups supporting the contras include Missions in Motion, Christian Emergency Relief Teams, and Salt and Light.[47]

The largest institution that united religious fervor and military might was the Christian Broadcasting Network (CBN), which raised money that it maintained was for Nicaraguan refugees on the Honduran side of the border. However, Tom Hawk, who worked in that area for years as the head of the evangelical group World Relief, "described the border area relief efforts as irresponsible, inexperienced, detrimental to refugees and overtly political."[48] Although there were real Nicaraguan refugees in Honduras, often supplies and camps for the refugees were a cover for the contras. CBN received assistance from the Air Force and Navy to ship its "humanitarian" supplies to Central America, and military bases in the United States stored CBN goods before shipping.[49]

Another group that raised funds in the mid-1980s for "Nicaraguan refugees" was Friends of the Americas, headed by Diane Jenkins, wife of Louisiana state representative Woody Jenkins, himself active in contra fundraising. Diane Jenkins appeared on CBN to solicit funds for Friends of the Americas, and she was the first recipient of the Ronald Reagan American Ideals Award. Woody Jenkins admitted that his interest went beyond pure humanitarianism or Christian charity and that he wanted to see the Sandinistas removed from Nicaragua. Contra leader Steadman Fagoth said he received two tons of food from Friends of the Americas and others in July 1984.[50] Although some private funding groups, such as Friends of the Americas and the World Anti-Communist League (WACL), are not religious institutions, their close cooperation and coordination linked them to Reagan's holy war against Nicaragua.

There were direct links between private fundraising efforts for "humanitarian relief" and the Nicaraguan Democratic Force (FDN). CBN's Operation Blessing gave $3 million to the Houston-based Nicaraguan Patriotic Association, whose vice president was the Houston representative of the FDN.[51] In addition, CBN gave $2 million to the Knights of Malta for its Central America operations and invited contra leaders Adolfo Calero and Steadman Fagoth to appear on CBN's television show, the 700 Club.[52]

The Nicaraguan Refugee Fund was founded through an agreement with the FDN's Nicaraguan Development Council.[53] Because of its ties to the

White House, the Nicaraguan Refugee Fund received much publicity—particularly for a dinner in Washington, D.C., in April 1985. Lending a religious air to the event, CBN's Pat Robertson gave the invocation and led the Pledge of Allegiance. The Moral Majority, the 700 Club, and the *Washington Times* reserved whole tables. Prominent conservative contra supporters—including Jeane Kirkpatrick, Joseph Coors, Woody Jenkins, J. Peter Grace, and Penn Kemble—were on the official dinner committee. Reagan spoke at the dinner and embraced a young girl whom he claimed was one of the suffering Nicaraguan refugees. Later reports showed that the child had been born and raised in the United States.[54]

Another major religious force to promote the conservative cause, both in the United States and in Latin America, was the Unification Church, founded and headed by the Korean Reverend Sun Myung Moon. Through the church, Moon built an enormous business empire, a munitions factory in South Korea, television channels in South America, hotels in the United States and Uruguay, and media outlets (including the *Washington Times*). An arm of the Unification Church, CAUSA, was very active in Latin America, running seminars in various countries to promote the cause of anticommunism.[55]

In 1982 CAUSA joined the CIA cause, proposed to the contras that the different factions unite, and then offered to help them. CAUSA provided supplies, cash, and emergency relief to the contras in Honduras in 1984, including $11,000 in cash to a contra group to help pay rent and telephone bills. "Gun-toting guerrillas in Honduras [were] clad in red CAUSA T-shirts" and a member of a student Moonie organization reportedly fought with the FDN in 1985.[56]

Informal links between CAUSA and the Reagan administration were enhanced by the free flow of former public officials into this ostensibly private organization. CAUSA's board of directors included the retired head of the Defense Intelligence Agency (DIA), Daniel Graham, and the commander of the USS *Pueblo* when it was captured by North Korea, Lloyd Bucher. Former U.S. ambassador to Honduras, Philip Sanchez, became CAUSA's head in 1986.

The Nicaraguan Freedom Fund (NFF), one of the many front groups of the Unification Church channeled $350,000 to the Americares Foundation in Connecticut.[57] Americares, in coordination with CBN, had sent more than $20 million in medical aid to El Salvador, Honduras, and Guatemala as of April 1985.[58] Some $680,000 went to Miskitos linked to the U.S.-backed contras, according to a Knights of Malta official in Honduras. Said Americares president, "My feeling is that none of the aid goes to contra forces, but I couldn't say that absolutely none of it does."[59] Dame of Malta Clare Booth Luce of the *Washington Times* board of directors was one of the original directors of the NFF, along with William E. Simon, Jeane Kirkpatrick, and Midge Decter. J. Peter Grace chaired the six-member advisory board of Americares, which included fellow Knight of Malta William E. Simon and Vice President George Bush's brother Prescott Bush, Jr.

The same names appeared repeatedly on lists of organizations and major organizational backers supporting private funding of the contra war. They included a blending of fundamentalist Christians, wealthy conservative Catholics, Unification Church interests, paramilitary groups, and ex-U.S. military personnel. Their interests, donations, boards of directors, and memberships overlapped. Some of the major movers of these efforts were J. Peter Grace, Joseph Coors, CAUSA International and the *Washington Times*, Jeane Kirkpatrick, William E. Simon, the Knights of Malta and the Americares Foundation, World Anti-Communist League and other Singlaub groups, and the Christian Broadcasting Network and related Christian groups.

Reagan's International Allies

The Reagan administration's two most important international allies in the religious crusade against the Sandinistas were the conservative hierarchy of the Nicaraguan Catholic church—especially Monsignor Obando—and the Vatican. It would be wrong, however, to imply that either was a simple tool of U.S. policy—as Nicaraguans occasionally did when referring to Obando. A more accurate interpretation would be that there was a convergence of worldview that often led to cooperative effort. The conservative bishops and the pope were concerned that the hierarchical organization and authority of the Church—its magisterium—were being threatened by greater grass roots participation in both religion and politics in post-1979 Nicaragua. These fears and a misplaced anticommunism often led Obando and the new Polish pope to pursue policies that dovetailed neatly with those of Washington.

OBANDO AND LIKE-MINDED BISHOPS

Throughout the first six years of the Reagan administration, Archbishop (later Cardinal) Miguel Obando y Bravo and other conservative bishops were clearly the Reagan administration's most stalwart foreign allies in the undeclared war against the Sandinistas. Even before Reagan's first inauguration, tense relations existed between conservative Nicaraguan Catholics and the Sandinistas. However, the years 1981 and 1982 saw a quickening of the process of polarization. Obando was elevated to a position of considerable preeminence internationally as well as locally—not so much because of native ability or theological prowess but because he was a major irritant to and opponent of the Sandinistas. In January 1982, the Institute on Religion and Democracy honored him with its first Religious Freedom Award and escorted him around Washington. From then on he not only was a frequent visitor to the United States but also traveled throughout the world carrying the message of religious "persecution" in Nicaragua. As Conor Cruise O'Brien later observed, "[The] Archbishop's complaints helped the President with the demonization of Nicaragua: The President, in claiming that the Church was persecuted in Nicaragua, could cinch that claim by quoting the Archbishop."[60]

In February of 1982, the Bishops—or at least Obando speaking in their name—issued a pastoral letter accusing the Sandinistas of serious human rights violations against Nicaragua's Miskito population. This charge was issued without any prior discussion about the matter with officials of the government and after the bishops themselves had turned down a government invitation to send a fact finding mission to visit the camps to which many Miskitos had been relocated.[61] Coming as it did at a time of extremely overblown and inaccurate rhetoric from the Reagan administration concerning Sandinista "genocide" against the Miskitos, this pastoral was seen by many Nicaraguans as essentially aiding and abetting the enemy.

From this point onward Obando would repeatedly trumpet the alleged human rights violations of the Sandinistas. However, neither he nor the Nicaraguan bishops' conference would make any statements about well-documented and much more serious contra atrocities. The blatant use of a double standard was often quite striking. For instance, while he and most of the bishops remained silent on a well-publicized and very shocking incident in which the contras kidnapped, tortured, and killed two outstanding lay Catholic workers, Felipe and Mery Barreda, Obando saw fit to denounce in a Sunday homily a subsequent attempt on the life of contra leader Eden Pastora. Obando himself would sidestep accusations of one-sidedness by arguing that "it would be ideal if we could denounce human rights violations from whichever side they come. But here there is no freedom of information. The information we have comes from the side of the Sandinista Front."[62] In fact, to obtain reliable data Obando could simply have consulted many of the church's own pastoral workers who had witnessed numerous contra attacks and taken detailed testimony from survivors.

The same bishops were also markedly intolerant of any priests and sisters who strongly condemned contra atrocities or U.S. policy or even tried to encourage people to participate in the political process. Such individuals were labeled members of the "popular church," considered the enemy, and, in over thirty instances, removed from their parishes. For instance, in July 1984 at the funeral of several youth who had been tortured and killed by ARDE, Father Pedro Belzunegui said, "Christ said: Blessed are the poor, those who suffer and cry, but also cursed are those who make them suffer. Because of this, from this Church, we want to say: Forever cursed be the criminal CIA that clothes itself in the blood of our brothers and sisters." Bishop Pablo Antonio Vega subsequently had the priest transferred to Guatemala, calling him a "propagandist about things that are none of his business."[63]

In numerous other ways Obando and his clerical allies came to be identified with U.S. policy and the anti-Sandinista cause. In May 1984, for instance, the archbishop went to the United States seeking private funding for his ongoing anti-Sandinista activities. A logical source of support was W. R. Grace and Company. In a memo subsequently leaked to the press, John J. Meehan, an aide to J. Peter Grace, told his boss of a meeting he had with Obando in which the latter outlined a plan to set up anti-Sandinista cadres under the guise of leadership-training workshops. The memo assessed the plan: "These leadership courses represent the best organized opposition in Nicaragua to the present Government's efforts to change the country into a Marxist-Leninist society. The archbishop has given all of his resources and skills to developing leaders who can oppose the Sandinistas and his program has been growing for about four years." Meehan suggested to Obando that he use Father Peyton's Family Rosary Crusade.[64] Father Peyton had previously worked extensively in Latin America with financial support from the conservative Catholic DeRance Foundation.

Obando received substantial funds from the United States, both through Catholic Relief Services and the Agency for International Development. Though the archbishop repeatedly denied links to the CIA, the *National Catholic Reporter* observed in 1984 that "four of the archbishop's principal financial supporters . . . have been repeatedly linked with CIA operations and anticommunist church organizations in Latin America in the past. These contributors are: the U.S. Agency for International Development (AID), W. R. Grace, Misereor and Adveniat."[65]

Within Nicaragua the Commission for Social Promotion in the Archdiocese (COPROSA) coordinated Obando's activities. The Konrad Adenaur Stiftung (the foundation of West Germany's Christian Democrats) and Misereor and Adveniat (agencies of the West German bishops) were heavy contributors to COPROSA, "but COPROSA refused to reveal [to the *National Catholic Reporter*] dollar amounts given by the two organizations." AID donated $250,000 in 1981.[66]

By 1985 Obando's support for the U.S. project in Nicaragua was obvious. For instance, the first mass at which Obando officiated after being elevated to the rank of cardinal in May 1985 was held in Miami, Florida, before a congregation composed largely of Nicaraguan exiles. Contra leaders Edén Pastora, Adolfo Calero, and Cristobal Mendoza Rocha (a former Somoza Security agent) were seated prominently near the altar.

Shortly after that highly symbolic act, Obando remarked that he did not object to "being identified with the people who have taken up arms."[67] Bishop Pablo Antonio Vega echoed the new cardinal's support for the contras in a statement in Bonn, West Germany. When asked about official and private aid that the contras received from the United States, the bishop answered that "a people who do not feel that their civil and social rights are guaranteed also have the right to look for help where they can get it."[68]

THE VATICAN

Vatican support for Reagan policy in Nicaragua was neither as unconditional nor as constant as that of the conservative Nicaraguan bishops. At first John Paul II—a Pole, an anti-Communist, and a pope deeply concerned with preserving the magisterium of the Catholic Church—seemed to be working in near-perfect harmony with Washington and Obando. Eventually, however, as the contra war dragged on without any tangible military success, the Vatican—with its millennia-old experience in seeking accommodation with established regimes of various colorations—began to back away from its originally strong anti-Sandinista stance. From the start, the Reagan administration had worked to involve the pope in its anti-Sandinista cause. In June 1982, President Reagan and then–Secretary of State Alexander Haig visited the Vatican and discussed with John Paul their mutual concern that the spread of "repression" and "Communist tyranny" in Latin America be stopped. One year later, Reagan took away the legal obstacles to closer cooperation with the Vatican by moving through Congress the repeal of an 1867 law forbidding the use of federal funds for a diplomatic representative to the Vatican. In December 1983, Reagan administration officials stressed the policy benefits of formal ties with the Holy See that would result from greater access to the Vatican's worldwide channels of information. "This Pope especially has been very brave in taking stands with which we agree," said one U.S. official.[69] Shortly thereafter, Reagan named the first U.S. ambassador to the Holy See, William A. Wilson, who received a papal blessing for Reagan's foreign policy: "On many issues the principles on which your Republic was founded closely parallel with the principles of the Holy See. . . . The condition of today's world depends largely on the way in which the United States exercises its global mission of service to humanity."[70]

The Reagan administration devoted much energy to the pope's Central America trip in 1983. U.S. Ambassador at Large Vernon Walters, who had previously served as deputy director of the CIA, visited the Vatican on October 18, 1982. Secretary of State George Shultz was at the Vatican in December 1982, and George Bush met with the pope and Vatican Secretary of State Casaroli on February 7 just before the papal trip began. The content of papal talks in each country closely followed official U.S. policy at the time.

On occasion, however, the Reagan administration overstated support by the Vatican for its crusade against the Sandinistas. For instance, in April 1985 Reagan himself publicly announced that the pope had agreed with his military solution for Central America. That assertion was emphatically denied by the papal nuncio to the United States, the Vatican, and Washington's Archbishop James Hickey.[71]

Nicaragua's conservative bishops also guided the Vatican in an anti-Sandinista direction. On various occasions they sent messages or went personally to Rome to tell their version of what was going on in their country and to urge appropriate anti-Sandinista responses. The content of an unsigned confidential document reportedly written by some of the Nicaraguan Church hierarchy and by advisers from the Latin American Bishops' Conference (CELAM) just prior to the pope's visit in March 1983 is illustrative of the type of message being conveyed to Rome. Leaked and subsequently printed in Spain, the paper was designed to provide background for the visit and to suggest an overall strategy for dealing with the Sandinistas. Its attitude toward the revolutionary government is unequivocal:

The fundamental reality that the Nicaraguan Church and the Vatican have to confront with complete clarity and without questioning is this: that the Sandinista government is a Marxist-Leninist government; that it is, in short, an enemy. The fact that it is an enemy means that a policy of accommodation cannot succeed. Each concession by the Church will be followed by another government demand, in an unending spiral, because the intrinsic aim of the government is the complete monoploy of political and ideological power.[72]

At the same time the paper observed that although Catholicism was more deeply rooted in Nicaragua than in the rest of the area, including perhaps in all Latin America, the Sandinista government was "weaker than any other communist regime"; the fragile internal and external situation was forcing it to a certain amount of compromise; and Monsignor Obando was extremely popular. "The Church must unite itself around this primate as has been the case in Poland."[73]

The paper also included specific recommendations. It stated that the Catholic Church should make clear to the Sandinista government that Obando must be at "the center of gravity" of Church-State communications. Nicaragua should have its own nuncio, not share one with Honduras, for "it is necessary to have a Nuncio who can work in strict collaboration with Monsignor Obando and a united Episcopal Conference (a Polish Nuncio)." The Church must point out specific doctrinal errors, denounce them authoritatively as being opposed to the magisterium of the Church, and point to the specific individuals and organizations that support them. Members of the Church who work to undermine the leadership of Obando must be removed from their positions of institutional authority and influence.

For their part, the Sandinistas were acutely aware of the need to avoid a deterioration of relations with Rome. They understood the power of the Vatican. As one Sandinista official (who did not wish to be identified) said in 1986: "The Vatican has made and unmade presidents and kings; it has made and unmade financial empires. Like the United States, its power cannot be overestimated. It has even made someone like Obando a world figure. That is not something to take lightly."[74] Accordingly, the Sandinistas, too, sent a number of delegations to Rome in an effort to convince John Paul II that religion and revolution could coexist in Nicaragua to the mutual benefit of both. But, through the first half of the 1980s, the voices of alarm coming from Washington and Nicaragua's conservative church hierarchy held the day.

During the first six years of the Reagan administration, tension between the Vatican and the Sandinistas mounted. The pope repeatedly made statements implying that the priests in the Nicaraguan government should resign. According to Daniel Ortega, one of the conditions for the 1983 papal visit to Nicaragua, initially conveyed to the Junta in the last quarter of the previous year, was that it remove the priests from office.[75] The pope also sent a message to Nicaragua denouncing the popular church. The pope's frequent attacks on some aspects of liberation theology as well as his decision in May 1985 to elevate the viscerally anti-Sandinista Archbishop Miguel Obando y Bravo to the rank of cardinal also served to exacerbate tensions between Rome and Managua.

The most dramatic example of the deterioration of relations between the Vatican and the Sandinistas came with the pope's visit in March 1983. The Nicaraguan government had gone to great expense and effort to welcome the pope. Between 600,000 and 700,000 people—around 40 percent of the adult population of the country—attended the papal mass held in the 19th of July Plaza.[76] Yet from the start everything seemed to go wrong. Junta leader Daniel Ortega's welcoming speech was overly long and apparently misunderstood by the pope. On the other hand, all the pope's utterances echoed the viewpoints of the conservative clergy. The people were told to obey their bishops. The "popular church" was denounced. And, though human rights violations were lamented, all the references were to apparent government misdeeds. Worse still—especially for mothers of victims of the contra war—the pope steadfastly refused to pray for Nicaraguans killed by the contras. There was tremendous confusion in the crowd as revolutionary Christians shouted, "We want peace," and a smaller group of Obando's supporters chanted, "Long live the Pope; long live Obando." Television pictures of an angry pope yelling "silencio" were beamed around the world, and the Western press generally made it appear that the Sandinistas had deliberately humiliated the Holy Father.[77]

Though Rome-Managua relations remained poor through 1985, a variety of signs in 1986 indicated that the Vatican was slowly beginning to reverse its position on Nicaragua by pursuing a less confrontational stance. In April the Vatican issued a document titled "Instructions on Christian Freedom and Liberation," which seemed to backpeddle on much of Rome's previously very negative position on Liberation Theology.[78] Later Nicaraguan Vice President Sergio Ramírez was received at the Vatican for conversations. That summer the Sandinistas expelled Bishop Pablo Antonio Vega. (Vega had given a series of speeches in the United States and elsewhere that many felt had contributed to the Reagan administration's successful effort to get a $100 million appropriation for the contras approved by Congress, and, in a press conference in Managua on July 2, he not only had refused to condemn U.S. support for the contras but also had endorsed the "right" of the people of Nicaragua to "defend" themselves against their own government.[79]) Significantly, however, though the Vatican responded with pro forma denunciations of the expulsion, it maintained "studious silence on Vega's proposal that he be appointed to head a prelature in exile, meaning a prelature for the contras."[80] And, when the exiled bishop immediately embarked on a speaking tour of the world to denounce the Sandinistas, it ordered him to come to the Vatican and thereafter effectively silenced him. That summer the Vatican assigned a new nuncio exclusively to Nicaragua. Paolo Giglio, however, was certainly not the Polish nuncio the conservative bishops had requested. In fact, he arrived in Managua with a conciliatory message and orders for Obando to return to dialogue with the Nicaraguan government. Remarkably, an "unusually conciliatory statement by Obando follow[ed] the first round of talks with Sandinista officials in September."[81] In sum, the Vatican appeared to have shifted away from a policy of direct confrontation with the Sandinistas. Though John Paul would perhaps continue to view the Nicaraguan revolution as "a Central American variation of Poland and therefore . . . never publicly recognize the revolution's legitimacy,"[82] he had begun to pursue more pragmatic, less confrontational tactics than those espoused by either the Reagan administration or Nicaragua's conservative bishops.

Conclusion

In its first six years in office the Reagan administration used a variety of tactics to manipulate religion and the religious issue as one part of its effort to destabilize and destroy its chosen enemy in Nicaragua. These included an elaborate propaganda campaign of half-truths, distortion, and outright falsehoods; CIA dirty tricks; close cooperation with right-wing Catholic and Protestant organizations and other ultraconservatives in the United States; and the coordination of anti-Sandinista policy with Nicaragua's conservative Catholic hierarchy and a strongly anti-Communist Pope. Although the effect of these U.S. machinations was impossible to measure precisely, they probably had contributed significantly to the polarization that had taken place not only within the churches of Nicaragua but also between certain segments of them and the revolutionary state. However, at the time this chapter was being written, it appeared that this situation might be ameliorated if the shift in Vatican strategy visible in 1986 continued into the future.

Meanwhile, in the United States, although the Reagan administration's torrid rhetoric had had an impact on some segments of the U.S. public, it certainly had not convinced the mainline Protestant and Catholic church leadership. As Bishop James Malone, head of the U.S. Catholic Bishops' Conference, put it: "The difference between Vietnam and Central America is that the Catholic Church stands between us and Central America."[83] He might just as well have spoken for the Protestants, too. A number of national church task forces had been commissioned and charged with carrying out careful investigations of Central American and Nicaraguan reality. Between 1981 and April 1985, seventeen major U.S. denominations had formally protested U.S. intervention in the region; thirteen of them also condemned the U.S.-inspired and U.S.-financed paramilitary efforts to overthrow the Nicaraguan government. In the words of then–Assistant Secretary of State Langhorne Motely, "Taking on the Churches is really tough. We don't normally think of them as political opponents, so we don't know how to handle them. It has to be a kid-glove kind of thing. They are really formidable."[84] Thus, for all of Reagan's heavy handedness and lack of concern for accuracy, for his ability to make accusations without any substantiation and, after the charges had been disproved, make them again as if they were new, he still could not convince the majority of Americans or the leaders of the U.S. Catholic and mainline Protestant denominations that Sandinista Nicaragua was so much a part of the "evil empire" that it was worth U.S. lives to eliminate or even that it should be eliminated.

Notes

1. Several useful English language sources on this subject are Michael Dodson and T. S. Montgomery, "The Churches in the Nicaraguan Revolution," in Thomas W. Walker, ed., *Nicaragua in Revolution* (New York: Praeger Publishers, 1982), pp. 161–180; "Religion and Politics," in Thomas W. Walker, ed., *Nicaragua: The First Five Years* (New York: Praeger Publishers, 1985), pp. 119–143; and Conor Cruise O'Brien, "God and Man in Nicaragua," *Atlantic Monthly* 258, no. 2 (August 1986):50–72.

2. Houtart as quoted in José Argüello, "Nicaraguan Catholicism: Church and Change," *Christianity and Crisis*, July 22, 1985.

3. Instituto Histórico Centroamericano, *Envío*, No. 30 (December 1983), p. 2B.

4. Second General Conference of Latin American Bishops, *The Church in the Present-Day Transformation of Latin America in the Light of the Council* (Washington, D.C.: United States Catholic Conference, 1973).

5. Instituto Histórico Centroamericano, *Envío*, No. 30 (December 1983), p. 9B.

6. O'Brien, "God and Man in Nicaragua," is particularly useful in explaining this attitude.

7. *Nuevo Diario*, November 6, 1985.

8. *Barricada*, December 20, 1984.

9. *Barricada*, December 18, 1984.

10. Thomas W. Walker, "Nicaragua: Catholic Unity Dissolves in Revolutionary Nicaragua," *Mesoamerica*, September, 1982, p. 8.

11. Patricia Hynds' interview with Gustavo Parajón, January 23, 1986.

12. Instituto Histórico Centroamericano, *Envío*, No. 15 (September 1982), p. 14.

13. Letter to the Board of World Mission, Moravian Church in America, in *North American Moravian*, January 1984.

14. "Sturdie Downs: 'Our Mission Is to Follow Christ,'" *Interchange* 15, no. 5 (May 1986), p. 4.

15. Stephen Schlesinger and Stephen Kinzer, *Bitter Fruit: The Untold Story of the American Coup in Guatemala* (New York: Anchor Press, 1983), p. 155.

16. Roland Flamini, *Pope, Premier, President: The Cold War Summit that Never Was* (New York: Macmillan, 1980), pp. 97–99.

17. Penny Lernoux, *Cry of the People* (New York: Doubleday, 1980), pp. 286–289.

18. Lernoux, *Cry of the People*, p. 286.

19. Nelson A. Rockefeller, *The Rockefeller Report on the Americas: The Official Report of a U.S. Presidential Mission for the Western Hemisphere* (Chicago: Quadrangle Books, 1969). See also Gary MacEoin, *Revolution Next Door* (New York: Holt, Rinehart and Winston, 1971), pp. 107–108.

20. Cited in Gary MacEoin and Nivita Riley, *Puebla: A Church Being Born* (New York: Paulist Press, 1980), p. 50. See also Lernoux, *Cry of the People*, pp. 142–147.

21. *Washington Star*, July 23, 1975; *Le Monde* (Paris), July 25, 27, and 28, 1975; *National Catholic Reporter*, May 29, 1977.

22. Gary MacEoin, *No Peaceful Way* (New York: Sheed and Ward, 1974), p. 49.

23. The Committee of Santa Fe, *A New Inter-American Policy for the Eighties* (Washington, D.C.: Interamerican Security Council, 1980), p. 20.

24. Committee of Santa Fe, *New Inter-American Policy*, p. 20.

25. CIA, "Manual del Combatiente por la Libertad," n.d., p. 9.

26. Tayacán [CIA], *Psychological Operations in Guerrilla Warfare* (New York: Vintage Books, 1985), p. 57.

27. Tayacán, *Psychological Operations*, pp. 62, 83, 94, 95.

28. From an interview by Betsy Cohn with Edgar Chamorro, December 20, 1986.

29. Nina Shea, "'Justice' in Nicaragua," *New York Times*, October 31, 1986.

30. Many of these distortions slipped by the U.S. media. Occasionally, however, they were exposed. See, for instance, Philip Taubman, "U.S. Seeks to Sway Opinion on Nicaragua," *New York Times*, November 14, 1984.

31. Thomas Quigley, "When Research Masquerades," *Commonweal*, April 5, 1985, p. 208.

32. Robert Parry, *Associated Press*, September 20, 1983.

33. White House, "Radio Address of the President to the Nation," Washington, D.C., December 14, 1985.

34. Hynds' interview with the Committee of U.S. Church Personnel Living in Nicaragua.

35. Interview by Betsy Cohn and Patricia Hynds with Juan Hernandez Pico, March 4, 1986.

36. Americas Watch, *Human Rights in Nicaragua: Reagan, Rhetoric and Reality* (New York: Americas Watch, July 1985), p. 14.

37. White House, "Radio Address," December 14, 1985.

38. *National Catholic Reporter*, February 4, 1983.

39. Martin Lee, "Their Will Be Done," *Mother Jones*, July 1983, p. 27.

40. Institute on Religion and Democracy, "A Revolution Against the Church?" 1981, p. 16.

41. James M. Wall, "Anti-communism Binds IRD to White House," *Christian Century*, November 28, 1984.

42. AIFLD's role was less publicized but more extensive in the ouster of Juan Bosch in the Dominican Republic in 1963 and in the coup against João Goulart in Brazil in 1964. AIFLD always worked closely with Catholic Action to set up pro-U.S. labor unions.

43. Walter LeFeber, *Inevitable Revolutions* (New York: W. W. Norton, 1983), p. 281.

44. James McBride, "To Occupy Until Jesus Comes: The Politics of the Christian New Right," *Radical Religion* 5, no. 4 (1981):11.

45. *Time*, February 17, 1986, p. 63.

46. *Time*, February 17, 1986, p. 65.

47. Tom Barry, Deb Preusch, and Beth Sims, *The New Right Humanitarians* (New Mexico: Resource Center, 1986), p. 24.

48. Vicki Kemper, "In the Name of Relief," *Sojourners*, October 1985, p. 13.

49. Barry et al., *The New Right Humanitarians*, p. 50.

50. John Dillon and Jon Lee Anderson, "Who's Behind Aid to the Contras," *The Nation*, October 6, 1984.

51. Kemper, "In the Name of Relief," p. 16.

52. Barry et al., *The New Right Humanitarians*, p. 50.

53. Robert Parry, *Associated Press*, June 29, 1985.

54. *Washington Post*, May 12, 1985.

55. For more information on CAUSA and its activities worldwide see Joanne Omang, "Moon's 'Cause' Takes Aim at Communism in Americas," *Washington Post*, August 28, 1983, and Scott Anderson and Jon Lee Anderson, *Inside the League* (New York: Dodd, Meade and Co., 1986).

56. Anderson and Anderson, *Inside the League*, p. 234.

57. *New York Times*, August 13, 1985.

58. *Pentecostal Evangel*, August 18, 1985, p. 25.

59. *Washington Post*, December 28, 1984.

60. O'Brien, "God and Man in Nicaragua," p. 57.

61. For a discussion of the Miskito relocations and the U.S. manipulation of that issue see Chapter 5 of this book.

62. *Newsweek*, November 18, 1985.

63. Instituto Histórico Centroamericano, *Envío*, No. 50 (August 1985), p. 5B.

64. From a photocopy of the original memo from John Meehan to J. Peter Grace, May 9, 1984.

65. *National Catholic Reporter*, August 31, 1984.

66. *National Catholic Reporter*, August 31, 1984.

67. Quoted in Deborah Huntington, "Between God and Caesar," *NACLA Report on the Americas*, September/October 1985, p. 44.

68. *La Prensa*, September 19, 1985.

69. *Christian Science Monitor*, December 12, 1985.

70. *Osservatore Romano*, April 10, 1984.

71. *Washington Post*, April 19, 1985.

72. *The Pope in Nicaragua: Analysis of His Visit* (Madrid: IEPALA Editorial, 1983), p. 171.

73. *The Pope in Nicaragua*, p. 173.

74. Interview by Patricia Hynds with a Sandinista official on January 31, 1986.

75. From an Ortega interview with the Task Force on Central America, the United Presbyterian Church (USA), in Managua late in November 1982 (as recounted by task force member Thomas W. Walker).

76. O'Brien, "God and Man in Nicaragua," p. 60.

77. For instance, one of the repeated allegations that was subsequently picked up and used by the *White House Digest* was that "the place in the square nearest to the Pope were reserved for Sandinista activists, preequipped with microphones" ("Persecution of Christian Groups in Nicaragua," *White House Digest*, February 29, 1984, p. 8). In fact, the section of the plaza nearest the pope was occupied by the international press corps—including author Patricia Hynds—none of whom had microphones.

78. O'Brien, "God and Man in Nicaragua," p. 65.

79. From a typed transcript of that press conference supplied by Antonio Valdivieso, Ecumenical Center.

80. Penny Lernoux, "Vatican Policy on Nicaragua in Transition," *National Catholic Reporter*, December 5, 1986, p. 4.

81. Lernoux, "Vatican Policy on Nicaragua," p. 4.

82. Lernoux, "Vatican Policy on Nicaragua," p. 4.

83. *Washington Post*, April 23, 1985.

84. *Washington Post*, April 23, 1985.

SEVEN

Electronic Penetration

HOWARD H. FREDERICK _____

From the time the Reagan administration came to office, various departments of the executive branch developed, expanded, and applied the doctrine of low-intensity warfare in the Central American context. That doctrine was based on the accumulated experience of the Germans in World War II, the British in Malaya, Kenya, and Ireland, the Philippine government against the Huk, the French in Algeria, and especially the United States in Vietnam. Trying to avoid the mistakes of the past, the Reagan administration transformed Central America into a testing ground for active counterinsurgency and regional counterrevolution. Andrew Messing of the National Defense Council called the region an "accessible laboratory" for the study of low-intensity conflict.[1]

According to the advocates of low-intensity warfare, victory is guaranteed not by military superiority but by carefully executed political and ideological tactics that render the enemy ineffective, demoralized, and isolated. Direct invasion by troops and the large-scale use of military force are reserved for an eventual seizure of territory from an enemy already incapable of presenting significant resistance. In the case of Nicaragua, the constant threat of an invasion and the continual psychological pressure on the government and people required the country to be in a perpetual state of tension, which contributed to a waste of resources and erosion of resolve.

The U.S. war against Nicaragua was as much an ideological struggle as a military one. Armed counterinsurgency and psychological war were part of one common strategy. In fact, the CIA's manual on psychological warfare in Nicaragua stated outright that "the human being should be considered the priority objective in a political war. And conceived as the military target of a guerrilla war, the human being has his most critical point in his mind.

Some of the material in this chapter previously appeared in Howard H. Frederick, "Radio War in Nicaragua," in Armand Mattelart, ed., *Communicating in Popular Nicaragua* (Paris: International General, 1986), pp. 70–81. The publisher's permission for reuse is gratefully acknowledged.

Once his mind has been reached, the political animal has been defeated, without necessarily receiving bullets."[2]

Not widely known in the United States, the Reagan administration's use of propaganda as a weapon against the Nicaraguan revolution was apparent to the Sandinistas from the start. In 1985, for instance, Nicaraguan Vice-President Sergio Ramirez Mercado, in a speech to students at the School of Journalism at the Central American University in Managua, identified five themes that Nicaragua's enemies had been using for several years to discredit and delegitimate the revolution in public opinion:

1. The revolution pursues a totalitarian system; 2. Nicaragua is attempting to be a base for Soviet penetration in Central American to challenge the interests of U.S. national security; 3. Nicaragua is the field of confrontation in the East-West struggle; 4. Nicaragua is attemtping a revolution without borders and systematically exports its revolution; 5. Nicaragua's excessive militarism only shows its expansion goals; its Army is ready, in the offensive sense, to invade and occupy other countries of the area; and in conclusion, as long as the Sandinist Front does not initiate a true national dialogue to include those up in arms, there will be no possibility for peace in the country.[3]

In theory, much of the U.S. propaganda campaign—or war of ideas against the Nicaraguan people—was supposed to have been waged by the surrogate forces, or contras, which the U.S. organized from 1981 onward to fight the Sandinistas. In 1983, the CIA's manual advised and admonished contra commanders that "in guerrilla warfare, every combatant should be as highly motivated to carry out propaganda face to face as he is as a combatant. . . . The techniques of psychological operations [maximize] the social-psychological effect of a guerrilla movement, converting the guerrilla into a propagandist."[4]

In fact, however, the contras themselves—perhaps because of the brutal way in which they normally treated Nicaraguan civilians—proved to be of little use as conduits of propaganda. Radio and television were far more effective.

At first blush, one might assume that the Sandinista government would have had a distinct advantage over any external enemy in waging an electronic war of ideas within Nicaragua's own borders. Like any nation, Nicaragua had the ultimate power and right in times of war to control local television and radio broadcasts in the name of national security. In reality, however, the Nicaraguan government was at a distinct disadvantage. The telecommunications infrastructure at the command of the United States (either through its own facilities or those of client states in the region) dwarfed that of the Sandinista government and flooded Nicaragua with a constant barrage of slanted, often false, anti-Sandinista programming.

Exactly how this campaign was organized was still partly a matter of speculation in 1986. After all, this aspect of low-intensity warfare is largely covert. But a familiar modus operandi was there. Throughout the world, numerous electronic wars were being waged to destabilize public opinion. Some were the tools of modern statecraft: Through the Voice of America, Radio Liberty, and Radio Free Europe, the United States daily focuses more than a million watts on Eastern Europe. Others are operated by the intelligence services and clandestine organizations. The administration had announced a new 50,000-watt AM radio station called Radio Liberacíon to be operated by the contras.[5] Charges of CIA manipulation through bribery of the printed media in the region had begun to surface.[6] The parts of the iceberg that were clearly visible, together with Reagan-inspired disinformation campaigns around the world, clearly point to the use of electronic means to penetrate the Nicarguan citizenry. This is the focus of this chapter.

Nicaraguan Telecommunications

Located in the heart of the region, Nicaragua is the largest nation in Central America. However, it is really two countries, a Spanish-speaking Pacific Coast and an English- and Miskito-speaking Atlantic Coast. The two are separated by jungles and mountains, thus creating a difficult situation for broadcast engineers, who for years had hoped to unite the country electronically. In the prerevolutionary period, only one radio station (Nacional) could reach the east coast and then only at night.[7] Television was limited to only the narrow Spanish-speaking Pacific coast. Even in 1986, with all the efforts of the Sandinista government, the Sandinista Television System (SSTV) covered only about 60 percent of the country and radio only slightly more.[8] (See Figure 7.1.)

Nicaragua's radio infrastructure had its roots in the history of repression by U.S. forces and the Somoza dictatorship. Radio broadcasting began in 1931, during the occupation by U.S. Marines, as a means of fighting insurgent guerrillas. Frustrated by poor telecommunications, the Marines set up Radio Nacional to assist their efforts at routing Augusto César Sandino and his troops, who were fighting a guerrilla war against U.S. occupation.[9] The Somoza family maintained control over Radio Nacional until the 1979 Sandinista revolution. Throughout this period, numerous independent commercial and religious stations were active.

At the time of the revolution in 1979, the Somoza family controlled about a third of the national economy. When the regime collapsed, the new government inherited sixteen radio stations, two television stations, and one newspaper, all previously owned by the dictator.[10] In 1979, some forty-eight radio stations were operating in the country.[11] In 1986, forty-nine radio stations were operating, of which thirty-two were in private hands and seventeen belonged to the Corporación de Radiodifusión del Pueblo (CORADEP), the People's Broadcasting Corporation, which inherited Somoza's radio assets. (See Figure 7.1.)

Nicaraguan television was set up with North American equipment (NTSC standard) in the mid-1950s. By 1967, five stations were operating, but by 1979 that number had dropped to only two commercial stations. Channel

126

Figure 7.1 Coverage by Nicaraguan television and radio.

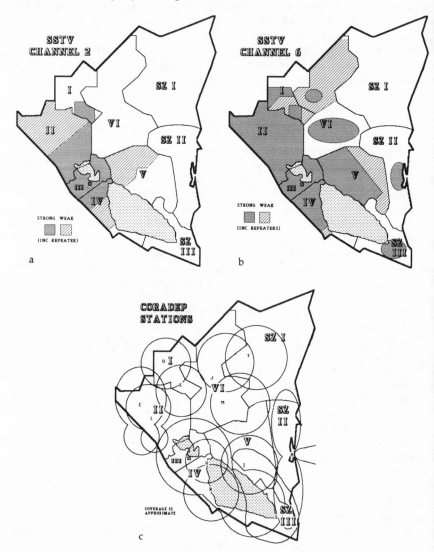

Note: Roman numerals on these and other maps in this chapter identify the regions and special zones into which Nicaragua was divided in 1982.

6 was completely owned by the Somoza family and supported Somoza's Liberal party. Eighty to 90 percent of its twenty-hour broadcast schedule originated in North American studios. Especially popular were dramatic series, action programs, and public affairs from the U.S. perspective. The only local programs were two fifteen-minute newscasts, commercials, Liberal party political programs, and a cultural program on Sunday.

Channel 2 had a more independent broadcasting philosophy but was also privately owned with minority shares controlled by the Somoza family. After the triumph, the new government bought the non-Somoza interest in Channel 2 and merged it with Channel 6 into the Sandinista Television System (SSTV). Although the new broadcasting managers kept 80 percent of the former staff, there was a desperate lack of trained broadcasting personnel such as directors and camera operators. The equipment was largely maintained by U.S. technicians. Within the first year of operations, SSTV integrated many young people into the stations and sent them to Mexico, Spain, and France for training. Cuban broadcasting engineers were also invited for technical expertise.

CORADEP, together with Radio Sandino (operated by the FSLN), the Voice of Nicaragua (run by the national government), and SSTV thus served as the main voices in support of the Sandinista revolution. The burden of responding to foreign electronic penetration fell largely on their shoulders.

Penetration of Foreign Television

As of the mid-1980s, television watching was still extremely popular in Nicaragua. SSTV estimated its 1986 daily audience at 1,300,000 to 1,500,000 million, or almost 50 percent of the population.[12] The number of television receivers is put at 200,000, of which 50,000 were color. People in Nicaragua often watched television in group settings. One conservative estimate put group viewing at five people per set, but many more people gathered around sets at state producer collectives. Indeed, the more humble the neighborhood, the greater was the frequency of group viewing.

In 1986, nine foreign television stations penetrated Nicaraguan territory. (See Figure 7.2 and Table 7.1.) Seven of the signals came from Costa Rica, which enjoyed a favorable topographical position in relation to Nicaragua. Honduras and El Salvador, lying to the north beyond mountainous regions, each had one television station that could be received in Nicaragua.

Because of the characteristics of the television signal and the geography of the region, reception was not uniform throughout Nicaragua. Honduran Channel 5 reached deeply into Regions I, II, and VI and could be received well in the cities of Chinandega, Somoto, Estelí, and Ocotal and as far south as Jinotega. Even the higher elevations of Managua could see this signal, weather conditions permitting. Salvadoran Channel 2 also reached much of this region with a weaker signal.

But Costa Rica was clearly the superpower among foreign television broadcasters, with seven of its stations receivable on Nicaraguan territory.

128

Figure 7.2 Strength of foreign television penetration of Nicaragua.

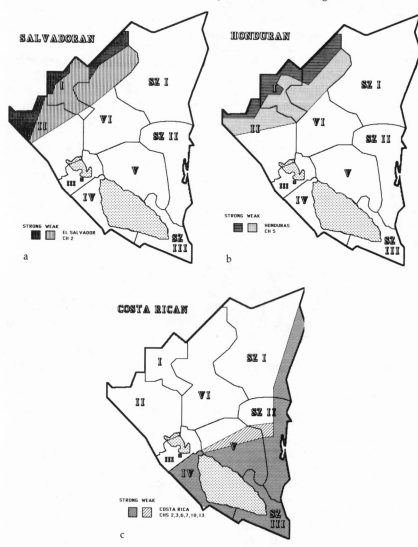

TABLE 7.1
Foreign Television Penetrating Nicaraguan Territory

Originating Country	Channels	Total Number of Stations
Costa Rica	2, 3, 4, 6, 7, 10, 13	7
El Salvador	2	1
Honduras	5	1

All of southern Nicaragua received Channel 7. The Chontales area of Region V could also pick up Channels 4 and 10. Bluefields on the Atlantic Coast in Special Zone II had strong signals from Channels 7 and 13 and weaker signals from Channels 2, 4, and 6. Indeed, Channel 7 reached as far north as Puerto Cabezas in Special Zone I. The areas of Carazo, Granada, and Rivas in Region IV could easily receive Channels 7 and 13.

In contrast, the SSTV did not reach many of the areas penetrated by foreign television signals. (See Figure 7.1.) For example, the strategic areas of Region I, site of numerous attacks by contras based in Honduras, was well served by Honduran and Salvadoran television but was not fully covered by Nicaraguan signals. The two repeaters at Estelí (one for each SSTV channel) had spotty coverage in this region. Nor could SSTV match the strength of Costa Rican television in most of southern Nicaragua. The strategic Atlantic Coast region near Bluefields, for example, had better coverage from its southern neighbor than from Nicaragua's own television.

One should also note that Nicaraguan television signals rarely extended beyond the country's borders. However, when a significant event occurred in Nicaragua, as when the Pope visited, Nicaraguan programming could be shared with neighboring countries through the Central American microwave network.

The programming of these foreign stations was similar to Nicaraguan programming before the revolution. The predominant content included action/adventures, violence, police, and dramatic series. The entertainment programs did not have content directed at the Nicaraguan people per se, but the placement of these programs against the Nicaraguan offerings often created a drain on SSTV's natural audience. Furthermore, because of U.S. economic blockade, Nicaragua could not provide the highest quality of imported programs to counteract foreign offerings.

In contrast to foreign entertainment programs, though, foreign television news often had content directed at Nicaragua. All these channels frequently covered U.S. intervention and the Nicaraguan counterrevolution in a sympathetic fashion. Furthermore, when the SSTV news aired at 8 P.M., these stations often placed their best programs up against it.

Acknowledging these problems, SSTV officials believed the only way to respond to penetration was to create better local programming and to produce programs about the areas that were being affected by the penetration. Following a pluralist programming philosophy, SSTV by 1986 was producing 35 percent of its television day locally, whereas 65 percent remained foreign. Of this foreign programming, Latin American shows accounted for 30 percent; the United States, 25 percent (reduced from 45 percent before the blockade); Western Europe, 30 percent; and socialist countries, 15 percent.[13]

Penetration of Foreign Radio

In 1985, seventy-four foreign AM and FM radio stations were penetrating Nicaraguan territory (see Figure 7.3 and Table 7.2). One-third of these foreign stations were broadcasting from Costa Rica; another one-fifth, from Honduras. Other regional broadcasters from Belize, Colombia, Cuba, El Salvador, Guatemala, Mexico, Netherlands Antilles, Panama, the United States, the USSR (Cuban relay), and Venezuela were heard in the country.

Because of the characteristics of AM and FM radio signal propagation, reception was not uniform throughout the country. Region I, site of intense contra activity, could hear thirty-two foreign stations. Only two Nicaraguan government stations broadcast in this region. Region I's neighbor, mountainous Region VI comprising the departments of Matagalpa and Jinotega, also the site of contra actions, was penetrated by twenty-eight stations. Special Zones 2 and 3 on the Atlantic were especially susceptible to foreign radio penetration because of their low-lying topography and proximity to the coast. For example, Special Zone 2, also the scene of numerous counterrevolutionary actions from troops based in Costa Rica, had twenty-eight non-Nicaraguan stations available on the ordinary radio. There was only one Nicaraguan station in that zone.

In contrast, the government-owned and -operated CORADEP network had only seventeen stations with signals of varying qualities to cover the entire country. (See Figure 7.1.) They had primary responsibility for responding to the seventy-five external stations penetrating Nicaragua. Formed on April 26, 1981, by Decree 109 of the Junta of National Reconstruction, the People's Broadcasting Corporation (CORADEP) operated its stations with old, poorly maintained equipment of North American manufacture (a situation exacerbated by the 1985 U.S. trade embargo). Everything from tape to microphones was scarce. Transmitter capacities ranged from one to ten kilowatts. CORADEP had two stations in Region I (Estelí and Ocotal); two in Region II (Chinandega and León); four small stations in Region III (Managua); two in Region IV (Granada and Rivas); one in Region V (Juigalpa); and two in Region VI (Matagalpa and Jinotega). In the Special Zones CORADEP had one station each in Puerto Cabezas, Tasba Pri, Bluefields, and San Carlos.

In opposition to the weak CORADEP coverage, five foreign AM stations were clearly the radio superpowers in Nicaragua, with coverage far superior

Figure 7.3   Numbers of foreign AM/FM radio stations penetrating Nicaragua.

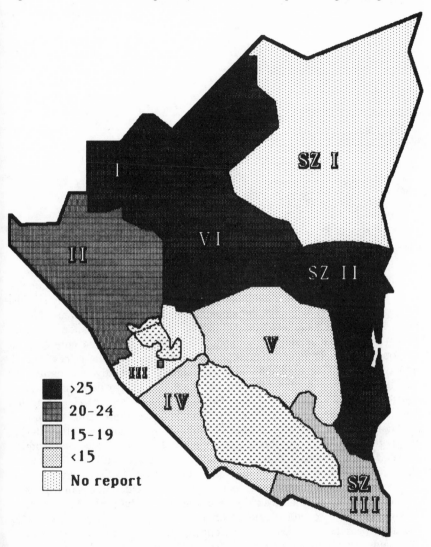

to any Nicaraguan station. These included four Costa Rican stations (TIHB Reloj, TILX Columbia, TIRI Impacto, and TITNT Monumental), and the Voice of America. Three other stations (TISCL Santa Clara from Costa Rica, YSSS Radio El Salvador, and HRN Voice of Honduras) could also be heard widely throughout the country. (See Figure 7.4).

Seventy-four exterior stations heard in Nicaragua were correlated by region, power, and signal quality. (Region III and Special Zone I were not

TABLE 7.2

Foreign AM and FM Radio Stations Penetrating Nicaraguan Territory

Originating Country	Nicaraguan Region							Total No. Stations Penetrating Nicaragua as a Whole
	I	II	IV	V	VI	ZE2	ZE3	
Belize	1	0	0	0	0	0	0	1
Colombia	3	1	0	1	1	3	0	7
Costa Rica	6	6	6	6	9	18	16	26
Cuba	3	0	0	2	2	5	0	5
El Salvador	2	3	0	0	2	0	0	4
Guatemala	0	1	1	0	3	0	0	5
Honduras	12	7	2	2	10	1	0	18
Mexico	2	2	0	1	0	0	0	3
Neth. Antil.	2	1	0	0	0	0	0	2
Panama	0	0	1	0	0	0	0	1
USA	1	1	1	1	1	1	0	1
Venezuela	0	1	0	0	0	0	0	1
Totals	32	23	11	13	28	28	16	74

reported in these data.) Region I and Special Zone II, where action by counterrevolutionaries was greatest, received a flood of high-quality signals. In Region I, which comprises the departments of Estelí, Madriz, and Nuevo Segovia, seventeen stations from Honduras, two from El Salvador, two from Costa Rica, and one each from Mexico, Colombia, and Cuba entered with a "good" signal. Thirteen stations penetrate this region with a "fair" signal, and two stations entered with a "poor" signal. The equivalent figures for Special Zone II, containing the Bluefields area of Zelaya department, were nineteen "good," four "fair," and five "poor." For Region VI (Matagalpa and Jinotega), those figures were ten "good," eleven "fair," and six "poor."

Another rough measure of radio infiltration was total kilowatts entering the region. Here again, Region I led with 2,001 kilowatts of incoming radiated power. Special Zone II was in second place with 743.5 kilowatts (kw), followed by Region II (710.5 kw) and Region VI (534.5 kw).

An examination of kilowatts per population yielded the same pattern. Special Zone III on the Costa Rican border was subjected to 8.0 watts of foreign radio per capita. Region I on the Honduran border received 6.67 watts per capita, whereas Special Zone II, containing the strategic city of Bluefields, was subject to 6.65 watts per capita. Region IV, in contrast, received only 0.79 watts per capita.

Shortwave stations, of course, have a far greater international reach. Though they were not included in this study, all major international broadcasters had serviceable signals throughout Nicaragua and Central America. A U.S. Congress study during the debate on Radio Martí claimed that foreign international broadcasters had far more hours of Spanish programs directed at the Caribbean/Central American region than did U.S. stations. Religious station HCJB, the Voice of the Andes, led the list with

Figure 7.4 Reception quality of leading foreign AM stations in Nicaragua.

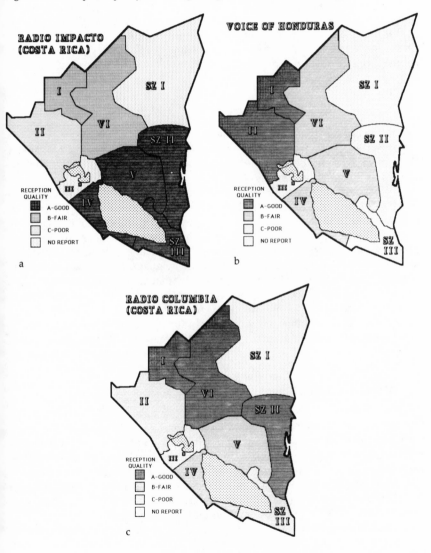

427 hours per week, followed by Cuba, 280; British Broadcasting Company (BBC), 186; Soviet Union, 133; the Federal Republic of Germany, 98; Voice of America, 84; China, 67; Albania, 56; South Korea, 56; and the German Democratic Republic, 54.[14]

Besides these strong international AM voices, numerous regional shortwave broadcasters directed their beams to include Nicaragua. In Region II, the author was able to pick up signals from nine regional shortwave stations. These stations were particularly interesting because they included two clandestine stations and three religious stations as well as commercial stations.

Content of Foreign Radio

The following remarks on the ideological perspectives of these stations were based on transcripts of nonmusic content made from recordings in Chinandega (Region II), Nicaragua, during July 1985 as well as transcripts of the Foreign Broadcast Information Service.

The war of ideas against Nicaragua had four orientations. Perhaps the most pervasive penetration of alien values came from foreign commercial stations. Not only were their economic messages often at odds with the goals of Nicaraguan government, but their overall ideological line was markedly anti-Sandinista and procontra. The second orientation included several clandestine/insurgent stations with language and content that was so at variance with normal radio programming that all but the most committed listener may have tuned them out. Next, and most powerful, were governmental stations such as the Voice of America. Finally, the fourth group, foreign religious stations, was generally composed of the evangelical/proselytizing variety that many devout Nicaraguan Catholics might have disregarded.

COMMERCIAL STATIONS

The foreign commercial stations whose signals could be received in Nicaragua aired material both directly and indirectly inimical to the revolutionary process in Nicaragua. First, through commercial advertisements they pushed values of consumerism. Of course, this was no conspiracy—they were simply trying to sell products to citizens in their own countries. But in Nicaragua these messages must have caused anxiety. For although most of the productive capacity of the country had remained in private hands, U.S. programs of economic destabilization and the contra war itself had cause an economic situation in which most Nicaraguans had little access to anything except the bare necessities. Radio Valle, broadcasting from Choluteca, Honduras, to an area which included Regions I and II in Nicaragua, was typical of many small commercial stations in that revolutionary country. Advertising dominated the nonmusic content of the station. Headache medicine and youth potions ("for bad moods and good figures") appealed to the symptoms of life's stresses, and tire and battery ads appealed to the desire for physical and psychic mobility. Eye drops, nail polish, numerous brands of coffee, and appliances—all contributed to an impression in the mind of the average Nicaraguan that life was better outside the country. If the negative impact of this commercialism was largely unintended, the political slant and content of the news and commentary on foreign commercial stations audible in Nicaragua appear to have been more deliberate. Take, for instance, Costa Rica's Radio Columbia, one of the region's true super-stations of commercialism. Although quick to point out apparent violations of Costa Rican territorial integrity by the Sandinista Popular Army, Radio Columbia never mentioned Costa Rican acquiescence to the counterrevolutionaries operating inside its territory. One civic affairs announcement on Radio Columbia, sponsored by the Costa Rica Institute for the Entrepreneurial Sector, summarized the Costa Rican self-perception of democracy that this station was fond of projecting: "Costa Rica is a free, independent and sovereign country. Costa Ricans know what this means because they live it daily. You don't fear persecution or unjust imprisonment. Because you, Costa Rican, are a citizen in a free country. Costa Rican democracy is a model for the world."

Especially biased against the Nicaraguan revolution was Radio Impacto, heard throughout Nicaragua. Broadcasting with 50,000 watts from San Pedro de Montes de Oca, Costa Rica, Impacto was viewed by the Sandinistas as a vehicle for contra disinformation. Its station identification stated its perceived self-image: "from San José, Costa Rica, capital of Latin American democracy."

Radio Impacto could be counted on to carry the news and views of the counterrevolution as well as of the internal opposition forces in Managua. About one-quarter of the items on a typical Impacto newscast dealt with Nicaragua. In a sense, Radio Impacto was much like Radio Free Europe and Radio Liberty, stations that broadcast only to the socialist countries of Eastern Europe and bill themselves as alternative home services. During the Nicaraguan elections in November 1984, I heard Impacto warning its listeners on the Atlantic Coast that contra attacks were likely and that people should stay away from the polls for their own safety. (The attacks did not take place.)

Perhaps the most blatant incident of disinformation during my monitoring of foreign radio signals was that of HRN, the Voice of Honduras, broadcasting at 10 kilowatts from Tegucigalpa. As the self-proclaimed "voice of the Honduran government and people," HRN crossed that gray boundary dividing commercial from governmental broadcasters. On July 4, 1985, the station broadcast the following report during a morning talk show:

We interrupt this program with the latest news. Attention friends of HRN in the entire country. The Nicaraguan People's Army is currently bombarding the village of Alauca. This morning at 7 in the morning the bombardments began in this village on the Nicaraguan border.

We are informed that a great number of the residents of this village have abandoned their houses. For that reason, Alauca, which has about 1,500 people, remains totally isolated. A great number of people have arrived at

El Paraíso and others have left their homes to find refuge in other locales in the region.

We want to point out that this is another violation of our country's integrity by the Nicaraguan People's Army.

Thus began the broadcast report of a fictitious attack by the Nicaraguan army on Honduran territory. Subsequent checking revealed no other mention of the attack in the Honduran or U.S. press. Radio Sandino from Managua denied the charge: "HRN is an old Honduran radio station controlled by the U.S. embassy and sets the pace of its reports against Nicaragua."[15] Even the Honduran president's information secretary stated that "the climate being created by the communications media is a warmongering climate."[16]

CLANDESTINE STATIONS

At least three anti-Sandinista clandestine stations had a direct bearing on events in Nicaragua: la Voz de Sandino, Radio 15 de Septiembre and Radio Miskut. A fourth, Radio Liberación, was under construction at the time this was being written. Although it claimed to be broadcasting from within Nicaragua, Radio 15 de Septiembre was thought to be located in Valle de Angeles, thirty kilometers northeast of Tegucigalpa. Run by Frank Arana, a Nicaraguan expatriate,[17] it was the official voice of the Nicaraguan Democratic Front (FDN), the contra organization operating in Honduras. Its orientation was vehemently anti-Sandinista.

Broadcasts monitored in July 1985 contained interviews with FDN commanders and Nicaraguan peasants, who revealed details of Sandinista "repression" and "harassment." They also included statements by FDN leaders about battles, death counts, and promises of further violence, military music, coded messages, and announcements. One interview with "Johnny" and "Henry," both instructors of a regional command, boasted that "one day we will walk freely in Nicaragua. Don't worry, we will be in the cities. We will kill the contemptuous Sandinista army that is killing our women and children. We don't want a communist regime. We are commandos for freedom and democracy." To the sounds of martial music, the announcer proclaimed Radio 15 de Septiembre, "voice of the Christian freedom commandos. . . . The puppets of Castro will be destroyed."

Many claims were made about the support of the Nicaraguan people for the contra forces. Commander "Dennis" said "about 80% of the people are on our side. About 40% in the cities are on our side." The Nicaraguan people, he claimed, were against the "Sandino-communists." "The number of tanks makes no difference because the people support us. . . . We have about 20,000 commandos." Announcers excoriated the Sandinista Defense Committees and the so-called divine mobs allegedly operated by the government.

FDN leader Adolfo Calero Portocarrero was often at the microphone exhorting his supporters and trying to win converts: "With God and patriotism we will destroy communism. Our forces are growing each day.

. . . Our people should not believe what *Nuevo Diario* and *Barricada* [Managua newspapers that support the Sandinistas] are saying. Radio Sandino and Radio Nacional [sic] are full of lies. Soon we will be in Managua. They are not capable of confronting our troops. This is the reality."
Radio 15 de Septiembre featured statements by ordinary Nicaraguans who had "escaped Sandinista tyranny." One woman complained of the Sandinista militia raping women and oppressing Nicaraguan peasants. "You have two small meals a day to keep the Sandinistas in power. Young Nicaraguans, your families are starving. 1985 will be the year of victory."
At the opposite side of the country, broadcasting from northern Costa Rica, was the Voice of Sandino, the official station of the Democratic Revolutionary Alliance. Ex-Sandinista Edén Pastora was often heard conducting lessons in guerrilla warfare for Nicaraguans who oppose the government:

A beehive—at night you cut a hole in the beehive, place it at the edge of the road, tie a 50-meter rope to it, and pull on the rope when the enemy was close—becomes a weapon. . . . A nail sticking out of a piece of wood covered with mud becomes a powerful weapon, especially if you smear horse or human manure on the tip. This immediately becomes a mortal weapon. When the nail penetrates a shoe it punctures the sole of the soldier's foot and causes gangrene or tetanus.

Fight, fight, fight is our war slogan! Our slogan is no longer "Free Homeland or Death" because we no longer want to die. Our slogan is now: Free Homeland or Kill![18]

The Misura organization, run by Miskito Indian contra Steadman Fagoth, was operating Radio Miskut in the Honduran town of Rus Rus, close to Fagoth's house. The station broadcasts in Miskito to the indigenous populations along the Atlantic coast region of Nicaragua. No transcripts or recordings of this station were available for this study.
In 1986, renewed U.S. Congressional funding included yet another electronic weapon in the low-intensity war against Nicaragua. As part of the contras' campaign to win the hearts and minds of Nicaraguan citizens, Radio Liberación was expected go on the air in 1987 to transmit anti-Sandinista songs, soap operas, editorials and commentary by contra leaders. Broadcasting from El Salvador, this 50,000-watt station would have five times the power of the largest transmitter in Nicaragua. Day and night it would reach most of the country with a strong signal. But unlike its predecessors, Radio Liberación would broadcast on the AM band.
To be run under the name of the United Nicaraguan Opposition, Radio Liberación was likely to have a far greater impact than previous contra efforts on shortwave. The signal itself would be beyond the Sandinistas' capacity to jam effectively. The cost of electricity and transmitter maintenance, and the need for dozens of such devices, would make that option prohibitive. As a result, polished programs produced in Miami and Washington would reach deeply into Nicaraguan public awareness in the middle of the most

listened-to band on the radio dial. One planned program, "Pancho Madrigal," reportedly would recount angry recriminations about life under the Sandinistas.[19]

GOVERNMENTAL STATIONS

The Voice of America (VOA) had been heard for years throughout Nicaragua from transmitters in the Caribbean. But because the VOA had just launched a new AM transmitter in Costa Rica, the signal quality was among the best heard in Nicaragua. Sometimes this signal obliterated even Nicaraguan stations such as Radio Mundial on an adjacent frequency. These facilities retransmitted the VOA's Spanish service, directed at Central and South America. Though it was a hemispheric, and therefore generalist, news and information service, numerous news items focused on Nicaragua. Here, for example, is a sample of Voice of America's coverage during the sixth anniversary of the Nicaraguan revolution:

> July 18, 1985: The Sandinista government tomorrow commemorates the sixth anniversary of its revolution at a time when the country is confronting serious economic problems and a guerrilla war of four years' duration. Sandinista leaders say 400,000 people will attend the ceremonies but among the mass media covering the event will not be an American Spanish-speaking crew that was deported.

> July 18, 1985: In interviews published on the evening of the celebrations, President Daniel Ortega reiterated his belief that the United States is planning to invade his country. . . . In Washington, President Reagan's security advisor Robert MacFarlane repeated that the U.S. has no intention of invading Nicaragua.

> July 19, 1985: The United States has offered a reward of $100,000 for information leading to the arrest of the murderers of six Americans in El Salvador last month. . . . The reward was offered after an accusation by the U.S. government that Nicaragua could be directly involved in terrorist plans against Americans in Honduras.

> July 20, 1985: The Nicaraguan government aided the terrorist attack carried out last month in El Salvador.

No mention was made of Nicaragua's progress in six years or its ongoing struggle against an external military threat. The reports clearly insinuated that Nicaragua was responsible for the deaths of six Americans in El Salvador. This reinforced a constant propaganda theme—that Nicaragua was trying to foment revolution elsewhere in the region.

The VOA, like the clandestine contra stations, gave ample coverage to Nicaragua's enemies. When Edén Pastora's helicopter crashed, daily news items followed his rescue and recovery. The hierarchy of the Nicaraguan Catholic Church was especially highlighted:

July 24, 1985: Nicaraguan Catholic bishops oppose a national fast planned by the so-called liberation theology [sic] in support of Foreign Relations Minister Miguel D'Escoto's hunger fast. . . . It warned that only the bishops have the authority to invoke a religious act. . . . Minister D'Escoto has been suspended as a priest by the Vatican because he assumed a governmental post. . . . Father D'Escoto is protesting U.S. support of Nicaraguan rebels trying to overthrow his government.

The "so-called liberation theology," the VOA failed to inform, comprised many of Nicaragua's churchgoers. The report legitimized the minority hierarchy's absolute powers. The item also called the contras "rebels" and attributed their aims clearly to overthrow. The Voice of America's orientation often put it in the same camp with other destabilizing stations such as Radio Impacto and the Voice of Honduras.

One interesting development was the Voice of America's overt attempts to circumvent Costa Rican law, which prohibited foreign nationals (individuals or corporations) from operating a radio station in the country. But the law did not prohibit the Voice of America from operating a Costa Rican–owned transmitter facility. After learning that the VOA would be violating Costa Rica neutrality by setting up a repeater facility, a group of conservative Costa Rican media executives, journalists, and politicians set up the Costa Rican Association for Information and Culture. One of the leaders of this group was Lilia Berrocal, owner of seven other stations, three of which were already penetrating Nicaraguan territory. Berrocal defended the move, saying that "the people of northern Costa Rica have been exposed to extensive propaganda from the Nicaraguan Communication system."[20]

The Voice of America, through formal agreements with Costa Rican citizens, installed a repeater station at Ciudad Quesada, in north-central Costa Rica and began broadcasting on January 19, 1985. The transmitter made a semblance of being a local station by sending out locally produced material of the Costa Rican Association of Information and Culture. The installations were made up of four seventy-meter towers, directional at 100,000 watts. Besides the $3.2 million authorized to build the facility, the VOA was to give $168,000 each year to the private association that controlled the transmitter.

Though the agreement was criticized by the Costa Rican Congress as circumventing the country's neutrality, it was initialed in the home of President Luis Alberto Monge.[21] As partial compensation to feelings that Costa Rica's neutrality had been violated, the agreement stated that the VOA could use the transmitter only 60 percent of the time.

Other U.S. activities in the region pointed to an increase in the Central American radio war. The United States was promoting an AM/FM transmitter in Honduras to beam Voice of America programs to Nicaragua. The station was to be located at the airfield in San Lorenzo, on the Gulf of Fonseca.[22] Honduran law stipulated that radio stations on its territory were not permitted more than one-third non-Honduran ownership.

Part of the Voice of America's expansion in the hemisphere was a $150 million shortwave and mediumwave relay station in Puerto Rico to cover the Caribbean and Central and South America. This project was slated for completion in 1990. Finally, site preparation and engineering studies were reportedly under way for a VOA transmitter in Belize.

RELIGIOUS STATIONS

Finally, some brief mention must be made of the religious stations broadcasting to Nicaragua. More than 90 percent of Nicaraguans are practicing Catholics; many found themselves in opposition to the Catholic hierarchy, which supported Nicaragua's enemies. Several religious stations sent signals to the country, but the content of these broadcasts was evangelical Protestant. The Lighthouse of the Caribbean (Faro del Caribe) from Costa Rica had North American preachers who insisted that "God helps only those who use the Bible." The Evangelical Voice from Honduras was owned by the Conservative Home Baptist Mission Society in Wheaton, Illinois. It blamed the region's problems on lack of faith: "Souls are dying today because Christians are not preaching the word of God. Christians are sleeping." External religious stations opposed both the Catholic hierarchy and the liberation theology movement.

International Law Implications

The Reagan administration's strategy for overthrowing the Nicaraguan government included using mass international propaganda as an essential component in subverting public opinion and individual morale of Nicaragua's citizens. Much of this broadcast onslaught was being carried out by the U.S. Information Agency (VOA) and the Central Intelligence Agency (contra stations). Commercial stations in alliance with North American capitalism and liberally bribed by the CIA (see the sources mentioned in note 6) were also doing their part. Over time the extensive complicity of clandestine and commercial stations in these violations of international law was likely to emerge.

Foreign radio stations were directing broadcast provocations against Nicaragua that threatened regional peace and harmony. This aggression violated not only fundamental principles of international law but also specific international accords. The Declaration on Principles of International Law Concerning Friendly Relations and Cooperation Among States in Accordance with the Charter of the United Nations, October 25, 1970, specifically prohibited "propaganda for wars of aggression." This complemented the International Covenant on Civil and Political Rights of December 16, 1966, wherein "any propaganda for war shall be prohibited by law." The declaration precluded not only armed intervention but also "all other forms of interference or attempted threats . . . against [a state's] political, economic and cultural elements." This prohibition included subversive foreign broadcasts attempting to change Nicaragua's governing system or trying to foment discontent and to incite unrest.

The electronic aggression against Nicaragua violated numerous international legal agreements. UN General Assembly Resolution 110(II) on "Measures to be Taken Against Propaganda and the Inciters of a New War," passed on November 3, 1947, "condemns all forms of propaganda . . . either designed or likely to provoke, or encourage any threat to the peace, breach of the peace or act of aggression." The International Convention Concerning the Use of Broadcasting in the Cause of Peace, of September 23, 1936, "undertake[s] to ensure that transmissions . . . shall not constitute an incitement to war . . . [and] to prohibit and, if occasion arises, to stop without delay within respective territories any transmission likely to harm good international understanding." The Convention on the International Right of Correction guaranteed states the right to correct inaccurate information disseminated in other states. Finally, the International Covenant on Civil and Political Rights, adopted on December 16, 1966, explicitly bound states to prohibit, by law, any propaganda for war.

In the opinion of this author, stations HRN (the Voice of Honduras) and TIRI (Radio Impacto from Costa Rica) had violated these proscriptions and warranted being brought to account before the World Court. In addition, the attempt by the Voice of America and the CIA-directed contra stations to flood Nicaraguan airspace was a provocation against Nicaragua's sovereignty.

Conclusion

During the Reagan years, Nicaragua had become the target of a war that was as much psychological as military. Bombarded with propaganda-laden radio and television signals transmitted by the varied, powerful, and rapidly growing foreign telecommunications systems encircling their tiny country, the Sandinistas were at a distinct disadvantage. Remarkably, however, even after five years of this type of attack, the Sandinistas still retained the support of a large—probably majority—segment of the Nicaraguan population, whereas the contras were almost universally despised, even by citizens critical of the Sandinistas. Among other things, the Reagan administration had badly underestimated the Nicaraguan people's passion for national self-determination.

Acknowledgments

The author wishes to thank Robert Merlino, graduate student in the School of Telecommunications, Ohio University, for his help in this study.

Notes

1. Andy F. Messing, "Focusing on Low-Intensity Conflicts: Force Here, Social Justice There? Tend to them All, or Fail," *Los Angeles Times*, January 14, 1986, section II, p. 5.

2. Tayacán, *Psychological Operations in Guerrilla Warfare: The CIA's Nicaragua Manual*, with essays by Joanne Omang and Aryeh Neier (New York: Vintage Books, 1985), p. 33.

3. *Foreign Broadcast Information Service*, May 21, 1985, p. P11.

4. Tayacán, *Psychological Operations*, p. 34.

5. *New York Times*, November 5, 1986.

6. "U.S. and Contras Find Ally in Costa Rica's Three Major Dailies," *Christian Science Monitor*, August 18, 1986, p. 12; and Martha Honey, "Contra coverage—Paid for by the CIA," *Columbia Journalism Review*, March/April 1987, pp. 31, 32.

7. Bonnie J. Brownlee, "Broadcasting in Nicaragua," in Joseph Straubhaar and Elizabeth Mahan, eds., *Broadcasting in Latin America* (Philadelphia: Temple University Press, in press).

8. Interviews with Oscar Oviedo Mosquera, subdirector, People's Radio Broadcasting Corporation, Managua, July 1985; and Medardo Mendoza H., Sandinista Television System, April 1986.

9. Richard Millett, *Guardians of the Dynasty* (Maryknoll, N.Y.: Orbis Books, 1977), p. 76.

10. John Spicer Nichols, "The [Nicaraguan] Media," in Thomas W. Walker, ed., *Nicaragua: The First Five Years* (New York: Praeger Publishers, 1985), pp. 183–200.

11. Carlos F. Chamorro, "Experiencias de la Comunicación Revolucionaria en Nicaragua," paper presented at the International Forum on Social Communication, Mexico City, June 1982, quoted in Brownlee, "Broadcasting in Nicaragua."

12. Interview with Mendoza.

13. Ibid.

14. Howard H. Frederick, *Cuban-American Radio Wars* (Norwood, N.J.: Ablex Publishing Corporation, 1986), p. 20.

15. *Foreign Broadcast Information Service*, July 5, 1985, p. P19.

16. *Foreign Broadcast Information Service*, July 8, 1985, p. P21.

17. "War of the Airwaves," *Latin America Regional Reports*, August 16, 1985, p. 6.

18. *Foreign Broadcast Information Service*, April 22, 1985, p. P22.

19. Maureen Meehan, "Briefing: U.S. Pre-Empts Costa Rican Airwaves," *In These Times*, October 31–November 6, 1984, p. 5.

20. Marjorie Miller, "Contras' Radio to Offer Soaps and Discontent," *Los Angeles Times*, December 25, 1986, p. I14.

21. Walter Pincus, "U.S. Enhances VOA, Sets Pact in Costa Rica," *Washington Post*, September 11, 1984, p. 1.

22. Ibid.

EIGHT

The Diplomatic Front

WILLIAM GOODFELLOW

From 1981 onward the Reagan administration and the Sandinistas engaged in on-again, off-again negotiations. During summer 1981 and again during spring 1986, agreement seemed possible. However, at the end of six years both sides were even farther apart, and a negotiated settlement seemed unlikely at least until a new U.S. administration assumes office in 1989.

The Nicaraguan government, fearing that the Reagan administration's hostility threatened to destroy the revolution, was eager to negotiate an agreement that would block what the Sandinistas perceived as the U.S. government's campaign to overthrow them. Many in the government in Managua, however, doubted that such an agreement was possible while Ronald Reagan was president. Those who held this view, perhaps a majority, believed that the negotiations were useful to buy time and keep the Americans off balance until a new, more reasonable administration came into office. Víctor Hugo Tinoco, Nicaragua's deputy foreign minister and chief negotiator, took the long view in March 1986: "Some day, maybe not next month or next year, the Americans will sign an agreement with us."[1]

There never was a consensus within the Reagan administration for a negotiated settlement with Nicaragua that would leave the Sandinistas in power. Within the State Department there were career officers who have worked hard for an agreement and sincerely believed that a bilateral or regional treaty that contained the Sandinistas would best serve U.S. national interests. There is considerable doubt, however, whether those in the State Department favoring containment of the Sandinista revolution could have delivered even if a successful treaty had been negotiated. The CIA, the National Security Council, the White House staff, powerful figures in the Pentagon, and other influential voices on the Reagan Right never wavered from their commitment to "roll back communism" by overthrowing the

---

This chapter draws extensively upon reports written by Jesse Biddle, Jim Morrell, and William Goodfellow published by the Center for International Policy from 1983 to 1986.

Sandinistas. For them negotiations, either bilateral or regional under the sponsorship of the Contadora countries, were an impediment to using stronger measures to oust the government in Managua. Although the negotiations were a convenient smoke screen to hide the administration's real agenda and deflect domestic and international criticism, Washington saw the bilateral talks and in particular the Contadora negotiations as counterproductive because they offered the Sandinistas a high-profile public forum where they could appear reasonable. Moreover, negotiations nurtured what the administration considered the false hope that the Nicaraguan problem could be dealt with without resort to military force.

Off to a Bad Start

The new Reagan administration was hardly predisposed to good relations with the one-and-a-half-year-old revolutionary government in Managua. The 1980 Republican party platform had stated, "We deplore the Marxist Sandinista takeover of Nicaragua." Further poisoning relations was Nicaragua's support for the "final offensive" by the guerrillas in El Salvador against the U.S.-backed government. The Sandinistas facilitated the transshipment of arms and supplies from Cuba to the guerrillas of the Faribundo Martí National Liberation front (FMLN) in El Salvador and probably provided some logistical help as well. In addition to their ideological kinship with the FMLN, the Sandinistas felt their own security interests would be served by a victory of the Left in El Salvador. No longer would Nicaragua be the only revolutionary government in Central America.

By the end of February 1981 it became clear that the "final offensive" would not topple the Salvadoran government. Lawrence Pezzullo, then U.S. ambassador to Nicaragua, stressed to the Sandinista leadership the U.S. government's strong objections to the arms flow. The Nicaraguans quickly opted for a more pragmatic course, and according to Ambassador Pezzullo, by April the shipments had dropped to insignificant levels.[2]

On March 1 Secretary of State Alexander Haig stated that U.S. economic aid to Nicaragua, suspended during the last days of the Carter administration, would be resumed when the arms flow to El Salvador stopped. Later in March a high-ranking Nicaraguan official stated, "The Sandinista Directorate will accommodate the United States. The Directorate will follow a hands-off policy toward El Salvador. In return, it expects a restoration of U.S. aid and a general improvement in relations."[3] Although the State Department acknowledged that the arms flow to El Salvador had abated, U.S. economic aid was not resumed, and U.S. rhetoric became increasingly harsh.

The Enders Talks: August–October 1981

Thomas Enders, then assistant secretary of state for Latin America, gained a certain notoriety when in 1973 as chargé d'affaires at the U.S. Embassy in Phnom Penh he personally helped direct the B-52 bombing campaign in Cambodia.[4] Six feet, eight inches tall, described by his colleagues as pompous but brilliant, he must have seemed the personification of the U.S. government to the Sandinistas.

On August 12 Secretary Enders arrived in Managua for a series of six meetings. In his first meeting with then–Junta coordinator Daniel Ortega, Secretary Enders restated U.S. opposition to Nicaragua's support for the Salvadoran guerrillas and called for an end to Nicaragua's arms buildup. In return, Secretary Enders pledged that the United States would vigorously enforce U.S. neutrality laws regarding Nicaraguan exiles already undertaking paramilitary training in the United States. Moreover, the United States would publicly declare not to use force or the threat of force against Nicaragua. Finally, the United States would resume economic aid to Nicaragua and would establish cultural exchanges.

It is unclear how seriously the Nicaraguans took the talks with Secretary Enders. Foreign Minister Miguel d'Escoto expressed optimism when he told reporters in Managua, "It is premature to judge the American intentions. We are committed to and continue to be committed to bettering the increasingly deteriorating relationship with the United States. We have made it a priority to make every effort to reach an understanding, a *modus vivendi*, with the United States."[5]

In the most detailed account of the 1981 negotiations yet published, Roy Gutman, a reporter for *Newsday* in Washington, argued that "the United States itself helped scuttle the talks." According to Gutman, the United States never presented the Nicaraguans with a complete set of demands. Former Nicaraguan Ambassador to the United States Arturo Cruz was shown but never given a draft of the U.S. demands in the security section of the treaty. Cruz, quoted by Gutman, called the demands "like the conditions of a victorious power."[6]

The Nicaraguan negotiators, in addition to being insulted and angered by what they considered unreasonable U.S. demands, were unsure of Secretary Enders's mandate. Did his position represent the consensus of the Reagan administration or merely the State Department's position?

At their final meeting on August 13, Secretary Enders proposed to Junta coordinator Daniel Ortega the exchange of proposals in five areas. These included a nonaggression pact with Nicaragua in exchange for a promise from that country not to use force against its neighbors, plus proposals on other security issues, cultural exchanges, and U.S. economic aid.

The first of these proposals was delivered on September 8. It promised vigorous enforcement of U.S. neutrality laws regarding Nicaraguan exiles training in the United States. Attached to the proposal, however, was a notice saying that the remaining U.S. economic aid to Nicaragua had been canceled, hardly the sort of gesture intended to encourage good will and flexibility on the part of the Nicaraguans. Eight days later a second draft on nonintervention was delivered, but subsequent drafts were never presented.[7]

Because of their inexperience—the new government had been in power for only two years—and their deep distrust of the United States, the

Nicaraguans never presented a substantive reply to the U.S. demands. Also at work was national pride, the Sandinistas belief that as a sovereign nation they could negotiate as equals with the United States. As a Mexican diplomat noted in an interview with me in 1986, "We have never been able to convince the Sandinistas that although in theory Nicaragua and the United States are equals, in the real world it is a different story. We have never been able to convince them that they must swallow their pride and go more than half way, much more than half way, to satisfy the Americans."

Most observers doubted that the basis for an agreement existed in 1981 regardless of the response from Nicaragua. Ambassador Pezzullo, however, disagreed. "There are magic moments . . . little windows of opportunity, and then they close, and everybody's caught with their prejudice in place." He felt Secretary Enders "made a good-faith effort," but the unresponsiveness of the Nicaraguans and the passage of time doomed the attempt.[8]

On October 7 Daniel Ortega, speaking before the United Nations, delivered a blistering condemnation of U.S. intervention in Central America. The Americans saw the speech as a violation of an understanding not to escalate public rhetoric during the talks. Moreover, during summer 1981 the Sandinistas repeatedly closed down the opposition paper *La Prensa*, further strengthening the position of hardliners in the Reagan administration opposed to any negotiations with the Sandinistas.

In November 1981 the National Security Council (NSC) drew up a broad range of policy options for covert actions against Nicaragua, including the overthrow of the Sandinista government. The plan finally approved by the NSC included military aid to allies in Central America and a broad program for covert action. According to leaked NSC documents, the United States was to "work with foreign governments as appropriate" to conduct various covert operations "against the Cuban presence and Cuban-Sandinista supported infrastructure in Nicaragua and elsewhere in Central America."[9]

On December 2, 1981, President Reagan signed the legally required "Presidential Finding" that such covert activity was in the national interest. The secret war against Nicaragua was on.

The Mexican Initiative

As relations between Nicaragua and the United States deteriorated throughout 1981, the Mexican government became concerned about the direction of the Reagan administration's policies. Because of its geographic proximity and shared cultural heritage, Mexico found it hard to ignore the conflicts engulfing Central America. In 1979 Mexico helped thwart a U.S. effort to have an Organization of American States (OAS) peacekeeping force prevent the Sandinistas from assuming power after Somoza's defeat. In August 1981, Mexico and France issued a joint declaration recognizing the FMLN-FDR opposition in El Salvador as a "representative political force" and urging the government of El Salvador to negotiate with all parties to the conflict.[10]

As news of U.S. covert operations against Nicaragua began appearing in the press in January and February 1982 the Mexicans became alarmed. In a major effort to change the course of Washington's policies, President José López Portillo of Mexico presented a comprehensive peace plan on February 21 in Managua. Emphasizing that it would be a "gigantic historical mistake" for the United States to militarily intervene in Central America, López Portillo called on Washington to end its use of force in the region and to disband the contras and other Nicaraguan exiles training in the United States. He also called for a system of treaties of nonaggression between Nicaragua and the United States and between Nicaragua and its neighbors.[11]

President López Portillo's plan received widespread support, although not from the Reagan administration. Nicaragua and Cuba agreed to negotiate within López Portillo's framework. Over one hundred U.S. congressmen signed a letter urging President Reagan to accept the Mexican offer.

Second Round of U.S.-Nicaraguan Negotiations: Spring 1982

To appear responsive to international pressure and to quell growing domestic opposition to its policy in Central America, the Reagan administration presented an eight-point proposal to Nicaragua on April 8. The proposal, presented by then–U.S. Ambassador to Nicaragua Anthony Quainton, was for the most part a restatement of Secretary Enders's 1981 proposal with one important addition. The new proposal called for "the Nicaraguan government's continued commitment, in line with earlier pledges, to permit political pluralism, a mixed economy and nonalignment in foreign affairs as a determinant of future relations with the United States."[12]

On April 14 Nicaragua responded with a fourteen-point agenda and stated that it had no objections to discussing the eight U.S. points. However, the Nicaraguans insisted that the talks be held in Mexico with the Mexicans present as moderators. The United States responded on April 29, insisting that any dialogue should take place strictly between the United States and Nicaragua and that talks should be held at the ambassadorial level. Ambassador Quainton conveyed Washington's position to the Nicaraguans: "I must note that your response did not direct itself to the essential question of Nicaraguan support of the guerrilla and terrorist groups in other countries. Progress in this areas is essential for our dialogue to be successful. . . . Until there is some sign from you that you are willing to seriously address yourselves to these matters, we believe that these conversations ought to take place within normal diplomatic channels."[13]

On May 7, 1982, the Nicaraguans responded to the eight points of the U.S. proposal. The Nicaraguan response emphasized the lack of evidence to support the U.S. assertion that Nicaragua was trafficking arms and offering material support to the Salvadoran insurgency. Nevertheless, the Nicaraguans stated that they "would be willing to exchange viewpoints and discuss the issue" of limiting their arms and military forces.[14]

The last of the spring 1982 exchanges was issued on July 1 by the United States. The U.S. response complained about the unhelpful negative tone of the earlier Nicaraguan note, took issue with most of the Nicaraguan positions, and finally offered to send a U.S. technical assistance team to Managua to help the Nicaraguans locate the "command-and-control elements of the Salvadoran Guerrilla United Revolutionary Directorate" that Americans said were located in the vicinity of Managua.[15] An examination of the exchange of notes suggests that the Americans viewed the process as primarily a propaganda exercise. Although the Nicaraguans showed some receptivity to U.S. concerns, the United States increased its demands and decreased its commitment to dialogue.

The full extent of the Reagan administration's cynicism was revealed a year later when a National Security Council document was leaked to the press. The NSC policy paper, produced in April 1982 when the talks were in progress, called for a "more active campaign to turn around Mexico and Social Democrats in Europe" while "in the meantime keep them isolated on Central American issues." The policy toward Nicaragua, according to NSC, was working: "The Sandinistas are under increased pressure because of our covert efforts and because of the poor state of their economy." The NSC also called for "increasing the pressure on Nicaragua and Cuba to increase for them the costs of interventionism." Finally, it revealed the administration's rather limited commitment to negotiations when it stated that the United States should "co-opt [the] negotiations issue to avoid congressionally-mandated negotiations, which would work against our interests."[16]

Extensive press coverage of the second round of U.S.-Nicaraguan talks exposed the Reagan administration's bad faith. In August 1982 the U.S. abandoned bilateral negotiations in favor of a public campaign to project a more conciliatory stance. Behind the scenes, however, the administration was increasing its military pressures on Nicaragua.

Contadora Is Born

As relations between the United States and Nicaragua continued to deteriorate, U.S. allies in the region began to take a more active role in attempting to resolve the deepening dispute. On September 7, 1982, the presidents of Mexico and Venezuela issued a joint declaration on the Nicaraguan-Honduran border conflict. The declaration called on the United States to put an end to its "support, organization, and emplacement of former Somocista guards" and for Nicaragua to "avoid military engagement in its border with Honduras."[17]

On January 8 and 9, 1983, the foreign ministers of Colombia, Mexico, Panama, and Venezuela met on the small Panamanian island of Contadora. In a bulletin issued following the meeting, they made an urgent appeal to all Central American countries to reduce tensions and resolve differences through dialogue and negotiation. They emphasized that the conflicts in Central America must be removed from the East-West confrontation, external factors "which make them worse."[18]

The foreign ministers of Colombia, Mexico, Panama, and Venezuela—quickly dubbed the Contadora countries—met periodically through spring and summer 1983 and on September 9 issued the Contadora Document of Objectives, which provided the framework for all subsequent Contadora draft agreements. The Document of Objectives was signed by the Contadora foreign ministers and by all five Central American countries. It called for reduction of tensions, establishment of democratic, representative political systems with honest and periodic elections, and national reconciliation. Arms levels were to be reduced, foreign military bases forbidden, and military advisers eliminated. Furthermore, arms trafficking was to be stopped as was any support for groups attempting to undermine or destabilize Central American governments. The Document of Objectives ends with a pledge to begin negotiations to formalize an agreement between the five Central American countries and establish adequate control and verification mechanisms.[19]

The Contadora negotiators continued meeting throughout winter 1983 and spring 1984. At one point there were over one hundred technical advisers and diplomats in Panama working on a draft agreement. Finally on September 7, 1984, in Panama City the Contadora foreign ministers presented the "Contadora Act for Peace and Cooperation in Central America." The act followed closely the Document of Objectives of a year earlier and provided for elaborate verification procedures, including the right of on-site inspection by the Verification and Control Commission to investigate possible violations.

On the day it was issued U.S. Secretary of State George Shultz praised the draft treaty. He called it "an important step forward." Secretary Shultz noted its conditional acceptance by Costa Rica, El Salvador, Guatemala, and Honduras, and added, "Nicaragua, on the other hand, has rejected key elements of the draft, including those dealing with binding obligations to internal democratization and to reductions in arms and troop levels."[20]

The State Department was taken completely by surprise when two weeks later Nicaraguan President Ortega sent a letter to the Contadora countries agreeing to sign the Contadora agreement. "We inform you of the Nicaraguan government's decision to accept in its totality, immediately and without modifications, the revised proposal submitted September 7 by the Contadora group."[21] The Nicaraguan acceptance included the sections "dealing with binding obligations to internal democratization and to reductions in arms and troop levels" referred to by Secretary Shultz.

A State Department spokesperson, reflecting the department's surprise and confusion, said, "It's not at all clear to me that in the long run Nicaragua won't come to regret its precipitous action."[22] The U.S. government, losing its earlier enthusiasm for the agreement, was now calling it "unsatisfactory" and "one-sided."

Immediately after Nicaragua agreed to sign, the United States initiated "intensive consultations" with Costa Rica, Honduras, and El Salvador, who subsequently insisted on further revisions of the text. A month later the National Security Council could exalt in a secret memo, "We have effectively blocked Contadora group efforts to impose the second draft of the Revised Contadora Act." While publicly continuing to support the Contadora negotiations, the administration privately rejoiced, "We have trumped the latest Nicaraguan/Mexican effort to rush signature of an unsatisfactory Contadora agreement."[23]

Nicaragua's Concessions

In accepting the September 1984 Contadora act, Nicaragua agreed to

- Expel all Soviet-bloc military advisers, estimated by the State Department to number between 2,500 and 3,500.
- Stop all imports of new Soviet weaponry, from Mi-24/Hind helicopters to AK-47 rifles.
- Shrink its 60,000-person army and scrap part of its inventory of weapons.
- End all types of aid to the Salvadoran guerrillas.
- Enter into a dialogue with the internal opposition.
- Let in a verification commission with powers of on-site inspection to verify all these commitments.

Nicaragua's concessions satisfied all the Reagan administration's publicly stated policy objectives. They did not, however, remove the Sandinistas from power, which was the ultimate objective of U.S. policy. Moreover, Contadora called on the United States to accept limits on its military options in Central America. The United States would have had to stop its military exercises within thirty days and close down its military bases and schools in the region within six months. These provisions would have also applied to Nicaragua but would have had no effect because Nicaragua had never allowed foreign military bases or exercises on its territory. The September 1984 draft also would have placed limits on U.S. military aid programs in El Salvador and Honduras and would have expelled U.S. military advisers. Finally, the agreement would have ended U.S. support for the contras and would have made it a violation for Honduras and Costa Rica to have continued to allow the contras to use their territory to launch attacks against Nicaragua.

Manzanillo Talks

On June 1, 1984 Secretary Shultz made a hastily arranged trip to Managua where he spent two hours at the airport conferring with President Ortega. Secretary Shultz proposed bilateral talks between the United States and

Nicaragua. Late in June the talks got under way at the Mexican resort of Manzanillo. The administration's special envoy to Central America, Harry Shlaudeman, represented the United States, and Deputy Foreign Minister Tinoco represented Nicaragua.

At the Manzanillo talks, Nicaragua made the Contadora treaty the basis of its negotiating position, casting doubt once again on the State Department's claim that Nicaragua's announcement that it would sign the Contadora agreement was only a propaganda ploy. Once again the State Department rejected Nicaragua's offer, saying the United States needed to continue its military exercises in Honduras, which the Contadora draft outlawed. The State Department explained, "Given the Sandinista position, agreement would have been possible only if the United States approved the September 7 draft without change, despite the imperfections acknowledged by Contadora participants."[24]

New Contadora Drafts

On October 19, 1984, the foreign ministers of Honduras, El Salvador, and Costa Rica, meeting in Tegucigalpa, Honduras, unveiled a new draft Contadora agreement of their own. Guatemala took a neutral position on the new draft, which was never endorsed by the Contadora countries. The U.S.-inspired "counterdraft" no longer prohibited U.S. military exercises in the region, it deleted the requirement for removal of U.S. bases, it altered the restrictions on military advisers, and it dropped the final protocol that would have bound the United States to uphold the agreement.

The so-called Tegucigalpa draft dampened the prospects for agreement because it was so clearly tilted against Nicaragua. The Contadora nations' next task was to try to incorporate provisions of the September 1984 draft that Nicaragua had agreed to sign with those of the U.S.-inspired counterdraft endorsed by Honduras, El Salvador, and Costa Rica.

On September 12, 1985, the Contadora foreign ministers issued their revised agreement. It incorporated many of the objections the United States had raised through its proxies Costa Rica, El Salvador, and Honduras. The new draft temporarily permitted joint U.S. military exercises in the region, although it limited them in size and duration. As Nicaragua's Deputy Foreign Minister Tinoco saw it, "Contadora felt it was necessary to make concessions to the United States in order to keep the negotiating process alive."[25]

The Nicaraguans were displeased, and on November 11 Nicaraguan President Ortega sent a letter to the presidents of the Contadora countries outlining Nicaragua's objections and making it clear that Nicaragua would not sign this time. President Ortega indicated Nicaragua's acceptance of 100 of the agreement's 117 provisions but objected to provisions that would allow U.S. military exercises to continue and would impose sharp cuts on Nicaragua's troop levels and armaments. Furthermore, President Ortega insisted that the United States sign a nonaggression pact with Nicaragua before his country would sign a new Contadora agreement.

On December 3, disturbed that the Contadora countries were overlooking the threat from the contras, Nicaragua seconded Costa Rica's proposal for a suspension of Contadora negotiations for six months. The Nicaraguans felt that the inauguration of new presidents in Guatemala, Costa Rica, and Honduras would work to their advantage, a decision that proved correct.

Caraballeda Declaration

Meeting at Caraballeda, Venezuela, in January 1986, the four South American countries of the Contadora Support Group—Argentina, Brazil, Peru, and Uruguay—revived the negotiations. With the Contadora countries they issued the "Caraballeda Message on Central America's Peace, Security and Democracy." The Caraballeda Message was essentially a summary of the provisions of the September 1984 Contadora agreement that Nicaragua had accepted. It called for simultaneous work on stopping aid to the contras and resolving the few outstanding issues preventing final agreement on a Contadora treaty.

Three days later, newly elected Guatemalan President Vinicio Cerezo took advantage of the presence of the other Central American presidents at his inauguration in Guatemala City and convinced them to endorse the Caraballeda declaration. Nicaragua, which had called for a six-month suspension of negotiations, returned to the negotiating table.

Panama City Meeting

For Nicaragua the Caraballeda declaration was a diplomatic victory. Virtually all the countries of Latin America were united in calling on Washington to stop supporting the contras. On April 5–6 in Panama City the Contadora and Central American negotiators again met. Mexico opened the meeting by proposing, in the name of all the Contadora countries, that the conference issue an appeal to the United States to suspend consideration of aid to the contras in order to allow time for negotiating and signing a new Contadora agreement. Costa Rica, Honduras, and El Salvador refused and insisted that aid to the contras was an internal U.S. matter outside the scope of Contadora negotiations. They insisted that treaty negotiations go forward without any condemnation of aid to the contras. Nicaragua, however, insisted on the appeal as proposed by Contadora, and the conference was deadlocked for three days.

In one final communiqué, twelve of the thirteen countries present agreed to a proposal to sign a Contadora agreement on June 6. Only Nicaragua refused to agree. The Latin solidarity of Caraballeda was shattered. Nicaragua refused to agree to disarm in the face of the Reagan administration's military escalation, dismaying even liberal members of the U.S. House of Representatives who had traveled to Panama City to observe the negotiations. When asked whether he thought Nicaragua was the obstacle to agreement, Peru's President Alan Garcia tried to explain Nicaragua's position:

How can you say so hastily that Nicaragua has been the problem? Nicaragua cannot trust good intentions and goodwill when there is a public, international, and open request of the U.S. administration to send $100 million in weapons to areas where the insurgents who oppose the Nicaraguan government operate. Therefore, I wouldn't go around hastily saying that Nicaragua is to be blamed. I would say that perhaps Nicaragua can do a bit more for this process but I feel that the responsibility lies with the bipolar conflict of the world which hurts us so much and which the Contadora Group wants to keep from reaching our countries.[26]

Habib Letter

The negotiations seemed to regain lost momentum when a letter from U.S. special envoy Philip Habib to Representative Jim Slattery (D.-Kan.) was made public. In his letter, dated April 11, 1986, Ambassador Habib said the United States interpreted the Contadora provisions as "requiring a cessation of support to irregular forces and/or insurrectional movements from the date of signature."

Ambassador Habib's letter seemed to bridge the gap between the Nicaraguan position, which was not to sign until the United States cut off the contras, and the U.S. position, which was not to cut off the contras until Nicaragua signed Contadora. The letter was greeted with enthusiasm by many in Congress who believed that it represented a shift in U.S. policy and a breakthrough in the negotiations, the first clear commitment to stop funding the contras if Contadora were signed by all parties.

Right-wingers in Congress and the Pentagon, however, reacted to Ambassador Habib's letter with near panic. Representative Jack Kemp (R.-N.Y.) demanded Habib's firing; the Pentagon released a study warning that signing of Contadora, which Nicaragua could then violate, would in three years require deployment of a hundred thousand U.S. troops to the region at an annual cost of $9.1 billion.

Although Ambassador Habib's letter had been duly cleared at the White House, the right-wingers easily prevailed in the "struggle for the president's mind," and on May 23 the administration in effect reneged on the Habib promise, saying Ambassador Habib should have promised a cutoff of aid to the contras on "implementation," not just "signature" of the treaty. The difference was enormous, particularly since the Reagan administration would be the sole judge of whether or not various provisions of the treaty were being fully implemented.

Movement in Managua

The apparent disarray in Washington puzzled the Nicaraguans. Deputy Foreign Minister Tinoco asked a visiting American in late May, "Who is speaking for your government? The Pentagon, the State Department, the Congress? Who are we to believe?"[27]

The outcry by the right-wing over the Habib letter, however, made an impression in Managua. If the Right in the United States was so convinced that signing Contadora would cut off the contras, maybe Nicaragua should sign after all.

On May 27 President Ortega struck a new conciliatory note. "We are willing to sign the Contadora peace document on June 6," he said, with no reference to Nicaragua's earlier conditions.[28]

June 6 Contadora Draft

The Contadora negotiators submitted their third, and they said final, draft agreement on June 6. The new draft adopted Nicaragua's concept of a "reasonable" balance of forces but also adopted the Guatemalan–Costa Rican system of assigning points to determine acceptable force levels. To sidestep the exercises and arms limitation problems, the new draft postponed them until after ratification. However, support of the contras would still have to end on signing. Withdrawal of foreign bases and military advisers was likewise keyed to signing.

On June 20 Nicaragua indicated it would accept the new agreement but stopped short of saying it would sign. Nicaragua "has always been willing to sign a peace agreement in the spirit of the Caraballeda declaration," the government announcement stated. It considered the Contadora agreement "the only instrument that can and should facilitate a rapid and efficient conclusion of the negotiating process to achieve peace in Central America."[29]

U.S. Rejects the Contadora Agreement

As Nicaragua became more and more positive about signing, the Reagan administration moved toward outright rejection of Contadora. The administration was opposed to "any lousy, fake, sham Contadora treaty," an official said on May 23. On June 24 President Reagan expressed the same thought somewhat more elegantly: "United States will support any negotiated settlement or Contadora treaty that will bring real democracy to Nicaragua. What we will not support is a paper agreement that sells out the Nicaraguan people's right to be free." "Real" democracy, as defined in Washington, emerged as a new and prohibitive condition. The administration quickly dismissed Nicaragua's support for the new draft. It was "propagandistic" and "an obvious effort to defeat" the president's contra aid request, the State Department said on June 22. Following the administration's lead, Honduras and El Salvador rejected the new draft. Costa Rica criticized the new draft but said it still wanted to sign "tomorrow." Only Guatemala pledged its full support to Contadora.

Nicaragua's statements in support of Contadora were drowned out by Honduras' and El Salvador's rejections and by votes in the U.S. Congress to approve President Reagan's request for another $100 million in aid for the contras. The chance for agreement was over. Contadora negotiators, speaking at the United Nations on June 26, the day after the U.S. House of Representatives approved the president's contra aid request, bravely stated that Contadora had "reached the end of a chapter, not the end of its work."

Agreement Unlikely Before 1989

Even if Nicaragua had joined the other four Central American countries in agreeing to sign the draft on the table in April, it was likely that the Reagan administration would have found a way to scuttle the agreement. The United States had enormous leverage over its allies in Central America, particularly in Honduras and El Salvador where the militaries were heavily dependent on hundreds of millions of dollars in U.S. military aid each year. The dominant role of the militaries in both countries would have made it very difficult for either Honduran President José Azcona Hoyo or Salvadoran President José Napoleón Duarte to sign a Contadora draft in defiance of U.S. wishes even if they had been predisposed to do so.

By the end of 1986 Contadora's short-term prospects seemed bleak. In both Washington and Managua, attention had shifted to the battlefield. Gone was talk of imminent signing, although the Contadora foreign ministries continued to emphasize that the Contadora process was still very much alive. Too much had been invested by all parties to allow the process to die. Attempts to negotiate a Contadora agreement seemed likely to continue, particularly if the war kept going poorly for the contras. However, the participants in the negotiating process were well aware that Contadora's success depended on Washington's acquiescence. The Contadora negotiators' best hope was to be able to continue averting a regional war until a more reasonable U.S. administration took office in 1989. As long as those committed to "rolling back communism" were in charge of U.S. foreign policy, the undeclared war against Nicaragua would continue.

Notes

1. Interview with Víctor Hugo Tinoco by William Goodfellow in Managua, March 5, 1986.
2. Interview with Lawrence Pezzulo by Center for International Policy (CIP) research assistant Jesse Biddle, July 2, 1983.
3. "Nicaragua Blinks in Showdown with U.S.," *U.S. News and World Report*, March 23, 1981.
4. William Shawcross, *Sideshow: Nixon, Kissinger and the Destruction of Cambodia* (New York: Simon and Schuster, 1979), pp. 265–272.
5. "Chronology of Nicaraguan Attempts at Bilateral Negotiations with the United States," Nicaragua Fact Sheets, Nicaraguan Embassy, Washington, D.C. (undated), p. 2.
6. Roy Gutman, "America's Diplomatic Charade," *Foreign Policy*, fall 1984, pp. 3–9.
7. Gutman, "America's Diplomatic Charade," pp. 7–8.
8. Gutman, "America's Diplomatic Charade," pp. 4–5.

9. *Washington Post,* May 8, 1983.

10. "Franco-Mexican Declaration," reprinted in Bruce Bagley, Roberto Alvarez, and Katherine Hagedorn, eds., *Contadora and the Central American Peace Process* (Boulder, Colo.: Westview Press, 1985), pp. 152–153.

11. "Speech of Mexican President José López Portillo in Managua, Nicaragua, on February 21, 1982," reprinted in Bagley et al., *Contadora and the Central American Peace Process,* pp. 100–101.

12. Proposal from the United States to Nicaragua, published in the *Washington Post* on April 10, 1982, reprinted in Bagley et al., *Contadora and the Central American Peace Process,* pp. 32–34.

13. Nicaraguan transcript of verbal presentation of U.S. response to Nicaraguan April 14 note. Presented by U.S. Ambassador Anthony Quainton in Managua on April 29, 1982 (unpublished).

14. Response from Nicaragua to the U.S. proposal of April 10, 1982; issued May 7, 1982, reprinted in Bagley et al., *Contadora and the Central American Peace Process,* pp. 34–39.

15. Reply of U.S. State Department to Nicaraguan appraisal of U.S. eight-point proposal; dated July 1, 1982, reprinted in Bagley et al., *Contadora and the Central American Peace Process,* pp. 39–42.

16. *New York Times,* April 7, 1983.

17. "Mexican-Venezuelan Declaration," reprinted in Bagley et al., *Contadora and the Central American Peace Process,* pp. 153–154.

18. "Informatin bulletin issued at Contadora Island, Panama, on January 9, 1983," reprinted in Bagley et al., *Contadora and the Central American Peace Process,* pp. 164–166.

19. "Document of Objectives," reprinted in Bagley et al., *Contadora and the Central American Peace Process,* pp. 176–180.

20. Secretary of State George Shultz in a letter to European Economic Community foreign ministers, September 7, 1984.

21. Letter from Nicaraguan president Daniel Ortega to Contadora foreign ministers, September 21, 1984.

22. U.S. Department of State briefing on the Contadora process, October 1, 1984.

23. U.S. National Security Council internal memorandum, October 20, 1984 (mimeo).

24. U.S. Department of State, "Fact Sheet: U.S. Efforts to Negotiate a Peaceful Settlement in Central America," February 25, 1986, p. 4.

25. Interview with Víctor Hugo Tinoco by William Goodfellow, March 5, 1986.

26. Tegucigalpa Cadena Audio Video, May 8, 1986, in Foreign Broadcast Information Service, May 9, 1986, pp. A4–A5.

27. Interview with Víctor Hugo Tinoco by William Goodfellow, in Managua, May 26, 1986.

28. Statement by President Daniel Ortega on Managua International Service, May 27, 1986, in Foreign Broadcast Information Service, May 29, 1986, p. 20.

29. Press communiqué, Nicaraguan Embassy, Washington, D.C., June 21, 1986.

PART 2

The Home Front

Introduction

When Ronald Reagan was first elected president in November 1980, U.S. relations with Nicaragua—and the U.S. public image of the Sandinista revolution—were still relatively good. However, by the time this book was being written less than six years later, the Sandinistas had been fully demonized and Congress had virtually declared war. This rapid metamorphosis had little to do with internal Nicaraguan reality. As the editor pointed out in Chapter 1, Sandinista policy remained fairly constant and, for a revolutionary government, remarkably pragmatic and moderate throughout the first seven years. The real intervening variable was the coming to power of a highly ideological U.S. administration that deliberately chose Nicaragua as convenient target enemy in its effort to demonstrate its resolve to stand up to and possibly roll back international "communism."

The four chapters in Part 2 are concerned with the devices used by the Reagan administration and others to facilitate and legitimize this abrupt about-face in U.S. policy. In Chapter 9 Eldon Kenworthy discusses the Reagan administration's massive and imaginative anti-Sandinista propaganda campaign. He notes the problems inherent in trying to market a policy of confrontation to a public wary of the costs of a possible second Vietnam, and he shows that the Reagan administration exhibited considerable skill in framing false assumptions and thus guiding public debate on the subject. In Chapter 10 Jack Spence details the way in which the U.S. media—by allowing the president to set the news agenda and by almost never investigating the validity of wild unsubstantiated charges against the Sandinistas—played a major role in the demonization of the Nicaraguan government. William LeoGrande in Chapter 11 examines the battle for aid to the contras in the U.S. Congress. He shows that although most members of the House felt that a confrontational policy was unwise and few were taken in by the Reagan administration's overblown rhetoric, even the Democrats eventually found it politically expedient to publicly concede the president's main points about the Sandinista "enemy." Having done so, it was only a matter of time before a persistent chief executive could box them into endorsing the contra war. In Chapter 12 Margaret Leahy discloses that a campaign—albeit amorphous and relatively unsuccessful—was even under way to intimidate and quiet academicians and others who traveled to Nicaragua and continued to contradict the Reagan view long after Congress and the media had succumbed.

NINE

Selling the Policy

ELDON KENWORTHY _____

> [I]ntentions have deliberately been kept cloudy. . . . [T]he main effort has
> been to reassure citizens while frightening the enemy. These goals are . . .
> inconsistent, and include various kinds of deceptions, especially in relation
> to one's own public.
>
> —Richard Falk, 1982[1]

Why did President Reagan's Nicaraguan policy require so much selling that
the administration created a new bureau for this purpose at the State
Department—the Office of Public Diplomacy for Latin America and the
Caribbean—along with a new White House–orchestrated Outreach Working
Group on Central America? Why was a "perception management" team
set up at the National Security Council and numerous "special reports"
released, aimed at Congress and the press, several substantial enough to
be called white papers? Why were there "Wednesday briefings" of influential
citizens and many televised speeches by the president, replete with fancy
graphics? Why was a blue-ribbon bipartisan commission on Central America
created, led by Henry Kissinger, and a rarely called joint session of Congress
convened to hear the president on Central America?

The short answer to these questions lay in the ambivalence key constituencies felt about a policy that, by mid-1982, rested on U.S. support for
a covert war aimed at overthrowing the Nicaraguan government. First, as
detailed in Chapter 11, the House of Representatives, until it finally succumbed in 1986, repeatedly voted down or watered down administration
efforts to aid the contras. Second, despite high ratings for overall performance,
President Reagan fared poorly in public opinion polls addressing his Nicaraguan policy, frequently "losing" by a two-to-one margin.[2] Finally, by
late 1985 all major U.S. allies in the region (the Contadora four plus four
South American governments organized to support Contadora) were on
record opposing Washington's involvement with the contras. The White
House failed in its attempts to revive CONDECA, the Central American
Defense Council, or to upstage Contadora with a Central American orga-

nization more susceptible to Washington's control (the short-lived Central American Democratic Community). Knowing it would be outvoted, the United States did not take its case against the Sandinistas to the Organization of American States, as it had in past instances when a Central American or Caribbean government was labeled a security threat.

For various constituencies that the Reagan administration could not ignore, its Nicaraguan policy presented costs and risks, both moral and material. The cooperation necessary for carrying out this policy rested on administration success in denying the risks and justifying the costs. These denials and justifications will be examined here. Although the motives of administration policy toward Nicaragua cannot be ignored, the emphasis here falls on legitimations—rhetoric that tries to make costs and risks acceptable. To show why a president known as "the Great Communicator" found legitimation difficult, I will first discuss Nicaragua in the context of U.S. foreign policy worldwide. After exploring this "big picture," I will examine legitimations specific to Nicaragua along with the rhetorical techniques used to sell them.

Discussions of administration attempts to manipulate public perceptions of Nicaragua often focus on distortions of fact. I will examine such distortions in the final pages of this chapter. Too much emphasis on factual error, however, diverts attention from the agenda-setting, debate-shaping assumptions that are more significant in the long run. Public debate on Nicaragua was corrupted more by unchallenged assumptions than by errors and omissions of a factual nature.

The Paradox of a Democracy Having an Empire

Richard Falk did not have Central America in mind when writing the words that began this chapter, but policies governing when and on whom Washington considers using thermonuclear weapons. Falk's statement is a reminder that to understand why so much misinformation was generated over Nicaragua, Nicaragua must be seen as the Reagan administration saw it— "geostrategically," or in the context of U.S. power worldwide. The defeat of the United States in Vietnam shattered a barrier in public consciousness that had isolated the dangers of nuclear confrontation from "operations" in the Third World. From the CIA coups of the 1950s through the counterinsurgencies of the 1960s, Third World interventions had been considered low-risk operations carried out by elite corps and kept from public awareness. The Pentagon's revival of low-intensity warfare in the 1980s was an attempt to regain the low profile that had accompanied pre-Vietnam interventions, including "successful" Green Beret actions in Guatemala and Bolivia.

Viewed by many as a unique trauma the U.S. public would outgrow, "Vietnam syndrome" actually represents the universalization of a core dilemma of U.S. foreign policy: that empire comes at a price many Americans are reluctant to pay. This dilemma impacts on presidents as they mesh imperial with domestic leadership. How can they persuade an indifferent or wary public to assume the human and material costs of maintaining global "commitments." That domestic politics can disrail imperial projects (e.g., Lyndon Johnson's not running again in 1968) means national leaders must allay or transform reservations the public holds about foreign intervention; they cannot merely ignore them.

No matter how the U.S. public is characterized—as privatistic and isolationist, or as pluralist and tolerant—it is hard to square quintessential American values with the mentality needed to sustain empire. Modern empires require citizenries high on arrogance or obedience, and preferably both. Americans are attracted to the fantasies of imperial rule—the movie "Rambo" had sequels because the hero never got killed—but quickly tire of the real thing. The central problem the Reagan administration faced in Nicaragua was that country's refusal to be another Grenada, much less a repeat of those moments when a shoe dropped in the White House sent a Latin regime packing. The "or death" alternative ringing in the chants of the Sandinistas, as in "free homeland or death," was no empty slogan.

In selecting "another Vietnam?" as the dominant metaphor for Central America, U.S. political cartoonists captured a widespread fear. As Falk reminds us, nuclear policy is a realm where presidents have had to overcome a similar reticence. Most citizens accept the dangers attendant on their government's being poised to plunge the earth into nuclear winter as the unavoidable cost of deterring the Soviets from destroying the United States or overrunning Western Europe. From the "massive retaliation" of the Eisenhower years, however, down to Presidential Directive 59 issued in the wake of the Iranian revolution, presidents have reserved the right to use nuclear weapons in a much broader range of situations (e.g., to maintain access to Persian/Arabian Gulf oil or to force an "honorable" peace out of North Vietnam). By his own admission, while president, Richard Nixon considered using nuclear weapons four times, none corresponding to the in extremis situation the public has in mind when it reluctantly endorses nuclear defense.[3]

To the public, then, high risks in foreign affairs are tolerable when presented as the only alternative to the capitulation or destruction of the United States. The "Red or dead" framing of the superpower conflict, launched as Washington took the quantum leap from atomic to thermonuclear weapons, elicited a begrudging "we'll risk dead." The public might not have accepted that risk had it been told that this policy was intended to give U.S. presidents "a range of options" for dealing with challenges to U.S. interests around the globe, including situations in which Soviet influence was minimal.[4] In short, the public understands one thing by such words as "security threat" and "vital interests"—defense and survival. Administrations invoke these concepts, however, to legitimate a much broader objective: maintenance of the pax americana issuing from World War II.

Nationalism in the Third World and the emergence of other powers in the first and second have made it difficult for either superpower to sustain the global influence it enjoyed a quarter century ago. Tending the empire has meant being alert to erosion at the edges, which poses a problem for presidents who must sell hundred-billion-dollar military budgets to the public as defense. The problem captured by "Vietnam syndrome" is not merely the selling of risks, then, but the selling of costs and risks in places either remote geographically or hard to equate with a direct Soviet threat. Although 56 percent of the Americans polled in April 1986 found Nicaragua troublesome, only 32 percent considered it a major threat to their security.[5] Therein lay President Reagan's problem.

In Vietnam, flawed policies led an initially supportive public to reverse itself. The Reagan administration entered the White House convinced that its ability to manage the empire rested on proving Vietnam an aberration. President Reagan sought to show the world that the United States was "back" and "standing tall." To demonstrate this, the White House had to show its "resolve" to use force in Third World settings, the Pentagon and CIA their skill in carrying out such missions (by themselves or through proxies), and the American public the willingness to see such projects through to the end. Central America and the Caribbean presented an ideal venue: minimal interference from other world powers coupled with a proximity to the United States that should make an appeal to the public on the basis of defense convincing.

By the time Grenada was ripe for a surgical attack, the administration had committed its prestige to demonstrating "resolve" in Central America. In the early months of Reagan's presidency, El Salvador was the primary target. "Mr. President, this is one you can win," Secretary of State Alexander Haig told Reagan privately.[6] After the situation in El Salvador stabilized, attention turned to Nicaragua and to the opportunity conservatives long had awaited to "rollback" a Marxist regime.

In an important sense, Reagan policy toward Nicaragua was only marginally about Nicaragua. The White House admitted as much on those occasions when it presented Central America as a test of U.S. "credibility" worldwide. Addressing Congress in 1983, the president asked: "If Central America were to fall, what would the consequences be for our position in Asia and Europe and for alliances such as NATO? . . . Our credibility would collapse, our alliances would crumble."[7] The Kissinger Report expressed the same "logic" when it argued: "The triumph of hostile forces in what the Soviets call the 'strategic rear' of the United States would be read as a sign of U.S. impotence."[8] What to Henry Kissinger was a "strategic rear," President Reagan called "our own backyard." The worst blow to U.S. credibility was assumed to lie in its not prevailing in its sphere of influence inasmuch as prevailing there must be a simple matter of "will." Failure to support the contras, the president said, would send "an unmistakable signal that the greatest power in the world is unwilling and incapable of stopping Communist aggression in our own backyard."[9]

One of the attractions "credibility" holds for policy makers is that its claims are irrefutable, based as they are on the perceptions of others and on futures. The recipients of the "unmistakable signals" rarely are specified, their actual response to U.S. moves rarely investigated. Another attraction is credibility's ability to turn into that "defense" the public is predisposed to support whatever event makes Washington look weak or stupid, whether or not the rival superpower is behind it. In the Kissinger formulation, the triumph of "hostile forces"—not necessarily forces aligned with the Kremlin—threatened U.S. security.

Although credibility is the logical solution to the problem of selling imperial risks to an enfranchised yet wary public, it has not captured the public's imagination. There remains an abstract, academic quality to this concept, comparable to how its principal proponent, Dr. Kissinger, is perceived. In selling his Nicaraguan policy, President Reagan found it expedient—or perhaps just natural—to incarnate the fear of Soviet gains at U.S. expense rather than deal with disembodied perceptions and signals. The incarnation he chose, for reasons embedded in his biography, was monolithic communism. World communism rivals credibility in its power to relate challenges to U.S. hegemony, wherever they occur, to the elemental defense of the American homeland.

To summarize, Falk's insight regarding "cloudy intentions" points to the mystification necessary to muster sufficient domestic political support for the policies needed to preserve an extensive empire. At the core of this mystification is the spinning of linkages: offense linked to defense, corporate interests to personal survival, attenuated alliances to moral obligations.[10]

Reagan Addresses the Nation

On Sunday evening, March 16, 1986, as Congress prepared to vote on an administration proposal to renew military aid to the contras, President Reagan delivered a major, televised address.[11] This speech also was broadcast, unedited, on Nicaraguan state television. The Sandinistas counted on most Nicaraguans finding Reagan's characterization of their reality so distorted that broadcasting the speech would discredit not only Reagan but his allies among their opponents. A speech thought persuasive in the United States also was considered persuasive in Nicaragua, the common characteristic being the rhetoric's distance from reality.

Picture the performance of a president trained as an actor, speaking from the Oval Office with its trappings of authority, aided by a map of Latin America that progressively turned red as the president detailed the spread of that "cancer," that "malignancy," whose vectors lay in Managua. The president made the four claims about the Sandinistas found in virtually every administration statement of this period. Pivotal was the assertion that (1) the Sandinistas are "a Communist organization," "the Communist Government of Nicaragua." In a radio address the week before, the president described the Sandinistas as "a cruel clique of deeply committed Communists at war with God and man."[12] Through such phrases as "like Communist governments everywhere, the Sandinistas . . . ," communism "explained" why the Sandinistas did the wicked things they do.

Communists (2) oppress their own population and (3) subvert their neighbors. Focusing on the threat to the hemisphere, Reagan described the Sandinistas as (4) "a Soviet ally," obedient to "Soviet mentors." Nicaragua was a "base" and a "beachhead" facilitating Soviet entry across "our own doorstep." Thus, Nicaragua's "campaign to subvert and topple its democratic neighbors," if left unchecked, promised "an outcome deeply injurious to the national security of the United States." The implication was clear: For the United States to be secure, the Sandinistas would have to go. In the president's words, "having this regime in Central America imperils our vital security interests." Invoking the Truman Doctrine of 1947, as Reagan had in earlier addresses, the president suggested that the United States once again faced Soviet expansionism. Yet the weight of the speech's ire fell on those who logically were intermediaries, accomplices.

Associated with Nicaragua were all our nemeses: "Arafat, Qaddafi, and the Ayatollah Khomeini." Eliminating the Sandinistas would take care of drug trafficking and illegal immigration.

The president accused the Sandinistas of violence toward their own people: "blacklists," "secret prisons," "brutality," and "mob violence." Despite possessing all the internationally recognized criteria of a legitimate state, the Sandinistas were dismissed as "an outlaw regime" that bore "the face of totalitarianism." The contras, on the other hand, were analogues of the "French Resistance that fought the Nazis" and the true heirs to a revolution "the Sandinistas betrayed." So structured, the "crucial test for the Congress" was not whether to aid exiles attempting to overthrow an established government but whether to "abandon the democratic resistance." Congress was asked to do what was easy to do as well as what was right, "so history will say of us, We had the vision, the courage and good sense to come together and act . . . when the price was not high and the risks were not great." "I am not talking about American troops. They are not needed."

Although "credibility" was not invoked in this speech, "communism" was used to tie Sandinista defiance of the United States not just to the Soviet threat or to Libyan terrorism but to downhome fears regarding drugs and illegal immigration. The central claim was defense: We must stop this "communism" that impinges upon us, that threatens "our own southern frontier." "My fellow Americans" did not include Latin as well as North Americans, as it had in some previous speeches ("Here in the Western hemisphere we are Americans from pole to pole").[13] On this occasion the threat to keeping "America safe," "America secure" conjured up the image of "Latin peoples by the millions" streaming north should "this Communist menace" go unchecked.

And should Congress fail to meet its responsibilities? Two weeks before the speech, the president's director of communications, Patrick Buchanan, published an op-ed with which the president expressed no disagreement.

"With the vote on *contra* aid," wrote Buchanan, "the Democratic party will reveal whether it stands with Ronald Reagan and the resistance—or Daniel Ortega and the Communists."[14] As the vote neared, a television commercial supporting the president said: "If Congress will act while there's still time, thousands of Americans will never be sent to fight and die in Nicaragua." Another commercial showed missiles erupting from their silos as the voice-over asked, "What can you do if the Communists use Central America as a base for nuclear missiles?"[15] Addressing the Senate Foreign Relations Committee, Secretary of State George Shultz said of Nicaragua: "I know which side I'm on; I know who the bad and the good guys are here."[16]

A televised address from the Oval Office is one thing; less "presidential" settings another. As the vote approached, the administration worked to reduce the options under discussion to the Central American equivalent of the "Red or dead" that had stifled policy debates in the 1950s. Hoping to turn Vietnam syndrome to their advantage, Reagan aides argued that failure to support the contras would result in U.S. troop commitments later. The administration staked out that privileged place in American political discourse of offering the only reasonable option bracketed by two unacceptable choices. "You can use American military force, which is the last thing we wish to do, or you can surrender, which is, I would think, unacceptable." Those were the "only" alternatives to resuming official U.S. military support for the contras, according to Elliot Abrams, undersecretary of state for inter-American affairs.[17]

The Policy That Could Not Go Public

Another step removed from the Oval Office were leaks and "backgrounders" (not-for-attribution interviews with senior administration officials). Public debate was manipulated by anonymous but "authoritative" statements critics could not challenge in a timely fashion. Despite its intelligence-sensitive nature, for example, word of a Soviet freighter bearing MiGs to Nicaragua was leaked on the day of the 1984 U.S. election. Later, when the ship was unloaded and no MiGs were on board, it scarcely mattered; the Soviet-Sandinista connection had received ample airplay.

Leaks and backgrounders also were used by administration factions to advance positions, close off options, and shoot down rivals. As internal battles spill into public view, we glimpse the extent to which formal speeches, such as the one just summarized, sell policy more than they reveal it. Take the administration's "commitment" to finding a negotiated solution. In the March speech the president said, "We have sought—and still seek—a negotiated peace and a democratic future in a free Nicaragua." Few listeners would have recognized in those final six words the administration's code for preconditions that effectively ruled out negotiation. The administration's real position had been revealed seven months earlier when, in a backgrounder, "a senior official" (either Abrams or National Security Adviser Robert McFarlane) told the *New York Times* that "the prevailing view in the

Administration is that you cannot negotiate a deal with Communists."[18] In another backgrounder, a senior official (obviously McFarlane) pointedly exempted Nicaragua from a second-term strategy of "creat[ing] incentives for Soviet friends or clients to have a more balanced relationship with the West."[19]

What emerged from the leaks, backgrounders, and the spontaneous interplay of press conferences was that the Reagan administration wanted the Sandinistas out—period. "When asked if the United States was out to overthrow the Sandinista regime, Mr. Speakes [the President's chief press aide] said: 'Yes, to be absolutely frank.' "[20] "Officials involved in Central American policy" told the New York Times that they wanted to "push Communism out of one country."[21] At a press conference on February 21, 1985, this exchange took place:

Q. Mr. President, on Capitol Hill the other day Secretary Shultz suggested that the goal of your policy is to remove the Sandinista Government in Nicaragua. Is that your goal?

A. Well, remove it in the sense of its present structure, in which it is a Communist, totalitarian state and it is not a Government chosen by the people. . . .

Q. Sir, when you say remove it in the sense of its present structure, are you not then saying that you advocate the overthrow of the present Government of Nicaragua?

A. Well, what I'm saying is that this present Government was one element of the revolution against Somoza. [A discourse on how the Sandinistas betrayed their revolution follows.]

Q. Is the answer yes then?

A. To what?

Q. To the question, aren't you advocating the overthrow of the present Government, if not to substitute another form of what you say was the revolution?

A. Not if the present Government would turn around and say—all right— if they'd say uncle, or all right, and come back into the revolutionary Government and let's straighten this out and institute the goals.[22]

"Revolutionary Government" now being contra-defined, if not contra-led, what the President was offering the Sandinistas was their participation in a government shaped by their enemies. If "overthrowing" a regime is equated with a knockout in boxing, the president was willing to settle for a TKO and to call it "a negotiated solution."

That at the center of Reagan policy lay the removal of the Sandinista government did not mean that the administration preferred military means. What the administration wanted, however, was not likely to be obtained by any other method. The White House continually pledged its support for "a diplomatic solution"—while calling the Sandinistas "terrorists," "genocidal," "Murder Inc.," a "cancer," and people who "hijacked" their own country. The diplomatic solution the administration had in mind could only be produced if the Sandinistas were on the ropes, "if they'd say uncle."

"[I]f Nicaragua still won't see the light," the president elaborated in 1986, "then the only alternative is for the freedom fighters to have their way and take over."[23] After each such interchange with the press, the State Department would insist that U.S. policy rested on the search for a peaceful, political solution.

Because the real policy carried risks the administration did not want examined, the real policy was kept off the agenda of congressional debate until disclosures of the administration's secret arms deal involving Iran, Israel, and the contras broke the spell. Hearings were held in Congress all along, but rarely did they address the large questions of what the policy really was and what risks it entailed. Congress focused instead on discrete events and appropriations. Through 1986, the only place where the real policy may have been examined with the care that the founding fathers intended when they wrote Article 1 of the Constitution was in the Select Oversight Committees that monitor the CIA—and those discussions were secret.

The Rhetoric That Masked the Policy

One way to frame the public relations task the administration confronted, given its real objectives, is to compare the evidence needed to sell the policy with the evidence revealed. It was not difficult to show that leading Sandinistas were Marxists, leaving aside what this means in Nicaraguan context. The problem was how to make of this a danger warranting the kind of military action that 70 to 80 percent of the U.S. people, according to opinion polls, feared—one that would draw U.S. soldiers into combat. Public fears could be mobilized around "another Cuba," interpreting Cuba to be a Soviet satellite that has given the Kremlin military bases and has a record of militarily aiding insurgencies abroad.[24] On this, however, the evidence was not compelling: Nicaragua was not "another Cuba" in this sense.

There was a second problem. The charge that Nicaragua was a "platform" for Soviet expansionism, of all the charges leveled at the Sandinistas, was the most negotiable (see Chapter 8). And that which is negotiable does not require a military solution. Although the Sandinistas showed little receptivity to negotiating away their rule inside Nicaragua, they gave every indication of being willing to barter their right to become "another Cuba." In September 1984, Nicaragua was the first Central American government to commit itself to sign the Contadora treaty, an act that caught Washington off guard. The entire Contadora process, as shepherded by Mexico, sought to assure the Reagan administration that there would be "no more Cubas" while guaranteeing the Sandinistas their right to rule, as Marxists even, provided that they had sufficient domestic support.

If the Marxist nature of the Sandinista regime was the problem, then the administration's strategy of military force was appropriate. For it would take force either to drive the tiger off or to make him change his spots.

Justifications for force, however, were couched in charges other than the Sandinistas' Marxism, the most invoked being Nicaragua's becoming "another Cuba." This charge, potent with the U.S. public, lacked compelling evidence and had a negotiable solution. The administration's response to this bind was linkage. What was most feared was tied, rhetorically, to what most easily could be proved yet distanced from a diplomatic solution. The key to Reagan administration rhetoric on Nicaragua lay in creating links where they did not exist while denying them where they did.

A second contradiction for the administration lay in its strategy for overcoming the "Vietnam syndrome." The administration played both sides of the street, scaring the public with "the Russians are coming" while reassuring it that the problem could be taken care of without sending "American boys" to battle. Only one assumption can square those messages: that a Central American army—and by Reagan's second term only the contras were available—could counter this "relentless" thrust of "world communism." The United States both entered and left the Indochina War thinking local armies could carry the day. Remembering that they could not, this "solution" was not convincing—which is not to say that many in Congress did not embrace it. Believing he was speaking off the record, Henry Kissinger said that either the administration's analysis of the situation "is wrong or the solution is wrong," adding, "It cannot be that it is such a vital interest and [that] it can be solved with $100 million."[25]

A third contradiction emerged from the administration's need for bipartisan backing for a policy that could not fully reveal itself. Given the Democrats' control of the House and the conviction of influential Democrats that a negotiated solution was possible on the "another Cuba" issue, plans for overthrowing the Sandinistas had to be presented as something other than they were, leading to the ultimate paradox of the contra war being sold as an aid to diplomacy.

The decision to support the contras had been made by the president in March 1981. By March 1982, the contras were blowing up bridges inside Nicaragua and the president's approval of the "secret war" had been leaked to the press. The Intelligence Committee of the Democratic-controlled House, insisting on clear guidlines for this CIA operation, was told its purpose was to interdict arms passing from Nicaragua into El Salvador. In December 1982, the entire House unanimously approved the Boland amendment: No money could be spent on actions aimed at overthrowing the Nicaraguan regime. Testimonies of those recruited by the CIA to run this war leave no doubt that overthrowing the Sandinistas was and remained the purpose of the operation.[26] Yet as late as June 1985—four months after the "say uncle" press conference—President Reagan sent the House a letter assuring it that support for the contras was not part of a plan to overthrow the Sandinistas, a letter that saved the policy from one of its many cliffhangers in Congress.[27]

Involvement with the contras led Washington to cancel a long-standing treaty obligation to the World Court, in anticipation of the June 1986 ruling against the United States. By March 1986, the State Department was arguing that Nicaragua, as a self-evident "aggressor state," was not entitled to "hot pursuit" (crossing borders to repel invaders).[28] As its commitment to the contras produced these contortions in its relationship to international law, the administration sold contra pressure as the handmaiden of diplomacy. "The Sandinistas will come to the negotiating table only when they see the carrot of peaceful settlement backed up by the stick of a well-equipped armed opposition."[29] Since the White House demanded that the Sandinistas first "sit down and talk with their opposition, both armed and unarmed,"[30] and since altering power arrangements inside one's country to placate outside forces is something no self-respecting government does, not surprisingly this rationalization of violence as diplomacy failed.

A final contradiction emerged with the overthrow of dictatorships in Haiti and the Philippines early in Reagan's second term, accompanied by a return to civilian rule in some Latin American countries. "Winds," "tides," and "waves" of "democracy" laced administration rhetoric in 1986. "Successes" in Central America were paraded before a deficit-minded Congress being asked to grant still more millions to that region. "Democracy" also was an issue on which the White House hoped to isolate Nicaragua from its supporters in Europe and Latin America. In the president's words, Sandinista rule was the "one tragic, glaring exception to that democratic tide."[31] Finally, "democracy" provided the needed link between the diplomatic settlement popular in Congress and the White House's goal of overthrowing the Sandinistas. "Democratic governments are more reliable signatories to agreements because their actions are subject to public scrutiny," is how one State Department official put it.[32] His boss, Elliott Abrams, was more blunt: "It is preposterous to think we could sign a deal with the Sandinistas and expect it to be kept."[33]

Here the contradiction lay in not letting go of the "Russians are coming" theme while embracing the "winds of democracy" rationale. At the same time that the administration was proclaiming gains in El Salvador, Honduras, and Guatemala, the map at the televised March 1986 speech turned progressively red as Reagan ticked off where "weapons supplied by the Sandinistas have been found" and where "radicals . . . trained in Nicaragua" operated. As every Central American country from Panama north turned red, the president recalled the "old communist slogan that the Sandinistas have made clear they honor: the road to victory . . . goes through Mexico." To embrace democracy as a foreign policy priority also raised questions about administration policy toward Chile, South Korea, and South Africa. "It is not our job to beat up on these friendly regimes," the ubiquitous "senior official" was said to have said while the born-again democratic emphasis was still receiving airplay.[34] Nicaragua conspicuously remained the only country on which the White House was prepared to impose "democracy" by force.[35]

What the Reagan administration sought in Central America was no different from what previous administrations had achieved: getting its way. By the 1980s, however, a U.S. president could be neither as preemptory as

Teddy Roosevelt had been when he "took Panama" or as sanctimonious as Woodrow Wilson when he set out "to teach" those republics "to elect good men." Nor could the region's contacts with other world powers be as tightly circumscribed as when, in 1945, John McCloy outlined Washington's strategy for the postwar era: "I've been taking the position that we ought to operate under this regional arrangement in South American [thereby keeping the United Nations and other powers out], at the same time intervene promptly in Europe." Prophetically, in his reply to McCloy, Secretary of War Henry Stimson feared that "these little South American peoples" might "throw a monkey wrench into the thing."[36]

Because Reagan could not announce his purposes as openly as his predecessors had done, real objectives were disguised in false, or at least secondary, goals that stood a better chance of overcoming the resistance of Congress, the public, and the few allied governments that mattered to the administration. This opportunistic approach to foreign policy yielded the contradictions previously described. That a policy fails the tests of coherence and objectivity, however, is not to say that it fails its "public relations" task. Given the superficiality with which Congress and the media approached Central America (see Chapters 10 and 11), given the refusal of most Democrats to challenge traditional assumptions regarding "communism" in "our backyard," and given the episodic, thin involvement of the public, those contradictions largely served their purposes.

Smoking Guns

Disinformation commonly is equated with inaccurate data, suppressed facts, and statements wrenched from context. So far a different order of dissimulation has been emphasized: agenda-setting and debate-manipulating assumptions which, in the U.S. political consensus, often escape even the critics. The interplay of these two forms of misrepresentation is best examined by focusing on specific issues.

At the heart of the White House's case against the Sandinistas were the interwoven assertions that Nicaragua subverted neighboring governments, built up its military for aggressive purposes, and functioned as a Soviet satellite. Four presentations of the administration's case substantial enough to be dubbed white papers were published between February 1981 and January 1987. Despite different titles and emphases, they seemed successive drafts of the same document, each better documented than the last, each more nuanced in its argument. In fairness to the Reagan policy, then, I shall concentrate on the most recent of these white papers: "Revolution Beyond Our Borders" (RBOB), published in September 1985.[37]

In the white papers, as in the public debate, attention initially focused on the "smoking gun:" hard evidence of arms being smuggled from Nicaragua to El Salvador. For several years the administration tantalized its critics by claiming to have evidence it could not reveal, to protect its intelligence network. Opponents poured over what information was released, looking for forgeries and false inferences.[38] In the midst of this misplaced concreteness, three assumptions that framed the white papers largely went unchallenged. The white papers assumed that Nicaragua had no right to aid guerrillas elsewhere, not even the right to provide safe houses, radio transmission, and R&R (rest and recreation). The second assumption was that, in supplying such aid, the Sandinistas confirmed their role as Soviet proxies in a Kremlin-directed campaign to subvert Central America. That is, Sandinista "internationalism" was assumed to be prima facie evidence of Soviet control. From these assumptions sprang a third: that a diplomatic solution to arms trafficking in Central America never could arise. Sandinista behavior in supplying Salvadoran rebels being both "criminal" and Soviet orchestrated, how could Managua's participation in a regional diplomatic solution be anything but a feint?

By the time RBOB was published, there were some "smoking guns." Evidence contained in this report undercut critics who took too literally ex-insider David MacMichael's assertions that no traffic in military supplies from Nicaragua to El Salvador occurred after April 1981. A CIA analyst of such matters with a top security clearance, MacMichael left the agency in April 1983 but continued to issue authoritative statements, such as his September 1985 testimony before the World Court: "I do not believe that such traffic goes on now."[39] On the basis of captured documents, defector testimony, serial numbers on U.S. rifles left in Vietnam, aerial photography, and a few well-publicized incidents in Honduras, RBOB made a probable case for the Sandinistas facilitating military equipment reaching the Salvadorans past April 1981. Much remained shrouded in secrecy, however. RBOB did not prove that these flows were "massive," did not pinpoint their paths—did not establish, for example, that Vietnamese-supplied weapons had to pass through Nicaragua—and brushed aside the diplomatic implications of periodic halts in Sandinista assistance to the Salvadorans.

In aiding armed struggles in neighboring countries, the Sandinistas were doing what governments left, right, and center traditionally have done in Central America. Smuggling weapons, lying about it, providing safe houses, helping to unify rebel factions: which country in the region, including the United States, has not done these things? In overthrowing Somoza, the Sandinistas had been assisted by Venezuela, Panama, Costa Rica, and Cuba. In attempting to overthrow the Sandinistas, the contras were aided by Honduras, El Salvador, the United States, and initially Argentina. Washington armed the contras, permitted them to recruit and train on U.S. soil, played an active role in unifying their factions, and at various times denied doing so. In each of the previous three decades, Washington provided similar assistance to dissidents attempting to overthrow some Latin American or Caribbean government.

So, whether one approves of such behavior or not, it was tendentious of the White House to present state-supported subversion of another state in this hemisphere as prima facie evidence of Soviet plotting. What the administration meant to say, but could not say openly, was that it reserved the right to be the only "internationalist" in the hemisphere. A debate too focused on "smoking guns" ignored these framing assumptions.

Smoking Rhetoric

Documented "smoking guns" were insufficient to prove the administration's contention that Nicaragua formed part of a "world Communist" plot to subvert all of Central America. As already suggested, such a public relations problem could be finessed by linking the administration's charge to more persuasive evidence, such as the buildup in the Sandinista armed forces. No one doubted that by 1984 the Nicaraguan army was three times larger than it ever had been and growing, along with becoming better equipped. To link this to the "subversion of Central America," the administration only had to show that the military buildup was offensive in intent. Thus it combed Sandinista rhetoric for anything that might support this interpretation.

Much was made of a statement by Tomás Borge, one of the nine Sandinista comandantes: "This revolution goes beyond our borders," the very phrase that gave RBOB its title and a phrase repeatedly invoked by the president, secretary of state, and undersecretary of state for the hemisphere. Just as Hitler spelled out his goals in *Mein Kampf*, Shultz told the Senate Foreign Relations Committee, in calling for a "revolution without frontiers" the Sandinistas had revealed their true intentions.[40] President Reagan asked: "Can we responsibly ignore the long-term danger to American interests posed by a Communist Nicaragua, backed by Soviet Union and dedicated—in the words of its own leaders—to a 'revolution without borders'?"[41]

That both men slightly misquoted Borge is indicative of their distance from the text. When Representative Edward Markey asked Shultz in 1983 for the source of the statement, three weeks passed before Markey was told it could not be found. Never having read Borge's speech did not prevent the president or the secretary of state from claiming that it explained Nicaragua's military buildup. "Why such a formidable buildup?," asked Schultz rhetorically in 1986. Tomás Borge gave the answer in 1981. "'This revolution,' he said, 'goes beyond our borders.'"[42]

Borge's speech was recorded and translated by Washington's own Foreign Broadcast Information Service (FBIS) as follows:

> The defense of our revolution has not been organized to conquer
> neighboring or faraway territories but to win peace. Our neighboring
> friends can rest assured that this revolution was carried out to defend the
> land on which we were born. . . . [Nicaragua] has joined the current of the
> revolutions of our time and it is a country with moral authority, not just in
> Central America or Latin America, but throughout the entire world. We are
> proud to be Nicaraguans. Our revolution goes beyond our borders. Our
> revolution was always internationalist from the moment Sandino fought in
> La Segovia. With Sandino were internationalists from all over the world.[43]

The emphasis, then, was on Nicaragua's having received help from others and having joined a worldwide historical movement. Clearly Borge felt the Sandinistas had a debt to discharge. Nothing in this speech suggests, however, that the Sandinistas planned to discharge this debt through military means or that they identified the worldwide revolution with communism.

According to RBOB, the Sandinistas' "growth in armed forces and acquisitions of major weapons systems were planned and, for the most part, implemented well before the time the Sandinistas allege any significant security threat existed."[44] Thus, their intentions were offensive. For evidence of such early planning, RBOB cites an internal Sandinista communiqué of October 1979, known as the "72-Hour Document." Although noting "that at present there are no clear indications of an armed counterrevolution by *Somocista* forces from abroad," the 72-Hour Document called on cadres to "build, strengthen and educate the Sandinista People's Army."[45] RBOB gives prominence to "the principle of revolutionary internationalism," which also appears in the 72-Hour Document.

Read in its entirety, this document reveals a Sandinista leadership more concerned with the loyalty of the new national army than with its size and firepower. Its contribution to the Central American revolution would reside, the document said, in "the consolidation of the Nicaraguan revolution." "We are strategically preparing to repel any aggression," states a document that anticipates such aggression as the response to Sandinista attempts to sever the bonds of economic domination.[46] The document does not identify the world revolution as Marxist or Communist.

Inasmuch as U.S. defense policy still bears the stamp of Pearl Harbor— far more than the Soviets, Washington plans for a world war beginning with a surprise attack—it is strange that the white papers assume the Sandinistas had amnesia. Given the history of U.S. military interventions in Nicaragua, why wouldn't a leftist regime there anticipate a need for arms? The 72-Hour Document reveals a strong historical memory: "We should remember that in 1933 he [Sandino] pointed out that while Yankee intervention appeared to have ended, political and economic intervention remained intact."[47]

In point of fact, as data in the white papers themselves indicate (Fig. 9.1), significant growth in Nicaragua's military capability followed threatening U.S. acts. By December 1981, the U.S. press carried stories of contras being trained on U.S. soil. By January 1982, a major contra plot to blow up an oil refinery near Managua was uncovered. By March not only had the contras penetrated deep inside Nicaragua, the presidential decision linking those attacks to U.S. policy had been leaked.

To link the Sandinista military buildup to subversion of Central America, the administration also changed the quantity of soldiers and the "sophistication" of weapons exceeded Nicaragua's defensive needs. In RBOB, the Sandinistas' military was described as "dwarfing in size, sophistication, and firepower those of their neighbors" (p. 31). Secretary of Defense Caspar Weinberger criticized the "tremendously increased flow of offensive weaponry" to Nicaragua.[48]

Figure 9.1   Soviet bloc military deliveries to Nicaragua.

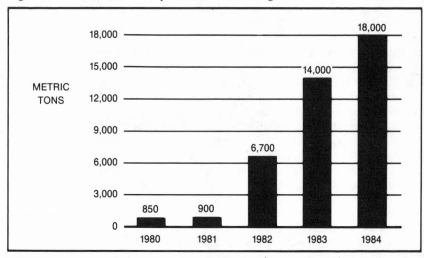

Sources: This graph appears in two white papers released by the U.S. Departments of State and Defense—"The Soviet-Cuban Connection in Central America and the Caribbean," p. 25, and "The Sandinista Military Build-up," p. 33 (both Washington, D.C.: Government Printing Office). These reports were issued or revised in 1985.

Airpower seems a fair test of "sophistication," especially in offensive capability. Well after RBOB was published and Weinberger spoke, Nicaragua apparently still had fewer than thirty combat aircraft, none of them supersonic, including fewer than fifteen Soviet Hind helicopter gunships. El Salvador, by contrast, apparently had forty U.S. Huey gunships along with some four dozen supersonic fighters or fighterbombers. Honduras also was far better equipped than Nicaragua.[49] Speaking off the record at the time Weinberger made his remark, "other officials . . . said that most of Nicaragua's recent imports are either clearly defensive, such as antiaircraft guns and missiles, or weapons useful for antiguerrilla operations [another form of defense]."[50]

As 1986 began, Sandinista forces stood at approximately 62,000—some 40,000 regular troops, the rest civilian militia on active duty. El Salvador's and Guatemala's regular troops were as large if not larger, and their auxiliary forces were either larger (Guatemala's) or better equipped (El Salvador's). Add to this Honduras' 20,000-person army, and President Reagan's claim, in his March 1986 speech, that "the Nicaraguan military machine is more powerful than all its neighbors combined" was simply not true.[51]

By mid-1983, President Reagan offered "symmetry" as a justification for supporting the contras. By doing to the Sandinistas what they putatively were doing to the Salvadoran government, the administration said, Nicaraguan leaders would think twice about continuing their subversion. This justification, of course, jarred with the simultaneous assertion that the Sandinistas were proxies in a Soviet-directed campaign. To make sense, "symmetry" had to assume that the Sandinistas had the power to halt the flow of weapons to El Salvador.

As even RBOB concedes in its historical narrative—though not in its analysis—at least twice the Sandinistas curbed their material aid to the Salvadoran revolutionaries. In this sense, "symmetry" worked but went unrewarded. After the failure of the "final offensive" in El Salvador in early 1981, "U.S. intelligence found that the arms traffic slowed or ceased by March."[52] In response, on April first Reagan cut off what U.S. aid to Nicaragua remained in the pipeline. Following the U.S. invasion of Grenada in 1983, the same pattern appeared, only now the argument that the Salvadorans could not absorb more Nicaraguan aid—which was how RBOB dismisses the earlier Sandinista cutoff—was implausible, as the complaints of Salvadoran rebels to the Sandinistas made clear. Through private channels Washington again was informed by Managua that the flow of arms to El Salvador had been shut down. Within weeks, the CIA was mining Nicaraguan harbors.

Although the genuineness of diplomatic initiatives is hard to assess at a distance, RBOB provides no hard evidence of a reluctance on Nicaragua's or Cuba's or the Soviet Union's part to reach a diplomatic solution in Central America that would have severely limited the subversive capacities of all three. Managua made bilateral approaches to its neighbors, seeking their cooperation in sealing borders. Although Costa Rica eventually reciprocated, Honduras declined under U.S. pressure not to inhibit the contras' entry into Nicaragua. In mid-1983 Castro responded to the request made of Cuba and the United States by the Contadora governments: that each show support for the treaty even though neither would be a signatory. Cuba said it would withdraw military advisers from Central America and halt military supplies if Washington did likewise. Moscow also voiced support for Contadora.

The Soviet Role

An honest treatment of Nicaraguan, Cuban, and Soviet intentions in Central America would have weighed, alongside phrases lifted from speeches, the priorities, resources, and opportunity costs of these governments. The president repeatedly claimed that "a faraway totalitarian power has committed enormous resources to change the strategic balance of the world by turning Central America into a string of anti-American, Soviet-styled dictatorships."[53] In a 1986 interview, he claimed "Nicaragua is literally already a satellite of the Communist bloc."[54] Given this emphasis, one would have expected the white papers to analyze Soviet resources and intentions. After all, whole departments of Washington's intelligence apparatus are devoted to evaluating such data. On this point, however, the white papers remain silent, allowing their readers to assume that the Kremlin had unlimited resources to gamble on distant Central America.

Arms and oil the Kremlin sent Nicaragua, advice and training as well. At every opportunity Soviet leaders wished Central American revolutionaries success. When it came to statements that count, however, such as mutual defense agreements, Moscow was circumspect: no agreements to come to Nicaragua's defense, no identification of it as part of the Soviet bloc. The Soviets permitted Nicaragua less sophisticated weaponry than they provided Peru. Had the white papers incorporated analyses of Soviet intentions by specialists on Soviet affairs at the CIA, this is what they would have contained. In the words of one such specialist: "Central America and the Caribbean—with the exception of Cuba—are peripheral to Soviet geostrategic concerns. Central America, moreover, is too far removed for Moscow to be able to adequately project its military power and, more importantly, it is a region where U.S. military and economic power is predominant."[55] With regard to other Central American revolutions, "the Soviet Union is seen by many rebels to have abrogated its revolutionary role," wrote a *New York Times* reporter after interviewing guerrillas from these nations.[56]

It might be argued that Cuba's role in Nicaragua surpassed the Soviets'; certainly more Cuban advisers were involved. Unable to deliver what the Kremlin could (oil for starters), Havana's relation to Managua remained more one of equals. "Nobody is running this thing except the Sandinistas," a "senior Western diplomat in Managua" told the *Wall Street Journal*. "The Sandinistas . . . aren't letting their Cuban advisers control the ministries."[57]

In arguing that the Soviets were using Nicaragua as a "platform" for subverting Central America, the white papers drew on documents that fell into U.S. hands in Grenada. In the March 1986 speech, the president said, "the American forces who liberated Grenada captured thousands of documents that demonstrated Soviet intent to bring Communist revolution home to the Western Hemisphere." Using these documents, the ranking Pentagon official specializing in Central America and the Caribbean estimated that the military aid promised Grenada by East Bloc nations over several years would equip "10,800 men under arms."[58] To Nestor Sanchez that seemed too large a military for Grenada's needs.

Missing from Sanchez's analysis was any consideration of hostile U.S. rhetoric and naval maneuvers during the two years preceding the U.S. invasion, an omission also found in most white papers' treatment of Nicaragua. With U.S. aggression factored in, the amounts and types of weapons listed in the captured documents seem entirely appropriate for the island's defense. Harvard political scientist Jorge Dominguez read "thousands of pages already declassified" of the captured documents and assumed he had been given those "most favorable to the US government position."[59] Dominguez reported no evidence of Soviet or Cuban plans to use Grenada as a transshipment point for Central American insurgents.

Conclusion

In the U.S. debate over Nicaraguan policy, assumptions supporting the administration position often went unchallenged while the White House worked to keep the debate focused on discrete facts and statements that served its purposes. The administration had to behave this way, given the underlying contradiction between its insistence on maintaining control over Central America and the reluctance of most U.S. citizens to assume the risks and costs of doing just that in a region transformed by nationalism. In the course of this analysis, several methods by which the Reagan presidency manipulated the public debate over Nicaragua have been mentioned. Discussion of the alternatives open to the United States was curtailed by presenting the administration's choice bracketed by one or two unacceptable alternatives. (Example: surrender U.S. interests, send in U.S. soldiers, or back the contras.) Dubious linkages tying alternative strategies to administration preferences blurred what clear choices did exist. (Example: presenting contra attacks as serving diplomacy.) Secrecy was used to preempt debate and disguise accountability. (Example: not discussing the real purposes of the CIA's involvement with the contras by claiming this operation was secret long after it ceased being so.) Accountability for decisions was masked by other means, including leaks, backgrounders, and nonbinding presidential letters to Congress. With a CIA operation at the center of the policy, debates that should have occurred in the open in the foreign policy committees of the Congress were confined to the closed "oversight" committees. The Republican chair of the Senate's Select Committee on Intelligence linked Niaragua to "a series of small conflicts that will shape our national security policy. . . . [T]he American public is going to be involved in that without knowing how it's being involved."[60]

The administration's tease regarding its intentions to overthrow the Sandinistas militarily served to divert attention from the economic warfare that remained a constant of Reagan policy. Pros and cons of economic sanctions against South Africa were widely debated, with the administration arguing that innocent people should not suffer. A comparable public debate regarding the U.S. economic boycott of Nicaragua never occurred.

Classic scare techniques, along with Red baiting, were trotted out whenever the administration feared losing a crucial vote. (Examples: "the Russians are coming," as are "hordes" of illegal immigrants "fleeing Marxism" in Central America.) The positions of other governments, both allied and opposed, were misrepresented to further the administration's case. (Example: Latin American governments were described as "secretly" supporting the contra-linked strategy when, in fact, they did not.)[61]

In its 1986 report, the U.S. Advisory Commission on Public Diplomacy lamented the "systematic misuse of such concepts as 'peace,' 'democracy,' 'terrorism,' and 'national liberation'" by governments in "the developing world, where political language is manipulated."[62] Perhaps. Writing a quarter century earlier, the Mexican Octavio Paz noted a similar problem—with us. "American realism . . . is of a very special kind, and American ingenuousness does not exclude dissimulation and even hypocrisy. . . . the North American does not tell lies, but he substitutes social truth for the real truth, which is always disagreeable."[63]

Acknowledgments

Help in collecting information for this chapter was rendered by Mark Arnold, Andrea Bilson, Laura Edelstein, William Fielding, Victor Hong, and Becky Pennick. The State Department's country officer for Nicaragua, Norma Harms, responded to my requests for government documents. Although I am sure she disagrees with my analysis, I appreciate her assistance. Thanks also are owed Walter LaFeber and Thomas Walker for comments on the draft.

Notes

1. Richard Falk and Robert Jay Lifton, *Indefensible Weapons* (New York: Basic Books, 1982), p. 170.

2. "Relax, Democrats: The Public Supports You on Nicaragua," *Washington Post National Weekly Edition*, April 7, 1986, p. 37.

3. "Nixon Reveals Four Times He Pondered Nuclear Bomb," *New York Times*, July 23, 1985, p. A17.

4. As Falk notes, "We now possess strong documentation for the assertion that every president going back to Truman and up through Nixon has actually threatened, usually in secret communications, the use of nuclear weapons so as to control the behavior of adversaries" (Falk and Lifton, *Indefensible Weapons*, p. 179). Typically, only half the U.S. defense budget is dedicated to deterring Soviet attacks on the United States and its NATO allies, according to Howard Morland, "A Few Billion for Defense," in the series "New Policy Papers," (Washington, D.C.: Coalition for a New Foreign and Military Policy, 1986).

5. "Relax, Democrats."

6. Laurence Barrett, *Gambling With History* (Garden City: Doubleday, 1983), p. 207.

7. "President Reagan's Address," *New York Times*, April 28, 1983, p. A12. Also on this theme, see the president's radio address of January 14, 1984, Department of State *Bulletin*, March 1984.

8. *Report of the National Bipartisan Commission on Central America* (Washington, D.C.: Government Printing Office, 1984), p. 93.

9. As quoted by Tom Wicker, "They're Coming Again," *New York Times*, April 2, 1985, p. A27.

10. The citizen for whom "frontier" evokes U.S. territory was first sold a leap abroad, as in John Kennedy's "Our frontiers today are on every continent," then a leap into militarized space with Ronald Reagan's "high frontier."

11. "Transcript of the President's Speech," *New York Times*, March 17, 1986, p. A12. Also printed by the State Department as its *Current Policy*, no. 805.

12. "Reagan Aides Open Compromise Talks on Aiding Contras," *New York Times*, March 9, 1986, p. A1.

13. "Text of the President's Address," *New York Times*, February 25, 1982, p. A14.

14. "The Contras Need Our Help," *Washington Post National Weekly Edition*, March 17, 1986, p. 29.

15. "Inside Washington," *Human Events*, March 1, 1986, p. 4.

16. "Shultz Says Nicaraguans Worse Off Than Filipinos," *Washington Post*, February 28, 1986, p. A11.

17. "Now that Contadora Is Dead," *New York Times*, January 8, 1986, p. A22.

18. "Reagan Aides See No Possibility of U.S. Accord with Sandinistas," *New York Times*, August 18, 1985, p. A1.

19. Leslie Gelb, "Taking Charge," *New York Times Magazine*, May 26, 1985, p. 70.

20. "Reagan Opens Campaign for Aid to Contras," *Washington Times*, February 19, 1986, p. 1. Two months later another senior Reagan aide, Donald Regan, told interviewers: "We have to get rid of it [the Sandinista regime] in some way or another. And what we want to do is to try to help those who are trying to overthrow that communist government" ("The Winds of War," *Washington Post National Weekly Edition*, July 28, 1986, p. 9).

21. "Reagan Aides See No Possibility."

22. "President's News Conference . . . ," *New York Times*, February 22, 1985, p. A14.

23. "Contra Takeover May Be Necessary . . . ," *New York Times*, August 20, 1986, p. A1.

24. A New York Times/CBS News poll taken in April 1986 showed a doubling in public support for military aid to the contras when citizens believed that Nicaragua would become "another Cuba." Thirty-four percent of those who said Nicaragua would give military bases to the Soviet Union favored military aid to the contras in contrast to 16 percent among those who believed Nicaragua would not give the Kremlin bases ("American Opinions on Aid to the Contras," *New York Times*, April 20, 1986, p. E3).

25. "'Off Record' Kissinger Talk Isn't," *New York Times*, April 20, 1986, p. A20.

26. Christopher Dickey, *With the Contras* (New York: Simon and Schuster, 1985), pp. 146, 210–211, passim.

27. "Reagan Letter on Aid to Nicaraguan Rebels," *Congressional Quarterly*, June 15, 1985, p. 1173.

28. "U.S. Limits Its Role At Court in Hague," *New York Times*, October 8, 1985, p. A5; "U.S. Aide Terms Nicaragua 'Aggressor State' in Region," *New York Times*, March 29, 1986, p. A4; "World Court Supports Nicaragua . . . ," *New York Times*, June 28, 1986, p. A1.

29. "President Declares He's 'a Contra, Too,'" *Washington Post*, March 15, 1986, p. A20.

30. "Reagan Appoints Habib as Envoy to Central America," *New York Times*, March 8, 1986, p. A4.

31. "Excerpts from Reagan's Speech on Aid for Nicaraguan Rebels," *New York Times*, June 25, 1986, p. A12.

32. James Michel, "U.S. Policy on Central America: the Need for Consensus," State Department's *Current Policy*, no. 828.

33. "Reagan Aides See No Possibility of U.S. Accord."

34. "U.S. Tries to Dampen Speculation . . . ," *New York Times*, April 20, 1986, p. A1.

35. Despite U.S. Embassy cables documenting fraud, Secretary of State Shultz took a Panamanian electoral commission's word that elections held there in 1984 were honest. Shultz attended the new president's inauguration. In the same year Shultz and Reagan repudiated a Nicaraguan presidential election deemed fair by several U.S. academic and Western European parliamentary delegations ("Shultz Explains '84 Panama Trip," *New York Times*, June 24, 1986, p. A6).

36. David Green, *The Containment of Latin America* (Chicago: Quadrangle Books, 1971), pp. 229–230.

37. "Revolution Beyond Our Borders," Special Report 132, published by the Department of States' Bureau of Public Affairs, September 1985.

38. The first white paper in particular invited this response. See, among others, "Apparent Errors Cloud U.S. 'White Paper,'" *Wall Street Journal*, June 8, 1981, p. 1. For an unprecedented congressional indictment of U.S. officials for misrepresenting intelligence findings, see the Staff Report of the Subcommittee on Oversight and Evaluation of the Permanent Select Committee on Intelligence, U.S. House of Representatives, *U.S. Intelligence Performance on Central America: Achievements and Selected Instances of Concern* (September 22, 1982).

39. "Latin Arms Trade Detailed in Court," *New York Times*, September 17, 1985, p. A9.

40. "Shultz Accused of Misquoting Sandinista Policy," *Washington Post*, October 4, 1983, p. A10.

41. "Excerpts from Reagan's Speech on Aid for Nicaragua Rebels," *New York Times*, June 25, 1986, p. A12.

42. Shultz before the Veterans of Foreign Wars, March 3, 1986, printed by the State Deparment as *Current Policy*, no. 801. Reagan made the same charge in a televised address May 9, 1984, printed in the Department of State *Bulletin*, June 1984, p. 24. For the Markey episode, see the previously cited "Shultz Accused of Misquoting Sandinista Policy."

43. Foreign Broadcast Information Service, "Interior Minister's Tomas Borge's 19 July Speech," July 21, 1981.

44. "Revolution Beyond Our Borders," p. 31, note 1. Also see p. 5.

45. U.S. Department of State, "The 72-Hour Document" (Washington, D.C.: February 1986), pp. 8, 15.

46. "The 72-Hour Document," p. 13.

47. "The 72-Hour Document," p. 10.

48. "Nicaragua Imports Seen as a Buildup for Defense," *Boston Globe*, November 13, 1984, p. 10.

49. "Stinger Missiles' Usefulness for Contras Is Questioned," *New York Times*, April 4, 1986, p. A6; "New Soviet Mi-17 Copters," *Latin American Monitor: Central America*, August 1986, p. 321; "U.S. Set to Offer Newer Jet Fighter to the Hondurans," *New York Times*, October 31, 1986, p. A1.

50. "Nicaragua Imports Seen as a Buildup for Defense."

51. "The 72-Hour Document," p. 2; "Nicaraguan Army . . . ," *New York Times*, March 30, 1985, p. A5; Arms Control and Foreign Policy Caucus, "Nicaraguan Military Power" (revised edition of the February 1985 paper).

52. Shirley Christian, *Nicaragua: Revolution in the Family* (New York: Random House, 1985), p. 195.

53. "Reagan Criticizes the Latin Debate," *New York Times*, April 18, 1984, p. A13.

54. "Transcript of Interview with President . . . ," *New York Times*, March 23, 1986, p. A23.

55. Peter Clement, "Moscow and Nicaragua: Two Sides of Soviet Policy," *Comparative Strategy* 3, no. 1 (1985), pp. 84–85.

56. James LeMoyne, "The Guerrilla Network," *New York Times Magazine*, April 6, 1986, p. 18. LeMoyne, a reporter with a great deal of experience in Central America, concluded: "The Soviet Union seems to play a limited role in the region" (p. 20).

57. "Despite Fears of U.S., Soviet Aid to Nicaragua Appears to Be Limited," *Wall Street Journal*, April 3, 1985, p. 1.

58. Nestor Sanchez, "What Was Uncovered in Grenada," *Caribbean Review* 12, no. 4 (fall 1983), p. 59. An administration white paper on Grenada released December 16, 1983 (*Grenada: A Preliminary Report*), suggested that only a quarter of these "10,800 men under arms" may have been destined for active duty, the remainder serving as reserves. Sanchez ignored this possibility in his article. Not only is a reserve army defensive in purpose, but it can soak up a lot of uniforms and rifles.

59. Jorge Dominguez, "US Fears Not Well Documented," *Boston Globe*, October 21, 1984, section A, p. 23. For an analysis of administration manipulation of public perceptions in the Grenada invasion, see Eldon Kenworthy, "Grenada as Theater," *World Policy Journal* 1, no. 3 (spring 1984).

60. "Overseeing the C.I.A. by Congress," *New York Times*, July 7, 1986, p. A1.

61. In a story filed from Mexico, the *Washington Post* asserted that "senior diplomats of four Latin American and three non-Latin U.S. allies" "disputed strongly" the administration claim that most Latin governments secretly "favor a tough line against Nicaragua." Said one "western ambassador," "That is just not what we are being told by the Latin Americans" ("Latin Mood Shifts Against Washington," *Washington Post*, March 17, 1986, p. A18). Administration manipulation of public opinion poll data from Costa Rica was detailed by National Public Radio's "All Things Considered," March 24, 1986.

62. United States Advisory Commission on Public Diplomacy, *Annual Report on the U.S. Information Agency* (Washington, D.C., 1986), p. 17.

63. Octavio Paz, *The Labyrinth of Solitude* (New York: Grove Press, 1961), p. 23.

TEN

The U.S. Media: Covering (Over) Nicaragua

JACK SPENCE

News coverage of Central America increased exponentially after 1978 with the onset of the crisis in Central America. From 1969 to 1977 the networks spent a total of one hour on Nicaragua—all on the 1972 earthquake. In the eighteen months following January 1978 there were six hours of coverage.[1] Increased media attention, however, stemmed not from a crisis in Central America but from a crisis in U.S. foreign policy. The crisis in Central America began years before the arrival of network camera crews. In the 1970s peasant access to land was reduced dramatically. The media ignored this fundamental crisis as well as Salvador's crucial 1972 election and the increasing political and economic deterioration of non-Somocista Nicaraguan groups at the hands of Somoza's corruption.

The two case studies of news stories on Nicaragua presented here suggest that, despite vastly increased coverage, the media slights crucial political Central American dynamics unless they happen to pertain to issues framed in Washington, particularly in the White House. The increased coverage of Central America was really coverage of Washington once El Salvador and Nicaragua had become "hot spots."

One case study reviews 181 *New York Times* articles from January through June 1986, a period in which Nicaragua stories were mostly framed by the 1986 contra aid debate. The second case study contrasts print and television coverage of Nicaragua's 1984 election with that of El Salvador's 1982 election.

Because Washington defines the news issues, news consumers cannot realistically see the situation in Nicaragua. For example, access to land and land ownership patterns continues to be one of the most important political issues facing Nicaragua's agrarian society. The 181 early 1986 *Times* Nicaragua stories contain one sentence alluding to this crucial issue.[2]

Most of the 1986 *New York Times* Nicaragua stories emanated from Washington. Innumerable presidential claims against the Sandinistas in 1986 were widely reported. Despite the obvious relevance of contrary views and a self-proclaimed media norm of balance, the president's charges went almost wholly unexamined. Many stories in both case studies from Central America became news because they provided data to a news frame established in Washington. Whether the "main" anti-government opposition would take part in the Nicaraguan election was the major news frame, but actually it was not an issue at all in coverage of Salvador's election because of Washington's consensus in favor of what it saw as Nicaragua's "main" opposition and against exiled Salvadoran political groups.[3] The contras were more controversial in Washington than the Sandinistas so the president's freedom fighter line did not entirely prevail when accounts provided evidence of contra corruption (of U.S. money). But Nicaraguan issues such as the effects of the war on Nicaragua, Sandinista programs, popularity, and support were not part of the news agenda as the case studies reveal.

Broken-Record Journalism

According to administration officials, the National Security Council determined on January 10, 1986, that $70 million in lethal aid and $30 million in nonlethal aid should go to the contras, an increase over the $27 million nonlethal aid of the previous year. Part of the campaign to convince Congress consisted of an all-out rhetorical assault on the Sandinistas. Each salvo received press coverage.

January 13 (op.-ed.)
  Event: none
  Source: Elliot Abrams
  Charges: "*no question* [emphasis mine] the Sandinista regime is repressive and undemocratic . . . is subverting neighboring democratic countries"; tightening repression of church, press, and opposition, "concrete evidence" [not cited] supports terrorism, increasing Cuban troop and pilot role, no free press and elections, betrays revolution, contempt for international law and Contadora, people do not want them.
January 22 (p. 1)
  Event: Reagan to seek contra aid
  Source: presidential aides
  Charges: increasing repression of church and press, increased Cuban combat role, support for terrorism.
January 30 (p. 10)
  Event: contra arms needs
  Source: administration
  Charges: new evidence [not cited] that port facilities would become a Soviet base.

February 14 (p. 10)
   Event: Reagan to seek contra aid
   Source: congressional supporters of Reagan policy
   Charges: freedom fighters forced to fight Soviet helicopters with "boots
      and bandages."
February 19 (p. 10)
   Event: Reagan to seek contra aid
   Source: Reagan
   Charges: freedom fighters with bandaids and mosquito nets versus attack
      helicopters piloted by Cubans.
February 20 (p. 6)
   Event: the charge
   Source: Reagan
   Charges: Sandinista "campaign of lies" in the United States to influence
      Congress.
February 26 (p. 3)
   Event: Reagan signs aid request
   Source: Reagan
   Charges: antidemocratic, subvert neighbors, boots versus gunships, brutal
      repression ("no room for doubt"), guns to Colombian terrorists.
February 28 (p. 3)
   Event: Shultz at Congress
   Source: Shultz (in a table-pounding performance)
   Charges: no individual liberties, "a cancer, right here on our land mass,"
      subvert with arms or guerrilla training Guatemala, Honduras, El
      Salvador, Costa Rica, Colombia, Venezuela, Brazil, Ecuador, Uruguay,
      and Chile.
March 3 (p. 4)
   Event: Shultz testimony
   Source: Shultz
   Charges: Sandinistas to allow Soviet-Cuban base.
March 4 (p. 1)
   Event: Reagan steps up contra aid drive
   Source: Reagan, Shultz
   Charges: Soviet-Cuban base, threaten canal and neighboring "fragile
      democracies," terrorism sanctuary two-day drive from Harlingen,
      Texas, aid radicals from Latin America, the Middle East, and Europe,
      subversion will lead to vast migration to United States.
March 6 (p. 1)
   Event: Reagan steps up aid drive
   Source: Reagan
   Charges: Sandinistas spread "sea of red," persecute Jews.
March 7 (p. 6)
   Event: Reagan tactics, resolve in Congress
   Source: Reagan official
   Charges: Communist base will consolidate.

March 7 (p. 7)
  Event: contras at White House
  Source: Reagan and contra leaders
  Charges: repression and subversion, Reagan says choice between backing
    him or Communists.
March 8 (p. 4)
  Event: Habib appointed
  Source: Reagan
  Charges: terrorism and subversion.
March 11 (p. 1)
  Event: Reagan speech to 200 supporters
  Source: Reagan
  Charges: contras equated with Hungarian freedom fighters.
March 17 (p. 1)
  Event: Reagan TV speech
  Source: Reagan
  Charges: *all* charges previously made, Sandinista regime a "beast," a
    "cancer," a second Cuba, a Libya, threat to Caribbean sealanes and
    Mexico, traffic in drugs, "no crime to which they would not stoop."
March 21 (p. 1)
  Event: House votes down aid amid assurances of a compromise
  Source: Reagan
  Charges: "A dark day for freedom."
March 23 (p. 1)
  Event: *New York Times* interview with Reagan
  Source: Reagan
  Charge: Nicaragua an expansionist Communist bloc state.
April 23 (p. 7) (after the bombing of Libya)
  Event: none
  Source: Reagan
  Charges: Sandinistas build a Libya, aid terrorists from Germany, the
    PLO, El Salvador, and Uruguay.
June 7 (p. 5)
  Event: Reagan presses for aid
  Source: Reagan
  Charges: terrorism, subversion, help Qaddafi agents.
June 8 (p. 1)
  Event: Reagan presses for aid
  Source: Reagan
  Charges: Sandinistas accept increased aid from Soviets.
June 10 (p. 3)
  Event: Reagan and Weinberger assail Nicaragua
  Source: Reagan, Weinburger
  Charges: Libyan agents, PLO embassy, increased censorship, hundreds
    of Soviet advisers, Cuban troops "swarming the streets of Managua
    by the scores."

June 17 (p. 3)
    Event: Soviet spy plane in Nicaragua
    Source: administration officials
    Charges: spy plane, Sandinistas attack Miskitos, Communists have no
    intention to compromise.

Propaganda, Events, and Pseudoevents

Why was this news? These charges were parts of twenty-three stories in
a subset of sixty in which the administration was addressing Congress
directly or through the media, or in which Congress was responding. Some
of the charges and repeated charges were not the centerpiece of the cited
story, but many of the stories were based on pseudoevents, vehicles to
transport the president's anti-Sandinista rhetoric. Or the charges were extra-
baggage in stories on minor areas of disagreement within the administration
or between it and Congress. It was announced that the president was going
to announce his aid plan, followed by another announcement of an announcement, the announcement itself, and several headlines in which the
news was that the president was pressing his case. But Reagan had made
similar charges for years. A small article next to the transcript of Reagan's
television address (March 17, p. 13) explained that if the networks certified
a presidential address as news they would give up advertising revenues in
prime time. The speech did not have one charge against the Sandinistas
that was new, or news. The endlessly reported charges became the rhetorical
equivalent of habitual "news" photos of a smiling president (any president)
waving on arrival or departure. This approach is like selling aspirin. It is
propaganda—except a departure for Camp David is not controversial. The
charges against the Sandinistas were.

Sixty stories of legislative news amounted to news of contest, not
presentation of substance. Would the Congress take the first-time step of
voting for overt lethal military aid to the contras? Though it took a month
of reporting, the media finally concluded what had been evident (at least
to the Sandinistas) for a month—that opponents of any overt lethal aid
had no chance of winning and, therefore, would not get any press. The
New York Times focused on the narrow substantial issue (the one being
debated) of whether the $70 million in lethal aid would be delayed, with
another vote, while Reagan sought diplomatic "solutions" or answers to
such questions as whether he would get the aid with no strings attached.
The *Times* reported the president's position that diplomatic progress would
be impossible if the Sandinistas refused to negotiate with the contras. But
in almost a dozen full pages of print, it did not report much more than
this. The substance of the positions was usually at the end of the story;
the main line of the story was whether the president would or would not
consider a compromise, whether the administration's rhetoric against congressional opponents and fence sitters had been too harsh. Pat Buchanan had
charged that these groups were on the side of the Communists—it was

news that the president softened this charge to say it had not been meant to imply opponents were intentionally on the Communist side, even though that is where they ought to know they were. Fine tuning minimal distinctions was news.

The *Times* reported contest not context. It ignored the military implications for the region, did not ask anyone to assess the strength of the proposed "strings," and did not place the congressional debate in the context of international law or the Contadora process. The obviously relevant pending World Court decision was not mentioned in the 171 stories that preceded the World Court decision itself. Senator, do you think voting aid for the contras is a violation of international law? Senator, do you think giving the contras more military aid, and perhaps a larger army than Honduras, might reduce Honduran sovereignty? These apparently were not newsworthy questions.

The congressional coverage, on the other hand, did have space to record the echoes of members from both sides of the aisle of the president's anti-Sandinista charges. Lugar wanted free and fair elections in Nicaragua (March 1, p. 4); Mickey Edwards said a Soviet beachhead was being established (March 5, p. 4); Dornan found a hard-core Communist regime; and Sasser, rebutting the president's speech, began by sharing his condemnation of the Sandinistas.

Rebutting the President: Evidence and Balance

WASHINGTON REPORTING—THE SANDINISTAS DEMONIZED

Modern journalism is supposed to be differentiated from the old-fashioned news form of trumpeting the proclamations of the king because the former includes dissenting views. Regarding the charges leveled against the Sandinistas, almost no contrary view could be found in the *Times*, particularly not in the sixty president/Congress stories or stories from Washington regarding international diplomacy or military affairs or Nicaragua itself. And the exceptions, as we will see, prove the rule.

This exclusion might be defended on the grounds that, after all, the Washington story was mainly the debate between the president and Congress, and, to take Elliot Abrams' word for it, the Sandinistas no longer had friends in Congress. This defense does not hold up. If there was "no question" that the Sandinistas were brutal dictators, why was it necessary for the *Times* to repeat the charges with such frequency unless the news hook was an apparent verbal obsession in the White House? The president sought to eliminate from public view favorable or even ambivalent evaluations of the Sandinistas. The *Times* tacitly accepted his views, seeking out no others, thus contributing to a drastic narrowing of acceptable grounds for public debate. The president's Red-baiting strategy worked. One story noted at the end that no evidence of that day's charge had been offered, but supporting evidence was never present.

The *Times* rarely gave a tip of the hat to balance. Four times the Nicaraguan Embassy was given a buried line or two. Once it got to state that it regretted that the aid was being considered. Another time its assertion that the findings of international human rights groups did not support the president's charge made the story.

Half a dozen times in sixty president/Congress stories the reporter added a background balance line. In one story, late in the campaign, the president had Cubans swarming the streets. Caspar Weinberger said (amid other charges) that there was really no debate about the brutal actions of the Nicaraguan leaders. In paragraph (or graf) 12 of this 15-graf story Gerald Boyd added, "Although the Reagan Administration often refers to the Nicaraguan government as Marxist, Sandinista leaders say their ideology is based only partly on Marxism. They say it is also a product of their country's history of conflict with the United States, which sent troops to occupy Nicaragua early in this century and later supported the long rule of the deposed Somoza family."

This comment was helpful because U.S. support of Somoza no longer resided in White House historical thinking but hardly responsive to the charges. And precisely the same "balancing" graf, again well into a multi-charge story, was used by Boyd in a March 7 story and before that by David Shipler on February 26. It was as if the *Times* had a software program that, at rare and odd intervals, automatically kicked in a boilerplate "balancing" graf beyond that story's halfway point.[4]

Three stories openly took issue with three of the president's many charges. On March 19, three days after the president's televised address, Alan Riding reported that the Brazilian government's skepticism and annoyance about the president's claim—accompanied by a map with spreading red ink emanating from Nicaragua—that Nicaragua (a country of 3 million) was subverting Brazil (a country of 140 million). Another story reported that the president's own Drug Enforcement Agency found no convincing evidence of Sandinista drug trafficking. One story on March 19 aired the doubts of a rabbi that there had been Sandinista persecution of Jews in Nicaragua. However, two more stories on this theme followed, generally favoring the president's view.[5]

These exceptions so violated the "no debate about . . ." rule that the president discussed them on April 9 in a *Times*-reported speech to the American Society of Newspaper Editors: "I'd hardly gotten through my televised address asking support for the freedom fighters in Nicaragua when some voices were questioning some of the charges I made against the Sandinista regime. For example, that the Sandinistas engaged in vicious acts of anti-Semitism and that they'd been deeply involved in the illicit drug trade. But . . . the Anti–Defamation League of B'nai Brith quickly issued a strong statement confirming the truth." And the president thanked the editors for printing those supporting views. One can only imagine the intensity of a presidential rebuke had the *Times* published stories debating other charges or airing positive opinions about the Nicaraguan government.

In short there was no balance and no supportive evidence to be found in the barrage of charges against the Sandinistas. A modicum of balance could be found in the views of Washington newsmakers who disagreed with the president's tactics but apparently not with his views on the Sandinistas. The *Times*, no less than Congress, rode the ideological narrows of the Potomac River.

THE FREEDOM FIGHTERS

The administration's unrelieved, unchallenged criticisms of the Sandinistas found their counterpoint in its gushing enthusiasm for the freedom fighters. Reagan's glowing spotlight on the contras and his dominant power in shaping the news agenda brought to the *Times* thirty-three articles about the contras, as opposed to the congressional debate on contra aid. The contras, in fact, received more stories (thirty-three to twenty-five) and more ink (727 column inches as opposed to 417) than did the Nicaraguan government.[6] The discrepancy increases by adding eleven stories (109 inches) on the internal anti-Sandinista opposition.[7]

Three of the thirty-three contra stories simply amplified the president's campaign with contra leaders Calero, Cruz, and Robelo featured in White House–sponsored news events. These stories did not allude to the CIA organization of the contras or its payments to Cruz and Calero.

Five other stories attributed the contras' reduced military presence to dwindling supplies and poor training and to the new Sandinista helicopter air power—precisely the conditions Reagan wanted to correct. But the contras did not emerge from these stories as soldiers victimized by an irresponsible Congress; they were disorganized and inept.[8]

Only one of the thirty-three stories, a full month before the first house vote, focused on contra human rights abuses. Stephen Kinzer verified a case in a human rights report by going to one of the towns included in the report (February 20, p. 7). Other stories on the contras made reference to these abuses, in particular a James LeMoyne story analyzing the diminished presence of the contras (March 9, p. 1E). One story, focusing on CIA involvement in Honduras, implicated the contras in disappearances and killings of Honduran leftists (February 14, p. 1). A Kinzer story, several weeks after the first House vote, described a contra attack on a village (the headline simply said "War Comes to a Nicaraguan Village," April 16, p. 3). The contras had burned some houses and taken away Sandinista officials. Kinzer had picked a village in which the Sandinistas were not likely to be popular, one inhabited by displaced Miskitos. Another story told of charges of contra cocaine and arms trafficking (April 11, p. 3).

Three stories aired claims that the contra leaders had been skimming money.[9] Another five articles chronicled power struggles in contra ranks: Pastora was dumped by his lieutenants, who were urged on by a CIA operative, and who then joined the Robelo/Cruz faction rivaling the Calero/Colonel Bermúdez faction (page 3 stories on May 11, 12, and 30). James LeMoyne evidently sided with the Cruz/Robelo wing against the "extreme" conservative, Somocista-dominated Calero wing as the battle was joined in a Miami convention (May 16, p. 5; May 23, p. 1). In the final story, a compromise was struck (May 30, p. 3). In these stories the freedom fighters did not measure up to Reagan's heroic images. But, stories of factionalism and corruption received far more and better timed journalistic play than evidence of a pattern of disemboweling Sandinista officials and other civilians. The implication of the *Times'* imbalance was that honest use of the taxpayers' money is important, atrocities less so if the victims are pro-Sandinista.

The coverage made little effort to see U.S. aid to the contras in historical perspective. Carter's negotiating stance when Somoza looked shaky was to keep the Sandinistas out of power, first by controlled, "open" elections with Somoza running, and then, as the military balance against him, to have him and a few notorious colonels removed but to keep his party and the National Guard intact. This approach was "pluralism"; its main aim was to keep the Sandinistas out. In Miami in 1986, U.S. brokers were after a similar coalition with many of the same players—Somocistas, the National Guard, and the most conservative conservatives, joined by a molified group of anti-Sandinista liberals.

Nor did *Times* reporters explore contra motives or compare them to the origins of the insurgency of El Salvador. In one tantalizing sentence in a story on why the contras were not more effective, a Western analyst suggested that the rebels in El Salvador fought better because they had real grievances.[10] They did not go to the hills because another force, opposed by the United States, was controlling most of the levers of power but because they were forced into armed rebellion when reform efforts were met with death squads. The opposition faced no such conditions in Nicaragua, but to have raised this as a dominant theme in the Nicaragua stories would have led to debating the "beyond debate" questions. The contras' corruption could be aired, and human rights abuses given passing references, but the reason for their existence could not be questioned.

The Internal Opposition and Freedom of the Press

The opposition to the Sandinistas inside Nicaragua can be divided into two categories—those who participated in the 1984 election and those who advocated abstention. Only the latter groups, those most ardently opposed to the Sandinistas, received early 1986 coverage in the *Times*, and they got a less critical press than the contras.

The news frame reflected the president's agenda; the groups were portrayed as victims of Sandinista civil rights abuses. In "U.S. Indian Says Sandinistas Bomb Villages," Russell Means claimed to have been a wounded witness on a clandestine tour with Miskito leader Brooklyn Rivera. The story (February 11, p. 6) did not mention that Rivera had earlier toured villages openly while negotiating with the government and could have done so again, nor that Means had earlier threatened to bring warriers to fight the Sandinistas. Four of fourteen grafs at the end contained a government denial and a reference to the government-sponsored autonomy process. But this extremely important process involving complex peace negotiations between the government, local Miskito commanders, and other Atlantic Coast ethnic groups did not merit more of the *Times'* attention.

"Nicaragua Businessmen Express Fear of Attacks by the Sandinistas" (March 6, p. 10) featured Enrique Bolaños of COSEP, an anti-Sandinista businessmen's association. He was worried that a recent Ortega speech singled out COSEP for criticism. Bolaños stated that a former head of COSEP had been killed by the security police and that his own land had been confiscated in 1985. No other versions appeared. The former COSEP chief was killed, all admit, while gunrunning; there is a dispute as to whether there was a firefight. The Sandinistas say the government offered Bolaños more good quality land in a region with fewer landless peasants. Bolaños would not listen to the offer nor would he have taken land expropriated from someone else, even Somoza.[11] The story had no criticism of COSEP or Bolaños, though a reporter would not have had to travel far in Nicaragua to find a critical comment.

In "Nicaragua Is Cracking down as Vendors Defy Price Curbs" (March 12, p. 4), the vendors said their blackmarket (my word) prices reflected higher costs, but the "unmoved" inspectors fined them anyway. At the end of the story, there was at least a short (and very rare) bit of text concerning the problems of underdevelopment and the government's claim that price controls are needed to help the poor. But explanation of the crucial Third World problem of food production and price policy was not possible in the "Sandinistas harass entrepreneurs" frame of the story. Scattered quotes geared to "balance" the vendors' viewpoint did little to clarify the complex and unfamiliar setting. And the "balance"—a quote saying without official prices the poor would suffer—was so buried that it had little impact on the Sandinista repressing vendors theme.

Many of the 181 articles critically mentioned Sandinista press censorship; one story (April 18, p. 3) focused on a proposal by editor Jaime Chamorro's pro-Sandinista brother Xavier to buy *La Prensa*, a plot by the government according to Jaime. The story does not mention that the family had previously bought out Xavier, who had majority support among employees but only a minority on the board of directors. Following the sale, views sympathetic to the Sandinistas were excised from the paper. In the second-to-last graf Kinzer did note that even though the harshest antigovernment articles are cut, critical articles appear regularly. To one seeking an assessment of the censorship this one balancing sentence hardly sufficed, but it was unusual, perhaps unique.

In one other striking example, Kinzer found "lively" political debate in Nicaragua (March 20, p. 8). He then noted that Reagan's anti-Sandinista speech was also broadcast on Sandinista television followed by a panel discussion with opposition participants. (One awaits the broadcast here of a formal address by Ortega followed by a panel with a pro-Sandinista representative.) Kinzer noted other opposition speeches and six freewheeling independent radio news shows. The article covered its bases, with quotes from opposition leaders complaining about restrictions or expression. Kinzer estimated that the limits on freedom of speech and press were nowhere near as thoroughgoing as in Cuba or other Communist bloc countries, a comparison accepting Reagan's Soviet beachhead framework but finding it not so true. But he did not draw a comparison with El Salvador—where right-wing death squads had killed tens of thousands whose political views they did not like—which had nevertheless received the U.S. good democratic housekeeping seal of approval.

These two notes—one at the end of an article, the other a heavily qualified exception to Reagan dogma—were small breaks in a four-year-long storm of allegations of no press freedom. In 104 articles in 1984 dealing with the Nicaraguan elections from the *Boston Globe, New York Times,* and *Washington Post,* 65 mentioned press censorship.

Although one might expect that the press would naturally focus on freedom of the press, coverage of this issue parallels the foreign policy agenda set by the White House. The daily press and television remained silent about the issue of freedom of the press in El Salvador, the Central American country rivaling Nicaragua in press attention since 1980. Had there been freedom of the press in El Salvador? The September 1985 Americas Watch Report on El Salvador took up the topic this way:

> Any discussion of press freedom in El Salvador must begin by pointing out the elimination of the country's two main opposition newspapers. *La Crónica del Pueblo* was closed in 1980 when members of the security forces raided a San Salvador coffee shop where the paper's editor and one of its photographers were meeting. Editor Jaime Suarez, a 31-year-old prize-winning poet, and Cesar Najarro, were disemboweled by machete and then shot. In 1981 *El Independiente* was closed when army tanks surrounded its offices. This was the culmination of a long series of attacks, which included the machinegunning of a 14-year-old newsboy, bombing and assassination attempts against editor Jorge Pinto. The Archdiocese's radio station, WMAX, spent several years out of commission after its offices were repeatedly bombed. Since 1981 the Salvadoran press has either supported the government or criticized it from a right-wing perspective. Daily newspapers do not publish criticism . . . from a leftist perspective, nor do they print stories critical of government forces from a human rights standpoint.[12]

Although the *Times* repeatedly drew attention to press conditions in Nicaragua since the inception of censorship in 1982, this glaring abuse of press freedom in pro-United States El Salvador went conspicuously unmentioned.

Even Kinzer's admission, at the end of the April 18 article, that critical articles regularly appeared in *La Prensa* understated the point. In three visits to Nicaragua in 1984 and 1985 I found articles every day with more hard hitting criticism of the Sandinistas than were found in U.S. dailies against any administration.

An issue of *La Prensa* (May 9, 1984) that I discovered by accident in a New York office prior to my doing a television interview on *La Prensa* illustrates the point. *La Prensa*'s middle of the page lead headline that day announced the World Court ruling that held that the court did have jurisdiction to try Nicaragua's case against the United States. At the top of the page *La Prensa* placed a large, grim picture of soldiers carrying a coffin. Next to this, a story featured a Nicaraguan opposition party. Below this, and above the main headline, appeared a Reagan attack on the Sandinistas with a large picture of Reagan. Below the main headline the editors chose two more stories highlighting opposition parties. And below them was a positive view of the Salvadoran election. (*La Prensa* in 1984 opposed participation in Nicaragua's election.)

The space on the front page was almost taken up by stories on the opposition and Reagan without one story featuring the Nicaraguan government. Imagine an issue of the *New York Times* without one story emanating from the current administration. Finally, in the bottom right corner a tiny story could be found about the Nicaraguan government giving military decorations to those who had downed a Honduran helicopter. The grim-looking coffin in the far corner of the page held one killed when the copter crashed.

In the main story, the headline on the court decision did not mention that Nicaragua won and the United States lost; it simply said that the court ruled that it had jurisdiction over the case, a point bitterly contested by the United States and ardently upheld by Nicaragua. There were six grafs on the first page, *all* of them devoted to the U.S. reaction to the decision, stating basically that it was meaningless. On the back page were a few grafs explaining the meaning of jurisdiction and then, a graf from the end, a sentence of reaction from the government of Nicaragua.

In the United States, Jesse Jackson on the Left and Barry Goldwater on the Right had both concluded that mining the harbors—the center of the World Court case—was an act of war. In the country being attacked, *La Prensa* had an account that heavily favored the attacking country and completely subordinated any opportunity for its own country's government to comment. These uncensored stories and the makeup of the page looked somewhat like those in the *New York Times*. Reagan was featured; Nicaragua got a sentence on the back page.

The series of 1985 *Times* articles framed by the contra aid vote closes with the crucial House vote, the definitive World Court decision against the United States, and an article from Managua on the Sandinista's closing of *La Prensa*, headlined "Sandinistas Say Closed Newspaper Backed U.S." (June 28, p. 4). Not until the last quarter of the last article, following numerous quotes from the opposition, and then one by the government that repeated the headline, did the author offer evidence pertinent to the headline. He said that the paper had been reluctant to criticize the U.S.-backed rebels and that its last edition had called for negotiations with the rebels, the position of the United States and the rebels.

None of the final articles assessed the impact of the war on Nicaraguan society, though they stressed the decree suspending *La Prensa* publication in civil libertarian terms. The *Times* systematically underplayed or eliminated the perspective of the Sandinistas—a product of the range of permissible debate and a legacy of "patriotic" journalism, as well as of the *Times'* own ideological leanings. Imagine, if possible, that an army financed by an alien power, one with longstanding bad relations, had been making cross border raids into Minnesota for some five years, and the violence had led to a death in one of every fifty families. A St. Paul daily, heavily financed by the same alien power, had published stories criticizing the Minnesota government but none about the alien financed and organized army. Of course, there would be heavy political pressure against the paper. The *Times'* elimination of the societal damage of the war, financed by the United States, and failure to consider the liberties that the U.S.-financed *La Prensa* did have in a time of war made it more difficult for a U.S. audience to understand censorship and easier for a Congress to vote for escalation.

Can "Brutal Dictators" Be Elected or Popular? The Issue Avoided

In the last article from this *New York Times* 1986 collection Kinzer sized up a Sandinista rally. His fifth sentence said, "The large turnout reflected the strong base of support the Government maintains, especially among young people, despite the continuing war, food shortages, galloping inflation and other problems." After journeying through many stories affirming the anti-Sandinista views of Reagan, the Congress, pundits, the contras, and the internal opposition—who all agreed the Sandinistas were repressive or brutal dictators—casual readers might blink in disbelief at this needle-in-the-haystack sentence. On their journey they would have encountered nothing—well, almost nothing—to suggest that anybody but Ortega could favor the Sandinistas or that the brutal dictators were elected.

Reporters were not wholly unconcerned with the hearts and minds of the Nicaraguan people. Three articles that might be called "the riddle of lack of support for the contras" implied, without addressing the issue, that the Sandinistas had little support (March 6, p. 1; March 9, p. E1; March 16, p. E2). They asked, in a time of "growing discontent" with the Sandinistas, why had the contras not received more support? The "growing discontent" theme made its first of frequent *Times* appearances in early 1980, a half year after Somoza's defeat.[13] If the reporters could so easily sense the pulse of discontent, should one assume that popular support had no pulse?

The first of the three stories, by LeMoyne, estimated the contras had support from conservative Catholic peasants—certainly a suggestion of a popular base in a Catholic peasant society. The author omitted evidence that contras dragoon peasant soldiers. Excontra leader Edgar Chamorro, in World Court testimony, said that after contras publicly machine-gunned local Sandinista leaders it was easy to get "volunteers." But the contras had little support from urban areas or from the middle class, LeMoyne explained. These groups saw the contras as former Somocistas, military types. In the second story, LeMoyne added that the contras had no program and "even worse" often brutalized Sandinista officials enabling the Sandinistas to wage an effective "propaganda" war.

In the third story, Kinzer also said the contras were not capitalizing on "Nicaragua's discontent." Many Nicaraguans were "frustrated and angry" that "life is in some ways worse than before." Kinser found "deep resentment in some quarters" over economic changes and a lack of Sandinista respect toward religion. Still the contras were not getting the support in the urban areas that the Sandinistas had mustered in their fight against Somoza. Why? People were afraid and weary of war, and they associated the contras with Somoza. In the midst of this article appeared a brief acknowledgment that the government provided subsidized food and goods to the needy (though it was not pointed out how large a group that was) and that the revolution's most enthusiastic supporters "include young people and tens of thousands that have benefitted from land distribution." Could the contras' popularity problems be in part due to the broad or deep popularity of the other side? It was not a question the *Times* cared to address.

Forgotten in *Times* coverage dedicated to charges against the "brutal dictatorship" was the fact that "brutal dictator" Ortega had been elected in November 1984 with a higher plurality (and a higher proportion of voting age population) than Reagan himself had gained in his 1984 landslide election. It was not relevant to mention that the contras led by Somocista officers were attempting to overthrow a government elected by secret ballot in competition with six other parties. This lack of attention stemmed from the media coverage of the election itself. A comparison with network and print coverage afforded the 1982 election in El Salvador shows that Nicaragua's election was skeptically downplayed; El Salvador's was hyped. The coverage differed dramatically on every point of comparison.[14]

For the 1982 Salvadoran election, network stories on election day and the day after averaged an extraordinary eight minutes (out of twenty-two per broadcast), for a total of forty-eight minutes. The networks' attention to the Nicaraguan election on election day and the day after amounted to 6 minutes 20 seconds, 13 percent of Salvadoran coverage. NBC did not broadcast on Sunday and gave the election no coverage on Monday. For CBS the election was a non-event on Monday. In 1982, the *Times* ran four front-page stories in two days. The Nicaraguan voting did not make the front page.

Media coverage of the 1982 Salvadoran election celebrated a return of democracy to El Salvador. The election was in media eyes the first free and fair election in the past fifty years. A "fledgling democracy" had been established. Media reports had pre-election doubts. NBC portrayed campaigning by Christian Democrat Duarte and right-wing Roberto D'Aubuisson as stump politics U.S. style. But it noted that many armed people were evident at campaign rallies and that D'Aubuisson had been tied to death squads. Richard Threlkeld on ABC (March 26) worried about fraud and that the entire Salvadoran Left might not vote. And the guerrillas, said the media, had called for a boycott and might attack the elections. As Threlkeld put it, the election was an "examination in democracy" to see if El Salvador deserved U.S. aid.

The doubts dramatically set the stage for the portrayal of a country passing its examination or being prevented from doing so by the violence of left-wing guerrillas. Before the election, the media briefly mentioned the possibility of the government threatening people to vote. But that issue faded by election day, whereas the issue of guerrilla pressure not to vote provided the spectacular "ballots over bullets" news frame. "Salvadorans Defy Bullets to Vote" headlined the *Boston Globe* (March 29, 1982, p. 1), and the media assumed guerrilla attacks near polling places were to "terrorize" the electorate. "Bang bang" battle coverage, always at a premium, got maximum attention. None of the media reported that the guerrillas had broadcast a cancellation of their earlier call to boycott; none thought it strange that these attacks did not kill one voter. (Reagan praised in four major addresses the same voter who was grazed by a stray bullet.) Even if we use an expansive definition of a polling place firefight (a half mile away, two hours before voting) from media reports, then fully 98 percent of the polling places were apparently violence free.

The media gave El Salvador the highest marks. Election day reports saw an enormous turnout, far exceeding expectations. But the media used expectations from the U.S. Embassy, which wanted to exceed expectations. The *Times* illustrated a multicolored sea of people marching down roads to the polls (March 28, p. 1). Cameras panned long lines of voters who had turned out, the networks said, despite guerrilla bullets. The media saw the election as a referendum on the leftist boycott of the election. Earlier stories had a buried sentence without expanation that the Left thought the election was a farce. Of course the Left had no access in this "referendum" to the Salvadoran media or any traditional electoral rights. Still, the media agreed that the Left had lost the vote.

A host of mutually reinforcing commentators drove these messages home. The media quoted members of the official U.S. observer team who found no fraud or coercion. The U.S. ambassador lauded the election on network morning shows. Strangely, the White House and State Department, also given extensive coverage, had similar views. Salvadoran politicians, mostly Christian Democrats, found this an astounding exercise in democracy—though there was no voter registration because many of the people were displaced and though innumerable Left political figures had been shot, tortured, or forced into exile. Of some forty-five voters quoted in three major papers and the major newsweeklies and on the networks, only one, speaking to a reporter who went to a slum where there had been a firefight, had anything negative to say about the election. (*New York Times*, March 30, 1982, p. 1). The others said they were voting for peace and democracy (and the coverage showed the guerrillas as the source of violence) or, more cryptically, because it was their civic duty. Reporters added their own voices to this chorus of praise. Frank Reynolds found "this exercise in democracy . . . gratifying, even inspiring" and, he said numerous times, a defeat for the Left. Dan Rather called it a "triumph"; Tom Brokaw, "one of the most remarkable election days anywhere."

There were a few postelection doubts. Would D'Aubuisson's party win, thereby creating more doubts about aid from Congress or would there be an ungovernable coalition? After all, exam grader Threlkeld noted, the Italians had been trying coalition government for forty years and still "hadn't gotten the hang of it." But optimism overrode these doubts. Reporters saw "hard bargaining" and the "give and take" of democracy, and death squad leader D'Aubuisson had become a "born-again politician."

The press ignored the election's repressive conditions. Since 1979, security forces and right-wing death squads had been implicated in assassinations of over 25,000 civilians, in a campaign to wipe out anyone with a remote connection to left of center political groups. The defense minister said not voting was tantamount to treason. Nonvoters faced the daunting prospect of passing through military checkpoints with ID cards unstamped on voting day. Many voting booths were not fully curtained, and ballot boxes were transparent, to be filled with sequentially numbered, nearly translucent paper ballots. Finally, it was likely that the civilian government would have limited governing power over the military.

If the media had given Nicaragua the same set of democracy examination questions it gave El Salvador, it would have been obliged, at the very least, to give Nicaragua the same "A" marks it had doled out in El Salvador. In Nicaragua, despite a history of fraudulent elections, there were no claims of fraud by participants or nonparticipants. Observers from the United States and Western European parliaments were favorably impressed.[15] Unlike in El Salvador, parties of the Left and Right and civilian political forces opposed to the election were able to operate within Nicaragua and make their views known (though a formal boycott campaign technically violated the election law). La Prensa, opposed to the election, could refuse to accept campaign ads or notices from participating parties. The Democratic Conservative party charged the censored La Prensa with censorship.

Despite the boycott and a contra call to vote null, the turnout was as high, and very likely higher, in Nicaragua than it had been in El Salvador. The percentage of null and defaced ballots was half that of El Salvador. The election had not been preceded by a two-year bloodbath aimed at killing off opposition politicians, trade union members, and schoolteachers deviating from the forces governing the country. Voting was nonobligatory and completely secret. Voter cards obtained during an obligatory registration (Salvador had no voter registration in 1982) were turned in so nonvoters would not carry evidence that they had not voted. The contra violence directed at the election was considerably more severe. Before the election seven election officials had been killed, and one candidate on the Sandinista ticket had been shot while campaigning and held in captivity for weeks.

The predominant news fare for the Nicaraguan elections did not concern these matters. Rather it focused on the boycotters and their objections to the election. The headline to the initial *New York Times* story, ten months before the election, set the tone—"Election Plan in Nicaragua Is Criticized by Opposition" (January 18, 1984, p. 3). In El Salvador, the boycotters received attention only to the extent that their military activities were held to threaten voters and disrupt the elections. The Salvadoran Left's reasons for nonparticipation received no attention. Once in a great while, a buried sentence noted one reason: their claim that Left candidates would not be safe. By contrast, in Nicaragua the military activities of the boycotters, heavily criticized by Americas Watch for a policy of violence against civilians, received no attention.

Of 104 stories from the *Boston Globe*, *New York Times*, and *Washington Post*, dating from January 1984 through the aftermath of the November election, boycotters and Reagan administration's objections to the election received, at a minimum, very substantial mention in 80. The only election story that made the *Times'* front page, four months before the election, featured Reagan calling it a Soviet-style sham.

The possible boycott of Arturo Cruz was the centerpiece of this coverage. His coalition (three small parties, COSEP, and trade unions) was always billed as the leading opposition group. Other opposition groups received no coverage until, late in the race and under U.S. Embassy pressure, they contemplated dropping out. Not one shred of evidence could be found in media coverage to suggest that Cruz had any more vote-getting pull than the Democratic Conservative party or the Independent Liberal party. One would have to make mind-boggling assumptions about the election returns (say, that every person who stayed home wanted to vote for Cruz) to imagine he would have significantly outpolled other opposition groups much less rivaled the Sandinistas.

The focus on Cruz's objections continued, even after coverage of CIA financing of COSEP, the strongest group in his coalition, and after July interviews with leaders of his coalition suggesting that they never seriously considered having Cruz run.

The press downplayed the voting. The next day a *Times* piece presented administration views that the election would worsen relations. As the results were coming in, the Nicaragua story moved to the front page—not a story on the issue of elections, but one on Reagan administration leaks that Soviet ships were bringing MiGs to Nicaragua. The anti-Sandinista bias in this coverage is another story, but the MiG crisis completely overshadowed election coverage as the administration MiG leaks (which proved to be false) intended. The media followed along.

Conclusion

Coverage of Nicaragua's Sandinistas amplified the president's condemnation. It did so literally by repeating the president's repetitions. Evidence supporting the president's charges was not relevant; stories never said "the charge could not be independently confirmed." The president did not wholly get his way in news reporting; the contras did not emerge from press accounts as boy scouts. But the critique of the contras in the press was more attracted to money-skimming charges than gross human rights abuses. The press did not offer views that questioned whether the United States should finance a war to overthrow an elected government because the legitimacy of the government was not an issue in Washington, as coverage of the 1984 election made clear. The only issue was whether diplomatic means might be possible or whether the contras deserved U.S. support.

The 1984 election coverage focused on a U.S.-backed opposition coalition. Even that group did not go so far as Reagan's "totalitarian dungeon" language, but is assessment of an unfair election framed the news, precisely the strategy being played by the State Department. In contrast to the bubbling coverage of the Salvadoran election, the *Times* headline for Nicaragua's election day saw voters "going through the motions." The press made no effort to see the contras or the internal opposition through Nicaraguan nationalistic eyes as yet another twentieth-century Nicaraguan political group playing the U.S. card to full, and in many cases personal, advantage.

The two case studies demonstrate that the press substantially replicated Washington biases covering over or distorting Nicarguan political dynamics in the process. Views outside acceptable Washington limits were eliminated. In so doing the press violated, or at best paid lip service to, its self-professed professional norm of balance. It only provided brief glimpses and buried pieces of evidence that might cause the very painstaking reader to question the Washington dominated view.

In the two case studies the only sustained examples of the questioning of presidential assertions came in wondering whether in 1984 the MiGs actually were arriving or whether in 1986 Nicaraguan troops had actually gone into Honduras. In the former case the White House was proved wrong but won anyway by establishing a consensus during the suspense that MiGs would be unacceptable. In the later case, in the midst of the contra debate, the frame was Washington centered: Was the White House credible, or was it exaggerating (shadows of the Gulf of Tonkin crisis) the troop movement's significance and extent? Had the Sandinistas once again misplayed their hand with Congress (though by that time it was evident to the Sandinistas, if not the *Times*, that the Congress was going to vote a substantial increase in aid)?[16] These were Washington news issues to which the Nicaraguans, given the dominance of Washington and its media in the region had to pay heed. But they do not present readers with a lens through which they can get a clear view of Nicaragua. Downplaying that government's views, or the views and conditions of its society, gives any Washington administration the upper hand to have its biases dominate the news and particularly weakens a semblance of a press-president adversarial relation when an aggressive administration repeatedly insists that certain questions are beyond debate.

Acknowledgments

I would like to thank Donna Kaye for an expert review of the manuscript.

Notes

1. El Salvador received a total of three minutes of coverage from 1970 to 1978 but almost eleven hours in 1982 alone. These and other data on quantity of network nightly news coverage are sums of raw data taken from various volumes of Vanderbilt Television News Archives, *Television News Index and Abstracts*.

2. The press has also ignored El Salvador's agrarian issue. Using a minimal definition of coverage of agrarian (any mention of "reform" or "social reform"), David Krusé found that only 3.3 percent of NBC's time on El Salvador from 1980 through 1984 mentioned the issue. It arose in 16 percent of *Times* stories, usually as just a word embedded in a sentence without analysis (David Krusé, *El Salvador and the Mass Media: Power, Symbolism and Reform*, unpublished manuscript).

3. Working to the disadvantage of Daniel Ortega, the Washington news frame helped and was helped by Napoleon Duarte. See Marc Cooper, "Whitewashing Duarte: U.S. Reporting on El Salvador," *NACLA Report on the Americas*, January 1986, pp. 7–10.

4. Two of these "balancing" grafs added a sentence of Sandinista claims to pluralism, mixed economy, and nonalignment.

5. The three March 19 stories were on page 4. The three *Times* stories on the Jewish persecution issue were "Rabbi Disputes Reagan Point About Jews in Nicaragua," March 19, p. 4; "Bias in Nicaragua Reported by Jews: Anti-Defamation League Says Accusation by Reagan in Speech Was Accurate," March 20, p. 9; "View of Jews of Nicaragua: Much Debate," April 20, p. 11.

6. The column inches measure stories leading with the topic, not references to the topic contained in all stories.

7. Three stories of members of Congress reporting on visits to Nicaragua largely reflect the views of the opposition ("House Delegation Leaves Nicaragua," March 16, p. 7; "U.S. Legislator in Managua Backs Use of Advisers," March 24, p. 2; "Traveling to Nicaragua Yields No Easy Answers," March 30, p. E3). This is not surprising since one delegation spent almost all its time with the opposition. This Potemkin Village tour seemed to be standard procedure.

8. "Most Contras Reported to Pull Out of Nicaragua," January 30, p. 10; "Anti-Sandinista Adviser Lists Aid Needs of Rebels" January 30, p. 10; "Contra Raids Trailing Off," February 21, p. 4; "Nicaragua Rebels in Retreat, Viewed as Reduced Threat," March 6, p. 1; "Battle-Weary Contras Await Reinforcements," March 9, p. E1.

9. "Contra Aid Troubling to Exiles," March 11, p. 9; "Who Got $27 Million Intended for Contras?" June 19, p. 27 (op.-ed.); "Officers Accuse Contra Chiefs Of Siphoning Off U.S. Aid Money," June 21, p. 1.

10. "Nicaragua Rebels in Retreat, Viewed as Reduced Threat," March 6, p. 1.

11. Jack Spence's interview with Enrique Bolaños, June 29, 1985, Managua.

12. Americas Watch, *The Continuing Terror: Seventh Supplement to the Report on Human Rights in El Salvador*, September 1985.

13. "Nicaragua Rebuilds, but Faces Hurdles," January 24, 1980, p. 3.

14. The analysis is based on network nightly news during the week surrounding the election and on coverage by the *Boston Globe, Washington Post, New York Times, Time, Newsweek,* and *U.S. News and World Report.*

15. Official observer teams from the Latin American Studies Association, the British and Irish Parliaments, the Dutch government, and the Socialist International (the organization of Social Democratic parties of Western Europe), and so on all gave the Nicaraguan election good grades. For their reports see the items cited in notes 14 and 15 of Thomas W. Walker's Introduction to this book.

16. The press demanded evidence of the Nicaraguan incursion and then ran quotes that it had been exaggerated by the White House. Kinzer had a good account of the Sandinistas strategy (March 30, p. E2).

ELEVEN

The Contras and Congress

WILLIAM M. LEOGRANDE

Central America was the first foreign policy issue taken up by the incoming administration of President Ronald Reagan, and he used it to set an example of his tough new foreign policy. Within three months of its inception, the administration tripled military assistance to El Salvador, cut off economic assistance to the Sandinista government in Nicaragua, and threatened direct military action against Nicaragua and Cuba to punish them for supporting the Salvadoran guerrillas.

Reagan's aggressive hard line in Central America immediately provoked opposition in Congress, but the Democrats were in disarray in the wake of Reagan's electoral landslide and the unexpected Republican majority in the Senate. Although Reagan's critics were vocal and persistent, they were confined largely to the liberal wing of the Democratic party. Rarely were they able to muster more than a third of the votes in either chamber. Their only significant victory in 1981 was legislation to make U.S. military aid to El Salvador conditional on progress toward human rights, agrarian reform, a political solution to the war, and justice for the murderers of U.S. citizens. But even this action was toothless; it required only that the president certify to Congress every six months that progress was being made toward these goals. The administration did this without apparent qualm or concern for contrary evidence.

The Origins of the Covert War

In fall 1981, the deteriorating fortunes of the Salvadoran armed forces prompted a full-scale review of U.S. policy in Central America.[1] During the policy review, the CIA proposed a variety of covert operations against Nicaragua. The least controversial was to continue financial assistance for internal opponents of the Sandinistas begun by the Carter administration and expanded by Reagan in March 1981.[2]

Among the paramilitary operations proposed, the most ambitious called for the CIA to assemble, train, arm, and direct a commando force of 500 Latin Americans, mostly Cuban exiles, to conduct paramilitary operations against Nicaragua from base camps in Honduras. The primary mission of this force would be to attack Nicaragua's economic infrastructure in the hope that the resulting economic hardship would produce political destabilization. Such a force would also enable the United States to attack "special Cuban targets" in Central America. The initial budget for this option was reportedly $19.95 million.[3]

A second option, proposed as a complement rather than alternative to the first, called for the United States to provide financial and logistical support for the efforts of Argentina's rightist military regime to train 1,000 Nicaraguan exiles for the purpose of overthrowing the Nicaraguan government. A third more limited option involved funneling military aid, particularly small arms, through the Honduran Armed Forces to Nicaraguan exiles already operating along the Nicaraguan-Honduran border.[4]

The CIA's plans touched off a heated debate within the administration over the objectives of U.S. policy toward Nicaragua. Some officials argued for a major covert effort to overthrow the Sandinistas. Others argued that such an effort would inevitably entangle the United States with the remnants of Somoza's hated National Guard—a futile alliance that would allow the Sandinistas to rally popular support. They also warned that efforts to depose the Sandinistas could spark a wider regional war, drawing the United States into direct military involvement. These officials argued that any covert operations against Nicaragua should have the limited objective of seeking to cut off any arms flow from Nicaragua to the Salvadoran guerrillas.[5]

After extended debate, President Reagan signed National Security Decision Directive 17 and a December 2, 1981, "Presidential Finding" granting the CIA broad authority to conduct covert operations in Central America.[6] The CIA was authorized to proceed with the creation of the 500-person commando force, to assist the Argentine effort to build an exile army, to establish liaison with exile groups operating from Honduras, and to work toward the creation of a broad political opposition front to the Sandinistas—in short, all the operations originally proposed were approved. Those within the administration who had argued that such operations would prove counterproductive won only a small victory; the objective of these programs would be limited, nominally at least, to halting the arms flow from Nicaragua.[7]

When the Presidential Finding was submitted to the Intelligence Committees of Congress, many members voiced concerns similar to those debated within the administration. There was strong bipartisan opposition to creating a commando force for attacking "special Cuban targets," and this aspect of the program was apparently dropped.[8]

By mid-1982 the military aid provided by the United States had transformed the exiles from a ragtag collection of small groups totaling no more than 1,000 persons into a well-equipped and professionally trained army of some 4,500, which called itself the Nicaraguan Democratic Forces (FDN).[9]

Most of the FDN's forays into Nicaragua from Honduras came in the eastern and central regions—far from the alleged arms smuggling routes along the western coast. Moreover, the contras never intercepted any arms and publicly disclaimed that they were trying to. This made it increasingly difficult for the administration to credibly maintain that the purpose of the operation was arms interdiction. By fall 1982, the administration was presenting a new rationale to Congress: The covert war was not designed to directly interdict arms but rather to punish Nicaragua in order to pressure the Sandinistas to cease their support for the Salvadoran guerrillas.[10]

Operationally, punishment meant contra attacks on border towns and targeting of economic assets—farms, warehouses, and so on. With this new strategy, the line between punishing the Sandinistas and trying to overthrow them became difficult to discern since the operations being mounted were exactly the sort originally proposed by the CIA as a way of deposing the government. By fall 1982, the contra army in Honduras was already three times the size of the invasion force at the Bay of Pigs in 1961; by fall 1984, it was ten times as large.

As the covert war widened and the U.S. role in it became more central, both the House and the Senate Intelligence Committees began to worry that the operation was spiraling far beyond the boundaries they had originally approved. In April 1982, liberal Democrats in the House committee failed in a bid to cut off funding for the covert war.[11] But, in an effort to hold the CIA to its original objective of arms interdiction and to send the administration a message that it was concerned about the direction of policy, the committee added language to the Classified Annex to the Fiscal Year (FY) 1983 Intelligence Authorization (P.L. 97-269) prohibiting U.S. aid to paramilitary groups "for the purpose of overthrowing the Government of Nicaragua or provoking a military exchange between Nicaragua and Honduras."[12]

This language was not designed to bring the covert operation to a halt; on the contrary, it was intentionally crafted to register the committees' growing uneasiness without interfering with the operation. The Reagan administration was able to interpret the law as allowing support for the contras so long as the purpose of the United States was not one of those proscribed. The intentions of the contras were irrelevant, legally at least.

This mild restriction remained a secret until December 1982 when Representative Tom Harkin (D.-Iowa) offered an amendment to the FY 1983 Defense Appropriations bill (which included appropriations for the intelligence community) to prohibit U.S. assistance to any group involved in paramilitary operations in Nicaragua. Representative Edward Boland (D.-Mass.), the chairman of the Intelligence Committee, argued that the Harkin amendment was unnecessary, assuring the House that the Intelligence Committee was carefully monitoring the situation. He offered as a substitute for Harkin's amendment the same language that had been included earlier in the Intelligence Authorization. The Republican leadership, seeking to avoid a vote on the Harkin language, supported Boland's substitute, which passed 411 to 0 and was subsequently incorporated into the Continuing Resolution (P.L. 97-377).[13] Although its passage merely reaffirmed existing law, the Boland amendment was another warning to the administration that it had not assuaged congressional concerns.

Cutting Off Aid to the Contras

By 1983, the administration's credibility and support in Congress had begun to erode. The visible failure of Reagan's Central America policy to achieve its stated objectives, its growing price tag, and the president's apparent determination to escalate U.S. involvement began to frighten moderates from both parties who had supported Reagan in the 97th Congress. Moreover, the Democrats' gains in the 1982 midterm elections tarnished the mantle of invincibility Reagan had acquired in the budget battles of 1981. The Democrats also gained enough House seats to alter the composition of key committees, including Foreign Affairs and its Inter-American Affairs Subcommittee. During the 97th Congress, Republicans and conservative Democrats had been able to block committee actions critical of Reagan's policy in Central America. During the 98th Congress, they could not.

The administration continued to expand the covert war in 1983 despite growing congressional opposition. In March, 1,500 contras invaded Nicaragua, and the intensified fighting led to a new series of press reports documenting the U.S. role in all phases of the war.[14] The new revelations convinced a number of members that the administration's real intent was to overthrow the Nicaraguan government, in violation of the Boland amendment. Senator Daniel Patrick Moynihan (D.-N.Y.), vice-chairman of the Senate Intelligence Committee, reported that a number of his colleagues had come to that conclusion. Senator Patrick Leahy (D.-Vt.) traveled to Central America on behalf of the committee to investigate U.S. operations and upon his return said that it appeared to him the administration was ignoring the intent of Congress. Representative Wyche Fowler (D.-Ga.) conducted a similar investigation for the House committee and returned with the same conclusion. Finally, Boland himself declared that the evidence was "very strong" that the administration was violating the amendment bearing his name.[15]

By being less than candid with the committees and ignoring warnings in September and December 1981, the administration lost the confidence of people like Moynihan and Boland, whose attitudes about the role of Congress in foreign policy were more traditional than activist. Boland and the Democratic leadership in the House became convinced that Congress could not control or limit the covert war because the administration would not deal with the Intelligence Committees in good faith. The only alternative, then, was to stop it. In spring 1983, the House Intelligence and Foreign Affairs Committees proposed the Boland-Zablocki bill (H.R. 2760) to prohibit the funding, directly or indirectly, of military or paramilitary operations against Nicaragua.[16]

During the same few weeks that Boland-Zablocki was being considered in committee, the Reagan administration's request for $110 million in emergency military aid for El Salvador was being slashed by the House Foreign Affairs Committee and the Appropriations Subcommittee on Foreign Operations. These setbacks led President Reagan to make an extraordinary speech on Central America to a Joint Session of Congress on April 27, 1983. Reagan tried to regain the offensive by casting the issue starkly in cold war terms, railing against the Cuban-Soviet menace and threatening to blame Congress for losing Central America if it failed to acquiesce to his demands. "Who among us," he concluded his speech, "would wish to bear the responsibility for failing to meet our shared obligation?"[17] In case there was any doubt about the import of this thinly veiled threat, UN Ambassador Jeane Kirkpatrick was more blunt a few days later when she complained that the administration's problems resulted because "there are some members of Congress who want to see Marxist victories in Central America."[18]

The Boland-Zablocki bill came to the House floor on July 27 and was bitterly debated for two days. In addition to cutting off funds for the covert war, the bill also included a provision authorizing $80 million (reportedly the sum requested by the administration for the covert war in FY 1984) in overt military aid for "friendly" Central American governments to be used for interdicting arms allegedly being smuggled from Nicaragua.[19] The overt aid provision was included to meet the administration's claim that the purpose of the covert war was to interdict arms flowing from Nicaragua to guerrilla movements in El Salvador and Guatemala. It was also required to win the support of Majority Leader Jim Wright (D.-Tex.) and enough other conservative Democrats to pass the bill.

The inclusion of overt aid, along with a series of policy statements in the bill that denounced Nicaragua for exporting revolution, angered several dozen of the most liberal members in the House. But ultimately, they were swayed by the argument that a repudiation of the covert war by the House would be an important political blow to Reagan's policy. For the liberals, the Reagan administration's vehement opposition to Boland-Zablocki was the most compelling argument in its favor. When the bill came to the floor, they swallowed their discomfort and supported it. The final tally on July 28 in favor of H.R. 2760 was 228 to 195.

Not surprisingly, the Republican-controlled Senate refused to take up Boland-Zablocki, but the House was not so easily dissuaded. On October 20, it voted 227 to 194 to add the Boland-Zablocki provisions to the FY 1984 Intelligence Authorization (H.R. 2968), and on November 2, it passed the Defense Appropriation (H.R. 4185), which included the prohibition on aid for the contras (which Boland had added in committee markup) without providing any overt aid for arms interdiction.

The Senate version of the Intelligence bill authorized a continuation of the covert war by giving the administration its full funding request. The contra aid issue stalled both the Intelligence and Defense bills in conference until a compromise was reached on the Defense Appropriation (P.L. 98-212). It provided $24 million for the covert war—substantially less than the administration had requested—and prohibited the president from supplementing that amount by using contingency funds or reprogramming.[20] This compromise was then included in the Intelligence Authorization (P.L. 98-215) as well.[21]

The administration was free, of course, to come back to Congress with a supplemental request, which it did in March 1984. But rather than following the normal procedure of submitting a request and having it referred to the relevant committees, the administration tried to short-circuit the legislative process. In a surprise move, Republicans in the Senate Appropriations Committee, acting at the administration's behest, added $21 million for the contras to an unrelated bill, a supplemental appropriation for emergency African famine relief, child nutrition programs, and summer jobs (H.J. Res. 492). This bill had already passed the House (with no contra aid in it), so the administration did not have to worry about hostile House committees killing the request. The administration hoped that once again a compromise between the House and Senate versions of the bill would produce at least part of the aid package it wanted.[22]

But the House conferees were unwilling to give in. On May 25, the bill came back to the House in disagreement, and it voted 241 to 177 to add a provision banning the use of any funds appropriated in the bill for military or paramilitary operations against Nicaragua—the same "Boland" language originally included the previous fall in the House version of the FY 1984 Intelligence Authorization.[23]

Between the Senate vote on the supplemental in March and the House vote in May, the press revealed that the CIA had mined Nicaragua's harbors, damaging ships from nearly a dozen nations, most of them allies of the United States. The administration then compounded the self-inflicted political damage by refusing to recognize the jurisdiction of the World Court to hear a complaint against the mining brought by Nicaragua. The mining and the withdrawal from the court were roundly condemned in the Congress. Even the Senate, which had never denied the administration its requests for funding the covert war, approved by a vote of 84 to 12 a nonbinding resolution calling for a halt to the mining.[24]

In this atmosphere the Senate took up the Conference Report on the supplemental appropriation for child nutrition and summer jobs to which aid for the contras had been attached. Faced with the prospect of losing the summer jobs bill because of the Nicaraguan aid provision, the Senate leadership gave up the fight. In June the Senate receded to the House position, stripping contra aid from the bill and accepting the Boland prohibition. Since by that time the $24 million appropriated the preceding November had been exhausted, the legal expenditure of U.S. funds to aid the contras came to an end.[25]

But the battle over Nicaragua was not finished. Having lost its bid for more aid during FY 1984, the Reagan administration simply shifted the fight to the pending legislation for FY 1985. The House Intelligence Authorization for FY 1985 (H.R. 5399) was reported from committee with the same ban on contra aid as in the FY 1984 bill, and it passed the House on August 2, 1984, by a vote of 294 to 118. The Republican leadership decided not to force a direct vote on the issue of covert aid, knowing that the effort would be futile.[26] Moreover, the administration knew it could rely upon the Senate to approve its request to keep the covert war going.

The Senate approved the administration's request for $24 million in contra aid for FY 1985, and the issue was joined in the conference on the FY 1985 Continuing Resolution (H.J. Res. 648). A year earlier, in a similar deadlock, House conferees had agreed to continue funding the covert war at something less than half the level requested by the administration. They adamantly refused to accept a similar compromise for FY 1985. "We are not about to agree," Boland insisted. "The House has voted four times to stop this war in Nicaragua."[27]

The issue deadlocked the conference for several days until a compromise was finally agreed upon. Although $14 million was appropriated for aid to the contras, none of the funds could be expended until after February 28, 1985. Moreover, they could only be released then if Congress approved by joint resolution (by majority vote of both chambers).[28]

This compromise settled the issue for the 98th Congress. Rather than fighting a major battle over an unpopular policy in the middle of Reagan's reelection campaign, the administration postponed the fight, hoping that the 1984 election results would give it a stronger hand in 1985. Not only did the Republicans expect Reagan to win reelection easily, thereby restoring his mandate and his influence on Capitol Hill, they also hoped his coattails would carry enough seats in the House to restore an ideological majority of Republicans and conservative Democrats who would support renewed aid to the contras.

The House Reverses Itself

Demoralized by the electoral debacle of November 1984, congressional Democrats were noticeably more reluctant to confront Reagan on Central America in 1985. This was especially true in the case of El Salvador, where the 1984 election of José Napoleon Duarte as president and the subsequent Christian Democratic victory in the 1985 legislative elections convinced many members of Congress that perhaps Reagan's policy was working after all.

But congressional opposition to Reagan's policy toward Nicaragua appeared to be less tractable. The House Democrats were firmly on record against a continuation of aid for the contras, and the Republicans had failed to gain enough House seats in the election to close the margin. Although the Democrats lost about two dozen seats in 1984, many of them were conservatives from Texas and North Carolina who had consistently voted in favor of the covert war. The election appeared to cost opponents of the covert war about thirteen to fifteen votes, well short of the thirty-two votes by which the Republicans lost the issue in May 1984. Even as resistance to Reagan's policy in El Salvador was crumbling, opposition to the covert war seemed solid.

On April 3, Reagan, acting under the terms of the compromise agreed to the previous fall, requested release of the $14 million. As Minority Leader Robert Michel (R.-Ill.) admitted, there was virtually no chance the House would agree.[29] In an effort to overcome the House's resistance, Reagan proposed a "peace plan" calling for negotiations and a cease-fire between the Sandinistas and the contras. He promised to spend the $14 million only for food and medicine, unless the Sandinistas refused to accept the contras' offer of negotiations, in which case military aid to the contras would be resumed. When even this proposal seemed doomed to fail, the President retreated even further, promising to use the $14 million only for nonmilitary aid.[30] That was enough to bolster his flagging support in the Senate, which voted 53 to 46 to release the $14 million (S.J. Res. 106).[31] Nevertheless, it was the closest Senate vote up to that time, and the outcome was in doubt until the very end. Had Reagan forced the Senate to vote directly on military aid, he might well have lost.

In the House, the situation was much more complex. Fearing that Reagan's peace plan might erode the majority against funding the contras, the Democratic leadership sought to devise a positive alternative to direct aid for the rebels. The result was H.J. Res. 247, sponsored by Michael Barnes (D.-Md.), chairman of the Western Hemisphere (formerly Inter-American Affairs) Subcommittee, and Lee Hamilton (D.-Ind.), the new chairman of the Intelligence Committee. It thus came to be known as the Barnes-Hamilton proposal. While continuing the ban on military aid for the contras, it provided $10 million for the International Red Cross and the UN High Commissioner for Refugees to aid Nicaraguan refugees and $4 million to help finance the Contadora peace process (led by Mexico, Venezuela, Colombia, and Panama).

To bring the Barnes-Hamilton proposal to the floor, the Democrats were forced to let the Republicans present an alternative of their own. Sponsored by Minority Leader Michel, it provided $14 million in direct, nonlethal aid (so-called humanitarian aid) to the contras to be administered by the Agency for International Development rather than the CIA. The Republicans hoped that by limiting aid to nonmilitary supplies and prohibiting CIA involvement, they could regain enough votes to keep the covert war going.[32]

To the extent that the House leadership's strategy was designed to ensure a solid victory against the release of the $14 million in military aid for the contras, it succeeded. The resolution to release the aid (H.J. Res. 239) was defeated 248 to 180—almost exactly the same margin registered in May 1984 when the issue had last been contested. But from that point, the leadership's strategy began to unravel. The first vote on Barnes-Hamilton produced a much narrower victory than the Democrats anticipated, 219 to 206. The vote on Michel's substitute could not have been closer. It was defeated 215 to 213, with the winning margin provided by members changing their votes moments before the final tally was announced.

Even this drama was surpassed on the vote for final passage of the underlying resolution (i.e., the second vote on Barnes-Hamilton). To everyone's surprise, Barnes-Hamilton was overwhelmingly defeated (303 to 123) by a bizarre coalition of Republicans and liberal Democrats.[33] The liberal Democrats, many of whom complained that they had not been consulted by the leadership when Barnes-Hamilton was devised, voted in favor of it on the first vote only because its defeat then would have made the passage of Michel's amendment more likely. Once the Michel proposal had been defeated and the choice was between Barnes-Hamilton or no aid at all, the liberals voted for no aid.

The liberals were also worried that the passage of Barnes-Hamilton would provide a legislative vehicle that the Senate could use to go to conference and insist upon direct "humanitarian" aid to the contras. Since the Senate had approved the release of military aid and Michel's proposal for nonlethal aid had failed so narrowly, the liberals were afraid that the end result of this process would be to restore aid to the contras. By voting against Barnes-Hamilton, they deprived the Senate of a vehicle because there was no House bill to go to conference.

The Democratic leadership knew that many liberals would vote against Barnes-Hamilton on final passage, but no one on the Democratic side imagined that the Republicans would vote against it at that stage. For them, the logical strategy was to support Barnes-Hamilton on final passage, even though they despised it, in order to create a vehicle for conference with the Senate. But the Republican leadership had as much difficulty with its most conservative members as the Democratic leadership had with the liberals. The Republican Right simply refused to vote for Barnes-Hamilton, which they regarded as tantamount to surrender in the war with Nicaragua.

Thus, the moderate Democrats were left alone in their support for Barnes-Hamilton. The press headlined the votes as a total defeat for Reagan's Nicaragua policy because all the aid proposals had failed. In fact, the votes indicated that the administration's position was stronger than anyone had anticipated and therefore encouraged the administration to return to Congress as rapidly as possible with a new aid request.

The surprise defeat of Barnes-Hamilton left moderate and conservative Democrats embittered. The whole purpose behind the bill had been to give them political cover—a politically defensible alternative that did not totally abandon the contras. The failure of Barnes-Hamilton left a number of those Democrats feeling politically vulnerable. Some of them publicly blasted their liberal colleagues for sinking Barnes-Hamilton and vowed that if they had known what was going to happen, they would have supported Michel's amendment.[34] Since the Republicans only needed to pick up two votes to pass Michel's amendment, the prospects for nonlethal aid looked excellent. They looked even better the day after the vote when the headlines reported that Nicaraguan President Daniel Ortega was on his way to Moscow.

Ortega had made half a dozen trips to Moscow over the preceding four years, and the political reverberations in the United States had always been slight. Thus the Sandinistas were wholly unprepared for the political firestorm caused by the April trip. Earlier trips had not received much attention in Washington because they had never coincided with any of the periodic upsurges of public attention to the issue of Nicaragua. But the April trip came just at the climax of an intense and acrimonious congressional debate and so became a front-page story.

The trip was a political disaster for opponents of contra aid. Reagan had charged that the Sandinistas were Communists and Soviet puppets. Ortega's trip seemed to prove him right. Some members of Congress literally believed that the trip was intentionally timed to insult and embarrass them. Others felt betrayed: They had gone out on a political limb for Nicaragua, and the Sandinistas had unthinkingly cut it off. But even among members whose response was less personal, the trip left a strong conviction that the Sandinistas could not be relied upon to act with any political acumen. At any moment they were liable to do something that would make it politically untenable to be seen as their defender. The fact that Ortega went to the Soviet Union in search of desperately needed oil was neither widely understood nor relevant to the political effect the trip had in Washington.

The administration launched its new drive for contra aid in the Senate, hoping that a successful vote there might produce some political momentum carrying over into the House. The administration and its Republican allies stayed in the background, allowing conservative Democrats to take the lead in proposing nonlethal aid. On June 6, the Senate adopted (55 to 42) an amendment to the State Department Authorization (S. 1003) by Sam Nunn (D.-Ga.) providing $38 million in nonlethal aid during FY 1985 and 1986.[35]

On June 12, the issue was joined once gain in the House on a series of amendments to a supplemental appropriation (H.R. 2577). It was a debacle for the House leadership, as the Democrats lost four successive votes by wide margins.[36] The first vote was on a proposal by Boland to extend the existing ban on military aid to the contras without regard to fiscal year. The Democrats were most confident of passing this amendment since the Boland language had passed by substantial margins three times since 1983. It was also a kind of poison pill for the Republicans; if they wanted nonlethal aid for the contras, they would have to accept a permanent ban on military aid to get it. But the Boland amendment was defeated 232 to 196.

The second vote came on an amendment by Richard Gephardt (D.-Mo.) that would have postponed any aid to the contras for six months and required another vote before money could be expended. The idea behind this proposal was simple enough—to give the Democrats time to regroup and to allow Ortega's Moscow trip to fade from memory. But for members who felt a political need to be on record favoring some sort of policy toward Nicaragua, this approach was worthless. Gephardt's amendment failed, 259 to 172.

The third amendment was a new version of the Michel proposal sponsored this time by Joseph McDade (R.-Penn.) to attract support from moderate Republicans in the northeast. The new Republican proposal had been worked out in negotiations between the Republican leadership and a group of conservative Democrats headed by Dave McCurdy (D.-Okla.). It provided $27 million in nonlethal aid for the contras as long as it was not administered through the CIA or Department of Defense. In addition to these restrictions, McCurdy also received a letter from President Reagan foreswearing any intent to overthrow the Nicaraguan government, pledging to resume bilateral negotiations with the Sandinistas, and committing the administration to efforts to remove Somocistas and human rights violators from the contra ranks. The amendment passed, 248 to 184, getting 35 more votes than it had gotten in April. Finally, Lee Hamilton offered a new version of the Barnes-Hamilton proposal to channel $14 million in refugee aid through international relief organizations. It failed 254 to 174.

In the wake of the Democrats' defeat in the House, the Senate Appropriations Subcommittee on Foreign Operations added Nunn's nonlethal aid proposal to the supplemental in markup, and it went unchallenged on the floor. The Senate Intelligence Committee then added the package to the secret portion of the Intelligence Authorization (S. 1261). Similarly, the House added the Michel proposal (this time sponsored by McCurdy) to the Foreign Assistance Authorization on July 10 without opposition.[37] When the minor differences between the House and Senate versions of the supplemental and the Foreign Assistance Authorization had been worked out in conference, the Congress had approved $27 million in nonlethal assistance for the contras for the remainder of FY 1985 and the first half of FY 1986.[38]

In the press and in the corridors of the Capitol, a variety of explanations were advanced to account for the stunning reversal of the House's position on aid to the contras. Most of the votes that changed from April to June were those of Democrats from the deep South or the border states. One explanation for their shift blamed the Sandinistas' growing authoritarianism and military ties to the Soviet Union and Cuba. According to this account, Ortega's trip to Moscow was the last straw, crystallizing animosity toward the Sandinistas that had been building among Democrats for several years. Conservatives were simply the first to become angry enough to break ranks and vote for contra aid.

A second explanation held that the president's harsh anti-Sandinista rhetoric and the Republicans' threats to blame the Democrats for being "soft on communism" had kindled political fear among Democrats from conservative districts. This fear was exacerbated by the failure of Barnes-Hamilton (which left the threatened Democrats without any "political cover") and by Ortega's trip to Moscow (which lent credence and drew public attention to Reagan's charges that the Sandinistas were Communists).

A third explanation looked to the internal processes of the House to explain the debacle, arguing that those who switched their votes in June were embittered by the liberals' wholesale desertion of Barnes-Hamilton in April. In deference to the leadership, many conservatives had grudgingly voted for Barnes-Hamilton and against Michel, even though they were uncomfortable with those votes both ideologically and electorally. When the leadership was unable (or in more Machiavellian reconstructions, unwilling) to keep the liberals from sending Barnes-Hamilton down to defeat on final passage, the conservatives felt betrayed. In June, they expressed their anger by handing the liberals and the leadership a crushing defeat. Dave McCurdy was certainly among those who felt betrayed. As a border state conservative and a member of the Intelligence Committee, McCurdy was influential among conservative and moderate Democrats. In 1983, he played an important role in lining up their support for the Boland-Zablocki bill, and until 1985, he voted consistently against aid to the contras. Immediately following the defeat of Barnes-Hamilton in April, however, McCurdy drafted his own plan for giving nonlethal aid to the contras and quickly recruited over a dozen Democrats as cosponsors, most of them other conservatives who had previously opposed contra aid. With the House so closely divided on the issue, McCurdy's small group constituted the margin of victory, and he emerged as a central figure in subsequent maneuvering.

Getting Back in the War

The $27 million in aid to the contras that Congress approved in June 1985 extended only through the first half of FY 1986 (until March 31, 1986). To obtain additional funding, Reagan was required to return to Congress for approval.[39] As early as January 1986, the administration indicated that it would seek a sizable increase in contra aid when the $27 million ran out in March. Even more important, the administration hoped to win a repeal of the ban on lethal military aid and the prohibition on CIA involvement in the war.[40]

On February 25, the administration submitted a request for $100 million in additional aid for the contras for the second half of FY 1986 and all of FY 1987. In an effort to break the back of congressional opposition, the administration went all out to win its full request.[41] Reagan spoke on the subject constantly, culminating the campaign with a nationwide television address on the eve of the congressional votes.[42]

The administration's strategy was to bludgeon the Congress into surrender. This strategy had worked well in summer 1985, when the administration had gained votes among southern Democrats by branding opponents of contra aid as soft on communism. In March, the administration returned to this theme with a vengeance. The bare-knuckled assault was led by White House Communications Director Patrick Buchanan. In an opinion piece for the *Washington Post* and in subsequent television interviews, he impugned the loyalty of Democrats opposing Reagan's Nicaragua policy, accusing them of being Moscow's allies. "The national Democratic Party has now become, with Moscow, the co-guarantor of the Brezhnev Doctrine in Central America," he wrote in the *Washington Post*. "With the vote on contra aid, the Democratic Party will reveal whether it stands with Ronald Reagan and the resistance—or Daniel Ortega and the Communists."[43]

This time, however, the strategy backfired. Buchanan's hyperbole was too crude and strident, too obvious an attempt at intimidation. The attacks were widely criticized in the press, and, rather than cowering, the Democrats fought back, accusing the White House of McCarthyism and even calling for Buchanan's resignation. Although Reagan never disowned Buchanan's vitriolic attacks, they subsided shortly after Senator Nancy Kassebaum (R.-Kan.), a supporter of contra aid, took the Senate floor to reproach the White House for abandoning "reasoned and rational debate." The administration was distorting the issue, she argued, by presenting it as a conflict between "Republicans in white hats and Democrats wrapped in red banners." Impugning the patriotism of anyone who disagreed with Reagan's policy was "simplistic" and "highly offensive," Kassebaum warned.[44]

The administration's rhetorical excesses regarding the Sandinistas did not subside, however. They were accused of every sin imaginable from drug smuggling to anti-Semitism. The president's televised address to the nation offered the full litany of charges, many of them so extreme and resting upon such dubious factual grounds that several national newspapers felt compelled to run stories assessing their accuracy (or inaccuracy)—a highly unusual practice.[45]

Having turned the contra aid issue into a veritable crusade, the White House rejected any compromise, insisting on the passage of its full, undiluted proposal.[46] At the last minute, when it was clear that the administration was at least ten votes short of a majority, Reagan offered some minor concessions in a letter to the House, but they were not enough.[47] The aid package was rejected, 222 to 210, a major political defeat considering how much attention and presidential prestige the administration had invested.[48]

Several factors contributed to the outcome. One was the vicious tone with which the administration had launched its appeal. Another was the fact that, despite the enormous effort mounted by the White House, public opinion remained adamantly opposed to U.S. involvement in Nicaragua. When pollsters first began asking about aid to the contras in early 1983, they found that about 60 percent of the public opposed aid to the contras and only about 25 percent favored it. These proportions remained unchanged over the succeeding three years. Polls taken in March and April 1986 showed 62 percent were opposed to aiding the contras and less than 30 percent in favor.[49] Another source of difficulty for the administration was the growing sense that its claims of wanting a negotiated settlement with Nicaragua were hollow and that it was unwilling to settle for anything less than the overthrow of the Sandinistas.

The growing opposition of Latin America to U.S. policy also became a factor in the debate. Until January 1986, the Contadora nations were always very circumspect in their criticism of U.S. aid for the contras. This caution allowed the administration to claim that in private they were much more supportive of U.S. policy than domestic political exigencies would allow them to acknowledge publicly. In January, however, the foreign ministers of the four Contadora nations (Mexico, Venezuela, Colombia, and Panama) and the four nations of the Contadora Support Group (Argentina, Brazil, Peru, and Uruguay) came to Washington to openly urge the administration to halt aid for the contras and resume bilateral talks with Nicaragua. They were rebuffed, but from that point onward, the administration's claims that most countries in Latin America secretly supported its policy had little credibility. Gradually, Congress was coming to realize that the administration's policy, despite its rhetoric, was incompatible with the Contadora process, with a peaceful negotiated settlement of the conflict, and with the policies of all our important Latin American allies.[50]

In tactical political terms, the key reason that Reagan was defeated in March was that the McCurdy group voted against him. McCurdy deserted the White House for several reasons. First, Reagan had not made good on the promises he gave McCurdy the previous June. The administration had pledged to purge human rights violators from the ranks of the contras and to re-open bilateral negotiations with Nicaragua. Nothing had been done on either front.

McCurdy was angered by what he saw as the administration's duplicity and a bit embarrassed at having gotten nothing but a worthless letter in exchange for helping the administration win a major victory in June 1985. At the same time, he was still intent upon playing a central role in the formation of U.S. policy toward Nicaragua.[51] Following the example set by Les Aspin (D.-Wis.) on the issue of the MX missile, McCurdy sought to position himself as the spokesperson for a group of moderates holding the balance of power between the administration and its Democratic opponents. From this vantage point, he aimed to mold U.S. policy by making the administration negotiate with him for his support.

The administration, however, was not keen to negotiate again with McCurdy. To win his support in June 1985, the administration had agreed to a bill that limited aid to nonlethal supplies and prohibited CIA involvement in its delivery. By 1986, with the Sandinistas making major gains on the battlefield, these limitations loomed large. Moreover, the administration was not pleased at having its policy held hostage by McCurdy, who was sure to demand more concessions in 1986. The consensus among Republicans was that they had been too quick to negotiate with McCurdy in 1985 and had given up too much to get his support. In 1986, they resolved to try to win without him.

The Democrats, on the other hand, had no hope of defeating the White House request unless a substantial number of the McCurdy group voted against it. To ensure McCurdy's opposition to the administration's request in March, Speaker Tip O'Neill promised him an opportunity to present his own plan for contra aid later in the year. McCurdy agreed, and most of the conservative Democrats who had followed him into Reagan's camp in June 1985 voted against the administration in March 1986.

A week later, on March 26 and 27, the Senate took up the administration's request, modified it slightly, and passed it by the narrow margin of 53 to 47. Political alignments around contra aid in the Senate mirrored those in the House, except that the Republicans began with the majority. As in the House, about two-thirds of the Democrats opposed any form of aid for the contras, whereas a substantial minority bloc of conservative southerners supported the administration. The Senate vote in March was close only because the moderate Republicans opposing contra aid in the Senate were numerous enough to offset the southern Democrats supporting it.[52]

Moderate Senate Democrats repeatedly tried, without success, to find a compromise position that would command broad support within the party and, by attracting moderate Republicans, have a chance of passage. Attempts to craft such compromises by Senator Joseph Biden (D.-Del.) in 1985 and by Senators Jim Sasser (D.-Tenn.) and Albert Gore (D.-Tenn.) in 1986 were overwhelmingly defeated. They were opposed both by liberal Democrats who, like their House colleagues, refused in principle to vote for any contra aid, and by the administration, which saw no need to make any real concessions in order to prevail in the Senate.[53]

In the House, the vast majority of Democrats continued to oppose any contra aid whatsoever, but this was clearly a minority position in the chamber as a whole. The McCurdy group still held the balance of power, and McCurdy's own position was still closer to the administration's than to the Democratic leadership's. As the political maneuvering began for the second round of contra aid votes in April, the issue was whether the Democrats could muster the votes to impose any significant restrictions on the administration's aid package. As the debate unfolded, the restriction that appeared to have the best chance of passage was one that allowed only $30 million in nonlethal aid to be distributed to the contras immediately and required a second vote by Congress in July before any of the $70 million in military aid could be released. Holding off military aid would delay a major escalation of the war and give opponents of contra aid another opportunity to block it in July.

Despite its defeat in March, the administration did not alter its legislative strategy. The White House remained convinced it could win without McCurdy and without making any real concessions. It focused on bringing renegade Republicans back into the fold and picking up a few conservative Democrats. The arithmetic looked favorable. Sixteen Republicans had voted against the White House in March. If that number could be reduced to the seven diehards who voted against the administration in June 1985, Reagan would win.

After being spurned by the administration, McCurdy's only hope for remaining a central player in the debate was to join forces with the Democratic leadership. After some negotiation, McCurdy agreed to sponsor the Democrats' restrictive amendment requiring a majority vote from both chambers of Congress in July before military aid to the contras could be released. A second amendment was developed by Robert Mrazek (D.-N.Y.) and Norman Mineta (D.-Calif.) to prohibit U.S. military personnel from training the contras in Honduras, Costa Rica, or El Salvador.[54]

When the House returned to the contra issue in April, the key fight was around the relationship of contra aid to the supplemental appropriation

(H.R. 4515). In March, the speaker had promised McCurdy that he would have a chance to offer a contra aid proposal as an amendment to the supplemental. The Republicans, however, did not want the aid package tied to the spending bill because the administration opposed other aspects of the bill and Reagan was threatening to veto it. They wanted the contra aid package to be considered as a separate measure, so that whatever aid package passed, it could go quickly to conference with the bill the Senate had already approved.

Not surprisingly, the Democratic majority on the Rules Committee refused to go along, instead reporting a rule that kept the contra aid issue tied to the supplemental. Though the Republicans protested the rule bitterly, it was narrowly approved, 212 to 208.[55] The rule provided that the administration's aid package as passed by the Senate on March 27 (S.J. Res. 283) would be taken up and that three amendments would be in order. First, a substitute by Lee Hamilton (a new version of the 1985 Barnes-Hamilton proposal) would be voted on, allowing the Democrats to establish that they remained opposed in principle to any contra aid. No one expected Hamilton's amendment to pass, however. If it was defeated, the rule provided that McCurdy's restrictive amendment would be taken up, followed by Mrazek's. Finally, there would be a vote on final passage of the proposal as amended.

As debate began on April 16, whip counts by both sides indicated that although the vote on the McCurdy amendment would be very close, the Democrats appeared on the verge of victory. Faced with that prospect, the Republicans pulled a surprise parliamentary maneuver to avoid voting and losing on the McCurdy amendment. They voted for the Hamilton amendment, thereby guaranteeing its passage. Under the rule, no further amendments were in order so the House had no opportunity to vote on the McCurdy or Mrazek amendments.[56] At that point the Democratic leadership "pulled" the bill from the floor rather than proceed to a vote on final passage of the Hamilton proposal. Otherwise, the Republicans might have used another parliamentary maneuver to strip Hamilton's amendment from the bill and get a vote on the unamended White House proposal.[57]

The Republicans avoided an embarrassing defeat on the McCurdy amendment, but they ended up with no contra aid at all. The reason behind the Republicans' decision, made in consultation with the White House, was the expectation that Reagan would veto the supplemental appropriation. It made little sense to expend great effort and to risk defeat on the McCurdy amendment in order to add contra aid to a bill that would probably never become law.

Instead, the Republican leadership proposed its own rule which would bring the contra aid package to the House floor as a separate bill. Knowing that the Democratic majority on the Rules Committee would never approve such a rule, the Republicans filed a discharge petition to force their proposal out of the committee. Few observers expected that the Republicans could muster the 218 signatures needed (they eventually got only 159), but the ploy did manage to keep the contra aid issue alive. To prevent McCurdy and the conservative Democrats from signing the Republican's discharge petition, Speaker O'Neill promised to allow yet another round of voting on contra aid in June when the House took up the military construction appropriation bill.

The Democrats were elated by the outcome of the votes in April. The moderate Republicans had withstood intense pressure from the White House, and McCurdy, good to his word, had lobbied hard against the administration among conservative Democrats. Over the next two months, events in Central America seemed to move against the administration. The contra leadership came to the brink of disintegrating as Arturo Cruz (who gave the contras a patina of respectability among Washington moderates) threatened to resign from the movement rather than remain a mere figurehead. But, after a marathon negotiating session among the contra leaders, he finally agreed to stay on, mollified by the promise of greater influence.[58]

The Contadora negotiating process seemed to be moving toward an agreement. All but a handful of issues were resolved, and Nicaragua, which had refused to sign a final agreement unless Washington agreed to stop aiding the contras, seemed to soften its position, hinting that it might sign an accord even without such a guarantee. Faced with the threat of imminent peace, the Reagan administration blew up in open and bitter feuding between the so-called pragmatists who saw Contadora as a potentially workable alternative to the ineffectual contras and the hardliners who saw any agreement as an obstacle to their efforts to oust the Nicaraguan government.[59] The disarray seemed to confirm the Democrats' argument that Reagan had no clear policy other than the blind use of force.

As the next round of voting grew near, Congress discovered that the contras had been less than scrupulous about how they spent the $27 million in nonlethal aid given to them in 1985. Although the 1985 law appropriating the funds specifically required the administration to establish procedures to guarantee that the funds were spent only for authorized purposes, an investigation by the General Accounting Office disclosed that over half the $27 million could not be accounted for at all. The press supplemented the stories of contra corruption with reports of their involvement in drug smuggling and gun-running.[60]

Everyone agreed that the June votes in the House would be extremely close, as they had been in March and would have been in April if the Republicans had not aborted the process for fear of losing. But it was difficult to imagine that in the intervening months anyone would have shifted to the administration's side on the merits of the issue.

The administration, however, was in search of just seven votes. Enormous pressure was brought to bear on the sixteen Republicans who had voted against the president in March. The White House cast the issue as one of party loyalty, hinting that this was a bench-mark vote that the president (whose popularity stood at a record 68 percent) would remember when he was deciding for which Republican candidates to campaign and raise money in the fall. Still, the whip count in April had shown the administration that it could not win enough of the Republicans to build a majority; it would have to seek out some of the Democrats in the McCurdy group as well. Instead of negotiating with McCurdy, the White House sought to splinter his group, picking off just enough members to win. The need to woo moderate Democrats dictated a change in the administration's tone. The harsh partisan rhetoric that characterized the debate earlier in the year was replaced by a conciliatory call for bipartisanship, and Reagan's vitriolic public denunciations of the Sandinistas were replaced by quiet presidential lobbying one on one with wavering members.[61]

The military construction appropriation bill (H.R. 5052) came to the House floor on June 25. The rule incorporated into the bill a proposal by McCurdy that included his April proposal on contra aid and added $350 million in economic aid to strengthen Central America's "democracies." The rule allowed four amendments: as a substitute for McCurdy, the administration's proposal sponsored by Representative Mickey Edwards (R.-Okla.) and Ike Skelton (D.-Mo.), providing $100 million for the contras in various increments through FY 1986–1987, and (taking a cue from McCurdy) $300 million in economic aid for the rest of the region; Hamilton's substitute proposal, essentially unchanged from April, opposing all contra aid; an amendment by Mrazek prohibiting U.S. personnel from training the contras in Honduras or Costa Rica within twenty miles of the Nicaraguan border; and an anticorruption amendment by Representatives Leon Panetta (D.-Calif.) and Barnes preventing the release of new funds for the contras until the $27 million approved in 1985 had been fully accounted for.

The first vote was the critical one—the choice between the administration's proposal and McCurdy's. The administration won, 221 to 209. Hamilton's substitute was defeated as anticipated, 183 to 245, but the Mrazek amendment passed, 215 to 212, indicating that even some administration supporters still harbored fears that a border incident involving Americans might touch off a wider war. The Panetta-Barnes amendment failed by a fairly wide margin (225 to 198) as the Republicans voted overwhelmingly against fiscal probity. They argued that the Democrats' demand for an accounting of the $27 million before releasing additional funds was really an effort to gut the aid program—which of course it was. But the vote revealed that the Republicans were prepared to look the other way while the contras embezzled part of the aid money if that was the price of keeping the war going. The military construction bill itself then passed easily, 249 to 174.[62]

On the key vote substituting the administration's aid package for the McCurdy proposal, eleven members who had opposed Reagan in March sided with him in June and gave him his margin of victory. Five were Republicans who simply gave in to partisan pressure from the White House. Six were Democrats. Of these, at least two were alleged to have received White House promises of material benefits for their districts in exchange for their votes. Four of the six were members of the Armed Services Committee, including chairman Les Aspin, whose vote almost certainly influenced those of his committee colleagues. For Aspin, the motive was largely ideological. Privately he had favored contra aid for over a year, but he hesitated to break ranks for fear of further complicating his already difficult relations with the party leadership and the liberals, relations strained by his championing of the MX missile.

The administration moved quickly to add the contra aid package to the military construction bill in the Senate, the next necessary step toward final approval. Senate opponents of contra aid had little hope of mustering a majority to reject Reagan's proposal. In March, the Senate had voted 53 to 47 in support of contra aid (the closest vote ever on the issue), and no one had voiced any subsequent change in their position. But Reagan's victory in the House had a sobering effect on Senate Democrats, who were accustomed to relying on the House to put the brakes on the administration's policy. Now they were the last bulwark against a major escalation of the war in Central America, and the sense that they stood at an historic turning point galvanized them to action.

Liberal Democrats began to organize a filibuster. The move was led by freshman Senators Tom Harkin (D.-Iowa) and John Kerry (D.-Mass.) but quickly picked up the support of senior members Alan Cranston (D.-Calif.), Edward Kennedy (D.-Mass.), and Intelligence Committee Vice-Chairman Patrick Leahy (D.-Vt.). The filibuster movement expanded rapidly at first but eventually foundered on two obstacles: division within the ranks of contra aid opponents and Majority Leader Robert Dole's (R.-Kan.) ability to control the flow of legislation to the Senate floor.

Not all opponents of contra thought that a filibuster was a good idea. In December 1982, Senator Christopher Dodd (D.-Conn.) had sponsored the first effort in the Senate to cut off contra aid, so his credentials as an aid opponent were unimpeachable. Yet he opposed the filibuster, fearing that it would allow Reagan to brand the Democrats as obstructionist and thereby damage their chances for regaining control of the Senate in the upcoming 1986 election. Better to give Reagan a vote on contra aid, Dodd argued, use the escalation of the war against the Republicans in the November election, regain control of the Senate, and then launch a concerted effort to stop the war.

Other more moderate Democrats were not so strongly opposed to contra aid that they were willing to engage in the gritty battle required to sustain a filibuster. Minority Leader Robert Byrd was a key figure in this group, and his opposition to the filibuster (he eventually voted for cloture to cut off the debate) made it especially difficult for the liberals to hold their moderate colleagues. Finally, the moderate Republicans who opposed contra aid were loathe to engender the wrath of their leaders and colleagues by blocking a final vote on contra aid when its proponents clearly had majority support. In the end, only five Republicans opposed cloture.

The Republicans' strategy for breaking the filibuster was to tie a resolution of the contra aid issue to the resolution of South Africa sanctions. Kennedy was intent upon introducing a tough sanctions bill before the Senate's August recess; Dole, acting on behalf of the administration, aimed to block it. Whenever Kennedy tried to attach the sanctions bill to a pending piece of legislation, Dole threatened to attach contra aid as well, thus forcing the Democrats to accept contra aid as the price for getting sanctions against South Africa. But Dole was also willing to trade one issue off against the other, offering to forego a Republican filibuster against sanctions if the Democrats would abandon the contra aid filibuster. The Democrats refused.

The Senate remained deadlocked around the two issues for a week and a half, until finally an elaborate agreement was reached governing debate on both South Africa sanctions and contra aid.[63] By the agreement, supporters of each bill still had to win a cloture vote to end debate. But postcloture debate was slashed from the usual thirty hours to four, and the two issues were tied together so that failure to achieve cloture on either one meant that debate on both would continue. By the time the agreement was reached, support for the contra aid filibuster had ebbed so badly that few of the organizers thought they could win a cloture vote. Surprisingly, they did win the first vote, 59 to 40 but lost the second a few hours later, 62 to 37.

The Democrats offered over a dozen amendments to the contra aid package, all of which were defeated. The Republicans were determined to allow no deviation from the bill passed by the House, for fear that further roadblocks to passage would arise in the Conference Committee. On August 12, the Senate rejected 54 to 46 a motion by Sasser and Dodd to strike the contra aid program from the military construction bill, and the following day it formally approved the contra aid portion of the bill, 53 to 47. The military construction bill then passed easily, making it only a matter of time before the Reagan administration had its $100 million in hand.[64]

How Reagan Won

With the House vote in June and the Senate vote in August, the Congress had come full circle—from the two-year-long battle to control the covert war, culminating in the May 1984 cutoff of funds, through the administration's successful two-year struggle to restore the program. Reagan's victory was impressive. At the height of opposition to the contra war in 1984 and early 1985, opponents held more than a sixty vote margin over the White House. Reagan gradually eroded the opposition coalition around its ideological edge by persistence, by refusing to take no for an answer. He simply returned to Congress, time after time, eventually wearing down the margin and wearing out his opponents. In the early years, when the House first rejected funding for the contras, Reagan held out for half or a third of the money— enough to keep the war going. When Congress finally cut off funding in 1984, the administration turned to U.S. allies like El Salvador, Honduras, Israel, and South Korea and to private corporations and individuals to keep the contras alive until the congressional verdict could be reversed.

The administration played heavily on the tried and true themes of anticommunism: The Sandinistas were Marxist-Leninists, puppets of Havana and Moscow. Unless stopped by Washington, they would continue exporting revolution to their neighbors, toppling dominoes south to the Panama Canal and north to the Texas border. The litany of Sandinista crimes recited by administration spokespersons was boundless: They had done away with all human rights, committed genocide against the Miskito Indians, driven the Jewish community into exile with anti-Semitic pogroms, smuggled drugs to poison the youth of America, and allowed Nicaragua to become a base for international terrorism.

The demonization of Nicaragua became so extreme that it caricatured itself. Few people who followed the issue closely took the charges literally—especially since the administration could rarely adduce much concrete evidence to back them up. But even though the exaggerated rhetoric was discounted, it had effect. It skewed the terms of debate, shifting the ground from the question of the effectiveness and propriety of the contra war to the issue of the Sandinista government's character.

This shift proved fatal for the administration's opponents. The Sandinistas, under the mounting pressures of war, acted in ways that gave ammunition to the administration's campaign of vilification. They moved into closer political and military alliance with Cuba and the Soviet Union and tightened internal controls against the unarmed opposition. The Democrats, of course, insisted that these developments were consequences of Reagan's war, but this argument was of little comfort. Whenever the Sandinistas did something that was politically indefensible in Washington, opponents of the covert war felt the ground slip out from under them a little bit more.

The Democrats tried to deflect the administration's assault on the Sandinistas' character by shifting the debate back to the merits of Reagan's policy, where they generally had the better of the argument. In hopes of doing this, they began conceding the evils of the Sandinista government. But they ended up conceding the argument without being able to shift its terms. Once the Democrats had conceded Reagan's premises, their posture was unavoidably defensive. If the Sandinistas were as bad as Reagan said—or even half as bad—then certainly the United States needed to do something about them. Reagan promised to do something; he would pressure them to behave, and those Communists would understand force. As an alternative, the Democrats offered support for the Contadora negotiations. But the argument for Contadora was crippled by the lack of real progress in the negotiations and the ambiguity about who was holding them up. Moreover, the Reagan administration held veto power over Contadora's success; by stalling, it could undercut the viability of the only alternative the Democrats were advocating.

The Democrats also tried to counter Reagan's attack on the Sandinistas by examining the moral character of the contras. The issue of contra human rights abuses was powerful in 1985, but by 1986 it had lost much of its punch. The administration neutralized it by denying the accuracy of reports about contra atrocities and then countering with stories of Sandinista atrocities. Rather than trying to sort fact from fiction, many moderates accepted the conventional wisdom that both sides had reprehensible human rights records. Thus did human rights cease to be an effective argument against contra aid.

Human rights was replaced in 1986 by the issue of contra corruption, which the Democrats also hoped would reveal the contras' moral turpitude. Surprisingly, it had little effect. Many members seemed willing to accept a certain amount of corruption among U.S. clients as a necessary price of Washington's global influence. And again, the administration simply denied the charges, and the Democrats had no smoking gun.

Both the human rights and corruption issues suffered from the serious weakness of being tangential. Most Democrats did not oppose the contra war because of human rights abuses or corruption, and they would have continued opposing it even if the contras had been as honest and decent as choirboys. The core of opposition to the war was based on the belief that it was ineffective and wrong. But by focusing on these peripheral issues rather than on the war itself, the Democrats left their argument vulnerable to Reagan's pledges to reform the contras.

Ultimately, the debates and votes in Congress over how much money to give the contras and under what conditions to give it to them served as a barometer measuring the resistance that the Reagan administration could expect, from the Congress and from the public, to its policy of escalating war. The administration's intense lobbying efforts were aimed less at the immediate goal of securing a few million dollars for the contras than at the longer term goal of breaking the back of the domestic political opposition to Reagan's aggressive use of military force to overthrow the government of Nicaragua.

In the flush of victory, the administration bragged of a new bipartisanship behind its policy, but its majority remained razor thin, its opponents still willing and able to do battle. No one believed that $100 million would end the war in Nicaragua, so it was inevitable that the administration would soon return to Congress for yet another increase in aid, yet another step up the ladder of escalation. And the battle would be joined once again.

Notes

1. Portions of this section and the following section are adapted from "The United States and Nicaragua," in Thomas W. Walker, *Nicaragua: The First Five Years* (New York: Praeger, 1985), pp. 425–446.

2. For details of the programs approved in early 1981, see "A Secret War for Nicaragua," *Newsweek*, November 8, 1982; Leslie H. Gelb, "Argentina Tied to Rise in U.S. Anti-Sandinist Acts," *New York Times*, April 8, 1983; Don Oberdorfer, "More U.S. Effort Yields Less Result," *Washington Post*, March 4, 1982. Regarding the less controversial aspects of the program approved in December 1981, see Leslie H. Gelb, "Reagan Backing Covert Action, Officials Assert," *New York Times*, March 14, 1982; Philip Taubman, "U.S. Reportedly Sending Millions to Foster Moderates in Nicaragua," *New York Times*, March 11, 1982.

3. Gelb, "Reagan Backing Covert Action." The *New York Times* obtained copies of both the options papers developed by the CIA for the National Security Council meetings in November and the "Presidential Finding" signed by Reagan in December. See also, Patrick E. Tyler and Bob Woodward, "U.S. Approves Covert Plan in Nicaragua," *Washington Post*, March 10, 1982.

4. Don Oberdorfer and Patrick E. Tyler, "Reagan Authorizes Plan to Counter Cuban Presence in Nicaragua," *Washington Post*, February 14, 1982; Philip Taubman, "U.S. Backing Raids Against Nicaragua," *New York Times*, November 2, 1982; Alfonso Chardy, "How the U.S. Covert Campaign Against Sandinistas Originated," *Philadelphia Inquirer*, February 16, 1983.

5. The elements of this debate are recounted in Philip Taubman, "CIA Is Making a Special Target of Latin Region," *New York Times*, December 4, 1982; Philip Taubman, "Background Noise on Overt Covert CIA Plot," *New York Times*, December 19, 1982.

6. The 1974 Hughes-Ryan amendment to the Foreign Assistance Act of 1961 and the National Security Act of 1947 requires that the president submit to the Intelligence Committees of Congress a "finding" whenever he initiates a covert operation. The Intelligence Committees are not empowered to approve or disapprove such findings, although they can refuse to authorize funds for any operation they oppose. For the applicable statutes, see *Compilation of Intelligence Laws and Related Laws and Executive Orders of Interest to the National Intelligence Community*, 99th Congress, 1st Session, Committee Print prepared for the Permanent Select Committee on Intelligence of the House of Representatives (Washington, D.C.: Government Printing Office, 1985), pp. 211–214.

7. Gelb, "Reagan Backing Covert Action"; Gelb, "Argentina Tied to Rise in U.S. Anti-Sandinist Acts"; Tyler and Woodward, "U.S. Approves Covert Plan"; "A Secret War for Nicaragua," *Newsweek*, November 8, 1982.

8. Chardy, "How the U.S. Covert Campaign Against Sandinistas Originated."

9. "A Secret War for Nicaragua," *Newsweek*, November 8, 1982.

10. Ibid.

11. "Congress Sought to Place Limits Early on U.S. Covert Assistance to 'Contras,'" *Congressional Quarterly Weekly Report* (hereafter, *CQ*) 43, no. 16 (April 20, 1985): 710–711.

12. *Congressional Record*, December 11, 1982, H1956.

13. Ibid., H9148-H9159. A continuing resolution is an omnibus appropriations bill for programs whose regular authorization or appropriation has not been passed by the start of the fiscal year.

14. See, for example, Philip Taubman and Raymond Bonner, "U.S. Ties to Anti-Sandinistas Are Reported to be Extensive," *New York Times*, April 3, 1983; Don Oberdorfer, "Washington's Role Troubles Congress," *Washington Post*, April 3, 1983.

15. Senator Moynihan's views were reported in Philip Taubman, "Moynihan Questions CIA's Latin Role," *New York Times*, April 1, 1983; Senator Leahy's views in Patrick Tyler, "Administration Accused of Violating Ban on Action Against Nicaragua," *Washington Post*, April 8, 1983; and Representative Boland's in Martin Tolchin, "Key House Member Fears U.S. Breaks Law on Nicaragua," *New York Times*, April 14, 1983.

16. The bill was named for Boland, chairman of the Intelligence Committee, and Clement Zablocki (D.-Wis.), chairman of Foreign Affairs Committee.

17. For the text of this speech, see President Ronald Reagan, "Central America: Defending Our Vital Interests," *Current Policy* No. 482 (Washington, D.C.: U.S. Department of State, 1983).

18. Quoted in "Congressmen Attacked Over El Salvador Stand," *New York Times,* May 5, 1983.

19. For the debate on Boland-Zablocki, see *Congressional Record,* July 27, 1983, H5721-H5762, and July 28, 1983, H5819-H5881.

20. The CIA has a contingency fund that it can use at its discretion to fund operations that are new and therefore have not been funded as a line item in the intelligence authorization or to fund existing programs that require money in excess of authorized levels. The contingency fund, however, cannot be used to finance programs that the Congress has explicitly refused to fund as line items.

Reprogramming is a normal mechanism for shifting appropriated funds between line item programs. The administration has the authority to reprogram funds if it notifies the relevant authorizing and appropriating committees and those committees do not object.

21. These acts superseded the Boland amendment of 1982, which expired at the end of FY 1983. For the text of the relevant section from P.L. 98-212, see *Compilation of Intelligence Laws,* p. 345.

22. "Senate Democrats Rebuffed; Latin Aid Package Approved," *CQ* 42, no. 12 (April 17, 1984):763–765.

23. "House OKs El Salvador Funds, Denies Aid to Contras," *CQ* 42, no. 21 (May 26, 1984):1231–1232.

24. "Hill Presses Reagan on Central America Policy," *CQ* 42, no. 15 (April 14, 1984):831–833.

25. At least the House thought it did. In fact, the administration circumvented the ban in several ways. Oliver North, a National Security Council staff assistant to National Security Adviser Robert McFarlane, played an active role in coordinating private contra aid efforts organized by the Republican Right (Joel Brinkley and Shirley Christian, "Nicaragua Rebels Getting Advice from White House on Operations," *New York Times,* August 8, 1985).

In early 1986, the press revealed that the administration had interpreted the Boland language prohibiting aid to the contras as applying only to aid for military or paramilitary activities. Millions continued to be spent for contra political activities. The House Intelligence Committee objected to this interpretation, but the Republican majority on the Senate Committee allowed it, so the administration was able to continue despite the House's objections (Robert Parry and Brian Barger, "CIA Gave Political Aid to Contras," *Washington Post,* April 14, 1986).

26. "House Authorizes CIA Funds, Bans Contra Aid," *CQ* 42, no. 31 (August 4, 1984):1878.

27. "On Foreign Aid, More Stumbling Blocks," *CQ* 42, no. 40 (October 6, 1984):2418.

28. The text of this provision from the Continuing Resolution (P.L. 98-473) is in *Compilation of Intelligence Laws,* pp. 346–348.

29. Joanne Omang and David Hoffman, "Representative Michel Sees House Rejecting Aid to the Contras," *Washington Post,* April 17, 1985.

30. "Reagan Agrees to Compromise on 'Contra' Aid," *CQ* 42, no. 40 (April 20, 1984):707–714.

31. *Congressional Record,* April 23, 1985, S4527-S4624.

32. The Republicans consistently referred to the Michel amendment and the later amendments proposing direct support for the contras as providing "humanitarian" aid. The term was a misnomer, however, because all the proposals defined "humanitarian" so broadly that it could include nonlethal military aid such as uniforms, jeeps, and aircraft.

33. The full debate on the April votes is in *Congressional Record*, April 23, 1984, H2310-H2428; and April 24, 1985, H2442-H2492.

34. Steven V. Roberts, "Reagan Still Pushing Rebel Aid, Backed by Disgruntled Democrats," *New York Times*, April 26, 1985.

35. For the June Senate debate, see *Congressional Record*, June 6, 1985, S7587-S7648, and June 7, 1985, S7726-S7759.

36. *Congressional Record*, June 12, 1985, H4115-H4200.

37. Neither the Senate nor the House Democrats saw any purpose in contesting these developments since the June votes had gone against them so decisively ("Senate Panel, House, OK Supplemental Funding Bills," *CQ* 43, no. 24 [June 15, 1985]:1181; "Intelligence Panel Adds 'Contra' Aid to its Bill," *CQ* 43, no. 25 [June 22, 1985]:1202; *Congressional Record*, July 10, 1985, H5399-H5400).

38. *International Security and Development Cooperation Act of 1985: Conference Report*, House Report 99-237, 99th Congress, 1st Session, July 29, 1985, pp. 63-73 and 142-146; *Making Supplemental Appropriations for the Fiscal Year Ending September 30, 1985, and for Other Purposes: Conference Report*, House Report 99-236, 99th Congress, 1st Session, July 2, 1985, p. 56.

39. These procedures are contained in P.L. 99-83 (the International Security and Development Cooperation Act of August 8, 1985) at Sec. 722(p) and in P.L. 99-88 (the Supplemental Appropriation Act of August 15, 1985) at Sec. 106.

40. Bernard Weinraub, "Reagan Will Seek $100 million in Aid for the Contras," *New York Times*, January 22, 1986.

41. Gerald M. Boyd, "Reagan Plans 'Flat-Out Effort' to Win Aid for the Contras," *New York Times*, March 2, 1986.

42. The text of the speech is in *New York Times*, March 17, 1986.

43. Patrick J. Buchanan, "The Contras Need Our Help," *Washington Post*, March 5, 1986.

44. *Congressional Record*, March 6, 1986, S2125-S2126.

45. Joanne Omang, "Claims on Contras in Dispute," *Washington Post*, March 18, 1986; Gregory Nokes, "Reagan's Contra Aid Blitz Raises Questions of Truth," *Miami Herald*, March 21, 1986.

46. Edward Walsh and Milton Coleman, "Idea of Compromise on Contra Aid Fades," *Washington Post*, March 1, 1986.

47. In the letter, the president promised to send only $25 million in nonlethal and "defensive" military aid (anti-aircraft missiles) to the contras immediately. The other $75 million would be delayed for three months but could then be released if Reagan certified that the Sandinistas had refused to negotiate in good faith with the contras. The text of the president's letter is in *Congressional Record*, March 19, 1986, H1429-H1430.

48. *Congressional Record*, March 20, 1986, H1444-H1493.

49. For polling data from 1983 and 1984, see William M. LeoGrande, *Central America and the Polls* (Washington, D.C.: Washington Office on Latin America, 1984), pp. 23-26. For 1985 data, see Barry Susman, "Americans Polled Oppose Overthrow," *Washington Post*, February 28, 1985; and Adam Clymer, "Most Americans in Survey Oppose Aid for Overthrow of Sandinistas," *New York Times*, June 5, 1985. For 1986 data, see Barry Susman, "In Poll Public Approves Denial of Contra Aid," *Washington Post*, March 26, 1986; and David K. Shipler, "Poll Shows Confusion on Aid to Contras," *New York Times*, April 15, 1986.

50. Robert J. McCartney, "Latin Mood Shifts Against Washington," *Washington Post*, March 17, 1986.

51. Steven V. Roberts, "A Wildcatter Drills for Power," *New York Times,* June 18, 1985.

52. *Congressional Record,* 26 March 1986, S3454-S3492, and 27 March 1986, S3564-S3693.

53. Steven V. Roberts, "Senate Approves Reagan's Request to Help Contras," *New York Times,* March 28, 1986.

54. The texts of these amendments and the Hamilton amendment (referred to later in this section) are in *Congressional Record,* April 14, 1986, H1809-H1811.

55. The text of the rule and the debate over it are in *Congressional Record,* April 15, 1986, H1820-H1832.

56. *Congressional Record,* April 16, 1986, HH1848-H1893.

57. See the discussion of this particularly complex parliamentary situation as it unfolded, in *Congressional Record,* April 16, 1986, H1890-H1893. For the relevant rules governing House business in this instance, see William Holmes Brown (parliamentarian of the House of Representatives), *Constitution, Jefferson's Manual, and the House of Representatives of the United States,* 99th Congress (Washington, D.C.: Government Printing Office), pp. 141–148.

58. Alfonso Chardy, "Contra Aid Bid Foundering in Congress," *Miami Herald,* May 2, 1986; James LeMoyne, "Contras Debate How to Widen Group's Appeal," *New York Times,* May 23, 1986; Dennis Volman, "'Contra' Unity Expected to be Bolstered by Talks," *Christian Science Monitor,* May 30, 1986.

59. Leslie Gelb, "Pentagon Predicts Big War if Latins Sign Peace Accord," *New York Times,* May 20, 1986; Bernard Gwertzman, "State Department Assails the Pentagon Over Study of Latin Peace Talks," *New York Times,* May 21, 1986; Joanne Omang, "Habib Called Wrong, Imprecise, in Letter on U.S. Latin Policy," *Washington Post,* May 24, 1986.

60. The text of the GAO report is in *Congressional Record,* June 26, 1986, H4258-H4259. See also, "Contra Aid: Tracing Where the Money Went," *CQ,* May 24, 1986; William Buzenberg, "Who Got the $27 Million Intended for the Contras?" *New York Times,* June 19, 1986; "Supplying the Contras: Big Business in Honduras," *Los Angeles Times,* May 9, 1986.

61. "For Reagan, a Key House Win on 'Contra' Aid," *CQ,* June 28, 1986.

62. The full debate is in *Congressional Record,* June 25 and 26, 1986, H4174-H4300.

63. "Rebuffing Democrats' Attack, Senate Approves 'Contra' Aid," *CQ,* August 16, 1986:1876–1881.

64. The full debate lasted three days. See the *Congressional Record,* August 11, 1986, S11175-S11235; August 12, 1986, S11335-S11413; August 13, 1986, S11475-S11526.

TWELVE

The Harassment of Nicaraguanists and Fellow Travelers

MARGARET E. LEAHY

> When you are losing your case on the merits, try to scare the other side into submission, and when that fails, impugn their integrity.
>
> —David Nyhan
> March 9, 1986[1]

Since its inauguration in 1981, the Reagan administration followed a policy that sought to overthrow the government of Nicaragua. To facilitate this objective, it concurrently sought to frame the picture of Nicaragua given to the North American public in a manner that supported its policy goal. Accordingly, Nicaragua was described as a Marxist-Leninist totalitarian state where a small Communist clique had betrayed the democratic goals of the 1979 revolution, engaged in a reign of terror against its own population, and sought to export such terror throughout Central America. A democratic alternative existed, however, in the form of the contras who, according to the president, were the moral equivalent of the founding fathers of the American revolution. The Sandinistas were evil; the contras good. And, in keeping with its democratic heritage, the government of the United States had to support good over evil by helping the patriotic resistance remove the traitors of the Nicaraguan revolution.

This characterization of Nicaragua did not go unchallenged, however. Tens of thousands of U.S. citizens traveled to Nicaragua following the 1979 triumph. Some went on construction brigades and helped to build health clinics and schools. Others went to work in these clinics as health personnel, whereas still others assisted in the literacy campaign or worked on various agricultural projects that sought to increase food production. Academics and researchers investigated various aspects of Nicaraguan life. And some people just went to look and see what was happening. The picture of Nicaragua these citizens offered upon their return to the United States differed dramatically from that of the administration and acted to undermine the perception needed to generate domestic support for an administration policy aimed at overthrowing the government of Nicaragua.

In an attempt to retain effective control of the flow and interpretation of information concerning Nicaragua, the Reagan administration and groups supportive of its policy agenda soon embarked on a variety of actions seemingly aimed not only at discouraging independent investigation and analysis of conditions in Nicaragua through harassment and intimidation but also at impugning the integrity and patriotism of those who painted a picture of Nicaragua different from that needed by the administration. And, just as the administration's rhetoric on Nicaragua became more strident over time so too did official and unofficial efforts to stifle debate intensify. What remained unclear, however, was the degree to which such actions were directed or orchestrated by the administration.

The Trouble with Travel

In 1981, then–Secretary of State Alexander Haig placed a travelers' advisory on Nicaragua. The purpose of a travelers' advisory is twofold. The first relates to the safety of U.S. citizens. If circumstances in an area could result in the endangerment of personal safety if citizens were to travel there, the secretary of state has the responsibility to warn the U.S. public of such risks by placing a travelers' advisory on the area. A travelers' advisory can also be issued for political purposes—to demonstrate U.S. displeasure with actions undertaken by a foreign government. By branding the nation as a high risk, the secretary of state seeks to isolate that nation politically and economically by discouraging U.S. citizens from traveling or investing there.

Sometimes these two purposes conflict, and foreign policy considerations outweigh safety concerns. According to one State Department official, during the 1978–1981 period, when violence against civilians was rampant in Guatemala, the secretary of state consulted the U.S. ambassador to Guatemala about the need to place a travelers' advisory on the country. The U.S. ambassador effectively vetoed the idea, stating that such an advisory would be "the kiss of death" for Guatemala, which needed the foreign exchange generated by tourism and foreign investment. Although there might have been a danger to U.S. citizens in Guatemala, the dictates of U.S. foreign policy made it politically undesirable to brand Guatemala a high risk. This same official suggested that politics similarly conditioned the decision to place a travelers' advisory on Nicaragua.[2]

By 1981 the contra forces attempting to overthrow the government of Nicaragua had begun operations in the northern provinces, and the government of Nicaragua had increased patrols and begun car searches along the Pan American Highway to guard against contra infiltration and attack. Using these searches as a pretext and claiming that such actions constituted harassment and a threat to U.S. citizens, the secretary of state issued a travelers' advisory. However, there was no evidence to suggest that U.S. citizens were in danger at any time, and as of early 1987, no United States citizen had been killed or seriously injured while traveling in Nicaragua.

According to the same official at the State Department, having been warned of the potential danger to their lives, and not taking appropriate precautions, individuals traveling to Nicaragua or their survivors might have problems recovering any claims against their U.S.-based insurance companies if anything were to occur. Although they would always have the redress of the U.S. courts to press their claims and they might possibly win in such circumstances, the officer suggested that this was just one mechanism that was used to dissuade people from traveling to Nicaragua.

The degree to which this advisory was successful was impossible to gauge. However, the advisory did have a negative impact on some who continued to make such trips. For example, the editor of this book, Thomas Walker, a professor of political science and the past chair of the Latin American Studies Association (LASA) Task Force on Scholarly Relations with Nicaragua, found that he was ineligible for mortgage insurance because his travels to Nicaragua put him in a high-risk category. By placing Nicaragua in a high-risk classification, the government automatically placed persons traveling there on a regular basis in the same category, and insurance companies responded accordingly, not out of particular political motivation but rather according to regular business practice.

On June 7, 1983, the United States took more direct action, closing down all six Nicaraguan consulates in the United States. According to the administration, this action was undertaken in retaliation for the earlier Nicaraguan expulsion of three U.S. diplomats accused by the Nicaraguan government of engaging in subversive activities. In addition, the United States claimed that because the consulates were used for intelligence purposes, their presence could not be tolerated. Although the Nicaraguan Embassy in Washington, D.C., was allowed to remain open and to issue travel visas, this action supported the administration policy of making it increasingly difficult for U.S. citizens to travel to Nicaragua. In a *New York Times* article that reported the closing of the consulates, the State Department was noted as "officially discouraging travel to Nicaragua."[3] The Nicaraguan government countered this action by waiving the visa requirement for all U.S. citizens, thus making travel even easier.

On May 1, 1985, President Reagan claimed that Nicaraguan policies "constituted an unusual and extraordinary threat to the national security and foreign policy of the United States" and declared a state of national emergency under which all direct trade with Nicaragua was prohibited and Aeronica, the Nicaraguan national airline, lost landing rights in the United States.[4]

None of these official actions stopped U.S. citizens from going to Nicaragua and returning to the United States with accounts that challenged the premises of administration policy. However, those who persisted in such travels soon found themselves confronted by more direct efforts at harassment and intimidation.

The Big Chill

Recent events strongly suggest the FBI and perhaps other federal agencies are once again collecting names and making lists, planting informants and watching organizations, opening mail and burglarizing offices.

—William Greider
May 23, 1985[5]

Early in 1985, reports began to surface of travelers returning from Nicaragua being harassed by the U.S. Customs Service and the FBI. The first widely publicized incident was the Haase case. On January 16, 1985, Edward Haase of Kansas City, Missouri, returned from Nicaragua thorugh the Miami Airport. At Customs, he was confronted and interviewed by an FBI agent who seized and copied Haase's personal address book and diary, a list of organizations concerned with Central American support work, and documents of a Nicaraguan support group with which Haase was affiliated. Haase immediately contacted the Center for Constitutional Rights in New York. Acting on Haase's behalf, the center contacted the supervisor of the Miami FBI office and requested that all copied materials be returned immediately to Haase. According to a later report by Anthony Lewis, the agent in charge, "Mr. Philips, refused to return the material. He said the F.B.I. was interested in it and that it was properly 'dissemicable.'" The material was under review, and when the review was completed, any information found important would be sent to the relevant federal agency.[6]

In February, the Center for Constitutional Rights filed a federal suit, charging that the seizure of such materials violated Haase's constitutional rights to free speech and free association. In a preliminary ruling, the court ordered the government to stop using, copying, or distributing the materials and to provide the court with information as to the previous dissemination of them. On May 14, 1985, the case against the FBI was dismissed. In dismissing the Haase suit, federal district court judge Thomas Pennfield Jackson stated that Haase had "all the equitable relief [he] could conceivably win" since the FBI had offered to return all copies of the documents and promised that they would not be used for investigative purposes. As a result of this ruling, Haase had no standing to seek a broader injunction barring federal agencies such as the FBI and Customs Service from subjecting travelers returning from Nicaragua to such questioning or searches in the future. In a further clarification of his decision, the judge also stated that the injunction against federal agencies was not needed, as there was no evidence to suggest that actions such as those particular to the Haase case were likely to occur again.[7] The court decision was appealed.

The judge's assumptions that the information obtained had not and would not be used for intelligence purposes and that cases similar to that of Haase were not likely to occur again were incorrect. Three days after the January seizure of Haase's materials, a Missouri man whose name appeared in the copied address book received a call asking him about Nicaragua, his political opinions, and his political activities. On April 2, 1985, Alice Heidy was returning from Nicaragua through the New Orleans airport. Her address book and notebook were seized by Customs officials and copied. On July 29, 1985, Mark Rogers had 125 pieces of literature seized by customs upon returning from Nicaragua through the Houston airport. George Rose and Heidrun Rose (a Canadian citizen) returned through the Houston airport on August 1, 1985. Various books, magazines, and newspapers were seized but later returned when found not to be in violation of 19 USC 1305, which prohibits the importation of subversive literature. Additional incidents at other airports were reported throughout 1985.[8]

In March 1986, upon arrival at the San Antonio airport, Michael Conroy, an economics professor at the University of Texas and chair of the Latin American Studies Association Task Force on Scholarly Relations with Nicaragua, found himself "flagged" by the Customs computer and, for the second time in less than one year, subjected to harassment by the U.S. Customs Service. Anthony Lewis described what happened: "When an immigration officer typed his name into the computer, the official looked up in alarm and directed him to Customs. There [as at the Houston airport in June 1985] his papers, notes, letters, books and newspapers were examined."[9]

In April 1986, the Center for Constitutional Rights filed a class action suit in federal court on behalf of ten named plaintiffs and other individuals and organizations interested in Nicaragua, charging that the FBI, the U.S. Customs Service, and their agents had violated the constitutional rights of the plaintiffs through a demonstrated pattern of Customs harassment.[10] Even though the Customs agents involved in the incidents charged in this suit usually cited 19 USC 1305 and its provisions precluding the importation of treasonable or subversive literature as the cause of their search or seizure of materials from the plaintiffs, in no instance was any of the plaintiffs charged under this statute. The suit claimed that in no instance were the materials examined, seized, or copied covered under the provisions of this statute. Rather, the suit argued, such actions were undertaken for political reasons.

The plaintiffs named in this suit were either individuals who had traveled or were planning to travel to Nicaragua or organizations that sponsor travel and research programs in Nicaragua. Alice Heidy, for example, was a member of the National Central American Health Rights Network (N-CAHRN), "a national association of physicians, nurses, and others committed to promoting health care in Central America, and to educating North Americans about the deleterious effects of Administration policies on the health rights of Latin American people."[11] Upon her return from Nicaragua, Customs seized and copied, among other things, her personal address book containing the names and addresses of other members of N-CAHRN and a notebook with information on N-CAHRN health projects in Nicaragua. Others, such as Michael Conroy and Thomas Walker, are members of the LASA Task Force that had sponsored research trips to Nicaragua in the past and planned additional trips in the near future. They, too, had materials examined or copied at Customs.

The suit claimed that the actions of the U.S. Customs Service, in addition to violating the plaintiffs constitutional rights, were

> the result of a policy, pattern, or practice of the U.S. Customs and the FBI to use the Customs inspection process to harass and intimidate travelers returning from Nicaragua, to disrupt the flow of information to U.S. residents about events in Nicaragua, to gather intelligence about likely opponents of the Administration's policies in Nicaragua, to discourage travelers to Nicaragua from bringing Nicaraguan publications back to the United States, and to discourage U.S. residents from traveling to Nicaragua.[12]

The suit asked the court to do two things: (1) to enjoin such practices by Customs and other government agencies and (2) to issue a preliminary injunction against such practices.

During the process of discovery, testimony given by Customs agents revealed some important information. First, individual agents had no clear idea as to the types of materials that could legally be classified as seditious and thus could be confiscated under 19 USC 1305. As a result, agents had confiscated materials simply because they were critical of U.S. policy toward Nicaragua or because individual agents believed the source of some of the documents—the Sandinista National Liberation Front (FSLN)—was a terrorist group. With these revelations, and under threat of court order, the U.S. Customs Service agreed to promulgate directives that would (1) clarify and narrow what materials were seditious and therefore subject to confiscation under the law and (2) establish strict controls on the consequent dissemination and disposition of such materials.[13]

Such a directive was issued on August 29, 1986. According to a report by Anthony Lewis, the directive now classifies and thus makes subject to seizure "only material that incites 'imminent acts of armed or other violence against constitutional government.'"[14] Final disposition in this case is still pending.

Persons who traveled to Nicaragua were not only subject to harassment upon their immediate return to the United States at Customs. Numerous incidents of harassment and attempts at intimidation undertaken by other official government agencies, such as the FBI, were also documented. For example, a New York man who worked on a construction brigade in Nicaragua in late 1984 found that his landlord was subsequently "visited" by the FBI three times.[15] Also in 1984, another man living in New York City returned from Nicaragua only to find that the FBI had questioned two of his friends about him and his political affiliations during his absence. Both friends felt intimidated by such questioning and, when they related the incidents to him, stated that if the FBI was investigating him he must have been involved in something illegal or subversive. The young man had been a volunteer health worker in Nicaragua. He felt intimidated and harassed by the actions of the FBI, stating in a letter to the Center for Constitutional Rights that his responsibilities to family and friends would "have to be weighed against my commitment to volunteer health services in Nicaragua if this harassment continue[d] or worsen[ed]."[16]

New York City was not the only area where such FBI visits occurred. Daisy Cubias, a member of the Central American Solidarity Association (CASA), lived in Milwaukee when she was questioned by the FBI after a trip to Nicaragua. FBI agents visited her at both her home and her work, asking her about other individuals she knew who were working with CASA. Stating that specific individuals were "under investigation," they inquired as to any knowledge Cubias might have about their possible involvement in "terrorist activities."[17]

Not only were those who went to Nicaragua and their friends, landlords, and families queried by the FBI; even those who had only shown a cursory interest in the Nicaraguan situation became suspect. In March 1985, for example, David Rostan, a New York City law student, found a card left by FBI agent Ken Goldsmith at his door. The card read: "Please call me, I'd like to talk about Nicaragua. This will be a friendly chat." The student had never been to Nicaragua but had recently attended a meeting on Nicaragua at City University of New York. The following month a friend of this student was visited by the FBI and questioned about him.[18]

At about the same time, break-ins at the offices of groups opposing the administration's Central American policies began to be reported from one end of the country to the other. From Boston to Seattle, from Detroit to Phoenix, and from various points in between, the pattern was the same. Normally, nothing of monetary value was stolen, but file and desk drawers were opened, with the files and organizational lists apparently examined and sometimes stolen. At the Old Cambridge Baptist Church in Massachusetts, which housed numerous organizations active on Central America, six office break-ins occurred between November 1984 and March 1986. In none of the cases were police investigators able to come up with suspects.

By April 1986, approximately twenty such break-ins had been reported around the nation. Although no one claimed responsibility, an incident that occurred in 1985 at the Washington, D.C., offices of *Sojourner,* an independent religious magazine that had published various articles contradicting the administration's version of Nicaragua, shed additional light on these matters.

During the predawn hours, when a worker returned to the *Sojourner* offices to pick up some materials, he "discovered four men in business suits standing around the rear entrance peering into the windows." After stating to the curious worker that they had simply come by "to visit," the four "hurriedly departed in a car with the [government] license number G-306." The police would not disclose the government agency to which the car was registered as "no laws had been broken."[19] Later, however, "with the help of a well placed source," the magazine "was able to trace the car's 1985 Virginia tag . . . to a block of numbers assigned to the National Security Agency. The source also informed the magazine that it [was] under investigation by several government agencies."[20]

Increasingly, spokespersons for civil liberties groups and organizations whose offices were targeted suggested that, rather than simple burglary attempts, these break-ins might well have been surreptitious entries conducted by or with the knowledge of agencies of the federal government and suspiciously reminiscent of a pattern of activities undertaken by federal agencies between 1956 and 1971, termed COINTELPRO.

According to the *Final Report of the Senate Select Committee on Intelligence Activities* (1976), COINTELPRO was "the FBI acronym for a series of covert action programs directed against domestic groups. In these programs, the Bureau went beyond the [legitimate] collection of intelligence to secret actions designed to 'disrupt' and 'neutralize' target groups and individuals," through break-ins, government infiltration, rumor and disinformation campaigns, and Red baiting. According to the report, "the Bureau conducted a sophisticated vigilante operation, aimed squarely at preventing the exercise of First Amendment rights of free speech and association, on the theory that preventing the growth of dangerous groups and the propagation of dangerous ideas would protect the national security [of the United States] and deter violence."[21]

Other investigations revealed that additional executive branch agencies had bowed to executive pressures during the Nixon administration, going beyond their legitimate investigative functions and engaging in actions similar to those of COINTELPRO. Although legislative actions during the 1970s prohibited such actions, questions began to arise in the mid-1980s as to whether the FBI and other government agencies had become similarly politicized and had acted outside the legitimate venue given to them by law in order to harass and intimidate the opponents of the administration's Central American policies.

Congressional Hearings

In 1984 and 1985, the House Judiciary Subcommittee on Civil and Constitutional Rights held hearings that raised some disturbing questions about the magnitude, purpose, and ultimate responsibility for actions undertaken by the FBI and other government agencies.

Under U.S. statutes the FBI investigates a wide range of crimes against the United States. To this end, the FBI is charged with the collection of criminal intelligence on, and the investigation of, individuals or groups that the bureau reasonably could suspect of committing crimes against the United States or of breaking federal law. In addition, the bureau conducts security clearances for prospective employees in certain components of government. In this capacity, the bureau investigates individual applicants. The bureau also has a specific foreign counterintelligence function. Here, in order to protect the national security of the United States, the FBI is charged with investigating attempts at espionage or other related hostile intelligence activities undertaken by foreign governments or their agents, including U.S. citizens or groups that the bureau might reasonably suspect of engaging in clandestine intelligence activities on the behalf of a foreign government that violate U.S. laws.

In the course of the 1984 hearings on the so-called Prohibition Against the Training or Support of Terrorist Organizations Act of 1984, testimony was offered alleging that, under the pretext of investigating terrorism, the FBI had engaged in a pattern of activities designed to harass persons and organizations that dissented from official administration policies.[22] Referring to this testimony in a January 1985 letter addressed to FBI Director William Webster, subcommittee chair Representative Don Edwards asked for "the investigative basis" of eighteen particular interviews.[23]

In his response, Director Webster wrote: "Of the 18 incidents, eight were not identifiable with any specific FBI investigations. Of the remaining ten incidents, all but two [were] classified or pending investigation," and the director would not comment on them in writing but offered to give Representative Edwards a classified briefing if he so desired. With respect to the other two incidents, the director responded that the FBI in Anchorage, Alaska, had indeed questioned a parish priest, a Catholic nun, and a community worker concerning a speech given by a Quaker pacifist during a church service commemorating the anniversary of the assassination of El Salvadorian Archbishop Oscar Romero. According to Webster, all these interviews were necessary as part of a "threat analysis" undertaken to ensure the safety of Pope John Paul II and President Reagan, both of whom planned visits to the area. The other incident involved five FBI contacts with a Los Angeles–based Central American refugee project that had been conducted between mid-1982 and early 1983. According to Webster, the FBI had investigated this group to ascertain the validity of allegations that the group had violated the Neutrality Act by recruiting or training persons to fight against the government of El Salvador. When the agents in charge ascertained that the allegations were unfounded, the investigation was closed.[24]

In a hearing held during April 1985 to review the FBI's budget request for FY 1986, members of the subcommittee were concerned in particular with (1) the magnitude of FBI interviews of persons opposed to administration policy in Central America, (2) whether the reasons for specific interviews were within the purview of FBI jurisdiction, and (3) the repercussions that such FBI interest might have on the constitutional rights of citizens.

In testimony given before the subcommittee, FBI Director William Webster admitted that his agents had visited at least 100 persons who had made trips to Nicaragua. When asked by Representative F. James Sensenbrenner, Jr., to inform the committee as to the "specific guidelines" that might "trigger the selection" of an individual returning from Nicaragua for interview, the director claimed that there had been "a specific foreign counterintelligence purpose in every one of the interviews" conducted but declined in open session to outline specific guidelines, stating that they were classified. The director also revealed that the interviews might have occurred as the result of specific tasks given to the FBI by other agencies of the executive branch. Under Executive Order 12333 (1981), the FBI, in addition to its foreign counterintelligence functions within the United States, was given the power to gather "positive intelligence" when tasked to do so by the National Security Council or the director of Central Intelligence.[25] In other words, other agencies under the jurisdiction of the executive branch could order the FBI to gather intelligence on individuals or groups for purposes other than those outlined above.

Throughout the hearings, members of the subcommittee questioned the director concerning both the foreign counterintelligence rationale offered for particular FBI interviews and the possibility of executive branch manipulation of the FBI for political purposes. The comments of Representative Kastenmeier were particularly telling in this second regard. Responding to Director Webster's testimony that taskings given to the FBI by the National Security Council and the director of Central Intelligence under Executive Order 12333 "were not a matter of public record," Representative Kastenmeier commented:

> [I]t may be that those who are inclined to take you to task for some things
> may be missing the source of the direction. That is to say, the President of
> the United States has a position with respect to Central America, and
> particularly Nicaragua, . . . and we have seen presidents use
> instrumentalities of the executive branch to forward their own points of
> view with respect to foreign policy in the past. . . . [W]hether or not one
> agrees with what the Bureau may be doing in its foreign counterintelligence
> program, the direction and tasking for that suggests higher accountability.[26]

Following the hearings, Representative Edwards addressed another letter to the director in which he asked for clarification on five additional cases that were drawn from public testimony given to the subcommittee. They involved

- Amy Good of Detroit, who was visited at home by two FBI agents who subsequently stated to Good's attorney that "the FBI was trying to interview all people returning from Nicaragua and was doing so for 'positive intelligence gathering.'"
- Jill Clark, "a member of the New Orleans chapter of the Committee in Solidarity with the People of El Salvador, [who] received three visits from the FBI."
- David Rostan, the New York City law student previously mentioned, whom FBI agent Ken Goldsmith contacted to have a "friendly chat" about Nicaragua.
- Daisy Cubias, the Milwaukee member of CASA, whose case was also mentioned earlier.

- Sally Brown, a member of Representative Patricia Schroeder's Denver office staff, who was questioned by the FBI "about an interfaith prayer service at the Central Presbyterian Church to commemorate the assassination of Salvadoran Archbishop Oscar Romero." Both Brown and the Colorado Council of Churches were contacted by the FBI and asked to identify persons who had been at the service.[27]

In his response, Webster once again claimed that all the investigations in question were legitimately conducted pursuant to either the Attorney General's Guidelines or Executive Order 12333. Of the five incidents, Webster said that "all but one [were] classified or pending investigation" and that he could not discuss them except in a classified briefing. With regard to the Brown incident, however, the director informed Representative Edwards that this was not an FBI case. Rather, Brown was contacted during an investigation "conducted by the Defense Investigative Service (DIS) during a background investigation of a Hughes Aircraft employee," and the director suggested that any further clarification would have to come from DIS.[28]

The content of Director Webster's briefing to Representative Edwards was classified. However, an extensive review of the testimony presented before the subcommittee demonstrates no clear correlation between a legitimate foreign counterintelligence purpose and the incidents related. The question also remains as to whether, in their taskings to the FBI, other executive branch agencies had initiated politically motivated investigations. The possibility that the FBI might have been used for political purposes raised for some the specter of a COINTELPRO II. This suspicion was given further credence by the pattern of break-ins discussed earlier.

Representative Edwards commented on the break-ins in his May 1985 letter to FBI Director Webster: "There is no indication that the FBI was involved in these break-ins. There is also no indication that they were the work of ordinary criminals. The incidents raise the question whether right-wing groups of which the FBI is aware, may be seeking to intimidate opponents of US foreign policy, with or without the knowledge of the Bureau."[29] Representative Edwards pursued the matter of the break-ins, writing to Director Webster in January 1986. Webster responded in writing on April 11, 1986, and in sworn testimony before the subcommittee (March 14, 1986) stated that the FBI was not responsible for the break-ins and did not know who was.[30]

However, for some the specter of government involvement or complicity in such actions remained. And such suspicions were reinforced by other concurrent governmental and nongovernmental actions. Just as the COINTELPRO practices of old used rumor and disinformation campaigns and Red baiting to disrupt and harass individuals and groups, so too did the most recent campaigns conducted against those who challenged the premises of administration policy.

Rumor, Disinformation, and Red Baiting

After returning from Nicaragua, a woman was visited at both her home and her job by FBI agents who asked her if she was aware of the fact that some members of a coalition with which she worked, the Ecumenical Refugee Council of Milwaukee, "were in the Communist Party." They told this woman, "You're going around with a bunch of terrorists, and we want to help you keep clean."[31] Similar accusations have been reported around the country by members of the Committee in Solidarity with the People of El Salvador (CISPES).[32]

Groups supportive of the administration have also been accused of Red baiting and intimidation. Accuracy in Academia (AIA), a spin-off of Accuracy in Media, emerged in 1985 with the avowed purpose of monitoring university professors who provided students with "incorrect information which leads to conclusions that may be distasteful from the point of view of our nation's heritage or national security. . . . Just plain bad facts."[33] This group at various times claimed to have lists of between one and ten thousand such professors teaching at U.S. colleges and universities.

The manner by which AIA compiled such lists was interesting. In a *New Republic* article recounting his life as a double agent for AIA, James Ledbetter reported that then–executive director of AIA, Lazlo Csorba III, told him he had gotten the initial list of "targets" from "a list of professors who had endorsed a rally opposing U.S. involvement in Central America."[34] For Csorba, opposition to the administration's policy in Central America made one's academic credentials and patriotism suspect.

What did AIA plan to do about such professors? According to its own publications, the group hoped to monitor classes and report to the university administration anyone who gave interpretations different from those the group members thought should be offered in support of U.S. interests. According to Reed Irvine, president and founder of Accuracy in Media, the parent organization of AIA, after that it would be "up to the administration [of the college or university] if they want[ed] a guy on the faculty who was consistently distributing misinformation to students."[35]

By the end of the academic year 1985-1986, AIA had publicized the names of some professors who it felt were providing "bad facts." In one report the following list was provided: Samuel Bowles of the University of Massachusetts at Amherst, Richard Fagen of Stanford University, Salvador Luria of the Massachusetts Institute of Technology, Cynthia McClintock of George Washington University, John Weeks of American University, John Womack and George Wald of Harvard University, Howard Zinn of Boston University.[36] AIA did not offer specific reasons for placing any of these professors on this list, but the McClintock inclusion is instructive with regard to the logic behind AIA targeting. The readings for the course for which Professor McClintock was targeted included U.S. government publications and a book by the Hoover Institution. To AIA, so far, so good. But Professor McClintock also used a film in that course that was critical of the contras.

It seems that the use of this film exposed her students to "bad facts." She became a target.[37]

According to Jordan Kurland, associate secretary general of the American Association of University Professors, such a targeting effort would not necessarily affect many of those whose names were initially listed by AIA; they were prominent members of the profession who were tenured at major universities. However, he suggested that such actions might affect the careers of lesser known professors, especially those who were without tenure or who taught at smaller, less prestigious universities.[38] Although some professors reportedly felt the need to tape their lectures to provide a record in case of later AIA misrepresentation, AIA efforts to limit the range of academic debate did not seem particularly effective in its first year or two of operation.

Other groups were not as subtle in their efforts to limit debate. In December 1984, for example, a slide show and talk on Nicaragua had to be canceled and the building evacuated when Omega 7, an anti-Castro, expatriot Cuban terrorist organization, claimed to have planted a bomb in the meeting hall. The next day, the secretary to the minister who was to have made the presentation received a call from someone once again claiming to represent Omega 7. "You're a bunch of communists," the caller said. "We're going to blow you up." The minister's office was located in a complex that housed a day-care center; as a result of these threats, the minister felt compelled to move his office.[39]

The actions of such groups were not without models from within the Reagan administration. In February 1985, Director of the Central Intelligence Agency William Casey revealed a secret Sandinista Disinformation and Public Manipulation Plan to a select few congressional representatives. In characterizing the plan he said: "What you have here is a Communist government, allied with the Soviet Union, undertaking a very well-organized effort with the help of certain Americans to change a vote in Congress."[40] Referring to the same document, Elliot Abrams, assistant secretary of state for inter-American affairs, said: "Some Americans would be shocked to find their names appearing in such a document as people the Sandinistas plan to use."[41] Although the secret plan was later revealed to consist mainly of information contained in the report of a New York City public relations firm that had been hired by the government of Nicaragua to develop routine lobbying strategies, the purpose and intent of the Casey-Abrams "revelations" were clear: Anyone who opposed the administration's Nicaraguan policy was suspect, being characterized as either a Communist agent or a Communist dupe. This theme was reiterated almost immediately by Patrick Buchanan, the White House communications director, who, in a *Washington Post* article, characterized the Democratic party and any others who opposed aid to the contras as standing with Moscow and the Communists.[42]

Even President Reagan got into the act when, during a press luncheon on March 11, he labeled the noted Latin Americanist, E. Bradford Burns, as a propagandist for the government of Nicaragua, and asked that "God help" the professor's students at the University of California at Los Angeles if this was the kind of thing he taught them.[43] The president accused Burns of "dispersing disinformation" based on an article he published in the journal, *Nicaraguan Perspectives*, that challenged the underpinnings of administration policy by outlining not only how the Nicaraguan people had benefited since 1979 but also how the contras, who were led by former National Guard officers and who engaged in atrocities against the Nicaraguan people, had no chance of winning support within Nicaragua.[44]

Referring to Buchanan and others, *New York Times* columnist Anthony Lewis said, "You can almost hear the voice of Senator McCarthy at Wheeling, West Virginia, 36 years ago this month. . . . But there is something more insidious about the Reagan smear campaign. Joe McCarthy was an outsider. The people running this operation hold positions in the United States government."[45] Lewis was right. Like McCarthy, the Reagan administration was attempting to quell dissent by branding dissenters as Communists. And, like its predecessor under J. Edgar Hoover, the FBI had begun to engage in questionable practices that led many to suggest that it too had succumbed to intimidation of dissenters in the name of the national interest. That the U.S. Customs and the National Security Agency might also have been involved in attempts at harassment and intimidation added fuel to the fire that saw the possibility of a new McCarthy era emerging.

By early 1987, however, there was at least one important difference from the McCarthy era. Intimidation, harassment, and Red baiting had not quelled dissent, and those attempting to present a view of Nicaragua that would preclude a popular stampede in support of the administration's war policies remained, for the most part, undeterred. Whether or not this would be enough to preclude more and greater involvement in attempts to overthrow the Nicaraguan government remained a question. It was, however, a ray of hope.

Notes

1. David Nyhan, "Waiving the Flag on Nicaragua," *Boston Sunday Globe*, March 9, 1986, p. A25.
2. Interview by Margaret Leahy, March 1986.
3. Philip Taubman, "21 Nicaraguanists in 6 Consulates Expelled by US," *New York Times*, June 8, 1983, p. 1.
4. Executive Order 12513, May 1, 1985.
5. William Greider, "Reagan's Moles," *Rolling Stone*, May 23, 1985, p. 51.
6. Anthony Lewis, "What Country Is It?" *New York Times*, February 28, 1985, p. A23.
7. William Hollan, "Suit Over Search Dismissed," *Kansas City Times*, May 15, 1985, p. B1.
8. Movement Support Network, *MSN News*, November 22, 1985, p. 2.
9. Anthony Lewis, "Policing Our Thoughts," *New York Times*, April 28, 1986, p. A25.
10. *Alice Heidy et al. versus United States Customs Service et al.*, Civ. Action No. 86-2365-JSL (Px).

11. *Heidy* vs. *U.S. Customs*, p. 4.

12. *Heidy* vs. *U.S. Customs*, pp. 34–35.

13. Conversation between Margaret Leahy and David Cole, Center for Constitutional Rights, October 1986.

14. Anthony Lewis, "Harassment at Customs," *San Francisco Chronicle*, September 17, 1986, p. 55.

15. Movement Support Network, *MSN News*, November 22, 1985, p. 2.

16. Letter to the Center for Constitutional Rights, December 1984.

17. Loretta Tofani, "Nicaragua Visitors Questioned," *Washington Post*, April 18, 1985, p. 1.

18. Movement Support Network, *MSN News*, pp. 4–5.

19. William Greider, "Reagan's Moles," *Rolling Stone*, May 23, 1985, pp. 51–52.

20. Movement Support Network, *MSN News*, April 1986, p. 17.

21. U.S. Senate, *Supplementary Detailed Staff Reports on Intelligence Activities and the Rights of Americans, Book III, Final Report of the Select Committee to Study Governmental Operations With Respect to Intelligence Activities*, Report no. 94-755 (Washington, D.C.: Government Printing Office, April 23, 1976), p. 3.

22. U.S. House of Representatives, *Hearings Before the Subcommittee on Civil and Constitutional Rights of the Committee on the Judiciary*, Ninety-Eighth Congress, 2d session, on H.R. 5613, *Prohibition Against the Training or Support of Terrorist Organizations Act of 1984*, August 2, 1984, Serial No. 82 (Washington, D.C.: Government Printing Office, 1984), pp. 34–53.

23. Letter of Representative Don Edwards to FBI Director William Webster, January 14, 1985.

24. Letter of FBI Director William Webster to Representative Don Edwards, April 25, 1985.

25. U.S. House of Representatives, *Hearings Before the Subcommittee on Civil and Constitutional Rights of the Committee on the Judiciary on FBI Authorization Request for Fiscal Year 1986*, April 17, 24, and 25, 1985 (Washington, D.C.: Government Printing Office, August 1985), pp. 8–9.

26. U.S. House of Representatives, *Hearings*, 1985, p. 22.

27. Letter of Representative Don Edwards to FBI Director William Webster, May 2, 1985, pp. 1–2.

28. Letter of FBI Director William Webster to Representative Don Edwards, May 24, 1985.

29. Letter of Representative Don Edwards to FBI Director William Webster, May 2, 1985, p. 2.

30. Letter of Representative Don Edwards to FBI Director William Webster, January 29, 1986. Letter of FBI Director William Webster to Representative Don Edwards, April 11, 1986. U.S. House of Representatives, *Hearings Before the Subcommittee on Civil and Constitutional Rights of the Committee on the Judiciary on FBI Authorization Request for Fiscal Year 1987*, March 14, 1986, proofs (Washington, D.C.: Government Printing Office), pp. 14–15.

31. Ross Gelbspan, "Break-ins, Threats Hit Political Activists," *Boston Globe*, December 30, 1984, pp. 21–25.

32. Movement Support Network, *MNS News*, April 1985, p. 5.

33. Joyce Garver Keller, director, People for the American Way, Chicago, 1985 (mimeo), p. 1.

34. James Ledbetter, "I Was a Spy for Accuracy in Academia," *New Republic*, December 30, 1985, p. 15.

35. Thomas J. Meyer, "Media Critic Forms New Organization to Monitor 'Disinformation' in Class," *Chronicle of Higher Education*, July 3, 1985.

36. Elliot Marshall, "New Group Targets Political Bias on Campus," *Science* 229 (August 30, 1985):841.

37. Keller, mimeo, p. 1.

38. Elliot Marshall, "New Group Targets," p. 842.

39. Gelbspan, "Break-ins," *Boston Globe*, December 30, 1984, pp. 21–25.

40. Anthony Lewis, "A Fear and Intimidation Campaign," *Patriot Ledger*, February 25, 1986, p. 20.

41. John Robertson, "O'Neil Denounces $100m Aid Plan for Contras," *Boston Globe*, February 21, 1986, p. 3.

42. Patrick J. Buchanan, "The Contras Need Our Help," *Washington Post*, March 5, 1986.

43. Anne C. Roark, "Reagan Hits Professor's Nicaragua Story," *Los Angeles Times*, pt. 1, March 12, 1986, p. 18.

44. E. Bradford Burns, "A Star Was Born," *The Nation*, April 5, 1986, p. 477.

45. Anthony Lewis, "A Fear and Intimidation Campaign," *Patriot Ledger*, February 25, 1986, p. 20.

Impact and Implications

Introduction

Part 3 focuses on the impact and implications of the Reagan administration's undeclared war. The intended and most obvious impact was on Nicaragua itself—in diminishing the ability of the revolutionary government to provide social services to that country's poor majority and thereby (it was obviously hoped) in eroding the image and legitimacy of the Sandinista revolution at home and throughout the world. In Chapter 13 Harvey Williams contends that, although "the hard-won social programs of the Nicaraguan people" would not easily be reversed, by 1986 they had clearly been damaged and made much more difficult by the contra war. In Chapter 14 Sung Ho Kim examines Reagan administration policy toward Nicaragua in terms of international law, morality, and prudence. He contends that a policy that is both illegal and immoral is also imprudent because it is particularly difficult to justify and sustain in a democratic society. In Chapter 15 Noam Chomsky brings the discussion full circle to focus on the implications of the Reagan war for and about the United States as a polity. In it, he digs beneath the self-serving, Orwellian rhetoric of the Reagan administration and the corporate media and identifies the double standards, warped definitions, and real motivations at work.

THIRTEEN

The Social Impact in Nicaragua

HARVEY WILLIAMS

From the outset, the Sandinista revolution was a popular revolution: popular in the sense that it depended upon the participation of a broad political base to achieve the overthrow of the Somoza regime and that the benefits of the revolution were to be widely distributed. Sandinista policy was developed with clear appreciation of the uniqueness of the Nicaraguan reality. Given the country's extremely limited level of industrial development, the revolution could not depend solely upon the urban proletariat. To be successful, the Sandinistas would need to acknowledge the importance of the vast number of marginally employed urban and rural poor and to incorporate them into the revolutionary process. In this instance, there was a significant parallel between the Sandinista policy and a key element of liberation theology, a preferential option for the poor.

The first public document of the revolutionary government made explicit the commitment to social as well as political and economic change. It specifically pledged the government to develop policies to promote the improvement of the quality of life for all Nicaraguans and outlined objectives in health, education, welfare, housing, and other areas.[1] Later policy statements reaffirmed these goals and defined the role of the government as not "a handout agency for the people but rather one of coordinating and giving technial assistance to the independent efforts of the people."[2]

During the first seven years following the Triumph, tremendous progress was made in meeting the needs of the masses through the development and implementation of programs in the social sector. Both within Nicaragua and internationally, the accomplishments of four key ministries—health, education, welfare, and housing—had been acknowledged as significant, even by critics of the revolution. These achievements were the result of a combination of conscious, flexible, and pragmatic planning on the part of the government and of mobilization, involvement, and commitment on the part of the people.

Analysis of the Sandinista social policies and programs during these first seven years is facilitated by defining three time periods. The first, from the Triumph in July 1979 through the end of 1980, was generally a time of planning and reorganization and of response to the immediate problems and damage created by the war. The second, the years 1981 and 1982, was a period of policy modification and adjustment and of rapid and relatively unimpeded program exansion. The third period, from 1983 into 1986, saw the full development of the Reagan administration's policy of low-intensity conflict, effectively bringing all social programs under siege and causing a policy shift toward program reinforcement and defense.

Reorganization and Recovery: 1979–1980

On coming to power in July 1979, the new government had to confront serious problems. The economy was in shambles. Both the social and the economic needs of the people had to be addressed. This was not merely a reactivation of processes temporarily halted. New programs needed to be designed and implemented to promote the revolutionary process. In their urgency to satisfy immediate needs with limited resources, planners and policy makers put together a patchwork of programs, borrowing heavily from a wide range of other countries and their own past experience. Although a Ministry of Planning was created, its function was more global than specific, and the individual ministries were left largely on their own to develop policies and programs within the announced general guidelines. During this period, interministerial coordination was limited, which led to some inconsistencies and even contradictions.

The Sandinista revolution had attracted considerable international attention. Following the Triumph, assistance came from both the East and the West. The Cuban government was particularly supportive, especially in offering technical assistance.[3] In the United States, the Carter administration was already reevaluating its acquiescence in Somoza's overthrow. Although some material and technical aid was approved, it was considerably less than the assistance granted following the earthquake of 1972.

Problems in the social sector were particularly serious. The policies of the new government promised programs that were either new or considerably larger than those that existed under Somoza. Because these programs were nonproductive, extreme care had to be exercised to avoid the misallocation of resources experienced in other developing countries.[4] From the very beginning, the role of the mass organizations in generating popular support and participation was a key factor in the success of social sector programs.[5]

HEALTH

The health delivery system under Somoza was disorganized, inefficient, and greatly biased toward providing curative care for a small minority of urban elites.[6] The major commitments of the Ministry of Health (MINSA) during the first period were toward the national unification of the health system and the restoration of prewar health facilities. Much of the latter was financed by money that was "in the pipeline" from Somoza era international support (particularly from the United States). Although it did little to correct the imbalance of services that favored the urban areas, it did increase the available facilities in those areas.

The creation of a National Unified Health System brought together several previously separate health groups: the social security system (which provided health care for the approximate 10 percent of the population covered), the Ministry of Health (which provided preventive care through health posts), the military hospital, and the various national and local social assistance boards (which maintained public clinics and hospitals). The National Unified Health System did not include private facilities, although it did develop a cooperative working agreement with some of the private, nonprofit providers. MINSA also took over the training of health personnel, increasing significantly the number of people trained at all levels, and provided training, materials, and health personnel for the efforts of several other government programs.

The most significant policy innovation for health was to make government health care open to all. Where facilities already existed, this enlarged scope greatly increased utilization by the masses and led to greatly increased expectations in underserved areas. In this early period, emphasis was on curative care, both because of the traditional system and because of the influence of the more highly trained professionals.

EDUCATION

As with health, the prerevolutionary situation in education was poor. The illiteracy rate (50 percent) and the yearly dropout rate (50 percent) were among the highest in Latin America, and schools were concentrated in the urban areas. The better schools were private, and their tuition charges excluded all but the children of the most wealthy.

The process of reorganization for the Ministry of Education (MED) was not as difficult, given the relatively centralized organization that existed under Somoza. Most of the effort was directed toward better integration of planning and curriculum development and expansion of programs in preschool, technical, special, and adult education. Although only 47 of the 128 war-damaged schools were repaired in this period, there was considerable construction of new schools, particularly those built by popular initiative with only technical assistance and supplies from MED. Community projects accounted for 85 percent of the 739 schools built in the first two years, most in rural areas.[7]

By far the most ambitious and well-known effort of MED, if not of the whole revolutionary process, was the Literacy Crusade.[8] Within one year after the Triumph, over 80,000 volunteers (mostly urban high school and university students) were mobilized. They carried out a five-month adult literacy program throughout the nation, from poor urban neighborhoods to the most remote locations in the interior. The results exceeded those anticipated, and the rate of adult literacy was raised from 50 to 88 percent. The Literacy Crusade received international attention, including the UNESCO award for distinguished and effective contribution on behalf of literacy. But the impact of the Literacy Crusade went far beyond the mere teaching of literacy. For all the participants, the brigade volunteers as well as their students, the experience promoted a sense of active participation and sharing in the revolutionary process, breaking down traditional barriers that had long existed between the rural and the urban, the old and the young, and the privileged few and the marginal masses. It also provided a model for the mobilization and participation of the masses in other social programs.

SOCIAL SECURITY AND WELFARE

These two programmatic areas were separate under Somoza and remained separate during the first period. The prerevolutionary Institute of Social Security covered only about 10 percent of the people, nearly all of whom resided in Managua. Although the system covered disability and retirement, its primary function was to provide medical care for its subscribers. With the reorganization of the government health system, the social security medical facilities were incorporated into the National Unified Health System. The Institute of Social Security devoted its efforts toward incorporating the majority of the people into the social security program. The use of social security funds to finance a health system for the whole population was a significant deviation from the traditional Latin American practice and demonstrated once again the Sandinista commitment to the society as a whole.[9]

The problems of organization for the Ministry of Social Welfare (MBS) immediately following the Triumph were great, primarily because such a ministry did not exist under Somoza. As in many other Latin American countries, most of the functions of social welfare were expected to be carried out by religious and private charitable agencies. The new MBS set for itself the goal of organizing under its supervision the diverse programs directed toward the resolution of social problems. These programs included homes for the elderly and for orphans, training and rehabilitation for drug and alcohol abusers, for juvenile delinquents, and for the disabled, and emergency relief for refugees and families in need. During this first period, the MBS not only developed a national coordination of the existing services, but it also created new programs. To the single child-care center that existed under Somoza were added seventeen new urban centers and fourteen rural centers. Among other new programs were three rehabilitation centers for the disabled, three centers for abused or abandoned children, three new homes for the elderly (plus subsidies for six private facilities), and nutrition programs that served over 250,000 children and pregnant or nursing mothers.[10]

HOUSING

The war contributed to the already serious housing situation that existed under Somoza. The Somoza regime never fully recovered from the effects of the 1972 earthquake, and most of the housing built in that recovery effort was designed for middle and upper income families.[11] Efforts of the new Ministry of Housing and Human Settlements (MINVAH) during this first period went into reorganization (combining the Somoza era Vice-Ministry of Urban Planning and the National Housing Institute) and into planning and the development of legislation. New laws introduced rent control and restructured mortgages. But the law with the broadest impact was that for the consolidation and ordering of illegal subdivisions. This law cleared the way for nearly half of the urban householders to acquire title to their land and outlined policies for the provision of supportive infrastructure. By way of satisfying immediate needs, some 1,146 new houses were constructed (mostly in Managua), and repairs were made to 4,676 houses damaged by the war.[12]

Adjustment and Expansion: 1981–1982

The 1981–1982 period was, as vice-minister described it to me, one of "relative bonanza." Most of the reconstruction work had been completed, and many of the problems of organization within the various ministries had been overcome. As part of the dynamic revolutionary process, a more clear and widely accepted view of the Sandinista goals was developed.[13] Local and regional organization was strengthened, and a new system of regionalization was enacted in order to decentralize and make more efficient the administration of government programs.[14] Although the U.S. government cut off aid entirely, total aid from all sources increased in 1981.[15]

The agrarian reform program showed great advances, and agricultural production began to increase toward prewar levels. Although military expenditures were high and climbing, they were still exceeded by public spending in the social sector. Quality of service and public spending in health and education, which had been the lowest in the region under Somoza, surpassed those of El Salvador, Guatemala, and Honduras, and nearly equaled those of Costa Rica.[16]

Popular participation continued at a high rate, and organizational effectiveness was increased. Most adults belonged to one or more of the mass organizations, and many others participated occasionally through special mobilizations. Participation was not limited merely to providing physical labor for government projects. Increasingly, the mass organizations were involved in planning, organizing, administering, and evaluating a wide range of public programs.[17]

But though internal development and international support increased during this period, aggression against the Sandinista government became stronger and better organized. The Reagan administration hardened its position against Nicaragua, launching frequent verbal attacks and increasing economic pressure. Not only were loans and PL 480 food credits, which came directly from the U.S. government, eliminated, but the Reagan administration began to use its influence in international loan programs to block international support.[18]

The counterrevolutionaries, fueled by covert assistance from the Reagan administration, began to step up their military operations against government targets. Operation Red Christmas in 1981 and extensive sabotage in early 1982 led to the imposition of a State of Emergency by the Sandinistas. The Nicaraguan Democratic Front (FDN) was officially formed in 1981 and given a "civilian directorate" in late 1982, and it was estimated that the number of persons under arms increased to over 5,000.[19] War damage to the economy during this period was estimated to be $40 million[20]—small by comparison to later years but still equal to one-third of the 1982 public expenditure for health. Increasingly, social programs and those that participated in them became the targets of the counterrevolutionaries.

HEALTH

MINSA received top priority among the social sector ministries during this period. The government budget for health was greater than for education, a rarity among Latin American countries. Improvement continued in all types of programs. Construction on four new regional hospitals was begun. The number of health posts was increased by over 25 percent, most in rural or underserved urban areas. There was a significant increase in the number of medical personnel at all levels. The number of consultations increased by over 20 percent.[21]

During this time there was a noticeable shift from a concentration of resources and services in urban areas to a dispersion toward underserved (primarily rural) areas. Dramatic increases in accessability and utilization were seen in poor urban neighborhoods[22] and in the interior.[23]

There was an even more noticeable shift from curative health to preventative health. The oral rehydration program was greatly expanded with the opening of more than 300 centers. During the first years of the revolution this program was called the major factor in the significant (30 percent) reduction of infant mortality. Major efforts in environmental sanitation included community programs for garbage removal and latrine construction.[24]

The programs that drew the most attention, including the recognition of the World Health Organization and UNICEF, were the preventive campaigns carried out by the health brigades during the Popular Health Workdays. Using as a model the successful Literacy Crusade, MINSA organized and trained community volunteers for a series of national inoculation campaigns. Popular participation and cooperation were widespread, and the results were dramatic: Polio and diphtheria were effectively eliminated, and the incidence of measles, tetanus, tuberculosis, and whooping cough was greatly reduced.[25]

But as the health programs became more widespread and more successful, the counterrevolutionaries saw them as appropriate targets for their campaigns. In spite of the fact that hostilities against civilians, and particularly medical personnel, violated several articles of the Geneva Conventions, three health workers were killed by the counterrevolutionaries during this period.[26] There were incidents of sabotage of expensive medical equipment, and several health facilities were damaged or destroyed. The worst incident took place in December 1981 when the counterrevolutionaries overran the Atlantic Coast community of Bilwaskarma. Doctors, nurses, and other health workers were beaten, raped, and kidnapped, and the hospital was destroyed.[27]

EDUCATION

In this second period, MED continued to expand both its physical structures and the enrollment of students. Although community-sponsored school construction dropped significantly, MED built more than three times the number of schools in this period than it had in the previous period. It gave special attention to underserved rural areas and to the construction of secondary schools in underserved areas of the interior. Enrollment neared 900,000 students, with primary and preschool showing the greatest increases.[28] Planning and curriculum development were expanded, and MED began to publish new textbooks. The regionalization and reorganization of MED were formalized in law in late 1982, officially creating a vice-ministry of adult education.[29]

The most significant growth took place in adult education. Following the Literacy Crusade, Basic Popular Education Centers were set up to reinforce and extend the crusade's gains. More than 150,000 adults continued in these programs. The total number of teachers grew from 12,975 under Somoza to over 40,000 in this period. Of these, some 20,000 were empirically trained teachers working in the Popular Education Centers.[30] Both the teachers and students participated at some risk, for it was the common understanding that they would be prime targets for the counterrevolutionaries. Toward the end of 1982, four adult education teachers and assistants were killed, and several others were kidnapped and threatened because of their activities.[31]

SOCIAL SECURITY AND WELFARE

The major change during the second period for these programs was the combination of the Ministry of Social Welfare with the Nicaraguan Social Security Institute to form a new ministry-level agency, the Nicaraguan Institute of Social Security and Social Welfare (INSSBI). INSSBI continued to incorporate new workers into the program and by the end of 1982 had nearly doubled the number of subscribers. Pension and disability benefits were granted to a number of special groups, including combatants, miners, brigade volunteers, retired government workers, militia members, circus workers, and those giving special patriotic service. There was a significant change in benefits paid in 1982: The proportion generated by death and injuries caused by counterrevolutionary aggression increased from zero to over one half the total.[32]

The social welfare programs began to show the effects of a reduced budget. Relatively few new child-care centers were opened (all in rural areas), and several pilot programs had to be curtailed. Increased emphasis was given to integrating the community and the mass organizations into the provision of services. Case workers facilitated the development of community support to help their clients deal with physical and mental disabilities, drug and alcohol problems, and physical abuse and abandonment.[33]

HOUSING

In both 1981 and 1982 MINVAH increased the number of housing units built, completing a total of 5,762 in this period—more than five times the number completed in the previous period. Although more than half were built in Managua, a shift began toward the underserved areas of the interior. Over 1,000 new units were constructed in a settlement for the relocation of Miskito Indians from the border region following the Red Christmas attacks of the counterrevolutionaries.[34]

There was also a shift toward facilitating housing for the very poor. MINVAH realized that its funds were too limited to anticipate building even low-cost housing for all that needed it. Therefore, two new programs were initiated: the Materials Bank and the Progressive Urbanizations. The former was a program for the production and distribution of housing materials that could be purchased at low cost and with low-interest financing. The latter was a sites and services program to provide low-cost controlled development (particularly in the urban centers). During this period 551 units were completed with the Materials Bank program and nearly 10,000 parcels distributed in progressive urbanizations.[35]

Also during this period, MINVAH administered a World Bank loan of $22 billion for urban reconstruction. In the project completion report evaluators stated that it was "probably one of the most effective urban projects supported by the Bank"[36] and commended MINVAH on its organization and the mass organizations on their support of the project. But even this glowing report did not keep the Reagan administration from blocking future loans.

Reinforcement and Defense: 1983–1986

During the 1983–1986 period a marked hardening took place in the position of the Reagan administration toward the Sandinistas. Although expressing verbal support for the Contadora process (initiated in January 1983), the Reagan administration seemed to be following the recommendations of the Rand Corporation's 1984 report: rejection of accommodation as untenable, emphasis on "diplomatic efforts to isolate the regime, raise the regime's costs, reduce the support it receives from Latin America and Europe,"[37] and strengthening of "the rebel forces to concentrate their attacks on economic targets."[38] This approach was part of a conscious shift to a new type of military strategy, called "low-intensity conflict."[39]

During this period the Reagan administration continued its diplomatic and economic campaign against the Sandinista government, eliminating Nicaragua's sugar quota, closing its consulates and restricting the issuance of visas to Sandinista supporters, continuing to block international loans and grants, and eventually, in May 1985, declaring a complete embargo.

Military intimidation increased. Following the U.S. invasion of Grenada, the Reagan administration expanded its military presence in Central America through an almost continual series of military maneuvers. Rather than actual preparations for direct military intervention, these maneuvers were part of the low-intensity conflict strategy. One goal was "to squeeze the economy by forcing a massive diversion of resources into defense. The strategy aimed to exacerbate social problems and tensions, eroding popular support for the revolution by making it ineffective in people's lives"[40] and to produce a heavy psychological impact on the civilian population.[41]

As the U.S. Congress moved from prohibiting covert aid to approving overt aid, the counterrevolutionary forces stepped up their attacks.[42] Through various forms, including intimidation and kidnapping, the estimated number of counterrevolutionaries under arms rose from some 5,000 to over 15,000. Although the mining of harbors and the attacks on international shipping and port facilities were halted after receiving wide international censure, the counterrevolutionaries increased their campaigns against civilian as well as military targets. Reports circulated almost daily of counterrevolutionary terrorist incidents.[43] The official policy became the "targeting" of all supporters and beneficiaries of the Sandinista revolutionary process, including the members of the mass organizations (who represented over half of the adult population),[44] a policy outlined in the CIA manual *Psychological Operations in Guerilla Warfare.*

> The results can be seen in the countryside, where some *contra* forces have been implementing this approach with varying success. Overall, there is a conscious effort to reduce the presence of the civilian government, to remove successful social programs and the ideological influence which comes with them. The strategy aims to create the impression of government weakness and *contra* strength. In practice, this means the targeted torture and assassination of teachers, health workers, agricultural technicians and their collaborators in the community. This is not, as many critics charge, "indiscriminate violence against civilians." Nor are the killings random acts of terror by incorrigibly brutal ex-National Guardsmen. Rather, the violence is part of a logical and systematic policy, and reflects the changing pattern of the war.[45]

The effects of the aggression of the Reagan administration and the counterrevolutionaries during this period were serious but not fatal. The total cost of the war was great, and estimates varied widely. The Nicaraguan government, in its case before the World Court in 1985, calculated the damages to total "US$372 million in direct losses and US$1.3 billion in indirect losses, a conservative estimate. The sum of these two figures is approximately equal to total export earnings over the last four years."[46] The proportion of the national budget that went for defense rose to 37 percent in 1983, passing health and education expenditures under the Sandinistas for the first time.[47] By 1985, defense expenditures had reached 50 percent of the national budget.[48]

Social sector programs were severely constrained in this period. A freeze was put on the extension of services for the urban areas, and investment in the social sector was reduced severely. Military obligations reduced the number of young men studying or employed in social programs. But the Sandinistas used the pressure from the aggression to reinforce the revolutionary process. "As early as 1983, they recognized that the strategic goal of low intensity war was population, not territory."[49] The Sandinistas continued to develop the support of mass organizations, responding to their complaints and concerns[50] and developing programs in their support. The priority programs of health, adult education, and agrarian reform were reinforced and expanded, particularly in the rural areas, offsetting the traditional preference for the more visible but less productive urban masses. The resettlement of peasants from scattered and vulnerable locations to new cooperative farms was viewed by most as positive. They ended up with more and better land and were less vulnerable to the attacks of the counterrevolutionaries, and they received the benefits of the government programs in health, education, welfare, and housing.[51]

Contrary to the wishes of the Reagan administration, the Sandinistas continued to receive aid and assistance from a wide range of sources. And even though official U.S. government aid was eliminated, U.S.-based private nonprofit organizations (including CARE, Oxfam America, American Friends Service Committee, and Church World Service) and solidarity groups continued to support the Nicaraguan people.

HEALTH

Throughout this period MINSA remained a Sandinista priority. Although investment in new facilities was severely curtailed after 1982, programs in preventive health and early treatment in rural areas were maintained. In spite of the fact that nearly 100 health facilities were destroyed or were closed as a result of hostilities in the area,[52] the total in service remained above the 1982 level. More impressive was the fact that medical consultations by region were in proportion to their respective populations for the first time in history.[53] Gains in trained personnel, immunizations, and reductions of mortality were maintained or improved. Although the U.S. embargo seriously affected the importation of medications and repair parts for medical equipment, it also stimulated innovative responses in equipment repair and herbal medicine substitutes. Difficulties in serving the more isolated areas actually served to reinforce popular participation through the mass organizations and local health committees.[54]

But the negative effects were also great. By 1985 an estimated 11,000 were dead and 5,000 wounded as a result of the aggression. Between 1983 and September 1985, thirty-five health providers were killed, eleven were wounded, and twenty-eight were kidnapped.[55] Among those killed were two internationalist physicians, one from France and one from West Germany. The latter was murdered in cold blood by the counterrevolutionaries after they had raped and shot two nurses who were working with him.[56] In clear violation of the Geneva Conventions, the counterrevolutionaries defined noncombatant international volunteers as prime targets for kidnapping and assassinations.

A clandestine rebel radio station warned last month that rebel forces regarded "all foreigners who come to implant communism in Nicaragua" as legitimate targets.
     At particular risk, because of their extended stays in remote parts of the country, are foreign doctors who have helped boost government health services while Nicaraguan physicians are being trained to replace those who left after the 1979 revolution. Alongside 500 Cubans, an equal number of European and North American doctors work for the Ministry of Health.[57]

From 1983 through 1985, more than 5,000 health workers were mobilized for defense, representing a serious drain of resources from the civilian population. The economic value of damages to the health infrastructure from 1980 through September 1985 was estimated to be nearly $1.8 million, over 70 percent in the eastern part of the country. Sixty-one health facilities were destroyed, including three belonging to the Nicaraguan Baptist Convention.[58]

Although polio and diphtheria appeared to be diseases of the past for Nicaragua, early advances against measles and malaria were being slowly eroded.[59] The incidence of dengue fever, a mosquito-borne disease that appeared to have been totally eliminated in 1982, showed a tremendous resurgence in 1985, reaching epidemic proportions and affecting over half the population of Managua, leading some to suggest the possibility of biological warfare. Despite a shortage of larvacide, a mass mobilization campaign to destroy mosquito breeding places was expected to reduce the incidence significantly.

EDUCATION

During this period MED was severely strained to maintain the gains made in the first years. Innovative programs, such as bilingual education for the Atlantic Coast area and rural work-study schools, were reduced or put on hold.[60] Enrollment, having reached a high of 939,793 in 1983, declined nearly 10 percent over next two years, then began to recover in 1986.[61] Investment in new facilities had nearly come to a halt by 1986, and expansion was limited to resettlement projects, as part of the policy to give priority to the productive sector. Given the economic limitations imposed by policies of the Reagan administration, major efforts were directed toward curriculum revision, improving academic quality and performance, stimulating creative alternatives to resolve material shortages, and reinforcing the popular support of education at all levels. There were also budget increases for new teachers and for scholarships for poor students in critical fields.[62]

Having been extended into the most remote areas of the country, in both regular and special adult education programs, MED personnel and facilities were particularly susceptible to attack by the counterrevolutionaries. Through 1985, MED suffered the following losses: 188 teachers and students killed and 106 kidnapped; 27 schools destroyed, 19 damaged, and 502 abandoned; 32,680 primary students and 11,359 adult education students left unattended; and 181 teachers left temporarily inactive. It was estimated that the number of students in 1986 would have been about 1,260,000 except for the aggression of the counterrevolutionaries and the Reagan administration.[63]

Even though Nicaragua continued to receive international support, the Reagan administration's "campaign to discredit the Sandinistas ha[d] resulted in reduced support for educational programs by some international organizations."[64] For example, "the Latin American Scholarship Program of American Universities (LASPAU), which had provided ten professors during the 1983 academic year"[65] was discontinued. And threats of U.S. military intervention were said to have led to the withdrawal of some 1,000 Cuban teachers.[66]

SOCIAL SECURITY AND WELFARE

INSSBI made its greatest gains in social security coverage during this period. By September 1985, the number of subscribers increased to 321,402, and the number of persons with social security coverage increased to 1,142,681. The latter figure was equal to 35.5 percent of the total population, nearly five times the proportion covered under the Somoza regime.[67] Most of this increase occurred after 1982 and was accomplished by extending coverage to persons in the interior of the country, particularly agricultural workers.

The number of child protection centers was greatly expanded during this period, particularly in the rural areas and in conjunction with the development of agricultural cooperatives and new settlements. Of the 181 child protection centers of all types functioning in 1985, there were 44 rural child care centers and 73 rural child nutrition centers.[68] The School of Social Work, which had been closed for reorganization since 1980, was reopened in 1984 and began training much needed professionals.

At the same time, INSSBI experienced an accelerating demand for its services because of the aggression of the counterrevolutionaries. By 1985, the number of persons displaced by the war had surpassed 250,000. The value of INSSBI programs to provide material assistance to less than half of these refugees exceeded $15 million.[69] The number of orphans resulting from the hostilities passed 7,000 by 1985. Although family and community support networks took the responsibility for many, by 1985 INSSBI was providing 1,136 pensions for orphaned minors.[70] Pensions for other war-caused deaths and disabilities constituted an increasing proportion of all social security payments. Although international aid continued to support INSSBI programs (particularly through food and other gifts in kind), cash donations, which reached a record high in 1983, had decreased by some 50 percent by 1985.[71] Another dark cloud on the horizon was deficit spending: The government was not making its required payments to the social security system or transferring INSSBI's share of the proceeds of the national lottery. By 1984 social security payments had nearly equaled contributions, and the reserves were threatened.[72]

HOUSING

The activities of MINVAH during this period continued at an accelerated pace. The number of housing units completed was higher than in previous periods. However, the most noticeable policy change was the shift of activity from Managua and other urban centers to the rural areas of the interior. For example, MINVAH completed a record high of 4,513 units in 1983, but only 26 percent were completed in Managua, as compared to over 60 percent before that year.[73] Although the resettlement efforts had been under way for some time, a major increase in activity took place in 1985.

> The campesinos were to be moved to new communities known as asentamientos, in areas of superior farming conditions and more defensible locations, where agricultural production disrupted by the war could be maintained or increased. Likewise, the relocation would increase the provision of social and technical services to the rural population, while reducing the risk of ambushes against technicians, teachers, and health workers. Organized relocation would also reduce the flow of displaced campesinos to the cities, which was overtaxing housing and social services.[74]

Original plans called for about 9,000 families to be relocated to some 200 settlements. But because of the reduced activity of the counterrevolutionaries in 1986, only about 4,000 families had to be relocated by that time. Housing provided by MINVAH in the new settlements ranged from conditioned sites with a minimal structure with roof to sites with completed, prefabricated units.[75]

Unfortunately, this plan had little immediate effect in deterring the flow of migrants to the cities, and the limited funds available to MINVAH were not used for urban development in this period. Asked what would be done for the many migrants residing in Managua and clamoring for housing and services, the head of MINVAH replied: "We do not propose to do anything. . . . We are not going to evict them but neither are we going to provide them with services such as electricity or water connections, and much less initiate programs to confer property titles. . . . We are simply going to ignore them."[76] This statement is an example of the revolutionary government's reluctance to encourage urban migration and the development of the marginal, nonproductive sector.

In spite of this pronouncement, the granting of property titles continued as fast as technical limitations would allow, and considerable housing was built by owners. In the rural areas, the Materials Bank program increased its activities. Alternative construction materials were developed to replace those previously imported and to make up for the decrease in lumber harvesting caused by counterrevolutionary activities in the forested regions of the country.

MINVAH received considerable technical support from international groups, especially in the form of volunteer construction brigades. But these were also targets of the counterrevolutionary attacks. Among others, two West German women were kidnapped and raped in 1983, a Swiss pacifist was killed in an ambush that also claimed the lives of five Nicaraguan women, and in 1986 eight West Germans (four men and four women) were kidnapped and held by the counterrevolutionaries for three weeks before being released.[77]

Conclusion

The social sector policies and programs of the Sandinista government of Nicaragua had broad popular and political support.[78] It was notable that a government with such limited resources could make as much progress in so many areas within the first seven years after coming to power. It was remarkable that Nicaragua achieved these accomplishments while defending against the aggression of one of the most powerful nations on earth. Whether by design or by happenstance, the Sandinistas refined and developed their social policies in a way that reached and involved the vast majority of the previously underserved poor. Social programs and the populations they served became so enmeshed in one another that it was impossible to separate the two: The people and the revolutionary process became one. What one observer remarked about health could be equally applied to all social programs: "By building toward a strong and equitable health care system, the Sandinistas may be doing more to secure themselves with their constituents than all the rhetoric and armed force in the world."[79] Although serious problems and limitations remained, even beyond the aggression of the counterrevolutionaries and the Reagan administration, it was unlikely that any power would easily be able to take away the hard won social progress of the Nicaraguan people.

Notes

1. Gobierno de Reconstrucción Nacional, *Primera Proclama del Gobierno de Reconstrucción Nacional* (Managua: Difusión y Prensa, 1979).

2. Gobierno de Reconstrucción Nacional, *The Philosophy and Politics of the Government of Nicaragua* (Managua: Dirección de Divulgación y Prensa, 1982).

3. Marc Edelman, "Lifelines: Nicaragua and the Socialist Countries," *NACLA Report on the Americas* 19, no. 3 (May/June 1985):33–56.

4. Emmanuel Jimenez, "The Public Subsidization of Education and Health in Developing Countries: A Review of Equity and Efficiency," *World Bank Research Observer* 1, no. 1 (January 1986):111–129.

5. For more extensive treatment of the Sandinista mass organizations, see Gary Ruchwarger, "The Sandinista Mass Organizations and the Revolutionary Process," in Richard Harris and Carlos Vilas, eds., *Nicaragua: Revolution Under Seige* (London: Zed Books, 1985), pp. 88–119, and Luis Serra, "The Grass-Roots Organizations," in Thomas W. Walker, ed., *Nicaragua: the First Five Years* (New York: Praeger Publishers, 1985), pp. 95–114.

6. For more information concerning the prerevolutionary period, see Thomas John Bossert, "Health Care in Revolutionary Nicaragua," in Thomas W. Walker, ed., *Nicaragua in Revolution* (New York: Praeger Publishers, 1982), pp. 259–272, and Harvey Williams, "Organization and Delivery of Health Care: A Study of Change in Nicaragua," in John H. Morgan, ed., *Third World Medicine and Social Change* (Washington, D.C.: University Press of America, 1983), pp. 285–298.

7. Ministerio de Educación (MED), *La Educación en Tres Años de Revolución* (Managua: MED, 1982).

8. See Valerie Miller, "The Nicaraguan Literacy Crusade," in Walker, *Nicaragua in Revolution*, pp. 241–258, for an early description.

9. Reinaldo Antonio Téfel, Humberto Mendoza López, and Jorge Flores Castillo, "Social Welfare," in Walker, *The First Five Years*, pp. 365–382.

10. Ministerio de Bienestar Social (MBS), *Informe de Actividades: 1979–1981* (Managua: MBS, 1981).

11. For more information concerning the prerevolutionary period, see Harvey Williams, "Housing Policy in Revolutionary Nicaragua," in Walker, *Nicaragua in Revolution*, pp. 273–290.

12. Ibid., pp. 279–284.

13. Gobierno de Reconstrucción Nacional, *Philosophy and Politics*.

14. Charles Downs, "Local and Regional Government," in Walker, *The First Five Years*, pp. 45–63.

15. Michael E. Conroy, "External Dependence, External Assistance, and Economic Aggression against Nicaragua," *Latin American Perspectives* 12, no. 2 (spring 1965): 39–67.

16. Ruth Leger Sivard, *World Military and Social Expenditures 1985* (Washington, D.C.: World Priorities, 1985).

17. Ruchwarger, "Sandinista Mass Organizations."

18. Conroy, "External Dependence," p. 52.

19. Bill Robinson and Kent Norsworthy, "Inside the Real War Against Nicaragua," *CENSA's Strategic Report*, no. 7 (May 1986), p. 2.

20. Nicaraguan Interfaith Committee for Action (NICA), *Nicaragua Update* 7, no. 5 (September/October 1985):6.

21. Ministerio de Salud (MINSA), *El Sistema Nacional Unico de Salud: Tres Años de Revolución* (Managua: MINSA, 1982).

22. For example, in Ciudad Sandino (a suburb of Managua) health facilities were increased from two parttime health posts with three doctors, a dentist, and seven nurses in 1977 to one health center, two health posts, and a pharmacy with a total of fifteen doctors, four dentists, twenty-eight nurses, and twenty-nine additional health workers in 1982 (Williams, "Organization and Delivery of Health Care").

23. David Siegel, "The Epidemiology of Aggression: The Effects of the War on Health Care," *Nicaraguan Perspectives*, no. 10 (spring-summer 1985), p. 23.

24. Thomas John Bossert, "Health Policy: The Dilemma of Success," in Walker, *The First Five Years*, pp. 347–363 and Williams, "Organization and Delivery of Health Care."

25. MINSA, *El Sistema Nacional*.

26. Committee for Health Rights in Central America (CHRICA), *Health Consequences of War in Nicaragua* (San Francisco: CHRICA, 1986).

27. "Black Scholar Interviews: Mirna Cunningham," *The Black Scholar* 14, no. 2 (March/April 1983):17–27.

28. MED, *La Educación en Tres Años*.

29. Rosa María Torres, *La Post-Alfabetización en Nicaragua* (Managua: Instituto Nicaragüense de Investigaciones Económicos y Sociales (INIES), 1983).

30. MED, *La Educación en Cuatro Años de Revolución* (Managua: MED, 1983).

31. "Sequel to the Literacy Campaign: Adult Education in Nicaragua," *Envío*, no. 17 (November 1982):14–21.

32. Instituto Nicaragüense de Seguridad Social y Bienestar (INSSBI), *Memoria 1982* (Managua: INSSBI, 1983), table 17.

33. Centro Latinoamericano de Trabajo Social (CELATS), *Política Social y Trabajo Social: I Seminario de Trabajo Social en Nicaragua* (Lima: CELATS, 1982).

34. Ministerio de Vivienda y Asentamientos Humanos (MINVAH), "Los Asentamientos Humanos de Centro América y Panamá: Nicaragua," paper presented at the 11th Meeting of the Permanent Central American Conference of Housing and Urban Development, Managua, August 19–25, 1984 (mimeo).

35. Harvey Williams, "Housing Policy," in Walker, *The First Five Years*, pp. 383–397.

36. World Bank, "Nicaragua, Credit 965-NI, Urban Reconstruction Report, Completion Report," June 24, 1983 (typed), p. 1.

37. Edward Gonzalez, Brian Michael Jenkins, David Ronfeldt, and Caesar Sereseres, *U.S. Policy for Central America: A Briefing* (Santa Monica, Calif.: Rand Corporation, 1984), p. 21.

38. Ibid., p. 21.

39. Sara Miles, "The Real War: Low Intensity Conflict in Central America," *NACLA Report on the Americas* 20, no. 2 (April/May 1986):17–48.

40. Ibid., p. 30.

41. Ibid., p. 32. Other acts of psychological harassment included the frequent overflights of low-flying supersonic reconnaissance aircraft, creating sonic booms that caused the people to believe they were being bombarded.

42. Average battles per day rose to 1.35 in 1983 and to 4.10 in 1984. Attacks against civilian and economic targets increased to 115 in 1983 and to 165 in 1984. See Juan Arrien, *La Educación en el Contexto de la Agresión Militar (1983–1985)* (Managua: MED, 1986), p. 4.

43. Extensive documentation exists on the terrorist activities of the counterrevolutionaries against civilians. See, for example, Dieter Eich and Carlos Rincón, *The Contra: Interviews with Anti-Sandinistas* (San Francisco: Synthesis Publications, 1985); Reed Brody, *Contra Terror in Nicaragua* (Boston: South End Press, 1985); and Teófilo Cabestrero, *Nicaragua: Crónica de una Sangre Inocente* (México: Editorial Katún, 1985).

44. Robinson and Norsworthy, "Inside the Real War," p. 10.

45. Sara Miles, "The Real War," p. 34.

46. "A Survival Economy," *Envío* 4, no. 52 (October 1985):2b.

47. Jaime Wheelock Román, *Entre la Crisis y la Agresión: La Reforma Agraria Sandinista* (Managua: Editorial Nueva Nicaragua, 1985), p. 84.

48. Robinson and Norsworthy, "Inside the Real War," p. 5.

49. Miles, "The Real War," p. 33.

50. "A Revolution That is Self-Critical," *Envío*, no. 17 (November 1982):9–13.

51. "Peasant Resettlements: Protection or Pacification?" *Envío* 4, no. 48 (June 1985):1b–11b.

52. CHRICA, "Health Consequences."

53. MINSA, *Sobre los Efectos de la Agresión en el Sector Salud* (Managua: MINSA, 1986) tables 3.1 and 8, mimeo.

54. Richard Garfield, "Revolution and the Nicaraguan Health System," *Medical Anthropology Quarterly* 15, no. 3 (May 1984):69–70.

55. MINSA, *Sobre los Efectos*, p. 5.

56. This incident is described in hideous detail by the perpetrators, in Eich and Rincón, *The Contras*, pp. 63–66.

57. Peter Ford, "Nicaragua: A Siren to Many Foreigners," *The Christian Science Monitor*, June 12, 1986, p. 7.

58. MINSA, *Sobre los Efectos*, pp. 10–12; NICA, "The Baptist Church in Nicaragua," *Nicaragua Update* 7, no. 5 (September/October 1985).

59. Pan American Health Organization (PAHO), *EPI Newsletter* 7, no. 6 (December 1985):7; PAHO, "Status of the Malaria Programs in the Americas," *Epidemiological Bulletin* 7, no. 1 (1986):1–5.

60. Katherine Yih and Alice Slate, "Bilingualism on the Atlantic Coast: Where Did It Come From and Where Is It Going?" *WANI*, no. 2–3 (December-May 1985):23–56; "A New Challenge: A People's Education in the Midst of Poverty," *Envío* 4, no. 48 (June 1985):1c–8c.

61. Central American Historical Institute (CAHI), "Education in Nicargua: More Students, But What Are They Learning?" *UPDATE* 5, no. 21 (May 23, 1986):1–4; Arrien, "La Educación."

62. Arrien, "La Educación," p. 6; CAHI, "Education in Nicaragua," p. 1.

63. Ibid., pp. 5–6.

64. Catherine Gander, "Nicaragua: 'Poor Man's' Adult Education," *NACLA Report on the Americas* 17, no. 5 (September/October 1983):46.

65. Charles Stansifer, "Observations on Salvadoran and Nicaraguan Education," *LASA Forum* 15, no. 1 (spring 1984):29.

66. Edelman, "Lifelines," p. 48.

67. INSSBI, *Organización de la Nueva Seguridad Social Nicaragüense: Problemática de su Crecimiento, Transformación y Financiamiento*, paper presented at the 24th Meeting of the Permanent Interamerican Committee of Social Security, Buenos Aires, November 25–28, 1985 (Managua: INSSBI, 1985), p. 8.

68. Ibid., p. 15.

69. INSSBI, *Logros 85* (Managua: INSSBI, 1986), p. 10.

70. INSSBI defines an orphan as a child who has lost its father or both parents or who has been abandoned. According to INSSBI data, 1,500 of those classified as orphans had lost both parents. See Javier Bertin, "Nicargua Los Desconocidos de la Guerra," *Pensamiento Propio* 3, no. 27 (October 1985):23–26; INSSBI, *The Care of War Orphans* (Managua: INSSBI, 1985), p. 6.

71. INSSBI, *Seis Años de Revolución en el INSSBI* (Managua: INSSBI, 1985), pp. 3, 29.

72. INSSBI, *Organización de la Nueva Seguridad Social*, pp. 27–31.

73. MINVAH, *Los Asentamientos*.

74. "War Forces the Relocation of Civilians," *Nicaraguan Perspectives*, no. 11 (winter 1985-1986), p. 15.

75. "Peasant Resettlements," *Envío*.

76. Larry Rohter, "War Contributes to Exodus to Managua," *New York Times* (February 18, 1985).

77. Cabestrero, *Nicaragua*, pp. 77–80; *Witness for Peace Newsletter*, p. 4; Ford, "Nicaragua," p. 7.

78. The various political party positions on the draft constitution showed a very high degree of agreement on social sector policies ("Towards a New Constitution," *Envío* 4, no. 53 [November 1985], pp. 1b–18b).

79. Alfred Yankauer, "Venceremos," *American Journal of Public Health* 74, no. 10 (October 1984), p. 1084.

FOURTEEN

The Issues of International Law, Morality, and Prudence

SUNG HO KIM

On June 27, 1986, the International Court of Justice (World Court), by twelve votes to three, ruled that the United States was in violation of international law by "training, arming, equipping, financing and supplying the contra [Nicaraguan counterrevolutionary] forces or otherwise encouraging, supporting and aiding military and paramilitary activities in and against Nicaragua" and ordered the United States to cease such activities and to pay Nicaragua for damages caused by them.[1]

In one sense, this was a grave and sad event. Here the world's leading industrial democracy representing the virtue of procedural justice was found guilty of perhaps the most serious offense under the UN Charter and customary international law—aggression and armed intervention—by the most authoritative world institution embodying the ideal of rule of law in international relations. And yet the administration that led this country to a "guilty" path was showing little remorse, turning "its back not only on the International Court of Justice but on 40 years of leadership in the cause of world peace through law."[2]

In another sense, however, the ruling was only an embarrassing procedural mishap for the United States. The World Court, which does not sit above the sovereign states, essentially lacks compulsory jurisdiction unless such is voluntarily accepted by states filing declaration to that effect under the so-called optional clause (Art. 36, par. 2) of the Statute of the World Court. Had the United States not filed such a declaration (which it did in 1946),[3] by simply refusing to be a defendant it would have prevented the World Court from ruling on the Nicaraguan complaint, which in fact was not the kind of case that typically came up before the World Court. Because the Reagan administration took action in October 1985[4] to terminate the 1946 declaration, the United States will avoid the embarrassment of future unconsented World Court litigation. In any event, according to the Reagan administration, the court should not have assumed jurisdiction over essentially "nonjusticiable" issues of security and military matters on which the Nicaraguan case was based.

These narrowly circumscribed views from opposite perspectives offer no satisfactory answer to a broader but urgent question facing U.S. people in the 1980s: Was the Reagan administration following a wise foreign policy in pursuit of the true national interest of the United States in Central America by waging its contra war against the Sandinistas? This chapter addresses this question by focusing on the analysis and clarification of the issues in the making of normative judgments about the foreign policy of the United States. What, in other words, should be the appropriate U.S. foreign policy toward Nicaragua in the balanced considerations of law, morality, and prudence of power? I shall begin my inquiry with the most relevant questions of international law in this instance: What are the contemporary standards of international law with respect to intervention? How is the common practice of intervention to be reconciled with the principle of nonintervention in international law?[5]

The Principle of Nonintervention in International Law

"Intervention," according to Hans Morgenthau, "is as ancient and well-established an instrument of foreign policy as are diplomatic pressure, negotiations and war."[6] Few students of international law would take exception to this statement of obvious political fact. It has been said that the emergence of two superpowers after World War II with conflicting ideologies and national interests, each claiming its own hegemonic zones, has made this world a hotbed of big power practice—intervention. These objective conditions so conducive to interventionary practice, however, have been in marked contrast with the steadily growing number of international agreements or pledges by governments that they would seek friendly relations based on the principle of nonintervention and self-determination of peoples, among others.

Significant for the United States, the principle of nonintervention seemed to have evolved into a contractually binding international obligation within the inter-American system, when, with the ushering in of the "Good Neighbor" policy by the Roosevelt administration, the American Republics signed in 1933 at Montevideo the Convention on Rights and Duties of States, which proclaimed in its Article 8 that "No state has the right to intervene in the internal or external affairs of another."[7] In signing the convention, however, the United States attached a long reservation that in effect would reserve for the United States such rights as are generally recognized by international law.[8]

The lingering doubt about U.S. willingness to commit completely to the principle of nonintervention appears to have diminished when it joined other sister republics at Buenos Aires in 1936 to sign without reservation the Additional Protocol Relative to Non-Intervention, which formulated more elaborately the principle of nonintervention. Article 1 of the protocol provided that "the High Contracting Parties declare inadmissible the intervention of any one of them, directly or indirectly, and for whatever reason, in the internal or external affairs of any other of the Parties."[9]

The same principle has been reiterated in various forms in succeeding inter-American conferences at Lima (1938), Chapultepec (1945), and Mexico City (1945) and has become finally incorporated into the Charter of the Organization of American States, signed at Bogota in 1948. Thus, Article 15 of the OAS charter solemnly declares as one of the "Fundamental Rights and Duties of States" that "No State or group of States has the right to intervene, directly or indirectly, for any reason whatever, in the internal or external affairs of any other State. The foregoing principle prohibits not only armed force but also any other form of interference or attempted threat against the personality of the State or against its political, economic and cultural elements."[10]

The principle of nonintervention has since been widely accepted and proclaimed—as pointed out in the Preamble of the General Assembly Resolution 2131 (XX) of December 1965—by other regional organizations and groups, such as the Pact of the League of Arab States (1945), the Charter of the Organization of African Unity (1963), the Bandung Conference of Asian-African nations (1955), the First and Second Conferences of Heads of State or Government of Non-Aligned Countries at Belgrade (1961) and Cairo (1964), and the declaration on subversion adopted at Accra by the Heads of State and Government of African states (1958).

Almost from the very beginning, the United Nations—which was founded on "the principle of the sovereign equality of all its Members" (Art. 2, para. 1 of the UN Charter), which pledged themselves to "refrain in their international relations from the threat or use of force against the territorial integrity or political independence of any State, or in any other manner inconsistent with the Purposes of the United Nations" (Art. 2, para. 4)—has been active in promoting the principle of nonintervention as a basis of friendly international relations. Since its second session in 1947, the General Assembly has adopted numerous resolutions, recommending that UN members observe the rules of conduct conducive to the maintenance of peaceful international relations including the principle of nonintervention in the internal or external affairs of another state.

The most comprehensive to date of those resolutions dealing more exclusively with the principle of nonintervention is an eight-point declaration adopted on December 21, 1965, under the title, "Declaration on the Inadmissibility of Intervention in the Domestic Affairs of States and the Protection of Their Independence and Sovereignty."[11] It has since become a part of the "Declaration on Principles of International Law concerning Friendly Relations and Co-operation among States in accordance with the Charter of the United Nations," adopted by the General Assembly on

October 24, 1970, in commemoration of the twenty-fifth anniversary of the world organization.[12] In 1981 the United Nations renewed its efforts in this direction by adopting another "Declaration on the Inadmissibility of Intervention and Interference in the Internal Affairs of States."[13] The typical paragraph of nonintervention principle as it has been "solemnly" proclaimed by successive declarations reads: "No State or group of States has the right to intervene, directly or indirectly, for any reason whatever, in the internal or external affairs of any other State. Consequently, armed intervention and all other forms of interference or attempted threats against the personality of the State or against its political, economic and cultural elements, are in violation of international law."[14]

Though not a strict contractual obligation as a treaty is, these declarations, which have been expressly formulated as the "Principles of International Law" and adopted repeatedly by a unanimous or near-unanimous General Assembly, are no longer considered as a mere "recommendation" but are now widely recognized as a binding international obligation either as an authoritative interpretation of the UN Charter or as a new customary international law norm. The typical nonintervention declarations, however, prohibit intervention or interference without defining it, thus leaving open the most fundamental question concerning the concept of intervention and the principle of nonintervention in international law: What are impermissible acts of intervention or interference that are to be distinguished from the normal exercise of power and influence in multiple contexts of interstate relations? Unfortunately, nonintervention is a norm without clear consensus about its definition. Moreover, it is a contextually diverse concept in international law.[15]

The issues of impermissible intervention typically arise in three basic situations or contexts of influence behavior by states. First, an assistance to the incumbent government may become an issue of intervention if that government is itself a party to internal strife in the target country, particularly when such an assistance involves tactical deployment of military personnel of the sending state. Intervention on the side of a patron government obviously constitutes an infringement of the process of self-determination of that country; it may also disturb the public order of the world community when such an intervention provokes suspicion and hostile reaction by other powers that might then threaten to counterintervene on the other side of the internal strife of the target state. Despite these problems, the structural biases of the Westphalian political order in favor of the incumbent government would make it well-nigh impossible to delegitimize "patronage" intervention by a patron state on behalf of a client government.

In the second context of influence behavior of a state, any action or deliberate inaction aimed at inducing the incumbent government in a target state to do (or not to do) something that that government would otherwise not do (or do) may give rise to issues of intervention. Here impermissibility of intervention is dependent on the degree of coerciveness in the means of influence behavior and with the degree of authority-orientation in the ends sought (the extent to which influence is aimed at the authority structures in the target state).

The traditional controversy over the definition of intervention as a "dictatorial interference" given by L. Oppenheim[16] essentially amounts to an effort to determine, by way of definition, the nonintervention threshold of influence behavior in this context of direct intergovernmental interaction. What separates intervention from normal practice of statecraft is the elemental test of dictation or coercion. The earlier view of equating coercion with actual use or threat of force is now generally rejected by most contemporary writers as too narrow a definition of intervention. The growing frequency with which public international documents nowadays refer freely to, among others, economic forms of coercion also indicates that the idea of coercion or dictation is no longer confined to the use or threat of physical force. Thus, the 1970 Declaration on Principles of International Law concerning Friendly Relations and Co-operation among States proscribes "the use of economic, political or any other type of measures to coerce another State."

Finally, in the third situation, any action aimed at assisting anti-incumbent elements in a target state would provoke issues of intervention. Here the nonintervention threshold is obviously very low, and such an action may give rise to issues not only of subversive intervention but also of indirect aggression, which has come to be considered as serious as direct aggression.

Armed intervention involving military force, used directly against the target state or indirectly through armed proxies or mercenaries, is the most coercive form of intervention and, in the absence of comparable prior wrongs by the target state to warrant plea of self-defense, would constitute one of the most serious offenses under international law: direct or indirect aggression. When armed intervention is aimed not merely at policy changes by the target state but at the fundamental change in its authority structure, it is obviously the most serious form of aggression. Such was precisely the charge brought by Nicaragua against the United States before the UN Security Council and the World Court in spring 1984[17] and, in further efforts to influence the world public opinion, before the Permanent Peoples' Tribunal in October 1984.[18]

U.S. Intervention in Nicaragua: Self-Defense or Aggression?

In terms of history, the geopolitical context of intervention, and the scope of military operations, there was little parallel between Vietnam and Nicaragua. In other ways, however, Vietnam held some valuable lessons in international law for the United States in Central America.

A striking aspect of the war in Vietnam, as in Nicaragua, was that in large part the controversy surrounding the U.S. role in that war was debated in the language of international law. Both the specialists in the field of international law and the public at large asked the same question: Was the United States justified in the military intervention in Vietnam, first against the Communist insurgency in South Vietnam and then against the North Vietnamese forces.

The legal position of the U.S. government was that it was "assisting" the South Vietnamese government "at its request" in the exercise of the right of "collective self-defense" against indirect and direct aggression by the North Vietnam.[19] The framing of the legal claims in justification of the U.S. intervention in this manner was dictated by the existence of perhaps the most fundamental prohibitive rule under the UN Charter that the United States and most other sovereign states of the world had pledged to uphold as a binding legal obligation. That prohibitive rule, often considered to have gained the solemn status of *jus cogens*—a norm so peremptory as to void all other conflicting treaties or customary norms—is declared in Article 2, paragraph 4, of the UN Charter: "All Members shall refrain in their international relations from the threat or use of force against the territorial integrity or political independence of any state, or in any other manner inconsistent with the Purposes of the United Nations." An important exception to this rule, however, is provided in Article 51, which recognizes "the inherent right of individual or collective self-defense if an armed attack occurs."

The precise meaning of this exception to the rule of nonuse of force in international relations has been extensively debated in the various forums and learned circles, particularly with respect to the meaning of "if" and "armed attack" in the qualifying statement "if an armed attack occurs." One view, most closely identified with Ian Brownlie,[20] would have the Charter restrict the inherent right of self-defense only to the situation of a prior armed attack, thus interpreting "if" as a conditional, in the sense of "only if." The opposite view, as articulated by Sir Humphrey Waldock,[21] claims that the inherent right of self-defense is indeed inherent and broader, and "if" in this case is hypothetical, in the sense of "if, for example." Obviously, however, a broader interpretation opens up the possibility of an abusive one, for instance, of "anticipatory self-defense" with implications that could negate the whole purpose of Article 2, paragraph 4 of the Charter.[22]

As to the meaning of the "use of force" prohibited by the Charter and of the prior armed attack that would then justify the use of force in self-defense, the United States government took the lead in advocating that it meant both direct use of force in the conventional sense and indirect one using subversive elements or proxies. In fact, World Court Judge Stephen M. Schwebel of the United States, who sat in judgment on the Nicaraguan charge of indirect U.S. aggression, had argued, when he was U.S. Representative to the UN Special Committee on the Definition of Aggression, that "the Charter of the United Nations makes no distinction between direct and indirect uses of force" and that the "most pervasive forms of modern aggression tend to be indirect ones."[23] By an ironic twist of fate the United States was now accused of indirect aggression, which it had earlier claimed to be as serious a crime as direct aggression.

The publicists of international law, by virtue of special training and professional commitment, are supposed to have a unique role in articulating what international law is at any given time.[24] In making intellectual judgments about the alleged facts against legal claims by governments, however, they depend heavily on the expert knowledge of the political history of the case. As with the scholars of Southeast Asia in the era of Vietnam War, the Latin Americanists little over a decade later were expected to make their major contribution to the clarification of the facts alleged by the contending parties to the conflict. In the absence of a supreme court of the world, the final judgment would be made by the world public opinion and, in the United States, by U.S. public opinion. The efficacy of U.S. interventionist policy in Nicaragua was bound to be affected by these "legal" judgments.

The two most important considerations in making such a judgment are the nature and extent of the prior wrongs alleged to have been committed by Nicaragua and the proportionality of the U.S. responses to them. If the prior wrong by Nicaragua had constituted an armed attack against El Salvador, the latter would have been entitled to invoke the right of "individual and collective self-defense" and to request armed assistance from the United States.

In the light of a number of the UN General Assembly's law-making resolutions and other public documents, armed attack would include both direct and indirect ones. Thus, in the 1974 "definition of aggression" resolution of the General Assembly,[25] an act of aggression was defined as:

(a) The invasion or attack by the armed forces of a State of the territory of another State . . . ;
(b) Bombardment . . . or the use of any weapons by a State against the territory of another State;
(c) The blockade of the ports or coasts of a State by the armed forces of another State; . . .
(f) The action of a State in allowing its territory, which it has placed at the disposal of another State, or be used by that other State for perpetrating an act of aggression against a third States;
(g) The sending by or on behalf of a State of armed bands, groups, irregulars or mercenaries, which carry out acts of armed forces against another State of such gravity as to amount to the acts listed above, or its substantial involvement therein.

It is significant to note that although the resolution recognized an indirect form of aggression, it also required the test of gravity in such an act amounting to the direct conventional forms of aggression or "substantial involvement therein" before it could be considered an aggression. The question, therefore, is whether the alleged Nicaraguan involvement with the El Salvadoran guerrillas was indeed so grave as to be an equivalent of the conventional form of attack. If the answer is yes, the second requirement would concern the appropriateness or proportionality of the U.S. responses to the alleged Nicaraguan involvement in the Salvadoran guerrillas. To justify its action on the grounds of self-defense, the United States would have had to confine its actions only to the extent of defeating the alleged Nicaraguan aggression.

In the famous statement about the need for proportionality, U.S. Secretary of State Daniel Webster wrote, in 1842 to the British government following the *Caroline* incident of 1837, that for a claim of self-defence to be legally justifiable the British government had to show the existence of "necessity of self-defence, instant, overwhelming, leaving no choice of means, and no moment for deliberation" and "the act justified by the necessity of self-defence, must be limited by that necessity, and kept clearly within it."[26] This standard is obviously too strict, but it communicates an idea and concern that the failure to restrict the reason for self-defense and the justifiable response would result in giving governments a "legal excuse for escalating a conflict"[27] to the detriment of world order.

What, then, were the prior wrongs allegedly committed by Nicaragua? Despite some questions about accuracy and credibility of the State Department's white paper, "Communist Interference in El Salvador," issued on February 23, 1981,[28] it does appear that the Sandinista government had in some way been involved in the arms supply to the leftist guerrillas in El Salvador even after its revolutionary victory in July 1979. The precise extent of the Sandinista government's involvement in the alleged arms traffic, however, is not clear.

Why the Sandinistas felt obliged to help the Salvadoran guerrillas is obvious: They were revolutionary comrades in arms from years past. But once established as legitimate, the Sandinista government came under the same obligation as other states to observe international law, particularly with respect to the principle of nonintervention. Whether by design or mistake, the Sandinista government thus made itself vulnerable to the charge of prior wrongs justifying appropriate responses by the injured parties. Whatever the extent of the Nicaraguan intervention in El Salvador, the initial response by the United States appears to have been appropriate as long as it was intended for and limited to the actual "interdiction of arms" allegedly flowing from Nicaragua. Why, then, was it necessary for the United States to authorize covert activity by the CIA? If it was a justifiable counterintervention in collective self-defense, why did the United States feel it necessary to do it under the cover of secrecy? Was it because of the concern for effectiveness of the planned operation, especially when the alleged external Communist involvement with the Salvadoran guerrillas was itself clandestine?

This would have been a critical factual issue on which to base a judgment about whether the United States could be considered as exercising the right of individual and collective self-defense, say, during the early months of 1981. The widely reported suspension of the $75 million aid agreement approved by the Carter administration and economic pressures put on national and international lending agencies to deny credit to Nicaragua in the early months of the Reagan administration might therefore be regarded as a justifiable economic intervention in retaliation against the Nicaraguan connection with the Salvadoran guerrillas.

The subsequent developments, however, dwarf in significance the initial question of defensible action by the United States. Accounts widely reported in the U.S. media, research findings by U.S. scholars, reports by the interested public groups, and congressional debates on contra aid all point to an inescapable conclusion that, as the original Nicaraguan arms connection with El Salvador appeared to have ceased, the United States increased its anti-Sandinista campaign. Not only had the CIA-supported contra forces continued to increase; it also became obvious to everyone that their activities were directed not at supposed arms interdiction but at selected governmental, economic infrastructural, and civilian targets within Nicaragua in concerted efforts to destabilize the country. The Reagan administration obviously had a different goal. Thus, according to David MacMichael, a high-ranking CIA analyst on Central America until 1983, "the U.S. systematically misrepresented Nicaraguan involvement in the supply of arms to Salvadoran guerrillas to justify its efforts to overthrow the Nicaraguan government."[29]

Even if we assume as correct all the allegations ever made against Nicaragua by the United States government, they could not possibly justify the extent of subsequent U.S. intervention as an act of justifiable defensive counterintervention or collective self-defense. On the contrary, Nicaragua was threatened with subversive intervention by the United States and was theoretically entitled to invoke the right of individual and collective self-defense. The Soviet and Cuban military assistance to Nicaragua, which the United States viewed as a threat to this hemisphere, could then be justified as a defensive reaction, as long as it was proportional to the U.S. threat against Nicaragua. Nicaragua, Cuba, and the Soviet Union would not dare to invoke openly such a right not because they had no legal right to do so but because of the fundamental political fact that the United States was a widely acknowledged hegemonic actor in the region.[30]

What the preceding analyses suggest is that the plea of self-defense by the United States would have been so farfetched that any attempt to rely on it to justify the U.S. action in the Central America would have invited only a sense of disbelief, if not an open ridicule, by world opinion. It was obvious to many that the United States was intervening in the internal affairs of another country with absolutely no legal excuse: request by the incumbent government, invitation by an established insurgency holding territory and operating as a de facto government, authorization by a competent global or regional organization, evidence of gross human rights violation by the target state, or danger to the lives and property of U.S. nationals abroad. By withdrawing from the World Court proceedings, the United States was in effect admitting that it had no legal case. Blatant untruth in wanton disregard of the facts would have discredited the United States even more. Besides, it was apparently not a great concern of the Reagan administration to comply with the principle of nonintervention in international law. The rhetoric of the Reagan administration characteristically placed more emphasis on moral claims that it was fighting against evil forces of totalitarian communism. How sound, then, were such moral claims?

Morality and Covert War
in Central America

Claiming to be responding to the demands from the younger generation that he clarify his "views on the relationship of moral considerations to American foreign policy" expressed in his famous first book, *American Diplomacy 1900–1950* (1951),[31] George F. Kennan wrote again on the problem of morality and foreign policy in 1985–1986.[32] He argued that government, being an "agent, not a principal," owed its primary obligation to "the *interests* of the national society it represents, not to the moral impulses that individual elements of that society may experience." "The interests of the national society" defined basically as "its military security, the integrity of its political life and the well-being of its people," according to Kennan, "have no moral quality" and "arise from the very existence of the national state in question and from the status of national sovereignty it enjoys."[33]

The fundamental problem of political realism in foreign policy, however, is that it goes against what seems to be a deeply ingrained need of most people to justify their conduct in moral terms that are often self-serving. Only the Rawlsian "veil of ignorance" might put people in the "original position" from which to make correct moral judgment.[34] Most people in real life, however, make their judgments from "interested" positions and are probably not even aware that they are often ideological reflections of such positions.

It is not surprising, therefore, that political idealism, defined in terms of a proposition that foreign policy goals and means must be morally justifiable, is in a state of fundamental conceptual confusion for failing to distinguish between moralizing as value preferences that give meaning to life among the like-minded people and moralizing as an exercise in judgment about "good" relations between the peoples with divergent and conflicting value preferences. One is morality of solidarity (ideology); the other, morality of coexistence (international morality).

A good example of moralizing for solidarity in the era of the Reagan administration can be seen in the typical rhetorical style of its one-time ambassador to the United Nations, Jeane J. Kirkpatrick. In her well-known article, "Dictatorships and Double Standards," Kirkpatrick defends U.S. support of "traditional autocracies" against a greater evil of "revolutionary autocracy." The evidence that traditional autocracies are still preferable to a revolutionary autocracy is that "[s]uch societies create no refugees" whereas "revolutionary Communist regimes" do so by claiming "jurisdiction over the whole life of the society and make demands for change that so violate internalized values and habits that inhabitants flee by the tens of thousands in the remarkable expectation that their attitudes, values, and goals will 'fit' better in a foreign country than in their native land."[35] In a world like this, the United States is a shining example of virtue, which owes no apology to anyone in the world. Thus, in the concluding words of Kirkpatrick, a posture of continuous self-abasement and apology vis-a-vis the Third World is neither morally necessary nor politically appropriate. No more is it necessary or appropriate to support vocal enemies of the United States because they invoke the rhetoric of popular liberation. It is not even necessary or appropriate for our leaders to forswear unilaterally the use of military force to counter military force. Liberal idealism need not be identical with masochism, and need not be incompatible with the defense of freedom and the national interest.[36]

This is a masterful demonstration of skill in moralizing for solidarity, the function of which is not necessarily to enlighten the public on complex issues of foreign policy but to rally patriotic emotion in an exclusionist frame of reference. This is what a country needs when it is at war with an enemy so vile and fierce that coexistence would be impossible, unthinkable, or patently immoral. For crusading anti-Communists, "revolutionary Communist totalitarianism" is a vile force, analogous to the Nazi menace faced by the Western democracies during World War II. What divided U.S. opinion since the end of World War II was this kind of moral judgment about the nature of Marxist-Leninist states as well as the prudential judgment about what to do with them. The sharp differences of opinion with respect to these questions separate not only the idealist but also the realist camp.

To the Left in the idealist camp are the advocates of human rights and distributive justice who find affinity with what Charles Krauthammer calls a "minimalist form of realism"[37] represented today by George F. Kennan. The left-wing political realists and idealists prescribe for the United States the policies of détente, nonintervention, and multilateral diplomacy. To the Right in the idealist camp are the crusaders of liberty and anticommunism with whom the Reagan administration has been closely identified, who find themselves in company with the militant realists[38] in relying on U.S. military strength and a policy of unilateral intervention.

If the issues of priority between morality and power separate idealists from realists, the judgments about the nature of the threat to the United States and what to do about it separate the Right from the Left. The fact that the division between Right and Left replaced that of idealism and realism as a dominant characteristic of U.S. foreign policy debate came to reflect the centrality of the question: What is the nature of the revolutionary struggles in certain parts of the Third World and the role of the Soviet Union in them?

On this question, the Right tends to see the Soviet Union as the principal antagonist, using Cuba as its major proxy in the business of exporting Communist revolution. Now, Nicaragua is added to the list to make up the Soviet-Cuba-Nicaragua axis as a fundamental threat to the United States. Poverty, social injustice, and autocratic regimes are not the principal causes of revolutionary violence in the Third World; the Marxists-Leninists from Moscow-Havana-Managua are. The Left, however, views social injustice as a major reason for revolutionary turmoil and the Soviet Union only as an opportunistic agent. If the Right is sustained by a patriotic sentiment, the

Left relies on the empathy many Americans have for the impoverished and suffering people at home and abroad—the sentiment that can be described as the noblesse oblige of the U.S. middle class. It may also be a compassionate sentiment in the finest tradition of Judeo-Christianity that urges the brotherhood of all mankind. The U.S. Left today clearly is not a politically dogmatic Left; nor is it a moralistic one. It seems to flow from the simple kindness of heart. In eloquent words reflecting such a sentiment on the war in Vietnam, John G. Stoessinger writes:

> Johnson used the strategy of the strong against the weak with Ho Chi Minh. He believed that he could bend the enemy to his will so that the North Vietnamese could avoid pain, death, and material destruction. It was a plausible strategy for someone who was rich, loved life, and feared pain. But Johnson confronted the strategy of the weak. The weak defied the American president by their readiness to struggle, suffer, and die on a scale that seemed beyond the bounds of reason. . . . Such defiance forced Lyndon Johnson to confront the necessity of carrying out the threat of ultimate escalation: to bomb North Vietnam into the stone age. In short, to commit genocide. At that point, Johnson hesitated, remembering Hitler and Hiroshima. And ultimately, the only answer was withdrawal.[39]

The lessons of Vietnam seem clear. Neither the powerful nor the weak can afford to ignore moral constraints on foreign policy in a hegemonic war. The use of treacherous means by the weak will deprive them of their only strength: the ability to suffer and endure pain, death, and destruction that might arouse moral sensibilities in the hearts of the powerful but reasonable adversary. Treachery by the powerful, on the other hand, deprives them of the only enduring basis of political control: the willing compliance by the weak.

The effective limits to U.S. foreign policy in Vietnam were thus set by both the moral character of American people, who finally said no to what their government was capable of doing with its enormous fire power, and the moral fervor of the Viet Cong and the North Vietnamese in what they believed to be the courageous act of national self-assertion in a defensive war. The rhetoric of anticommunism, the moralism of democracy, and the legal claims of collective security and defensive counterintervention against Communist aggression from the North became increasingly hollow to many Americans as they witnessed the horrors of war in the mass media and different accounts of U.S. intervention presented by learned people whose loyalty to the United States could not be questioned.[40]

The only choice that remained for the U.S. government was massive disinformation, censorship of news, wholesale arrest of antiwar demonstrators, or even a government-sponsored "accuracy in media and academia" campaign—in short, the suspension of democratic rules. The American people would have been willing to live by a lesser democracy had they really believed that the country was in clear and present danger. But the specter of totalitarian slavery looming over San Francisco Bay by the domino effect if the United States let Vietnam fall to Communist aggression was not taken seriously. In the end, to many Americans the Saigon government was nothing more than corrupt dictators interested only in maintaining their privileged status in that impoverished country while masquerading as freedom fighters against totalitarian Communists. Similarly, to many Americans, the Reagan administration's objection to the Sandinista government as an evil totalitarian was not very convincing when compared to the brutal dictatorship of Anastasio Somoza, which the popular revolution overthrew in 1979.

Beyond the simple morality of compassionate Americans, additional moral constraints have been imposed on U.S. foreign policy, and they are "founded on traditional American principles of justice and propriety."[41] These are unilateral, self-imposed constraints in affirmation of the moral character of the United States as a society. Americans cannot suspend them without losing their soul except in a national emergency. Hegemonic intervention by a great power that typically takes place within its sphere of influence cannot, by the very nature of it, be considered such an emergency. Even when the major adversary power is directly involved in the situation, U.S. moral principles cannot be suspended. To the contrary, U.S. moral principles should be able to rally Americans behind the foreign policy needed to deal with such an emergency. The plea that such principles must be suspended to deal with an emergency is either a betrayal of the American soul or an admission that it really is not an emergency. What are these moral principles?

Kennan wrote that "secret operations—a branch of governmental activity closely connected with, but not to be confused with, secret intelligence" are out of character with U.S. morals. Approving U.S. covert action to apprehend the kidnappers of the *Achille Lauro* as one of the "rare moments when a secret operation appears indispensable," however, he warned against such an action becoming "regular and routine feature of the governmental process, cast in the concrete of unquestioned habit and institutionalized bureaucracy."[42]

Because the free press and open media are so fundamentally American, the sort of institutionalized disinformation so characteristic of a more closed society such as the Soviet Union proves to be dysfunctional in the United States. The credibility gap, as evidenced during the Vietnam War era, is a very serious moral and political issue of the social contract between the people and government in the United States. Covert operations, in short, cannot remain covert very long, and a storm of controversy is likely to arise if Americans find out that their government has engaged in or supported objectionable covert activities. They will ask, Does our destabilization campaign to overthrow another government include plans to assassinate its leaders and terrorize innocent civilians? The answer to such a question reported in the U.S. press balanced against the perception of national emergency has a way of swinging crucial congressional votes.

These, then, are the most important moral constraints on U.S. foreign policy, which many foreign observers have come to admire in American people. The policy outcome in the case of Nicaragua would therefore be a function of executive initiatives taken by the Reagan administration and the judgment made by the American people through its congressional and functional representatives with respect to the appropriate means of achieving foreign policy goals based on the kinds of perceived threat the Sandinista government posed to the United States.

What about moral constraints that come from an entirely different frame of reference, one based on moral judgments about what the people of one country may owe to those of another by virtue of the fact that they are all human beings? If we define international morality thus in "other-regarding" terms,[43] it seems clear that the principal moral claim made by the Reagan administration for its intervention in Nicaragua was the avowed goal of establishing a pluralistic democracy in that country.

Assuming that the United States was morally obligated to ensure pluralistic democracy in Nicaragua and that it was the best political system for a highly stratified Third World country where the privileged few were in control of the political and economic resources of the country, the hollowness of the U.S. claim became apparent when the records of the Sandinista government were juxtaposed with those of the U.S.-supported Somoza government it replaced or other Central American countries supported by the United States. In fact, it was rather remarkable that, even under the state of siege produced by the subversive intervention of its neighboring superpower, Nicaragua could remain as free and democratic—certainly by the Third World standards—as it was reported to be by various objective and prestigious international observer groups.[44]

What the Reagan administration was objecting to in Nicaragua, then, was not its alleged dictatorial nature. Its objection was to a Marxist-Leninist government, especially when it came into existence within the traditional sphere of influence of the United States. The Sandinista government's promise of mixed economy, political and civil liberties for the Nicaraguans, and noninterventionist and nonaligned foreign policy[45] was not sufficient for the Reagan administration, which took an "essentialist" view that the threat to the United States came from the Marxist-Leninist nature of the Nicaraguan government.

This essentialist view as it was applied to Nicaragua raised some troublesome questions for the American people. If the Reagan administration was indeed correct in saying that the Sandinista government was a threat to the region and U.S. security, it could not be saying that with all the military, political, and economic resources of a superpower it was vulnerable to attack from Nicaragua. What it was saying was that the region was vulnerable to a revolutionary change inspired by the Sandinista victory in Nicaragua. The Nicaraguan government did not even have to be involved in the would-be revolutions in Central America. Its mere existence in the region as a successful revolution against oppression and social injustice might be enough to inspire other revolutions in Central America.

It thus seems that the most probable goal of the Reagan administration in its campaign against the Sandinista government was, failing its overthrow, to discredit the regime or turn it into an unbearable burden to the Nicaraguan people through the sustained economic and political strangulation of the country. In that way no one would look to Nicaragua as a model for future. On the other hand, it appears that the Sandinista government was determined to prove the Reagan administration wrong by adhering—within the limit of national emergency created by the U.S.-backed contra war—to a nonaligned foreign policy and mixed economy with guarantees of basic political and civil liberties for people and all political groups in Nicaragua.

In this curious battle between the Reagan administration committed to making the Sandinista revolution "go sour" and the latter refusing to turn ugly, one would have to stretch the imagination to say that morality was on the side of the U.S. policy. But, is this not a sentimentalist moral judgment? Is there not a higher morality of public order?

U.S. Hegemonic Interest and "Prudent" Foreign Policy Toward Nicaragua

One does not have to be a right-wing political realist or crusading neo-internationalist to recognize that the United States as a superpower is bound to claim for itself special privileges of power beyond the minimum sovereign right of territorial integrity and political independence. But no rational power, however indifferent to the legal, moral, or other such normative constraints, can afford to behave in a reckless and imprudent way that is harmful to its own interest. Without prudence, power has no meaning. So the final question before us is, Was the Reagan administration's Nicaraguan policy a prudent policy?

In the often-quoted classic statement about political prudence, Machiavelli declared that "it is much safer to be feared than loved, if one of the two has to be wanting,"[46] because "men love at their own free will, but fear at the will of the prince, and that a wise prince must rely on what is in his power and not on what is in the power of others, and he must only contrive to avoid incurring hatred."[47] What has not been quoted so often is his reminder that "one ought to be *both* feared and loved" (emphasis added),[48] for power that relies on fear alone is not likely to last very long. This is particularly true with the imperial or hegemonic power, for the subjugated people are in a potential state of rebellion unless they benefit from the security or glory of the empire.

The ancient Han Chinese were frequently conquered by the barbarians who, however, became "sinonized" by a "superior" Han culture, which ultimately ruled. The British Empire ruled so successfully not only by means of a powerful navy, balance of power, and the divide and rule principle but also by virtue of its civility, rule of law, and competent civil service, which won for several centuries admiration and willing compliance by many of its colonial peoples. What really sustained Rudyard Kipling's "White Man's Burden" were both the bayonets and Shakespearean sonnets.

Even in the good old days of imperial rule, the successful empires did not rule by fear alone. The whirlwind of change has since come to the peripheral world that would have made it difficult even for the most virtuous empire to rule. That change was brought on by the passions and legitimizing forces of nationalism or ethnicism. This is particularly true in that part of the Third World that had been subject to colonial or hegemonic control by outside power in the past and where brutal traditional autocracies were believed to be the link between the hegemonic state and dependent state. The major blind spot in U.S. foreign policy, especially during the Reagan administration, appeared to be the failure to recognize this basic fact.

Marxist-Leninist revolutionaries are not always the prime cause of the Third World disturbance; nationalism or communalism is. In fact, the success or failure of the Third World capitalist elites or Communist counterelites has depended significantly on their opportunistic and historical connection with the forces of nationalism. In Vietnam the strength of communism, especially under the leadership of Ho Chi Minh, was in its identity with Vietnamese nationalism. In South Korea the weakness of Communist appeal was the result in no small degree of the liberating role of the capitalist United States in its independence from Imperial Japan. The Soviet difficulty in Afghanistan reveals the strength of Afghan religion, tribalism, and incipient nationalism. Both traditional elites and Marxist counterelites are now held hostage to the forces of nationalism or other bonds of group identity such as ethnicism, tribalism, or sectarianism, whichever happens to be in command of the passions and aspirations of people in the country.

In Central America, the United States bears a special burden of having been the chief imperialist in the region during most of the twentieth century. Although rejecting traditional empires and fancying itself to be a sister republic to the South, the United States has often—though not always—practiced what might be called absentee imperialism in Central America. Thus, to the people of Central America the United States is both hypocritical in masking its hegemonic ambition with the Monroe Doctrine and callous in denying responsibility for cruelty perpetrated by its surrogate autocrats.

In an era of mass communication with rising levels of nationalistic consciousness and shrinking emotional distance between peoples in Latin America, nothing is more likely to arouse anti-U.S. sentiment than the direct U.S. armed intervention in Central America. Without willing compliance by people in client states, the political and economic cost of maintaining hegemonic order is likely to outweigh its benefit. One essential requirement of prudent U.S. foreign policy is the intellectual understanding of the point at which the benefit of hegemony decreases as its cost increases.

Conclusions

No doubt a direct U.S. military intervention could in a matter of weeks drive the Sandinista government out of Managua, but then the new contra government would have to deal with hundreds of thousands of Sandinista guerrillas. The Sandinistas in power might be constrained by international law and the political reality of U.S. hegemonic interest in Central America, but what would constrain the Sandinistas in the mountains and urban hideouts? Would not such an intervention likely produce greater fermentation of anti-U.S. revolutionary passions in the region? On the other hand, would not the successful Sandinista revolution, if left alone to mature and prosper, become a catalyzing role model for others in the region?

Faced with this dilemma, the Reagan administration apparently pursued its policy of a protracted war of harassment and economic strangulation of Nicaragua. It was a no-win but a low-cost policy for the United States. Nicaragua was not a Vietnam. It is a tiny country of a little over 3 million people at the doorstep of the United States. What it took in terms of dollars needed to sustain the contra war was a pittance to the supereconomy of the United States. Because Nicaragua was located in a well-acknowledged sphere of influence of the United States, its rival hegemonic power, the Soviet Union, was unlikely to provoke a major interhegemonic crisis by openly challenging U.S. hegemony there by counterintervention involving the actual deployment of the Soviet or Cuban troops.

The survival of the Sandinista government, thus, did not seem to depend on the U.S. fear of a major international crisis. It depended primarily on the Sandinista government's and Nicaraguan people's determination to resist U.S. intervention and their ability to suffer and endure pain while avoiding postures that might alienate liberal opinions in the United States. If the Sandinista government should succumb to desperation and abandon its policies of moderation, it would prove the Reagan administration's point that traditional autocracy is a lesser evil than totalitarian communism. On the other hand, if through nonalignment, independent development, and political and economic democracy the Sandinista government should survive, it would become history's first Third World nation to have successfully put an end to its traditional autocracy without the resultant revolutionary excesses or totalitarianization of a society—a rather fascinating alternative to a rule by right-wing "death squad" or left-wing "terror." The presence of a revolutionary but nonaligned government in Central America could in fact be a blessing in disguise to the region and to the long-range hegemonic interest of the United States if it should serve as a warning to its neighboring governments, forcing them to reform and thus preempting runaway revolutions.

In conclusion, an appropriate U.S. foreign policy would have to reject the doctrinal inflexibility with self-serving moralism typical of the Reagan administration. It would have to combine healthy skepticism of conservative United States and prudent political realism with liberal visions of ideological polyphony of the Third World. Such a policy in Central America would have required nonintervention in the internal affairs of Nicaragua in expectation that Managua would continue to recognize the external political reality that the United States as a hegemonic power in the region reserved the political right of hegemonic intervention only to prevent opportunistic enhancement of the rival hegemonic powers. For such a policy, there was no need for covert (as distinct from legitimate secret intelligence) activities. A creative and flexible U.S. foreign policy that can ensure a better life for a majority of people living under U.S. hegemony is the only true and winning competition against totalitarian communism in the Third World!

Notes

1. *New York Times,* June 28, 1986, pp. 1 and 4. The three dissenting World Court judges were from the United States, Great Britain, and Japan.

2. Thomas M. Franck, "Icy Day at the ICJ" [an editorial comment on U.S. withdrawal on January 18, 1985, from ICJ proceedings], *American Journal of International Law* 79 (1985):379.

3. 61 Stat. 1218; Dept. of State *Bulletin* 15 (1946):452.

4. *New York Times,* October 7 and 8, 1985.

5. Particularly noteworthy among the recent comprehensive studies on the principle of nonintervention is R. J. Vincent, *Nonintervention and International Order* (Princeton, N.J.: Princeton University Press, 1974).

6. Hans J. Morgenthau, "To Intervene or Not to Intervene," *Foreign Affairs* 45 (1967):425.

7. *Treaties, Conventions, International Acts, Protocols and Agreements Between the United States of America and Other Powers, 1923–1937,* Senate Document No. 134, 75th Congress, 3rd Session, compiled by Edward J. Trenwith (Washington, D.C.: Government Printing Office, 1938), p. 4809; see also Marjorie M. Whiteman, *Digest of International Law,* vol. 5 (Washington, D.C.: Government Printing Office, 1965), p. 421.

8. Trenwith, *Treaties, Conventions,* p. 4810.

9. Ibid., p. 4822; see also Ann Van Wynen Thomas and A. J. Thomas, Jr., *Non-Intervention: The Law and Its Import in the Americas* (Dallas, Texas: Southern Methodist University Press, 1956), pp. 62–63.

10. United States, *Treaties and Other International Acts Series* 2361 (April 30, 1948): see Whiteman, *Digest of International Law,* vol. 5, p. 423.

11. UN General Assembly Resolution 2131 (XX); *Yearbook of the United Nations, 1965* (New York: UN Office of Public Information, 1967), pp. 94–95.

12. UN General Assembly Resolution 2625 (XXV); *Yearbook of the United Nations, 1970* (1972), pp. 788–792.

13. UN General Assembly Resolution 36/103, December 9, 1981; *Yearbook of the United Nations, 1981* (1985), pp. 147–149.

14. UN General Assembly Resolution 2625 (XXV); see note 12.

15. For a penetrating legal analysis of intervention in its diverse contexts, see John Norton Moore, "The Control of Foreign Intervention in Internal Conflict," *Virginia Journal of International Law* 9 (1969):205–342.

16. L. Oppenheim, *International Law—A Treatise,* vol. 1, 8th ed., H. Lauterpacht, ed. (London: Longmans, Green and Co., 1955), p. 305.

17. Nicaragua's appeal to the World Court came five days after the U.S. veto of a UN Security Council draft resolution that would have "condemn[ed] and call[ed] for an immediate end to a mining of the main ports of Nicaragua." See U.N. Doc. S/16463 (April 4, 1984), reprinted in *International Legal Materials* 23 (1984):669.

18. See Marlene Dixon, ed., *On Trial: Reagan's War Against Nicaragua* (San Francisco: Synthesis Publications, 1985).

19. See, especially, Lawyers Committee on American Policy towards Vietnam, *Vietnam and International Law: An Analysis of the Legality of the U.S. Military Involvement* (Flanders, N.J.: O'Hare Books, 1967).

20. Ian Brownlie, *International Law and the Use of Force by States* (Oxford: Clarendon Press, 1963), pp. 275–280.

21. See his analysis in J. L. Brierly, *The Law of Nations*, 6th ed., Sir Humphrey Waldock, ed. (New York: Oxford University Press, 1963), pp. 413–432.

22. For a penetrating analysis of this point, see Louis Henkin, *How Nations Behave: Law and Foreign Policy* (New York: Praeger, 1968), pp. 231–236.

23. Stephen M. Schwebel, "Aggression, Intervention and Self-Defence in Modern International Law," *Recueil des Cours* 136 (1972):458, quoted in Abram Chayes, "Nicaragua, the United States, and the World," *Columbia Law Review* 85 (1985), f.n. 101, p. 1466.

24. See, for example, Kevin W. Quigley, "A Framework for Evaluating the Legality of the United States Intervention in Nicaragua," *New York University Journal of International Law and Politics* 17 (1984):155–185.

25. Gen. Ass. Res. 3314 (XXIX), 29 UN GAOR Supp. (No. 31) at 142, UN Doc. A/9630 (1974).

26. As quoted in Brownlie, *International Law*, p. 43.

27. Quigley, "A Framework for Evaluating," p. 176.

28. The text of the white paper in *New York Times*, February 24, 1981, p. 8.

29. *New York Times*, June 11, 1984, as quoted in Dixon, *On Trial*, p. 131.

30. For analysis of the concept of sphere of influence and its foreign policy implications for the United States in Latin America, see Edy Kaufman, *The Superpowers and their Spheres of Influence* (New York: St. Martin's Press, 1976); Harold Molineu, *U.S. Policy Toward Latin America: From Regionalism to Globalism* (Boulder: Westview Press, 1986).

31. George F. Kennan, *American Diplomacy 1900–1950* (Chicago: University of Chicago Press, 1951).

32. George F. Kennan, "Morality and Foreign Policy," *Foreign Affairs* 64 (1985/86):205–218.

33. Ibid., p. 206.

34. John Rawls, *A Theory of Justice* (Cambridge: Harvard University Press, 1971).

35. Jeane J. Kirkpatrick, "Dictatorships and Double Standards," *Commentary*, November 1979, p. 44. Noam Chomsky takes issue with Kirkpatrick's contention about refugees; see his *Turning the Tide: U.S. Intervention in Central America and the Struggle for Peace* (Boston: South End Press, 1985), p. 8.

36. Kirkpatrick, "Dictatorships and Double Standards," p. 45.

37. Charles Krauthammer, "The Poverty of Realism," *The New Republic*, February 17, 1986, p. 22.

38. A new magazine about U.S. foreign policy published by Irving Kristol, *The National Interest*, reflects this school of thought.

39. John G. Stoessinger, *Crusaders and Pragmatists: Movers of Modern American Foreign Policy* (New York: W. W. Norton, 1979), p. 200.

40. See, for example, George McTurnan Kahin and John W. Lewis, *The United States in Vietnam* (New York: Dial Press, 1967); Marcus G. Raskin and Bernard B. Fall, eds., *The Viet-Nam Reader* (New York: Random House, 1965).

41. Kennan, "Morality and Foreign Policy," p. 208.

42. Ibid., p. 214.

43. See Stanley Hoffmann, *Duties Beyond Borders: On the Limits and Possibilities of Ethical International Politics* (Syracuse, N.Y.: Syracuse University Press, 1981), p. 190.

44. See Introduction to this book.

45. As exemplified by its acceptance of the Contadora peace initiatives and the 1986 draft constitution of the country with an impressive list of basic rights of individuals that "cannot be suspended" by the president even under the state of emergency (see Article 184 of "First Draft of the National Constitution of the Republic of Nicaragua," document prepared for National [U.S.] Conference on the Nicaraguan Constitutional Process held in New York, April 1986, mimeo.).

46. Niccolo Machiavelli, *The Prince and the Discourses* (New York: Modern Library, 1940), p. 61.

47. Ibid., p. 63.

48. Ibid., p. 61.

FIFTEEN

U.S. Polity and Society: The Lessons of Nicaragua

NOAM CHOMSKY

In a front-page story of March 9, 1986, the *Miami Herald* outlined Reagan's request to Congress for aid to the contra armies, quoting its crucial paragraph authorizing the CIA and any other "department or agency in the executive branch" to take over the war effort. "Officials said that if Congress rejects the package, then Reagan may feel free to use other measures to contain Nicaragua." An accompanying story reported that 60 percent of the U.S. population opposed aid to the contras, whereas 49 percent agreed that the situation in Nicaragua poses a significant threat to national security. When the request was approved by the House, a government official commented: "This is for real. This is a real war," confirming the judgment of Nicaraguan President Daniel Ortega that the House action "amounted to a declaration of war."[1]

The *Herald* story was unremarkable; one could cite dozens of similar examples. It happened to be particularly jarring to me personally because the *Herald* was the first newspaper I saw on returning to the United States from a week in Managua, where I had been lecturing at the Jesuit university and had observed firsthand the tiny and impoverished country that the United States must "contain," struggling to survive under the military, economic, and propaganda war organized by the hemispheric superpower.

The contents of the *Herald* story, though unremarkable, are informative with regard to U.S. society and culture. They may serve to open the question of what we may learn about ourselves from this latest episode in a history forecast by Simon Bolívar in 1829 when he remarked that the United States seems "destined to plague and torment the continent in the name of freedom." Several phrases merit comment: the references to (1) administration plans, (2) the role of public opinion, and (3) the need to contain Nicaragua.

Administration Plans and the Rule of Law

It is, in the first place, quite accurate for officials to warn that a lawless administration will simply find other ways to pursue its goals if Congress were to bar direct takeover of the war.[2] One did not have to await the World Court decision to hear that U.S. operations against Nicaragua are in "violation of international law and the Neutrality Act of 1794."[3] Nevertheless, the easy acceptance of lawless behavior is instructive. As Jack Spence comments in Chapter 10, "the obviously relevant pending World Court decision" was ignored in prior commentary. The decision itself was generally dismissed by elite opinion as a minor embarrassment. Its contents were suppressed or falsified, the World Court—not the United States—became the criminal, and the rule of law was held inapplicable to the United States.

The World Court determined that U.S. actions constituted "an unlawful use of force" and violations of treaties. It ruled that "these violations cannot be justified either by collective self-defence [the U.S. claim] . . . nor by any right of the United States to take counter-measures involving the use of force in the event of intervention by Nicaragua in El Salvador, since no such right exists under the applicable international law." The court found no credible evidence of Nicaraguan support for guerrillas in El Salvador since early 1981, noting further that Nicaragua could not be charged with a higher responsibility to halt arms flow than El Salvador, Honduras, and the United States, all of which claimed to be unable to do so despite the "extensive resources deployed by the United States." The court also observed that El Salvador had not charged "armed attack" until August 1984, four months after Nicaragua had brought its claim to the court.[4]

In its editorial response to the World Court's decision, the *New York Times* downgraded its significance: "The 'laws' the Court seeks to articulate are more accurately values, rooted in traditions that America should honor even in a hostile forum," the editors stated, while denouncing "the Court's tendentiousness." "But," they added, "even the majority acknowledged that prior attacks against El Salvador from Nicaragua made 'collective defense' a possible justification for America's retaliation."[5] The editors voiced no criticism when this same "hostile forum" ruled in favor of the United States in May 1980 in the matter of the Iran hostage crisis, nor have they been reluctant to denounce official enemies for their violation of the rule of law. Furthermore, contrary to what they assert, the court explicitly rejected the claim of "collective self-defense" as a justification, even if the United States could establish its factual allegations.

Contra lobbyist Robert Leiken "blamed the court, which he said suffers from the 'increasing perception' of having close ties to the Soviet Union."[6] But even rational commentary held that the United States should not be bound by the World Court's decisions. Thus Thomas Franck of New York University Law School argued that the United States should not accept World Court jurisdiction because "America—acting alone or with its allies—still needs the freedom to protect freedom" (as in Nicaragua).[7] If other powers have a comparable right to use violence to protect what they will call "freedom," then the framework of global order constructed after World War II reduces to empty pieties. Note further that the author, quite typically, does not consider it necessary to establish that the U.S. goal is to "protect freedom." This is a higher truth, standing alongside Reagan's "priority of installing democracy in Managua," "Uncle Sam's controversial effort to force the Sandinistas not to export their revolution,"[8] and other proclamations of the state propaganda system echoed as a matter of course in news and opinion columns in disregard of the facts—a pattern all too familiar among powerful states, past and present.

On the "conservative" side of the political spectrum, Irving Kristol explains that "the argument from international law lacks all credibility" because the Soviet Union had already "breached this rule" of nonintervention by "supplying armaments, technicians, 'specialists' in both the military and civilian spheres," thus justifying the use of force by the United States in counterintervention. The same argument was given by UN Ambassador Vernon Walters, who denounced "the arms shipped to Nicaragua, openly and brazenly," in the debate leading to the U.S. veto of a Security Council resolution calling on all states to observe international law.[9] By the same logic, the USSR has every right to attack Denmark and surely Turkey— countries that pose a vastly greater threat to the USSR than Nicaragua does to the United States, countries in which, furthermore, the United States has "intervened" in the Kristol-Walter sense and would "intervene" on a still more massive level if they were under military attack by a Soviet proxy army.

It also follows that the USSR has the right to counterintervene in El Salvador in response to U.S. intervention in support of the "war of extermination and genocide against a defenseless civilian population"[10] waged by its client state. The U.S.-backed assault was described in these words in October 1980 by Bishop Rivera y Damas, the successor of the martyred Archbishop Romero; a few weeks later José Napoleón Duarte hailed the killers and torturers for "valiant service alongside the people against subversion"[11] as he was sworn in as president of the Junta to ensure the flow of arms for the necessary chores after the murder of four American churchwomen, the role he has played throughout, to mounting applause in the United States as the terror began to achieve its aims. And surely Nicaragua had a right to counterintervene in September 1980, when it began to send a trickle of arms to the victims, according to U.S. government documents. Needless to say, these logical consequences are not drawn.

In short, the United States is exempt from the rule of law, to which, however, it may grandly appeal in condemning others for violation of their solemn commitments. Thus no bill of indictment of the Sandinistas is complete without a denunciation of their alleged violation of their "commitment to the Organization of American States to political pluralism, human rights, free elections, non-alignment, and a mixed economy," Ronald Reagan's words to Congress in justification of aid to the contras. A formal finding by the Congress denounced the Nicaraguan government for having "flagrantly violated" this "commitment," adding that "the United States, given its role in the installation of the current Government of Nicaragua, has a special responsibility regarding the implementation of the commitments made by that Government in 1979."[12] The denunciation is standard in the media. Putting aside the accuracy of the charges, no such "commitment" exists, as the World Court observed (par. 261), noting also that the Organization of American States had resolved that the solution of the problems of Nicaragua is a matter "exclusively" for the Nicaraguan people. But Nicaragua is nevertheless bound by this nonexistent obligation, and it is the U.S. duty to determine whether it has been upheld and to enforce it. The United States, in contrast, is not bound by the UN Charter—the foundation of current international law and part of "the supreme law of the land"—or other elements of international law, or by its 1956 Treaty with Nicaragua, also violated by the United States according to the World Court with only U.S. Justice Stephen Schwebel dissenting.[13]

U.S. client states inherit this exemption from legal obligations. Thus while the charge concerning Nicaragua is a fabrication, a similar charge does hold with regard to the State of Israel, which was admitted to the United Nations on the express condition that it would observe UN resolutions on return or compensation of refugees. The rule of law is a subtle instrument, as interpreted in a lawless and violent state.

The World Court decision and the reaction to it carry other lessons. Crucially, this U.S. rejection of the rule of law is nothing new. The United States destroyed the Central American Court of Justice, established at U.S. initiative, when it ruled against the United States in regard to its interventions in Nicaragua in 1912 and 1916. The only novelty in the present case is that the United States does not have the power to dismantle the World Court.

There is also a certain significance to the World Court's condemnation of the United States for the attack by contra forces against San Juan del Norte on April 9, 1984. In 1854, the U.S. Navy burned down this port town to avenge alleged insults to U.S. officials and Cornelius Vanderbilt. These facts, and much else, are relevant to the reaction here to the current criminal attack against Nicaragua. It will not do merely to refer occasionally to "the United States' past inglorious role" in Central America[14] while proclaiming its firm commitment to democracy, human rights, and other good things. There is, after all, a history that serves to test these commitments. Ideologues understandably prefer to forget the history or to pretend that the United States is now embarking on a new path of righteousness, a stance that we would not tolerate on the part of official enemies. U.S. institutions have not changed, and there is little recognition of the sources of U.S. conduct in the Central America–Caribbean region or elsewhere, or even of its nature. Consequently, there is no reason to suppose that current policies deviate from historical practice, and they do not, either in their character or the display of noble intent in which they are clothed. From all this we learn something more about ourselves, or would, if we chose to learn.

The dismissal of the historical record reaches quite startling proportions. In a cover story in the *New York Times Magazine* by its Central America correspondent James LeMoyne, he observes that "virtually every study of the region . . . has concluded that the revolutions of Central America primarily have been caused by decades of poverty, bloody repression and frustrated efforts at bringing about political reform."[15] Furthermore, every serious study has concluded that the United States bears a certain responsibility for these conditions, hence for the rise of "the guerrilla network," but no hint of that will be discovered in this article. LeMoyne discusses the role of Cuba, the Soviet Union, North Korea, the PLO, Vietnam, and others, but one participant in the drama is missing, except for the statement that in El Salvador, "the United States bolstered the Salvadoran Army, insisted on elections and called for some reforms." Also missing is the fact that the army that the United States "bolstered" conducted a program of mass slaughter and torture to destroy "the people's organizations fighting to defend their most fundamental human rights," just as Archbishop Romero predicted they would do shortly before his assassination while vainly pleading with President Carter not to "bolster" these forces that "know only how to repress the people and defend the interests of the Salvadorean oligarchy." This combination of convenient historical ignorance and praise for the benevolence of our intentions is typical of media and other commentary.[16] Few seem able to appreciate the significance of the observation by former Costa Rican President Daniel Oduber that the "thugs" who threaten "the lives of Central Americans and their families . . . are not the Leninist commissars but the armed sergeants trained in the United States."[17]

Public Opinion and Democracy

Let us turn now to the second point raised in connection with the *Miami Herald* story: the plan to pursue the illegal activities outlined in defiance of the will of the public. The public is similarly opposed to the other major programs of the Reagan administration,[18] a fact that underscores some lessons about the U.S. form of democracy: In a system of elite decision and occasional public ratification, it matters little what a passive and unorganized public may prefer.

We learn more about our culture and society from the report in the *Herald* article that half the U.S. population regard Nicaragua as a threat to our national security. Though Reagan has been singularly unsuccessful in convincing the public to support his policies, the form of reactionary jingoism (mislabeled "conservatism") that he represents has been highly successful in setting the general mood and the terms of debate. Again, this is nothing new. Wars and periods of domestic turmoil in the United States have regularly given rise to propaganda campaigns, conducted by business and educated elites, to overcome the incipient efforts of segments of the normally irrelevant population to become involved in shaping public policy. This was true of both world wars, and the Vietnam War too evoked impressive efforts to overcome "the crisis of democracy" perceived by elite groups.[19]

The war against Nicaragua illustrates a typical feature of U.S. democracy. Public opinion is irrelevant as long as the public is inert. To ensure this result, it is necessary to conduct what is called the "engineering of consent," an inspired Orwellism that has been a staple of democratic theorists and the public relations industry for many years, referring to the need to control what people think in a society in which obedience cannot be guaranteed by force. This task falls to the media. In Chapter 10 of this book, Jack Spence reviews how news coverage reflected the "patriotic agenda"; the same is true of the range of opinion permitted expression. The standard procedure is to present official positions without comment, accepting all pretensions about democracy, human rights, and so on, and then to adopt these doctrines as the framework for reporting and analysis. The occasional subsequent exposure of some of the more flagrant falsehoods in the small print is largely irrelevant once the appropriate mood has been established. The U.S. government learned this lesson in the course of its World War I propaganda exercises, when its Committee on Public Information discovered "that one of the best means of controlling news was flooding news channels with 'facts,' or what amounted to official information."[20] This technique has been applied since with great success, with the cooperation of the media and educated opinion, teaching those who choose to know something significant about the workings of American democracy.

More important than the deceit is the willingness of educated elites and the media to permit the centers of state and private power to set the terms of discussion. During the Indochina War, for example, one could debate whether the Vietnamese were guilty of aggression in Vietnam but not whether the United States was guilty of aggression in its attack against South Vietnam—an event that did not occur in official history, though it did occur in the real world, as surely as the USSR attacked Afghanistan. Similarly, we may debate whether Nicaragua sent arms to people attempting to defend themselves against the U.S.-organized slaughter in El Salvador, but any further question is off the agenda—for example, the thought that this might be a humanitarian obligation, comparable to the United States' providing arms to victims of some Soviet-organized campaign of torture and massacre. The legitimacy of U.S. operations in El Salvador is also off the agenda; they are efforts to achieve reforms and mitigate atrocities, whatever the facts. From such examples we learn another important lesson about the functioning of democracy when the ideological institutions—the media, the schools and the universities—reflect a narrow consensus of elite groups that control the state and private economy.

What appears to be outright deceit often reflects a much deeper subordination to prevailing doctrine. A case in point is the reference to "democracy" in Central America. Thus we read, in a typical news account, that Congress is considering aid for the "Nicaraguan rebels" and the "four Central American democracies."[21] Plainly, not even the minimal conditions for democracy exist in El Salvador and Guatemala, with the political opposition silenced or slaughtered and the popular organizations decimated by the U.S.-backed security forces. In Honduras, much of the population is starving while the country is under military rule behind a thin civilian facade. Even in Costa Rica, the only one of the four countries where the term "democracy" can be pronounced without a shudder, the conditions for meaningful democracy barely exist, with the media almost entirely in the hands of ultra-Right representatives of the business community and the economy kept afloat by U.S. aid conditional on Costa Rican support for U.S. crusades in the region.

But to accuse the press of deceit for such reference to the "democracies" would be to miss the point. In U.S. political theology, the term "democracy" has a technical meaning: It refers to a system of governance in which elite groups that dominate the private economy are ensured control, with the public permitted to ratify elite decisions periodically. If the public becomes organized to enter the political arena and participate in shaping affairs of state, that is not "democracy," but rather a "crisis of democracy," which must be overcome, whether by death squads as in Central America or by more subtle means at home. Thus the "four democracies" are indeed "democracies" in the Orwellian terms of U.S. usage, whereas Nicaragua is definitely not one, since business- and landowner-based groups were not represented much beyond their numerical proportion in the preelection system of governance, as Thomas Walker observes, and in the 1984 elections privileged elites linked to U.S. state and business interests were not guaranteed the required advantages: control over the media and the political system in addition to the power that flows from control over investment decisions— all of this a severe affront to "democracy." The United States traditionally favors free elections when conditions guarantee that power will remain in the hands of the privileged minorities it favors, a fact removed from the public eye though familiar to serious scholars. Gordon Connell-Smith observes that "while paying lip-service to the encouragement of representative democracy in Latin America, the United States has a strong interest in just the reverse," apart from "procedural democracy, especially the holding of elections—which only too often have proved farcical." The reason is that the United States "has been concerned with fostering the most favorable conditions for her overseas investment," whereas meaningful democracy might direct state policy to popular domestic concerns.[22]

The media, then, are simply observing more general doctrinal conventions when they report on the "fledgling democracies" of Central America[23] and Reagan's hopes to induce Nicaragua to join the "democratic wave," and they cannot be accused of deceit in any narrow sense of the term.

The most effective editorializing is carried out within the news columns, where the principles of state propaganda are simply presupposed. Turning to the opinion pages, we also observe the practice of "engineering of consent." Take one crucial example: the debate over Nicaragua in the opinion pages of the national media in the first three months of 1986, when attention was focused on the impending congressional votes on contra aid.

During this period, the *New York Times* and *Washington Post* ran eighty-five pieces by columnists and invited contributors. Opinions on the Sandinistas ran from harshly critical (virtually all) to critical but more conditionally so; thus 100 percent uniformity was maintained on the central issue. Alleged apologists for the Sandinistas were bitterly denounced (anonymously, to ensure no possibility of response), but none was allowed a voice. It is particularly impressive that the two most striking features of the Sandinista regime were almost entirely ignored amid a chorus of abuse: the constructive social programs and the fact that in sharp contrast to U.S. clients such as Duarte in El Salvador, the government has not engaged in large-scale torture and slaughter. The latter point is nowhere mentioned, reflecting a general tendency to dismiss atrocities in our domains as defects of little significance. As for the first point, apart from an oblique reference by Abraham Brumberg,[24] there is only one phrase referring to the Sandinista programs in health, literacy, land reform, and development—by Tad Szulc (*NYT*, March 16), in the course of a denunciation of the "generally appalling leadership" in this "repressive society" and "its failures." These programs are crucial to understanding the U.S. attack against Nicaragua, a matter to which we return; correspondingly, no mention of the basic reasons for the U.S. war was permitted in these opinion columns.[25]

Exactly the same is true of editorial opinion. In eighty *New York Times* editorials on Nicaragua from 1980 through mid-1986, I found two phrases on these crucial features of the Sandinista government.[26]

There was debate in the eighty-five opinion columns: over the proper way for the United States to respond to Sandinista abuses and crimes. In contrast, one will find no debate over whether we should establish a terrorist army to attack El Salvador, where the crimes are vastly worse. This sharply limited debate helps maintain the impression that we live in an "open society," but as in the case of Indochina and many other issues, it is important to ensure that the debate proceeds within the framework established by the centers of power so that its presuppositions are established as the bounds of thinkable thought.

As in the case of Indochina, this travesty is accompanied by the pretense that a great debate is raging, the Reaganites versus the Sandinistas' "major diplomatic and public relations campaign aimed at convincing domestic and international opinion that they are 'David' fighting the U.S. 'Goliath'" (in the words of Robert Leiken). Thus Leiken writes that "the marvels of the 'new' Nicaragua are proclaimed far and wide by its numerous international supporters as the solution to the oppression and underdevelopment that have beset Central America and as a model, not just for Central America, but for Latin America and the entire third world"; "the American public is caught in a bitter propaganda war over Nicaragua," between the Reaganites and the Sandinistas' "well-organized network of 'opposition' figures, 'witnesses,' 'correspondents,' and professional writers of letters to editors."[27] The fact that this "propaganda war" proceeds in the national media at the ratio just illustrated is insufficient for those who see anything less than total conformity as a dangerous impropriety.

The news columns explain that the spectrum of responsible opinion extends from Mark Falcoff of the American Enterprise Institute to contra supporter Robert Leiken. Falcoff tells us that "the Democrats on the Hill keep pretending that this Government in Managua is a Social Democratic humanist regime bumbling its way toward democracy" (for a discussion of the real situation, see William LeoGrande's Chapter 11). And Leiken comments that "both sides are basically hysterical," refusing to "cope with reality," the nonhysterical reality being that Nicaragua is caught in a "contest between Moscow and Washington" with the superpowers represented locally by the "Soviet-backed expansionist Sandinista regime" for which popular support has "virtually vanished" and the peasant-based "resistance," which expresses "the antihegemonist sentiments of the Nicaraguan people" and must undertake a "protracted struggle" of "armed resistance to the Sandinistas," leading the defense of Latin America against "Soviet hegemonism."[28] Beyond the respectable Falcoff-Leiken spectrum, the *New York Times* informs us, the "issue's subtleties" are "buried in epithets," were "mudslinging," entirely unserious.

Containing Nicaragua

Let us turn to the third point raised at the outset in connection with the *Miami Herald* news report. Perhaps its most striking words are the bland reference to the perceived need for "measures to contain Nicaragua," no doubt a vital necessity in the face of the "unusual and extraordinary threat" it poses "to the national security and foreign policy of the United States"— Ronald Reagan's words as he declared a "national emergency to deal with that threat" on May 1, 1985 (Presidential statement, *NYT*, May 2, 1985). That the United States must "contain Nicaragua" is not a topic of debate— though one may ask whether "debate" would be the proper reaction in circles that retain a measure of sanity. Rather, it "is now a given; it is true," on a par with the fact that "the Sandinistas are communists of the Cuban or Soviet school"; that "the Reagan administration is right to take Nicaragua as a serious menace—to civil peace and democracy in Nicaragua and to the stability and security of the region"; that we must "contain . . . the Sandinistas' aggressive thrust" and demand "credible evidence of reduced Sandinista support for El Salvador's guerrillas"; that we must "fit Nicaragua back into a Central American mode" and turn "Nicaragua back [sic] toward democracy," and, with the "Latin democracies," "demand reasonable conduct by a regional standard."[29] The source of these certainties is near the dovish end of the spectrum of expressible opinion, critical of the contras as "an imperfect instrument" to achieve our goals. These goals are laudable, by definition. That too "is a given; it is true," hence a matter that passes beyond the limits of discussion.

What is the nature of the "Central American mode" and "regional standard" to which we would like to fit Nicaragua back as we turn it back toward democracy? To anyone familiar with the Central American mode that the United States has instituted and maintained and the regional standard it has set as it installed and backed some of the most violent terrorist states of the modern era after a long history of support for brutality and corruption, these words can only elicit amazement. We see again the utility of historical amnesia and of the tunnel vision that enables us to put aside unacceptable facts about the contemporary period.

Presumably the Central American mode includes Guatemala, where a brief experiment with capitalist democracy was aborted by U.S. intervention in 1954 establishing a terror-and-torture state kept that way with regular U.S. intervention under Kennedy and Johnson and receiving U.S. military aid through the Carter years. President Reagan explained that the worst of the monsters we supported was the victim of a "bum rap" and "totally dedicated to democracy." The country now enjoys "democracy" after the population has been thoroughly traumatized, with death squad killings on the increase and the newly elected president acknowledging frankly that he can do nothing given that the roots of actual power are in the military and the oligarchy and that the civilian government is merely "the managers of bankruptcy and misery."[30]

The Central American mode must also include El Salvador, where Church-based human rights groups recorded over 37,000 killings by death squads and security forces through 1984 (the actual numbers are unknown) and where we may rejoice that political killings by the security forces have been reduced to over four a day now that the government death squads have "decapitated the trade unions and mass organisations," a conservative British correspondent observes, so that "numbers are down and the bodies are dropped discreetly at night into the middle of Lake Ilopango and only rarely wash up on to the shore to remind bathers that the repression is still going on."[31] There massive state terror organized by the United States and presided over by José Napoleón Duarte has largely achieved its intended goals of ensuring that "popular organizations" will not raise the threat of meaningful democracy.

The *Washington Post* editors are quite right to say that the United States wants to "fit Nicaragua back" into the Central American mode, though not quite in the sense they intend their readers to understand.

The regional standards advocated by the United States are illustrated in the 1985 Human Rights Report of the Council on Hemispheric Affairs, which designates Guatemala and El Salvador as the hemisphere's worst human rights offenders, the "only two governments in the hemisphere that abducted, killed, and tortured political opponents on a systematic and widespread basis," the sixth successive year that they achieved this honor.[32] The only other candidate in Central America was "the C.I.A.'s proxy army" of "hit-and-run terrorists."[33] It will not escape notice that these three "prime human rights violators" are close U.S. allies and clients and that our Honduran client would join the collection if human rights were extended to include the right to work, to food, to health services, and so on, as in international conventions. Could there be a lesson here about the United

States? The answer within the ideological institutions is no, since the United States stands for all good things, whatever the facts may be.

No less interesting is the *Post*'s demand for "credible evidence of reduced Sandinista support for El Salvador's guerrillas"—the necessary way to fix the burden of proof, given the inability of the U.S. government to provide credible evidence of its claims regarding such support. As noted, the World Court dismissed the publicly available evidence as of little merit, adding that even if the claims were valid they would be irrelevant to the criminal nature of the U.S. attack. A look at U.S. government documents explains their rather disdainful reaction. Consider the most recent, the September 1985 Department of State Special Report on Nicaragua.[34] This report informs us that seaborne operations in the Gulf of Fonseca have been, and still are, "the primary method of infiltration" of arms from Nicaragua. The Gulf of Fonseca is approximately 30 kilometers wide. At the World Court, former CIA analyst David MacMichael testified that the U.S. Marine Corps maintains a radar facility on Tiger Island in the Gulf of Fonseca with equipment "designed to survey air and water traffic in the Gulf and surrounding areas—coastal areas," in addition to constant operation of U.S. naval vessels and U.S. Navy SEAL teams on surveillance missions. The surveillance system, he testified, was able to locate and track boats moving through the area and for "a very long distance" beyond, "up and down the Pacific Coast of Central America." Despite these extensive means, no interceptions were made in this tiny area—showing, perhaps, that the United States is a "pitiful, helpless giant," as Richard Nixon lamented, quite unable to deal with an enemy of the amazing prowess and sophistication of Nicaragua.[35]

New York Times military specialist Drew Middleton quotes with apparent seriousness a U.S. general who said that "'a militarized Nicaragua is far more dangerous' to United States interests in the region than the fighting in El Salvador." The danger is that Nicaragua will "overawe" Costa Rica while "preparing to give powerful, direct support to rebels in El Salvador and, eventually, to attack Honduras" ("which is currently benefiting [*sic*] from the presence of United States Army and Air Force units") with Cuban air support—while the United States stands helplessly by. The Nicaraguan army is "prepared for offense," and according to intelligence sources, "the absorption of advanced equipment by the army has gone remarkably well, as well or better than the program with the Syrian army"[36]—a statement that can only elicit amusement on the part of anyone familiar with military realities in the two regions.

Congressional critics of Reagan's plans "say they would settle for containing the Sandinistas" and "curbing Nicaraguan help for Latin American insurgencies." True, "the Sandinistas are nasty guys," but they "can be better contained" by nonmilitary means, the *Washington Post* editors explain. "Mr. Reagan should have held to these undeniable transgressions" of the "Sandinista junta"—such as its having "meddled in its neighbors' affairs" (something we would never do) and "complicated the region's security problems" (something we cannot do by definition)—"and then devoted himself to the truly hard questions: How can the Sandinistas best be contained and what can the United States do to promote democracy in Nicaragua?" in accordance with our historical dedication to this enterprise.[37]

Across the spectrum of articulate opinion, it is agreed that we must "contain Nicaragua." "Nicaragua is a cancer, and we must cut it out," Secretary of State George Shultz thunders to "sustained applause" at Kansas State University. "Negotiations are a euphemism for capitulation if the shadow of power is not cast across the bargaining table," Shultz adds; accordingly, the purpose of our aid, Assistant Secretary of State Elliott Abrams explains, "is to permit people who are fighting on our side to use more violence." Richard Lugar, chairman of the Senate Foreign Relations Committee, "has warned Nicaragua that unless it changes its ways the United States may consider using force against it." "We all lament the absence of freedom and pluralism" in Poland, he explains, but Nicaragua "is located in the Western Hemisphere," where, we are to understand, the United States has always fostered "freedom and pluralism."[38] The doves counter that the use of force may cause us serious problems, so that alternatives should be considered first.

These words evoke some historical memories. A high-ranking Western observer in Managua warned that on its present course, the United States "will be seen more and more as a kind of deviant democracy, with a kind of crypto-fascist foreign policy."[39] I am just old enough to recall Hitler's ravings about "containing Poland," protecting Germany from the "terror" of the Czechs and the "aggressiveness" of the Poles, and excising "the cancer" of the Jews. Current Washington rhetoric again teaches us something about ourselves, if we care to learn.

The same is true with regard to the almost fanatical lying, on such a scale that even the *New York Times* offered a gentle admonition in reaction to Reagan's March 16, 1986, address calling on Congress to support his attack against Nicaragua, which achieved new levels of deceit.[40]

Although the media are full of contempt for "the Sandinistas' paralyzing paranoia" and "Managua's adolescently anti-American rantings,"[41] an objective look will show that the shoe is on the other foot. We do not have to go very far from the hysterical U.S. cultural scene to read that the United States is following a policy of "madness" in Nicaragua, supporting a "band of cutthroats" who are "spurred on by their bizarre cowboy leader, the President of the United States"—this, from Canada's leading newspaper, the *Globe & Mail* (Toronto), which is conservative and generally pro-United States. The director of the Royal Institute of International Affairs in London, David Watt, describes "the chasm that lies between current American perceptions of the world and the world's perception of America," observing that "with the possible exceptions of the Israelis, the South Africans, President Marcos of the Philippines and a few right-wing governments in Central and South America," most of the world is highly critical of the Reagan administration's policies and its "debasing the language of international intercourse with feverish rhetoric."[42]

Libertarian Standards or Service to State Power?

The charges against Nicaragua also teach us some lessons about ourselves. There no doubt are reasonable standards by which the crimes alleged, which are sometimes real, merit condemnation. A rational person will, of course, ask whether the critics apply the same standards to themselves and to U.S. client states; if not, the charges have exactly the merit of denunciations—often accurate—of the atrocities of official enemies by Communist front organizations. Let us ask what we learn about our society and culture by applying this rational criterion.

Few actions of the Sandinistas evoked more outrage than the State of Siege announced on October 15, 1985. "There is no reason to swallow President Ortega's claim that the crackdown is the fault of 'the brutal aggression by North America and its internal allies,'" the *New York Times* assured us, adding that this new demonstration of Nicaragua's lack of "respect for democracy and human rights . . . will further damage [the] mediation" by the Contadora countries—which the United States was seeking to undermine (see Chapter 8 by William Goodfellow). Robert Leiken tells us that "the wave of Sandinista repression in October of 1985" justifies our support for the contras.[43] The outrage was widely echoed. We therefore ask whether the same standards are applied elsewhere—in neighboring El Salvador, for example, where two days later the government renewed the State of Siege that had been in force since March 1980 when Duarte joined the Junta, at a time when "the masses were with the guerrillas," as he was later to concede.[44]

The Salvadoran State of Siege suspended constitutional guarantees including "*inter alia* freedom of movement and residence, freedom of thought and expression, inviolability of correspondence and the right of assembly," also the right to be brought to a court within seventy-two hours, freedom of press and phone calls, and so on.[45] It has been renewed monthly since, in particular, on October 17, 1985. El Salvador is not under attack by the proxy army of a superpower operating from foreign bases. The alleged "symmetry" between El Salvador and Nicaragua is transparent nonsense,[46] except in one respect: In each country much of the population is subject to the ravages of a terrorist army serving its U.S. masters and their clients. The October 1985 renewal of the Salvadoran State of Siege, which had laid the basis for gruesome atrocities since 1980, passed without mention in the press, which was enraptured over U.S. success in bringing "democracy" to El Salvador. There was no editorial in the *New York Times*, nor has there ever been a word on this topic. On the contrary, the story in the *Times* in 1980-1981 was that "a weak centrist regime is beset by implacable extremes"; "the right-wing 'death squads' . . . have contributed as much as leftists to the murder of 10,000 people" in 1980, and Duarte, for all his devotion to human rights, is unable to curb them. Later, the *Times* conceded that it knew all along that neither extragovernmental right-wing death squads nor, certainly, leftists, were responsible for the slaughter: "Under the Carter Administration, United States officials said security forces were responsible for 90 percent of the atrocities," not "'uncontrollable' right-wing bands."[47]

As the military prospects for the U.S.-backed regime in El Salvador dimmed and there were fears of direct and costly U.S. intervention, we find occasional reference to the "brutality" and even "barbarity" of the government security forces and "the inability of weak civilian governments to curb these crimes" (*NYT*, November 18, 1983). As "the honorable Mr. Duarte," the "honest, reform-minded Christian Democrat," took office with U.S. aid and the military campaign gained effectiveness with the direct participation of the U.S. Air Force in coordinating bombing strikes against fleeing peasants and defenseless villagers,[48] the tone became more upbeat, though it was conceded that Duarte has been "less than rigorous in bringing death squad operatives to judicial account" (meaning, he has done little to curb the security forces he praises for their services). Nevertheless, we must give aid to this "centrist committed to human rights, reform and reconciliation," to the "reformist democrats led by Mr. Duarte," even though "at earlier stages, the left and right have combined to reduce Mr. Duarte to passivity."[49]

Throughout, the story has been the inability of the reformist government to control its own army, including the elite battalions fresh from their U.S. training that were responsible for the most horrendous atrocities. From March through December 1980, the escalating slaughter merited four *New York Times* editorials: March 17, praising the reformist "center"; April 28, on the "weak centrist regime . . . beset by implacable extremes"; November 29, on the massacre of the leaders of the political opposition, which raises "a severe challenge to [the] credibility" of the government; and December 24, on the new hopes now that Duarte had become president of the Junta—hailing the security forces for their "valiant service alongside the people against subversion," as the editors failed to observe. The press has largely suppressed the fact that Duarte has denied atrocities or denounced the victims as "Communists" (e.g., the victims of the May 1980 Sumpul River massacre—a story suppressed in the U.S. media) and refuses to accept reports by the Church human rights offices because the church workers are under the direction of "subversives." The truth of the matter, carefully concealed in the fables about the beleaguered "centrist government," is that "Duarte's cultivated pose of long-suffering sincerity has done little for the tens of thousands killed under the governments he has headed. . . . His greatest efforts have been directed toward winning hundreds of millions of U.S. aid dollars from a docile Congress, rather than toward ending the reign of terror by the very security forces who receive the increasingly easily-won U.S. assistance."[50]

Even the murder of the archbishop in March 1980 merited no editorial reaction in the *New York Times*, only a comment under "Topics"—without a word of condemnation of the Salvadoran government, then or ever, for its complicity, at the very least in blocking inquiry, for example, by a raid on the legal aid office of the archbishopric that destroyed evidence implicating the security forces in the assassination.[51] The destruction of the university by the army in June 1980, with many killed and large-scale destruction, merited not a word, while the general slaughter elicited evasions and falsehoods about the distribution of responsibility. In subsequent years, we read constantly of the hopes that the reformist center will be able to control the security forces for which it was lobbying in Congress but nothing remotely comparable to the denunciations of the Sandinistas, who cannot be charged with any crime that comes even close to the atrocities for which Duarte and other Salvadoran and U.S. leaders bear direct responsibility under the unmentionable State of Siege. In this regard, the *New York Times* was quite typical of the media and of educated opinion generally.

These facts reveal with some precision just how seriously we are to take the pretended horror over the declaration of a State of Siege in Nicaragua, which, as observed by Abraham Brumberg, was "by no means as onerous in practice as [its provisions] were on paper,"[52] surely incomparably less onerous in practice than the State of Siege in El Salvador since 1980.

To the time of writing, the same standards prevail. Few here seem concerned that in El Salvador "government agents routinely torture prisoners in their custody, conduct 'disappearances,' and commit political killings in attempts to eliminate opposition to the government," that "Salvadorans who allegedly violate human rights remain virtually immune from investigation and prosecution," and that "most victims are non-combatant civilians, including women and children," the primary targets being "refugee workers, trade unionists, and university staff and students" subjected to "arrest, torture, and killing."[53] Now that Duarte's U.S.-backed terror has "decapitated" and demolished labor and the popular organizations that might have laid the basis for meaningful democracy, the editors of the *New Republic* inform us that "the real model for supporting the push toward democracy in our sphere" is El Salvador, exulting in the success of their advice to Reagan to continue with the assault "regardless of how many are murdered," since "there are higher American priorities than Salvadoran human rights."[54] There is no reaction to the renewed attack by the Duarte government and the U.S. Embassy against the churches and human rights groups, with death threats, beatings, torture, expulsion of religious activists, the discovery of the mutilated corpse of a young man after he had appealed to the Red Cross to prevent the army from again displacing returnees from their homes by "burning of our houses, our crops, our lands." Meanwhile, a U.S. "police training program . . . included three of the most notorious death squad members in San Salvador" who will "have their techniques upgraded" here.[55]

Readers of the foreign press will learn some of the details, for example, the fate of Laura Pinto of the Mothers of the Disappeared, who had undertaken a European tour after being barred from the United States and was again imprisoned and tortured to force her to issue accusations against human rights activists. In Europe, the mothers had described brutal torture, murder, and disappearance, while Duarte in his familiar fashion dismissed them as "Marxists" and the U.S. government and media protected the population from their disclosures.[56]

The lack of concern here is typical of the response to atrocities on "our side," particularly if they are working, and may be compared to the casual dismissal of the extensive and careful—but totally irrelevant—documentation of contra atrocities. Two human rights investigators report that a high State Department official described official policy as one of "intentional ignorance."[57] The same is true of the U.S. press and cultivated opinion generally, with regard to El Salvador as well, except that in this case the "intentional ignorance" is combined with vast enthusiasm for the progress of "democracy." Again we discover the actual standards of the major media and many other critics of Sandinista abuses, which do not remotely compare with those of our admired clients.

Censorship of *La Prensa*[58] and its closing after the United States' virtual declaration of war in June 1986 have also elicited much outraged commentary. Again, we may ask whether it arises from libertarian standards or mere service to state power. The question is readily answered by an inquiry into the reaction when the independent media were not censored, but rather eliminated, in El Salvador in 1980-1981, with editors and journalists tortured, murdered, and mutilated or driven out of the country by assassination attempts, the Church radio station bombed and destroyed by security forces, and so on. These attacks, which far exceed anything that has taken place in Nicaragua, received not one word of censure—or mention—in the *New York Times* editorials, and they were known only to readers of reports of human rights organizations or the marginal dissident literature, with rare exceptions.

We gain a clear insight into the real attitudes toward freedom of expression held in the United States by observing the reaction to events in our leading client state during the weeks when outrage over suppression of critical opinion in Nicaragua was reaching its peak. In August 1986, Israeli authorities closed two Jerusalem Arab newspapers on the grounds that "although we offer them freedom of expression, . . . it is forbidden to permit them to exploit this freedom in order to harm the State of Israel." The closure was upheld by the High Court on the grounds that "It is inconceivable that the State of Israel should allow terrorist organizations which seek to destroy it to set up businesses in its territory, legitimate as they may be." A Jerusalem weekly had been closed in 1985 and another journal in 1983 on similar charges, permissible under regulations of the British mandatory authorities that amount to a permanent State of Siege, and have been maintained and applied with considerable harshness in Israel since its founding, regulations that permit the censors to bar anything that might in their judgment harm "public order." In July the Jerusalem municipality compelled the Muslim religious authorities to terminate the construction of a cultural center on which they had already spent over half a million dollars, revoking the first permit that Israel had granted them for new construction in East Jerusalem.

On June 26, *Ha'aretz* reported that the interior minister "extended for another year the decree which forbids Advocate Kamal El Dahar, spokesperson for the Progressive List [a Jewish-Arab political party], to leave the country . . . after being convinced that 'by going abroad he will endanger the country's security.'" The decision was upheld by the High Court on the basis of secret evidence. A few weeks later the government banned travel abroad for Father Riah Abu al-Assal, secretary of the Progressive List. In February 1986 the courts rejected the appeal of four young Arabs who were imprisoned for waving a Palestinian flag in a protest of September 22, 1982, against the Sabra-Shatila massacres; any act interpreted by the authorities as support for hostile elements (for example, a painting that includes the colors of the Palestinian flag) can lead to imprisonment, primarily for Arabs but for Jews as well (for example, Rami Livneh was sentenced to ten years in prison for "contact with a foreign agent," namely, political discussion with Palestinians). In late 1985, the Knesset passed a bill effectively outlawing political parties or legislation that calls for Israel to be a democracy in the Western sense, that is, the state of its citizens rather than "the sovereign State of the Jewish people" in Israel and the diaspora as the High Court determined. Meanwhile the press reported a sharp increase in torture in prisons, administrative detention without charge, expulsion, and other human rights violations.[59]

Israel is a rich society, militarily and technologically dominant in the region, not under attack by a superpower. It is the leading recipient of U.S. aid and a loyal client state that performs services for the United States worldwide, participation in near-genocide in Guatemala, for example. We therefore ask how much news coverage has been provided and protest voiced over censorship and other repression in Israel, in comparison to the reaction to repressive measures in Nicaragua under far more onerous circumstances?[60] There has been no coverage, no protest. We therefore know exactly how to understand the outrage expressed over repression in Nicaragua.

The integrity of the denunciations of Nicaragua can also be judged by the reactions, in the same circles, to regular U.S. practice. In 1943, the American Civil Liberties Union (ACLU) praised the "state of civil liberty" during World War II in contrast to that during World War I, when governmental and other pressures "resulted in mob violence against dissenters, hundreds of prosecutions for utterances; in the creation of a universal volunteer vigilante system, officially recognized, to report dissent to the FBI; in hysterical hatred of everything German; in savage sentences for private expressions of criticism; and in suppression of public debate of the issues of the war and the peace," as well as destruction of unions and political organizations, sentencing of presidential candidate Eugene Debs to ten years' imprisonment for a pacifist speech, internment of the conductor of the Boston Symphony Orchestra for declining to play the national anthem, barring of dozens of newspapers from the mails—all of these minor events in comparison to the postwar repression launched by the Wilson administration. But the ACLU's evaluation of World War II is surprising in the light of the (U.S. court–approved) dispatch of 110,000 Japanese-Americans to concentration camps, the 1940 Espionage Act and Smith Act, initiation of repressive activities of the FBI that persisted for at least thirty years, government strike breaking and destruction of the Socialist Workers party, full-scale martial law in Hawaii barring trial by jury, habeas corpus, and other due process rights, jailing of dozens of people for such seditious acts as counseling draft opposition, barring of dissident press from the mails and seizure of newspapers and other publications, surveillance of all international message traffic under wartime censorship, brutal treatment of conscientious objectors, and so on. Meanwhile Left-liberal opinion (*New Republic, New Leader*) called for restricting the Bill of Rights to "friends of democracy" and "exterminating" the "treason press" (*Nation*), while such revered moralists as Reinhold Niebuhr stressed the "greater measure of coercion" required during a national emergency and approved infringements on "the freedom of organizations to spread subversive propaganda" and community drives "to eliminate recalcitrant and even traitorous elements."[61]

Recall that opposition to the war was minuscule, the United States was by far the richest and most powerful state in the world, and its national territory had not been threatened with attack since the War of 1812. It is inconceivable that the United States during wartime would have followed the recent Nicaraguan practice: permitting German or Japanese legislators and advocates of a war against the United States to travel freely and to give press conferences calling for renewed attacks on the United States at the airport on departure or to return to travel freely after publishing anti-American diatribes in the Axis powers; allowing Americans to travel to these states to urge further military actions against the United States with impunity; and so on. Nor would it have tolerated for a moment a major journal that supported the Axis powers or even expressed neutralist sentiments.

We ask, then, whether current critics of Nicaragua urge that it would have been proper at the time to condemn the United States bitterly and support military attacks against it. The comparison is, of course, entirely unfair to Nicaragua. A closer comparison would be to the years when the United States was becoming constituted as a nation, with murderous assaults on the native population by George Washington's forces, extensive corruption, the ludicrous nineteenth-century Washington cult as part of the effort to create national unity, military expansion (including attempts to conquer Canada), threats of secession by New England, slavery—in what was even then probably the richest country in the world, with unparalleled advantages. The questions answer themselves.

When hypocrisy of the kind illustrated is found elsewhere, it is shameful enough, but we are talking about the United States, which is torturing Nicaragua while deploring its misdeeds. The spectacle surpasses hypocrisy: It reveals as well the supreme moral cowardice of American culture that has long been a source of shame for those who care about their country.

This review barely touches the surface. A fuller inquiry should consider how the media have handled U.S. government charges against Nicaragua.

Consider the *New York Times* treatment of the charge of Nicaraguan support for a terrorist operation in Colombia in November 1985. On January 7, 1986, the Colombian foreign minister stated in a news conference that "Colombia accepts Nicaraguan Foreign Minister Miguel d'Escoto's explanation and considers the incident closed." The *Times* did not report the fact; rather its editorial the following day asserted that "Colombia's patience has since been strained by evidence—which Nicaragua disputes—that the Sandinistas supplied guns to terrorists who staged" the November incident. On January 5 and 6 the *Times* had published stories on the Colombian charge against Nicaragua and Nicaragua's denial. On January 15, the *Times* reported that "American officials have linked Nicaragua to the Terrorism in Bogotá—a charge denied by the Nicaraguan Government" and published an op-ed item repeating the charges. The U.S. government charge was reported again in a news column of February 26, the Colombian reaction still ignored.[62] The example is again both typical and instructive.

The Real Reasons for the War Against Nicaragua

The reasons advanced by the Reagan administration for the current attack on Nicaragua merit no further discussion.[63] The real reasons for the U.S. attack, and the domestic hysteria accompanying it, are not difficult to discern, though they are inexpressible within the mainstream of intellectual opinion. The real crimes of Nicaragua are its moves toward independence and the attempts to direct resources to the needs of the poor majority.

The *Manchester Guardian*, July 6, 1986, accurately comments that

> Nicaragua is in no way a threat to the United States. It has held elections which were freer of violence and less spoiled by intimidation, and which offered a wider range of ideological choices than most elections in the region. It has pledged not to accept foreign bases, either for nuclear or conventional weapons, on its territory and has offered to sign a treaty with the United States to that effect. Its only danger to Washington is that it sets an example of independence which has been lacking for decades in the Central American isthmus.

A January 1983 report of the Inter-American Development Bank concluded that "Nicaragua has made noteworthy progress in the social sector, which is laying a solid foundation for long-term socio-economic development." The real crimes of Nicaragua are explained further by the charitable development agency Oxfam, which reports that "among the four countries in the region where Oxfam America works [Guatemala, El Salvador, Honduras, Nicaragua], only in Nicaragua has a substantial effort been made to address inequities in land ownership and to extend health, educational, and agricultural services to poor peasant families"; "from Oxfam's experience of working in seventy-six developing countries, Nicaragua was to prove exceptional in the strength" of the commitment of the political leadership "to improving the condition of the people and encouraging their active participation in the development process."[64] Oxfam adds that it is now compelled to shift its efforts from development to war relief, a grand success for the U.S. war, which also provides U.S. moralists with a welcome opportunity to denounce Sandinista failures.

The real reasons for the U.S attack are sometimes conceded. "Few US officials now believe the contras can drive out the Sandinistas soon," Boston Globe reporter Julia Preston states. "Administration officials said they are content to see the contras debilitate the Sandinistas by forcing them to divert scarce resources toward the war and away from social programs."[65] These horrifying statements are blandly reported, evoking no comment, quickly forgotten. The United States will not permit constructive programs in its own domains, so it must ensure that they are destroyed elsewhere to terminate "the threat of a good example."

The "threat of a good example" elicits fear and outrage for understandable reasons: It may prove to be a "virus" that will "infect" the region and even beyond, as Kissinger warned about Allende, as U.S. policymakers have always feared, as did their predecessors back to the days when the czar and Metternich were warning about the "pernicious ideas" of radical democracy that might spread from the United States, undermining the civilized world order over which they presided.

All of this is transparent, entirely familiar from the historical and documentary record in Latin America and elsewhere, but entirely inexpressible in a well-functioning doctrinal system—again, an instructive lesson.

We can perceive both the real reasons for the attack on Nicaragua and the nature of the system of indoctrination that effectively conceals them by attending to the devices employed to frighten Congress into supporting aid to the terrorist proxy army. In his speech on the eve of the House vote in June 1986, after warning of the threat to our existence posed by Nicaragua, Reagan worked his way to the final climactic flourish: "Communist Nicaragua," he declaimed, is "dedicated—in the words of its own leaders—to a 'revolution without borders.'" In short, the Nicaraguans themselves admit that they intend to conquer and destroy us. The same phrase served as the title for the State Department attempt to demonstrate Sandinista aggression, published in September 1985 in an obvious effort to counter the possibility that the concurrent World Court proceedings might evoke a spark of interest here.[66]

Reagan's invocation of this dramatic Communist admission of their aggressive intent was reported by the press without comment. In an interview with Nicaraguan Vice-President Sergio Ramírez, the Washington Post challenged him to explain away the statement by Tomás Borge in July 1981 that "this revolution goes beyond the borders," the alleged source of Reagan's charge. At the dovish extreme of the U.S. media, the editors of the Boston Globe wrote that "the State Department has never been able to document any arms shipment to back up the Sandinistas' boast about 'a revolution without borders,'" adding that "their failure to spread their revolution, and their humiliating silence about it, should be taken as a sign of reassurance, but is ignored in Washington."[67] "Conservative" commentators naturally exulted in the episode.

The media were well aware that the whole story was a fraud. When Borge stated that "this revolution transcends national boundaries," he made it entirely clear that he meant ideological transcendence: "This does not mean we export our revolution. It is enough—and we couldn't do otherwise—for us to export our example . . . we know that it is the people themselves who must make their revolutions." Although the fraud had been exposed at once by the Council on Hemispheric Affairs,[68] the president's advisers could have perfect confidence that the media would continue to fulfill their function at a critical moment, as they did.

Particularly noteworthy is the reaction of the doves. They oppose contra aid on the basis of the "humiliating silence" of the Sandinistas over their failure to back up their boast that the success of their revolution would inspire others. The doves feel no need to explain that the president was lying about the "boast" and that the real "boast" failed thanks to U.S. international terrorism. And most instructive, they find it "reassuring" that the Sandinistas' efforts "to address inequities in land ownership and to extend health, educational, and agricultural services to poor peasant families"—unique among seventy-six developing countries (Oxfam)—have failed, thanks to U.S. violence.

The deceit is also revealing with regard to policy realities. It is quite wrong to argue that Nicaragua poses no threat to "the national interest." Borge's actual words express the true threat quite clearly; state propagandists are right to be troubled by them. Starving peasants in Honduras, who look across the border and see health clinics, literacy campaigns, increased production of subsistence crops, and so on, might ask: "Why not us?" The rot may spread, infecting the region and beyond, threatening U.S. control in more crucial domains. But it cannot be conceded that the real danger is "the threat of a good example." Therefore, in its traditional way, the propaganda system presents it in a different light: It is the threat of eventual conquest, the threat that the people of the world who "outnumber [us] . . . 15 to 1 . . . [will] sweep over the United States and take what we have," as Lyndon Johnson warned.[69] We see here quite clearly the two variants of the domino theory: the version used to terrify the population and the real truth, plainly inexpressible in public and kept from the public by the loyal media.

The real concerns of U.S. elites follow from guiding geopolitical conceptions that are well documented in the internal record under a corollary that we might call "the rotten apple theory," to adopt the terminology of planners from Dean Acheson to the present. The fear is that one rotten apple may infect the barrel; "the rot may spread"—the rot being social and economic development in a framework that does not accord with the perceived needs of U.S. elites. Greece, Guatemala, Vietnam, Cuba, the Dominican Republic,

Chile under Allende, and other countries have evoked similar fears, along with responses ranging from terrorism and subversion to mass slaughter. Until we are prepared to face and discuss these topics, our belief that we are part of a democratic polity is more shadow than substance. The fakery about "revolution without borders" is not original. In March 1950, as the United States was deepening its commitment to the French effort to reconquer the former colony of Indochina, Dean Acheson accused China of planning to initiate "adventures beyond their borders," acting as a Soviet puppet.[70] The hypocrisy, masking real concerns, should be seen in the context of the general concept of containment, of fears that the people of the world will "take what we have" and that the embattled minority who control the doctrinal system to something approaching 100 percent can barely hold their own in the face of "propaganda assaults" by powerful adversaries, and so on. The underlying assumption is that everything belongs by right to the owners and managers of U.S. society, so that any infringement on total control is an insufferable crime, eliciting terror that all is lost. The case of Nicaragua merely highlights far more general features of our society and culture.

The United States plainly has the military capacity, and apparently the moral capacity as well, to pursue its historical vocation of torturing Nicaragua while strengthening "democracy" in the standard Orwellian sense of the term in El Salvador and other dependencies. The rational policy for a violent terrorist state with unparalleled resources and few domestic constraints would be to refrain from outright invasion and to persist in the CIA program of 1981 outlined by David MacMichael at the World Court hearings: to use its professional proxy army to "provoke cross-border attacks by Nicaraguan forces and thus serve to demonstrate Nicaragua's aggressive nature," to pressure the Nicaraguan government to "clamp down on civil liberties within Nicaragua itself, arresting its opposition, demonstrating its allegedly inherent totalitarian nature and thus increase domestic dissent within the country," and to undermine its shattered economy. The United States surely has the capacity to "'turn Nicaragua into the Albania of Central America,' that is, poor, isolated, and radical," as a State Department insider reportedly boasted in 1981.[71] As the intended results are achieved, domestic hypocrites will feign indignation over Nicaraguan abuses, applying standards that they do not for one moment accept, and will assure us that the problems of Nicaragua result from "Communist mismanagement," "Sandinista paranoia," and the "inherent totalitarian nature" of the Sandinistas.

"A priest in Nicaragua, who had been in Chile before, said that the US realised it had made a mistake and overthrown Allende too soon, while there was still a dream of what socialism could be. In Nicaragua they are trying to destroy the dream first."[72] That is the intelligent policy for a power with unparalleled resources of violence and cynicism. It is necessary to eliminate any hope for a decent life and true independence in the shadow of the Enforcer. Once "regional standards" have been restored by violence and we have fit the starving and miserable people in our backyard "back into their Central American mode," we may attend to their fate with the same solicitude we have shown throughout our history, meanwhile reveling in this renewed demonstration of our traditional benevolence.

Notes

1. Alfonso Chardy, *Miami Herald* (*MH*), March 9, 1986; James LeMoyne, Linda Greenhouse, "Week in Review," *New York Times*, (*NYT*), June 29, 1986.

2. See, for example, Robert Parry and Brian Barger, Associated Press, April 14, 1986, on CIA involvement in violation of congressional restrictions at a level that "may astound even the most jaded observer," Representative Sam Gejdenson commented.

3. Editorial, *NYT*, December 28, 1981.

4. International Court of Justice (ICJ) Year 1986, June 27, 1986, General List No. 70, pars. 251, 252, 157, 158, 233.

5. Editorial, *NYT*, July 1, 1986.

6. Jonathan Karp, *Washington Post* (*WP*), June 28, 1986. The Soviet judge had withdrawn from the case.

7. *NYT*, July 17, 1986. On the international reaction, including the opinion of Dutch legal experts that "the decision is legally binding," see Martin Cleaver, "The Hague," *Guardian* (London), June 28, 1986.

8. Stephen Rosenfeld, *WP*, April 11, 1986; William Beecher, *Boston Globe* (*BG*), June 20, 1986; and innumerable other articles.

9. *Wall Street Journal* (*WSJ*), April 11, 1986; Security Council, S/PV.2703, July 31, 1986, 42; Elaine Sciolino, *NYT*, August 1, 1986. The vote was eleven to one, with Britain, France, and Thailand abstaining. This was the twelfth time that Nicaragua had brought the issue to the Security Council.

10. Arturo Rivera y Damas, "Homily," October 26, 1980, cited by Raymond Bonner, *Weakness and Deceit* (New York: Times Books, 1984), p. 207.

11. José Napoleón Duarte, *Miami Herald*, December 23, 1980.

12. Reagan, "Report to Congress," April 10, 1985; formal finding by Congress, July 29, 1985, quoted in ICJ report cited in note 4, pars. 169, 170. In the real world, the U.S. government supported the Somoza dictatorship until its bloody end and then sought to retain the rule of Somoza's National Guard, which it rescued and soon reconstituted to attack Nicaragua, while offering aid in a manner designed to strengthen its allies in the business community who could be counted on to block social programs. See Peter Kornbluh's discussion in Chapter 2 of this book; Thomas W. Walker, *Nicaragua: The Land of Sandino*, 2d ed. (Boulder, Colo.: Westview Press, 1986); Noam Chomsky, *Turning the Tide* (Boston: South End, 1985).

13. Judge Schwebel was the State Department's deputy legal adviser when the World Court backed U.S. claims against Iran, a decision that he found "splendid." Youssef Ibrahim, *NYT*, May 25, 1980.

14. Editorial, *NYT*, March 1, 1982.

15. *NYT Magazine*, April 6, 1986.

16. See, for example, *NYT Magazine* cover story (Tad Szulc, "Radical Winds of the Caribbean," May 25, 1980), noting that "the roots of the Caribbean problems are not entirely Cuban" because the "Soviet offensive" is also to blame along with the consequences of "colonial greed and mismanagement" by European powers; the United States is blamed only for "indifference" to the brewing problems.

17. In Kenneth M. Coleman and George C. Herring, eds., *The Central American Crisis* (Wilmington, Del.: Scholarly Resources Inc., 1985), p. 196.

18. See Chomsky, *Turning the Tide*, chapter 5; and Thomas Ferguson and Joel Rogers, *Atlantic Monthly*, May 1986.

19. See among other sources, Robert J. Goldstein, *Political Repression in Modern America* (Cambridge: Schenkman, 1978); Noam Chomsky and Edward S. Herman, *Political Economy of Human Rights* (Boston: South End, 1979); Noam Chomsky, *Towards a New Cold War* (New York: Pantheon, 1982).

20. Steven Vaughn, *Holding Fast the Inner Lines* (Chapel Hill: University of North Carolina Press, 1980), p. 194.

21. Helen Dewar, *BG-WP*, August 14, 1986.

22. Walker, *Nicaragua*, pp. 45, 88, 104; Gordon Connell-Smith, *The Inter-American System* (Oxford: Oxford University Press and Royal Institute of International Affairs, 1966), pp. 23ff.

23. Steven Roberts, *NYT*, August 6, 1986.

24. Former director of the State Department journal *Problems of Communism*, who has given nuanced (and in my view, quite plausible) assessments of the Sandinista government elsewhere, most recently, in *Dissent*, spring/summer 1986.

25. Note that the issue is not the character of the individual pieces but the editorial decision as to what constitutes permissible debate. For a closer analysis, see Noam Chomsky's introduction to Morris Morley and James Petras, *The Reagan Administration and Nicaragua* (New York: Institute for Media Analysis, 1987).

26. March 9, 1986; July 24, 1984. The only other near-exception is a sentence on social reforms in "Editorial Notebook," a signed comment by editor Karl Meyer, June 27, 1983.

27. Robert Leiken, statement before the Committee on Foreign Relations, United States Senate, March 4, 1986; *New Republic*, March 31, 1986; *New York Review of Books*, June 26, March 13, 1986.

28. R. W. Apple, *NYT*, March 12, 1986. Robert Leiken, *New York Review*, December 5, 1985; Senate testimony, March 4, 1986; *New Republic*, March 31, 1986; *Soviet Strategy in Latin America* (New York: Praeger, 1982), pp. 87–88. The terminology and conceptions are standard in the Maoist cult literature.

29. Editorial, *WP*, weekly edition, March 31, 1986.

30. Council on Hemispheric Affairs, (COHA), *Washington Report on the Hemisphere*, April 16, 1986. Alan Nairn and Jean-Marie Simon, *New Republic*, June 30, 1986.

31. *El Salvador* (London: Catholic Institute of International Relations, February 1986); Americas Watch, *Settling into Routine*, May 1986; Ambrose Evans-Pritchard, *Spectator* (London), May 10, 1986.

32. *COHA's Human Rights Report*, Washington, D.C., December 31, 1985.

33. Editorials, *NYT*, April 23 and June 14, 1985. Even its most avid supporters concede the point; see Bruce Cameron and Penn Kemble, *From a Proxy Force to a National Liberation Movement* (manuscript), February 1986, urging the United States to undertake measures to create a "political base" for its "proxy army." A July 16, 1982, Defense Intelligence Agency (DIA), "Weekly Intelligence Summary" described the leading contra group as a "terrorist" organization headed by former National Guard officers (COHA, "Misleading the Public," April 3, 1986); nothing has changed since that time.

34. *"Revolution Beyond Our Borders": Sandinista Intervention in Central America*, U.S. Department of State Special Report No. 132, September 1985.

35. UN Official Document A/40/907, S/17639, November 19, 1985.

36. *NYT*, May 6, 1984.

37. Steven Roberts, *NYT,* April 6, 1986; editorial, *WP,* weekly edition, April 14, 1986; editorial, *NYT,* March 18, 1986.

38. AP, April 14, 1986; Robert Pear, *NYT,* November 25, 1985; AP, *NYT,* April 1, 1985. Reference to Nicaragua as a "cancer" is standard; see, for example, the president's March 16, 1986, address (*NYT,* March 17).

39. Randolph Ryan, *BG,* March 10, 1986.

40. Editorial, March 20, 1986. For a partial record of the falsehoods in this speech and elsewhere, see COHA, "Misleading the Public"; "Talk of the Town," *New Yorker,* March 31, 1986. See *Human Rights in Nicaragua: Reagan, Rhetoric and Reality,* Americas Watch, July 1985, for an earlier record.

41. Editorial, *WP,* March 31, 1986; editorial, *BG,* March 19, 1986.

42. Editorials, *Globe & Mail* (Toronto), March 18, 5, and 28, 1986; David Watt, "As a European Sees It," *Foreign Affairs: America and the World 1983,* Winter 1983, pp. 521–532.

43. Editorial, *NYT,* October 18, 1985; Senate testimony cited in note 27.

44. Edward Schumacher, *NYT,* February 21, 1981.

45. Amnesty International, *El Salvador: Recent Allegations of Torture of Political Detainees,* London, October 1985; *Report on the Visit of a Trocaire Delegation to El Salvador: November 1985* (Dublin: Catholic Agency for World Development, 1986).

46. On this matter, see Chomsky, *Turning the Tide,* p. 135.

47. Editorials, *NYT,* April 28, 1980, and February 19, 1981; Alan Riding, *NYT,* September 27, 1981.

48. Chomsky, *Turning the Tide,* pp. 21ff, 122 ff.

49. Editorials, *NYT,* June 3, 1986, and May 8 and 20, 1984.

50. *COHA's 1985 Human Rights Report.* For references not given here, see Chomsky, *Turning the Tide.*

51. "Topics," *NYT,* March 26, 1980; Chomsky, *Turning the Tide,* p. 103.

52. *NYT* op-ed, February 14, 1986; *Dissent,* spring 1986.

53. Amnesty International, *Amnesty Action,* January-February 1986.

54. *New Republic,* editorials, April 7, 1986, and April 2, 1984. See Chomsky, *Turning the Tide,* pp. 167 ff, for further details.

55. Reuters News Agency, *BG,* June 30, 1986; James LeMoyne, *NYT,* August 3, 1986; Julia Preston, *WP,* weekly edition, August 11, 1986; Chris Norton, *Christian Science Monitor* (*CSM*), July 10, 1986; COHA *News and Analysis,* July 28, 1986; Doyle McManus, *Los Angeles Times,* August 7, 1986. Also Americas Watch, *Settling into Routine.*

56. *New Statesman* (London), July 18, 1986; see Chomsky, *Turning the Tide,* pp. 22 ff, 110.

57. Donald Fox and Michael J. Glennon, "Report to the International Human Rights Law Group and the Washington Office on Latin America," Washington, D.C., April 1985, p. 21.

58. The opposition journal subsidized by the procontra U.S. organization PRO-DEMCA with grants from the U.S. government. "While *La Prensa's* opposition to Somoza is often cited to confirm the newspaper's democratic credentials, shortly after conservative Pedro Joaquin Chamorro, Jr., took editorial control in 1980, 80 percent of the staff resigned and founded the independent, pro-Sandinista paper *El Nuevo Diario*" (COHA, *Washington Report on the Hemisphere,* July 23, 1986).

59. *Al-Hamishmar,* July 25 and August 13, 1986; *Jerusalem Post* (*JP*), August 24, 1986; Moshe Negbi, *Politika,* August 1986; editorial, *JP,* July 17, 1986, arguing that "Israel is, after all, entitled to look askance at the continued publication" of such newspapers; *JP,* August 13, 1986; *Kol Ha'ir,* July 4, 1986; *Ha'aretz,* June 26, 1986; *The*

Other Israel, May-June 1986; *News from Within*, August 12, 1986; Attallah Mansour, *Ha'aretz*, February 5, 1986; Aryeh Rubinstein, *Jerusalem Post*, November 14, 1985 See Chomsky, *Turning the Tide*, pp. 73–74, for a very partial indication of the scale of censorship in Israel, which applies not only to current affairs but also to history Thus a book on the 1948 war was barred by government censorship for fifteen years; Ian Black, *Manchester Guardian Weekly*, June 1, 1986. On the increase in torture, etc., under the Labor government, see Noam Chomsky, *Pirates and Emperors* (New York: Claremont, 1986), chapter 2; on Livneh, see Noam Chomsky, *Peace in the Middle East?* (New York: Pantheon, 1974), p. 174.

60. Similar questions arise about human rights groups, most strikingly, the International League for Human Rights, which went so far as to suspend its Israeli affiliate on the sole grounds that the government attempted to destroy it by illegal means blocked by the courts, an action that aroused no concern here. Ibid., pp. 196–197. Noam Chomsky, *Fateful Triangle* (Boston: South End, 1983), p. 142.

61. Goldstein, *Political Repression*, and Margaret Leahy's Chapter 12 in this book; Richard Fox, *Reinhold Niebuhr* (New York: Pantheon, 1985), p. 293.

62. AP, *BG*, January 8, 1986, p. 81 in the sports section; editorial, *NYT*, January 8, 1986; AP, *NYT*, January 5, 1986; Stephen Kinzer, *NYT*, January 6, 1986; Bernard Weinraub, *NYT*, January 15, 1986; Elliott Abrams, op-ed, *NYT*, January 15, 1986; David Shipler, *NYT*, February 26, 1986. The *Washington Post* also failed to report the Colombian acceptance of Nicaragua's disclaimer of responsibility.

63. See Chomsky, *Turning the Tide*; Walker, *Nicaragua*; references in note 40.

64. Editorial, *Manchester Guardian Weekly* (*MGW*), July 6, 1986; *Oxfam America Special Report: Central America*, fall 1985; Dianna Melrose, *Nicaragua: The Threat of a Good Example?* (Oxford: Oxfam, 1985), pp. 26, 14.

65. *BG*, February 9, 1986.

66. *NYT*, June 25, 1986; see note 34.

67. *NYT*, June 25, 1986; *WP-MGW*, July 6, 1986; editorial, *BG*, July 14, 1986.

68. *Washington Report on the Hemisphere*, October 16, 1985. For a review of this and earlier frauds, see Chomsky, *Turning the Tide*, p. 270; also see Eldon Kenworthy's Chapter 9 in this book.

69. See Chomsky, *Turning the Tide*, pp. 66 ff, for further quotes and references.

70. March 15, 1950; see Michael Schaller, *The American Occupation of Japan* (New York: Oxford University Press, 1985), p. 226.

71. Cited by Thomas W. Walker, in Coleman and Herring, *The Central American Crisis*, p. 172.

72. Joseph Hanlon, *New Statesman*, October 19, 1984.

Acronyms

AFSC	American Friends Service Committee
AIA	Accuracy in Academia
AIFLD	American Institute for Free Labor Development
ALPROMISU	Alliance for the Progress of Miskitu and Sumu People
ANACH	National Association of Honduran Campesinos
ARDE	Democratic Revolutionary Alliance
BG	*Boston Globe*
CAUSA USA	Confederation of the Associations for Unity of the Society of the Americas
CDSs	Sandinista Defense Committees
CEBs	Christian base communities
CELAIS	Latin American Center for Social Work
CELAM	Second General Conference of Latin American Bishops
CEPAD	Evangelical Committee for Aid and Development
CHRICA	Committee for Health Rights in Central America
CIA	Central Intelligence Agency
CISPES	Committee in Solidarity with the People of El Salvador
CODHEH	Committee for Defense of Human Rights in Honduras
COHA	Council on Hemispheric Affairs
CONDECA	Central American Defense Council
COPROSA	Commission for Social Promotion in the Archdiocese
CORADEP	People's Radio Corporation
CORPI	Regional Council of the Indigenous Peoples of Central America, Mexico and Panama
COSEP	Superior Council of Private Enterprise
CSM	*Christian Science Monitor*
DIA	Defense Intelligence Agency
DIS	Defense Investigative Service
DN	(Sandinista) National Directorate
ECLA	Economic Commission for Latin America
EPS	Sandinista Popular Army
FBIS	Foreign Broadcast Information Service

311

FDN	Nicaraguan Democratic Forces
FMLN	Faribundo Martí National Liberation Front
FOA	Friends of the Americas
FSLN	Sandinist Front of National Liberation
GAO	Government Accounting Office
GATT	General Agreement on Tariffs and Trade
HRN	Voice of Honduras
IDA	International Development Agency
IDB	Inter-American Development Bank
IMF	International Monetary Fund
INSSBI	(Nicaraguan) Institute of Social Security and Social Welfare
IRD	Institute on Religion and Democracy
JP	*Jerusalem Post*
KISAN	Nicaraguan Coast Indian Unity
LASA	Latin American Studies Association
MBS	Ministry of Social Welfare
MDN	Nicaraguan Democratic movement
MED	Ministry of Education
MH	*Miami Herald*
MINSA	Ministry of Health
MINVAH	Ministry of Housing and Human Settlements
MISURASATA	Miskito, Sumu, Rama, and Sandinistas Working Together
MTT	Mobile Training Teams
NACLA	North American Congress on Latin America
N-CAHRN	National Central American Health Rights Network
NHAO	Nicaraguan Humanitarian Assistance Office
NICA	Nicaraguan Interfaith Committees for Action
NSC	National Security Council
NYT	*New York Times*
OAS	Organization of American States
PAHO	Pan American Health Organization
PRODEMCA	Pro-Democratic Forces in Central America
PSN	Nicaraguan Socialist party
RBOB	Revolution Beyond Our Borders
RMTC	Regional Military Training Center
SOUTHCOM	Southern Command (U.S. military, Panama)
SSTV	Sandinista Television System
SUKAWALA	National Association of Sumu Communities
UCLA	Unilaterally Controlled Latino Assets
UDN	Nicaraguan Democratic Union
UNHCR	UN High Commission on Refugees
UNO	United Nicaraguan Opposition
UPANIC	Union of Nicaraguan Farmers

USAID	U.S. Agency for International Development
USIA	U.S. Information Agency
WACL	World Anti-Communist League
WP	*Washington Post*
WSJ	*Wall Street Journal*

About the Editor and Contributors

The Contributing Editor

Thomas W. Walker is professor of political science at Ohio University, Athens, Ohio. He holds a B.A. in political science from Brown University, an M.A. in Latin American studies, and a Ph.D. in political science from the University of New Mexico. Walker is the author of *The Christian Democratic Movement in Nicaragua* and *Nicaragua: The Land of Sandino* (second edition, 1986, Westview Press); the coauthor, with John A. Booth, of *Understanding Central America* (forthcoming from Westview Press); and the editor/coauthor of *Nicaragua in Revolution* and *Nicaragua: The First Five Years*. In 1982, he was a member of the national Central American Task Force of the United Presbyterian Church's Council on Church and Society. From 1983 to 1984 he served as a founding co-chair of the Latin American Studies Association's Task Force on Scholarly Relations with Nicaragua.

The Chapter Authors

Noam Chomsky is Institute Professor in the Department of Linguistics and Philosophy at the Massachusetts Institute of Technology, where he has taught since 1955. He has published extensively on linguistics, philosophy, intellectual history, and contemporary affairs, has lectured widely in the United States and abroad, and is a member of numerous scientific and scholarly associations. Among his most recent books are *Turning the Tide: US Intervention in Central America and the Struggle for Peace* and *Pirates and Emperors: International Terrorism in the Real World*. Chomsky holds undergraduate and Ph.D. degrees in linguistics from the University of Pennsylvania. He has received honorary degrees from the University of London, University of Chicago, Loyola University of Chicago, Swarthmore

College, Delhi University, Bard College, the University of Massachusetts, and the University of Pennsylvania.

Betsy Cohn founded the Central American Historical Institute in Washington, D.C., in March 1982. Previously she worked in the development education department of Oxfam America writing materials on world hunger and Central America for Oxfam groups. Cohn has traveled frequently to Central America. She has appeared on radio and television, as well as at universities, high schools, churches, and community conferences on Central America and topics related to self-reliant development; her expertise is U.S. foreign policy and Nicaragua. Cohn holds a B.A. in Third World Studies from Boston College where she twice cotaught "The Political, Economic, and Ethical Dimensions of World Hunger."

Michael E. Conroy is associate professor of economics at the University of Texas at Austin where he also serves as the associate director of the Institute for Latin American Studies. Conroy has published in numerous journals, including *Third World Quarterly, The Journal of Regional Science, Southern Economic Journal,* and *Latin American Research Review.* His present research focuses on the survival strategies of the urban poor in Honduras, the Nicaraguan economic experiment, and regional outreach by the Nicaraguan government. Conroy earned a B.A. in economics and Latin American studies from Tulane University and an M.S. and a Ph.D. in economics from the University of Illinois at Urbana. In 1985/1986 he served as chair of the Latin American Studies Association's Task Force on Scholarly Relations with Nicaragua. He is also a member of the National Executive Board of PACCA (Policy Alternatives for the Caribbean and Central America).

Martin Diskin is professor of anthropology at the Massachusetts Institute of Technology, Cambridge, Massachusetts. Diskin has had extensive field experience among indigenous and peasant groups in Mexico over the past twenty-six years. In 1986, he and three colleagues completed a major study of the problematic of the Atlantic Coast of Nicaragua, published by the Latin American Studies Association (LASA) as a two-part article, "Peace and Autonomy on the Atlantic Coast of Nicaragua: A Report of the LASA Task Force on Human Rights and Academic Freedom," in spring and summer 1986 issues of *LASA Forum.* Diskin holds the Ph.D. from the University of California at Los Angeles.

Howard H. Frederick is assistant professor of international telecommunications at Ohio University, Athens, Ohio. He has also taught at Mary Baldwin College and in fall 1985 was an IREX (International Research and Exchange Program) exchange professor at the Karl Marx University in the German Democratic Republic. Frederick holds B.A. degrees in psychology and German from Stanford University, an M.A. in radio/television from San Francisco State University and a Ph.D. in international relations from American University, Washington, D.C. Among other studies, he is the author of *Cuban-American Radio Wars.*

Eva Gold is a research/writer at National Action/Research on the Military Industrial Complex (NARMIC), the research and resource unit of the Peace

Education Division of the American Friends Service Committee (AFSC). She has worked at NARMIC since 1977, and since 1981 has focused on U.S. military policy and presence in Central America. Gold has written numerous reports and articles published by NARMIC/AFSC and a variety of periodicals. Gold holds a B.A. from the University of Pennsylvania and an M.A. from Temple University.

William Goodfellow is director of the Center for International Policy in Washington, D.C. In that capacity, he has traveled frequently to Central America and has been deeply involved in covering the Contadora peace initiatives. In addition to numerous articles authored or coauthored in the center's *International Policy Report*, he has also published in the *New York Times, Los Angeles Times, Philadelphia Inquirer,* and *Newsday.* Goodfellow holds a B.A. in political science from Boston University and an M.A. from Goddard College.

Patricia Hynds is a Maryknoll lay missioner who works as researcher/writer/translator for Jesuit-directed, Managua-based Instituto Histórico Centroamericano's monthly Spanish/English publication, *Envío,* and for the publication of the affiliated office in Washington, D.C., the Central American Historical Institute. Hynds holds a B.A. in Spanish and Chicano Studies and an M.A. in Mexican American Studies from California State University at Northridge.

Eldon Kenworthy is associate professor of government at Cornell University in Ithaca, New York. He has published several articles on U.S. policy in Central America, including ones in *World Policy Journal, Current History,* and *Democracy.* Kenworthy holds a B.A. from Oberlin College and a Ph.D. from Yale University.

Sung Ho Kim is assistant professor of political science at Ohio University with research and writing interest in the normative problems of international relations. Kim attended the Law School of Seoul National University and holds a B.A. degree from Baldwin-Wallace College and Ph.D. from Columbia University.

Peter Kornbluh is an information analyst at the National Security Archive, a nongovernmental research institute in Washington, D.C. Much of the work for his chapter was done while he was a fellow at the Institute for Policy Studies, Washington, D.C. Kornbluh holds a B.A. in Latin American Studies from Brandeis University and an M.A. in International Relations from George Washington University. He is the author of *Nicaragua: The Price of Intervention* and the co-editor with Michael Klare of *The New Interventionism: Waging Low Intensity Warfare in The Third World.*

Margaret E. Leahy is visiting professor of political science at California State University at Chico. She is the author of *Development Strategies and the Status of Women: A Comparative Study of the United States, Mexico, the Soviet Union, and Cuba.* Her interest is in the area of social reconstruction and the revolutionary process. In 1984, she was in Nicaragua as an observer of the elections. Leahy holds a B.A. and an M.A. in international relations from San Francisco State University and received her Ph.D. from the School of International Relations at the University of Southern California.

William M. LeoGrande is associate professor of political science in the School of Government and Public Administration at the American University in Washington, D.C. LeoGrande has published widely in the field of Latin American relations with the United States and Latin American politics. His articles have appeared in the *American Political Science Review, Latin American Research Review, Foreign Affairs,* and *Foreign Policy.* LeoGrande holds A.B., M.A., and Ph.D. degrees from the Maxwell School at Syracuse University, Syracuse, New York.

Jack Spence is associate professor of political science at the University of Massachusetts at Boston. He has contributed articles on U.S. media coverage of Central America to *Columbia Journalism Review, Socialist Review,* and *NACLA Report on the Americas.* Spence holds an A.B. from Grinnell College, a J.D. from Harvard Law School, and a Ph.D. from the Massachusetts Institute of Technology.

Harvey Williams is professor of sociology at the University of the Pacific, Stockton, California, where he joined the faculty in 1977. He has published widely on Latin American topics, including several chapters on social sector programs in Nicaragua that have appeared in *Nicaragua in Revolution, Nicaragua: The First Five Years,* and *Third World Medicine and Social Change.* Williams holds an A.B. from the University of California, Berkeley, and an M.A. and Ph.D. from Vanderbilt University, Nashville, Tennessee.

Index